— Quantifying —
ARCHAEOLOGY

D1340388

— Quantifying — ARCHAEOLOGY

Stephen Shennan

EDINBURGH UNIVERSITY PRESS

For Sue

© Stephen Shennan, 1988, 1997
First published 1988
Reprinted 1990
Second edition 1997

Edinburgh University Press
22 George Square, Edinburgh

Typeset in Times and Helvetica
by Pioneer Associates, Perthshire
Printed and bound in Great Britain

A CIP record for this book is available
from the British Library

ISBN 0 7486 0791 9

CONTENTS

ACKNOWLEDGEMENTS

I would like to thank Mike Baxter, Clive Orton and Richard Wright for helpful comments and suggestions. Needless to say, they are not responsible for any errors.

The following material is reproduced by permission of the organisation specified: tables A, B and E, Cambridge University Press, from *New Cambridge Statistical Tables* (2nd edn) by D. V. Lindley and W. F. Scott, tables 12, 18 and 21; figure for exercise 12.2 and figure 11.10, Society for American Archaeology, respectively from *American Antiquity* 60 (4), 1995, and *American Antiquity* 61 (4), 1996; figure for exercise 13.3, the American Anthropological Association, from *American Anthropologist* 94 (3), September 1992; figures 14.5–14.6, John Wiley and Sons Inc, from *Sampling* by S. K. Thompson, 1992 and the American Statistical Association, from *Journal of the American Statistical Association*, vol. 85, 1990; figure 3.9, Chapman and Hall Publishers, from M. Wand and M. Jones, 1995, *Kernel Smoothing*, figure 2.3; figures 14.7–14.10, University of Southampton and English Heritage, from *Planning for the Past*, vol. 3, by T. Champion, S. J. Shennan and P. Cuming, 1995, figures 1 and 8–10.

I would also like to thank the following for permission to use their published material: the Biometrika Trustees for the tables of the χ^2 and t distributions; Stanley Thornes (Publishers) Ltd for the table of the standardised normal distribution from J. White, A. Yeats and G. Skipworth, *Tables for Statisticians*.

Every effort has been made to trace the copyright holders but, if any have been inadvertently overlooked, the publisher will be pleased to make the necessary acknowledgement at the first opportunity.

One

INTRODUCTION

The days of the innumerate are numbered
(Colin Renfrew)

The aim of this book is to make students of archaeology familiar with some of the basic quantitative methods used within the discipline as well as some of the more advanced ones which are widely used. The techniques are not specific to archaeology, they are used in a great variety of fields, but experience has shown that archaeologists do not gain a great deal from attending statistics classes for sociologists or biologists. Although the statistical theory and method are the same, the examples tend to be either boring or incomprehensible or both. This situation is particularly unsatisfactory for archaeology students because by and large they are not mathematically inclined, so if alien mathematical concepts are to be understood it has to be from a base in relevant subject matter, preferably involving worked examples.

It is hoped that by the end of the book students will themselves be able to use the simple techniques described and to understand the more advanced ones. But in many ways specific skills are less important than some more general attitudes the book aims to put across. The first of these is a knowledgeably sceptical attitude to the results of quantitative analyses rather than a 'knee-jerk' acceptance or rejection on the basis of uninformed prejudice. The second is a feel for the way in which archaeological questions can be translated into quantitative terms. The third is a basis of knowledge for talking to statisticians about data analysis problems. If you turn to a statistician for help and neither of you knows what the other is talking about, you will probably end up with the wrong answer to the wrong question.

The book assumes very little in the way of prior knowledge. Only the most basic mathematical operations of addition, subtraction, multiplication and division are required, together with a vague memory of roots and powers.

WHY USE QUANTITATIVE METHODS?

The key argument here is that quantitative reasoning is central to archaeology and that a better grasp of its implications is likely to improve our work as archaeologists. Clive Orton's book *Mathematics in Archaeology* (1980) provides an excellent demonstration of why this is the case by taking some of the standard questions which archaeologists ask, such as 'What is it?', 'How old is it?', 'Where does it come from?' and 'What was it for?', and showing how a quantitative approach can help to provide the answers. It follows, therefore, that quantitative methods should be seen, not as a distinct scientific specialism within archaeology, like artefact characterisation techniques, for example, but as part of every archaeologist's mental toolkit. Statistical, mathematical and computer specialists may often be required to cope with particular problems, but archaeologists must have sufficient quantitative awareness to recognise when problems arise which can be helpfully tackled in a quantitative fashion. No one else can do this for them.

Given that this is the case, it remains to be specified exactly where the mathematics and the archaeology come together. Part of the answer is in the simple description of the archaeological record: *counts* of potsherds or lithics of different types, *sizes* of pits, and so on. Such quantitative information is an essential part of all modern archaeological reports, and simple quantitative description is the first topic we will consider, in the next chapter. Methodologically, it is very straightforward; conceptually, it raises important issues which tend not to get the attention they deserve. The results of such quantitative summaries are tables of data and it is on the basis of these that archaeologists build their arguments and draw their inferences. The process usually involves the claim that some sort of patterning exists in the data being considered. One way of doing this is simply to look at the table of data and on the basis of this point out what appears to be important and significant within it. As Wright (1989) emphasises, this is unlikely to be very satisfactory. Mathematically-based techniques can help us to recognise patterning in archaeological data and to specify its nature. The area where mathematics meets the messier parts of the real world is usually statistics. It is precisely this fact that makes statistics in many ways a tricky subject, because mathematical and factual considerations are both involved, and because the patterns are only rarely very clear cut. Nevertheless, inasmuch as all interpretation of the archaeological record is concerned with identifying patterning, it is capable of benefiting from a quantitative approach. The point that, within certain constraints, we are *identifying* patterning rather than creating it is an important one to which we will have to return later. Without such an assumption archaeological evidence would not tell us anything, but one of the virtues of the quantitative approach is that it can tell us in particular cases what a lack of patterning actually looks like.

In this context it is unfortunate that the emergence of 'post-processual' archaeology in the 1980s has led to a reaction against the use of quantitative methods, perceived as associated with the processual approaches which have been rejected. While it is certainly the case that such techniques have been used by archaeologists of the processual school more than anyone else, and some at least of these entertained the over-optimistic view that quantitative data analysis could somehow provide direct insights into the past denied to more traditional approaches, the definition of patterning in data remains fundamental to the archaeological enterprise, whether demonstrating associations between rock art motifs or showing the existence of 'structured deposition' in the archaeological record, and quantitative methods have a vital role to play in this, not least as an antidote to our ever-present weakness for self-deception. In recent years there has been a tendency for archaeology to split between the retrieval and description of data, on the one hand, and discussions of high-level theory with little empirical grounding on the other. This weakness will persist until the zone in between is occupied by the rigorous analysis and interpretation of archaeological data patterning.

THE PLACE OF QUANTITATIVE METHODS IN ARCHAEOLOGICAL RESEARCH

Before turning to the techniques themselves it is appropriate to say something about the place of quantitative methods in the research process. The analysis itself generally comes at a very late stage in the sequence, immediately before interpretation and conclusions, but it is not a good idea to leave it until then before thinking about appropriate techniques of analysis for a particular study (cf. Fieller, 1993). At the research design stage the investigator should be deciding not just what to do but how to do it, including appropriate forms of analysis. Once these decisions are made they define the conduct of the research and nowhere is this more important than in ensuring that the data collected and the method of their collection correspond to the requirements of the techniques it is proposed to use, including the theoretical assumptions the techniques presuppose. Discovering the problems at the analysis stage is too late. Research is not a linear process, of course; it is a loop, because the conclusions will (or should) send you or somebody else back to the first stage again, to design a new investigation.

Two

QUANTIFYING DESCRIPTION

Collections of archaeological material do not speak for them-selves; it is necessary for archaeologists to specify aspects of the material which interest them, and these will be determined by their aims (or, very often, by what has become traditional within the discipline). The process of going from aims to relevant aspects of one's material is by no means straightforward. Some archaeologists would say that it has rarely been done success-fully and that consequently many if not most archaeological (re)constructions of the past are little more than fictions.

Let us consider an example. Suppose one is interested in studying social stratification through time in a given area. The next step might be to look at the archaeological record of that area and to decide that the best aspect for giving us an indica-tion of changing social stratification would be the variation, through time, in the quantity of metal grave goods deposited in the richest graves in the area. A diachronic picture showing the changing quantities of metal could then be drawn. However, if the quantities of metal deposited related not to the social power of the individuals buried but, for example, to changes in mining technology or in the trade contacts of the area, then the picture would not reflect changing social stratification, but something else. If, after we had mistakenly argued that metal deposition related to social stratification, we then went on to try and explain the reasons for growing social stratification, we would be making matters even worse, because we would be trying to understand a process that never occurred! Presented in this form, the pitfalls seem obvious enough, but they are very easy to fall into in practice, and much recent work has been devoted to improving our understanding of the enormous variety of processes which produce the archaeological record.

For the purposes of this text we will have to skirt round this problem most of the time and to assume that we have selected for investigation an aspect of our material which is appropriate to our interests. In practice, particularly at the level of describing material for an excavation report, for example, there is broad agreement about what categories of information should be recorded and presented, so that we do not have to agonise too much. But we can rightly raise the question whether what has become traditional in such matters is always what we want.

Once we have defined the aspects of our material in which we are interested, it is necessary to prepare a record of them ready for analysis. When data are being collected, the process of assigning a value or score to some aspect of the material in which we are interested constitutes the process of measurement. This is a much more general definition than simply measuring things with a set of calipers or weighing them on a pair of scales – measurement can be of many different kinds. If we are studying a collection of pottery, for example, there are many aspects in which we could be interested: the height or volume of the vessels, the decorative motifs used on them, the fabrics of which they are made, or their shapes. For each vessel in our collection we need to record the information in which we are interested. The result of this work will be a large table of scores and values for each aspect of interest to us (e.g. Table 2.1). The aspects of our material in which we are interested in a given study are usually referred to as the *variables* of interest. Each item that we are studying, whether the items are sites, regions, ceramics, lithics or whatever, will have a specific *value* for each variable.

TABLE 2.1. Example of the information recorded for a group of ceramic vessels.

	Height (mm)	Rim diameter (mm)	Fabric type	Rim type	Motif in position 1	Motif in position 2	...
Vessel 1	139	114	1	1	16	11	...
Vessel 2	143	125	2	1	12	9	...
⋮							
Vessel *n*	154	121	4	3	21	15	...

The process of measurement, especially the description of complex items such as pottery or graves, is by no means straightforward and requires a lot of clear thinking (see for example Gardin, 1980; Richards and Ryan, 1985). It is not, or should not be, simply a matter of sitting in front of a database program filling in the names of fields.

In the past there was little choice about ways of entering data: numbers had to be entered directly into the rather clumsy data entry modules of large statistics packages. These days it is much more usual to enter data into a database or spreadsheet program unless the data set is a trivial one. Spreadsheets, of course, have extensive statistical functions and if data can be easily structured for spreadsheet entry then they are in a form amenable to quantitative analysis. More complex data need to be organised in a relational database and there is an extensive literature on the way to construct these successfully in a way which captures the characteristics of interest and enables information to be retrieved in ways which are flexible, accurate and consistent (e.g. Elmasri and Navathe, 1989); unfortunately, most archaeologists seem unaware of it! An analysis of burials, for example, may involve information about the grave itself, the skeleton(s), possibly individual bones, the positions of the grave goods, their number and their attributes, such as detailed descriptions of pottery. These sets of information are likely to be best stored in separate tables within the database, following the formal rules for relational structure, and must be correctly linked together. Such a structure provides the flexibility to examine, for example, the relationship between the sex or age of a buried individual and the decorative motifs on pottery grave goods buried with them. On the other hand, the rules of good relational structure which make this possible may mean that outputting the data in a form suitable for statistical analysis can be quite complex.

Software does not remove the substantive problems of data description, although it may make it easier to make a good descriptive scheme work; it certainly does not save you from making mistakes. It is obviously vital to use terms and codes consistently and without ambiguity and to avoid logical inconsistencies between different parts of the descriptive system. Systematically describing pottery decoration for computer input can be especially difficult since it can involve making decisions about what are the basic units of the decorative scheme, what are simply variations within the basic structure, and many others (see Plog, 1980, for a good discussion of this).

A general question which often arises is what to include and what to omit from the description, even when you know what your aims are. For example, if you are studying a cemetery of inhumation burials with a view to understanding patterns of burial ritual and social structure, do you include information on the position of each grave good in the grave? Perhaps the exact position of the limbs of the skeleton is significant in some way? The usual answer is to err on the side of inclusion rather than omission, but in a very large study this may involve an enormous amount of work which may not prove relevant and which, if it involves fieldwork, is likely to cost a great deal of money as well as time. It may also produce a dataset which is simply too unwieldy to analyse (cf. Fieller, 1993).

The best way to sort out all the problems which may arise is to carry out a pilot study – a preliminary analysis of a small part of the data using the proposed descriptive system. The importance of this cannot be urged too strongly. It is no exaggeration to say that decisions taken at the coding/description stage will have a major effect on the outcome of the subsequent analyses and that time spent getting it right will more than repay itself.

It might be thought that there is an exception to the above comments: increasingly data are being captured by various kinds of automatic data logging techniques, perhaps in particular the use of video cameras to capture images which can then be manipulated using image analysis techniques. Even here, however, choices and decisions cannot be avoided prior to analysis (see Durham et al., 1994); if it is an image of an object, for example, we have to define what parts of the image will be analysed: the shape only? internal detail? the texture? a segment of the shape? Furthermore, as with all the more laborious descriptive methods, we end up with a table of numbers which we need to do something with.

LEVELS OF MEASUREMENT

Once we have produced a table or tables of data then all the information is there but it is not yet very accessible to us. We are not usually interested in the characteristics of each individual item, but in the assemblage of material as a whole. When we ask questions like 'How common are the different pottery fabrics?', 'Are the vessels a standard size?', answers are not immediately available from the table. We need to summarise our data (the values of our variables) in some way, whether by means of diagrams or summary numbers. Whatever form of summary we choose, however, we first need to consider the measurement characteristics of our variables, or what are known as *levels of measurement*. What are these levels or scales? They are, in order of their mathematical power from lowest to highest, the *nominal*, *ordinal*, *interval* and *ratio* scales.

The nominal scale is so-called because it involves no more than giving names to the different categories within it. You might not think of this as measurement at all, but as the process of classification: placing things in groups or categories, a basic first step in virtually any investigation. Suppose we were studying British Bronze Age funerary pottery and we categorised our pots, following a long-standing classification, as collared urns, globular urns, barrel urns and bucket urns. This would represent a nominal scale, appropriate for this particular set of pots, in which there were four categories. In this case the process of measurement would consist of assigning one of these categories or values to each of our pots. There is no inherent ordering among the pots implied by categorising them in this way. We could assign numbers to the categories, e.g.:

1 = collared urn
2 = globular urn
3 = barrel urn
4 = bucket urn

If we did this we would be using the numbers merely as symbols that are convenient to us for some reason – perhaps as a shorthand notation. It would be meaningless to add or multiply these numbers together.

If it is possible to give a rank order to all of the categories according to some criterion, then the ordinal level of measurement has been achieved. Thus if we categorised the sherds in a pottery assemblage as fine ware, everyday ware and coarse ware, we could say that this was an ordinal scale with respect to some notion of quality. We could rank the fine wares as 1, domestic wares as 2, and coarse wares as 3. Similarly, the well-known and much maligned classification of societies into bands, tribes, chiefdoms and states (Service, 1962) is a rank-ordering of societies with respect to an idea of complexity of organisation. Each category has a unique position relative to the others. Thus, if we know that chiefdom is higher than tribe and that state is higher than chiefdom, this automatically tells us that state is higher than tribe. On the other hand, we do not know *how much* lower chiefdom is than state, or tribe than chiefdom, we simply know the order – it is lower. It is this property of ordering which is the sole mathematical property of the ordinal scale.

In contrast to the ordinal scale, where only the ordering of categories is defined, in interval and ratio scales the distances between the categories are defined in terms of fixed and equal units. The difference between these two, however, is rather less obvious than the others and is best illustrated by an example. Is the measurement of time in terms of AD or BC on an interval or ratio scale? It is certainly more than an ordinal scale because time is divided into fixed and equal units – years. The distinction between the two depends on the definition of the zero point – whether it is arbitrary or not. Defining chronology in terms of years AD or BC is an arbitrary convention. Other different but equally valid systems exist, with different starting points, for example the Jewish or Islamic systems. If, on the other hand, we consider physical measurements, such as distances, volumes or weights, then the zero point is not arbitrary. For example, if we measure distance, whatever units of measurement we use, a zero distance is naturally defined: it is the absence of distance between two points; and the ratio of 100 mm to 200 mm is the same as that between the equivalent in inches, 3.94 and 7.88, i.e. 1:2. This is not true of our chronological systems: the ratio of AD 1000 to 2000 (1,000 years) is 1:2, but if we take the cor-responding years in the Islamic chronology, 378 and 1378 (also 1,000 years), the ratio is 1:3.65. Chronology then is an example of an interval scale but physical measurements are examples of ratio scales. In practice, once we get beyond the ordinal scale, it is usually ratio scale variables that we are dealing with in archaeology – physical measurements of the various types referred to above, and counts of numbers of items.

The reason for knowing about these distinctions is that they affect the statistical techniques which we can use in any particular case, whether we are using complex methods of multivariate analysis or merely drawing diagrams. In the chapters which follow, as the different techniques are presented, one of the first considerations will always be the level of measurement of the data for which the methods are appropriate. It is particularly easy to slip into using inappropriate methods these days when the work is always done by computer rather than by hand calculation, since the program will take the numbers you give it at face value and not question whether they are suitable for the operations being carried out.

The discussion so far has emphasised the distinctions between the various levels of measurement but it is worth noting that the scale of measurement for a particular property of a set of data is not necessarily immutable and indeed to some extent is a matter of choice.

Let us return to our example of dividing a pottery assemblage into fine ware, everyday ware and coarse ware, an ordinal scale based on an idea of fineness or quality. In principle, there is no reason why we should not quantify the fineness of the pottery fabric, for example in terms of the mean grain size of the tempering material, or the ratio of inclusions to clay. We would then have a ratio scale measure of fineness and we could place each sherd or vessel on the line from fine to coarse, measured in terms of fixed and equal units. Clearly such a ratio scale contains more information about the property in question than the ordinal scale of fine, medium and coarse and in that sense it might be regarded as preferable.

There is, of course, no reason in principle why we cannot reverse the process. Starting with measurements of grain sizes in our pottery fabrics, for example, we could then categorise them as fine, everyday and coarse. If we do this, however, we are neglecting information, which is generally not a good thing to do. Nevertheless, the argument is not completely straightforward and controversies have raged in the archaeological literature about when and whether it is appropriate to categorise ratio scale variables (see the contributions to Whallon and Brown, 1982, particularly those of Hodson and Spaulding).

The best guide is to make use of the level of measurement

that will provide an answer to the question being investigated for the least cost. To refer again to the pottery example, if our investigation requires no more than a distinction between fine ware, everyday ware and coarse ware, it is a waste of time and money to produce a detailed quantified description of every vessel's fabric. However, we may want to analyse a few examples of each fabric type to demonstrate that our distinctions between the fabrics are not totally subjective.

EXERCISES

2.1 Look at the series of German neolithic ceramic vessels in Figure 2.1, p. 14 (after Schoknecht, 1980), and devise a set of variables and values that you think provides the basis for a systematic description of them suitable for entry into a database or a statistics program. Apply your system to the vessels and produce table(s) of values of your variables for each vessel. What problems arose, if any? (Scale: 3:16.)

2.2 Try the same exercise with the set of illustrations of grave plans and their contents from a late neolithic cemetery in the Czech Republic which appear in Figures 2.2 to 2.7, pp. 15–20 (after Buchvaldek and Koutecky, 1970). The contents of the graves are also listed below since the nature of the objects is not always clear from the drawings and not all of them are illustrated. (Scale: plans 1:27, pottery and grindstone 1:4, other items 1:2.)

GRAVE 1   1. Amphora
          2. Decorated beaker
          3. Flat axe
          4. Flint blade
          5. Grindstone

GRAVE 2   1. Base sherds of beaker
          2. Decorated beaker

GRAVE 3   1. Decorated beaker with handle
          2. Decorated amphora
          3. Flint blade
          4. Piece of copper spiral

GRAVE 4   1. Piece of flint blade
               2. Sherds probably from two vessels

GRAVE 5   1. Amphora
               2. Decorated amphora
               3. Mace head
               4. Flint blade

GRAVE 6   1. Quartzite scraper

GRAVE 7   1. Amphora
               2. Decorated beaker with handle
               3. Decorated jar
               4. Cylindrical beaker with lug

GRAVE 8   1. Amphora
               2. Decorated amphora
               3. Decorated beaker with handle
               4. Hammer axe
               5. Flint blade

GRAVE 9   1. 2. Decorated beakers
               3. Jug
               4. Decorated beaker
               5. Jar
               6. Decorated amphora
               7. Amphora
               8. Flint blade

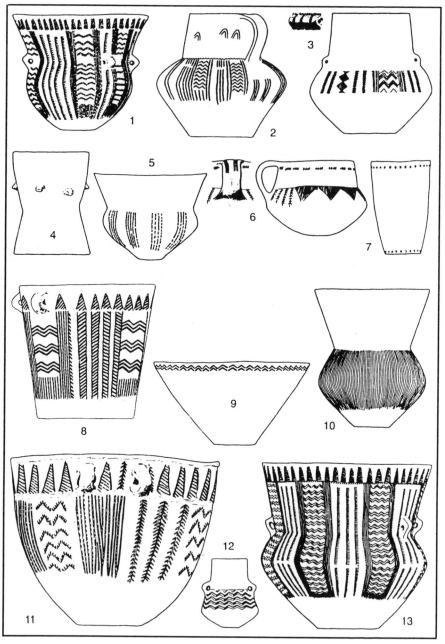

FIGURE 2.1. Decorated neolithic ceramic vessels from Germany.

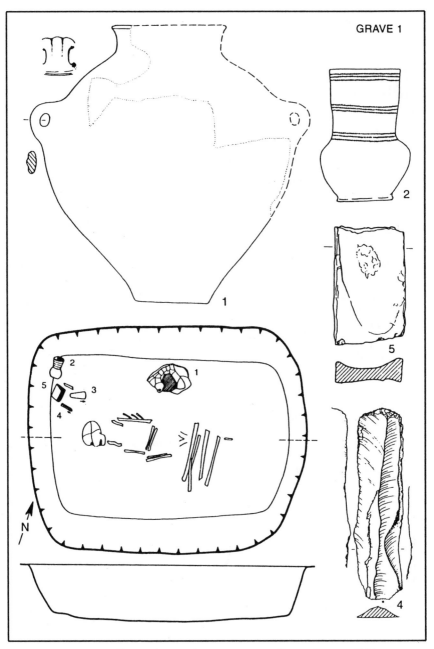

FIGURE 2.2. Grave plans and grave contents from a late neolithic Corded Ware cemetery in the Czech Republic (after Buchvaldek and Koutecky, 1970).

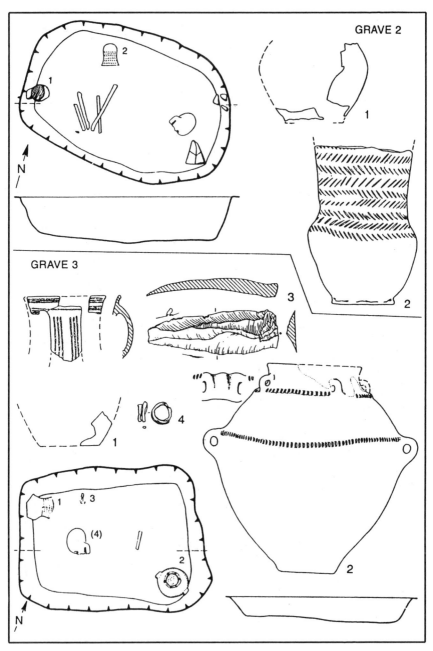

FIGURE 2.3. (*caption as on opposite page*)

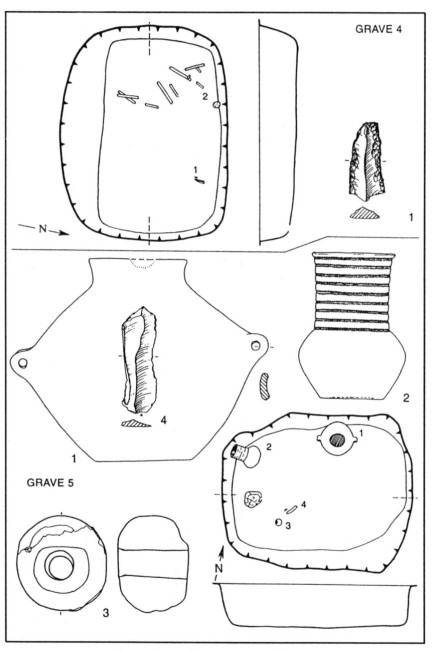

FIGURE 2.4. Grave plans and grave contents from a late neolithic Corded Ware cemetery in the Czech Republic (after Buchvaldek and Koutecky, 1970).

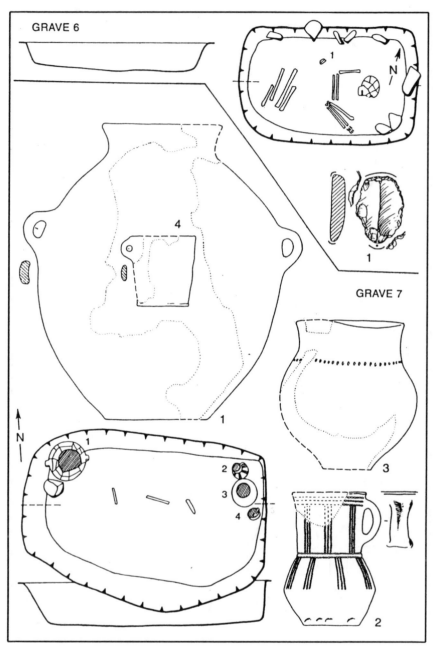

FIGURE 2.5. (*caption as on opposite page*)

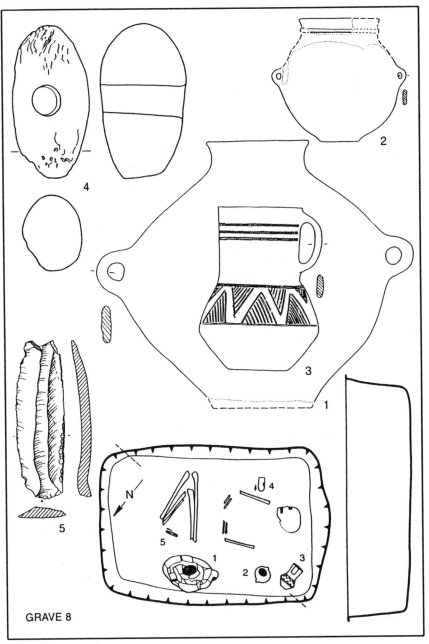

FIGURE 2.6. Grave plans and grave contents from a late neolithic Corded Ware cemetery in the Czech Republic (after Buchvaldek and Koutecky, 1970).

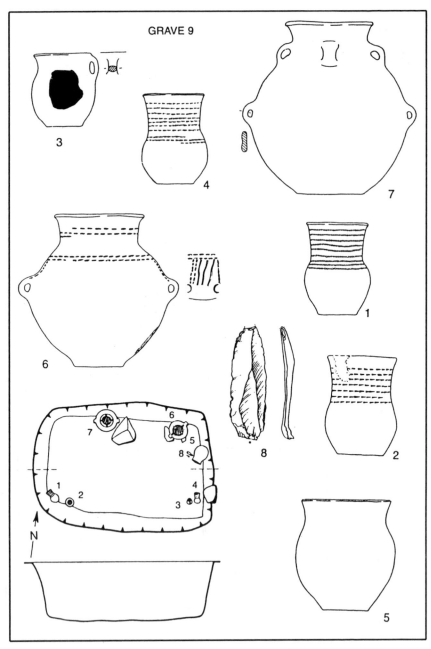

FIGURE 2.7. Grave plans and grave contents from a late neolithic Corded Ware cemetery in the Czech Republic (after Buchvaldek and Koutecky, 1970).

Three

PICTURE SUMMARIES OF
A SINGLE VARIABLE

In using quantitative methods in archaeology it is possible to get a long way in terms of understanding simply by devising some pictorial means to represent your data. Once data are represented visually the power of the human eye and brain to detect and assess patterns can be immediately employed, and some very complex methods of quantitative analysis boil down to little more than ways of obtaining the best possible picture of a complicated data set, as we will see below. Conversely, however, the human eye can see patterns when none are really there and this too is a point to which we will return later.

The use of graphs and charts to display information has always had an important role to play in statistics, but in recent years they have become even more important. The reasons for this are both good and bad. On the bad side the increasing availability of presentation graphics packages has led to a proliferation of fancy means of data presentation involving multiple dimensions and an enormous range of colours and hatchings. By and large these obscure more than they illuminate, which is fine if you're trying to con someone at a business presentation but not otherwise. The golden rule is to keep things clear and simple; principles of good visual representation are discussed and illustrated by Tufte (1983, 1990) in two books now widely recognised as classics.

On the good side there is now a much greater emphasis among statisticians than there used to be on the importance of *exploring data* for significant patterning. The idea is that

data = smooth + rough

In other words, a given set of observations can be divided into two components, a general pattern (the 'smooth') and the variations from that pattern (the 'rough'). The task of data analysts then is to distinguish the smooth from the rough in the most objective kind of way, being continuously sceptical as they do so. This forms part of the research loop, the continuing interplay between ideas and data, and exploring data in this way can be an important means of generating ideas, not just evaluating them.

This chapter is concerned with the various visual means of representing the distributions of single variables. The idea is to reduce the data to some kind of order, so that it is possible to see what they look like, to obtain an initial impression of the 'smooth' and the 'rough'. In general, this involves the presentation of *frequency distributions*, in which the observations are grouped in a limited number of categories.

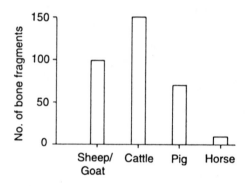

FIGURE 3.1. Bar chart of the number of bone fragments of different domestic animal species from a hypothetical British Iron Age site.

BAR CHARTS AND PIE CHARTS

Probably the best known are simple *bar charts* or *bar graphs*, which are familiar in everyday life and whose use in archaeology is long established. These permit a distinction in terms of whether the categories are simply at the nominal scale, or whether there is an inherent ordering of the bars. An example of the former would be Figure 3.1, which is a summary of the number of bone fragments of different types from a hypothetical British Iron Age site. There is no particular significance in the ordering of the species on the horizontal axis; it could be changed to any one of the different possible orderings and the information contained within it would stay the same.

An alternative way of presenting these data would be by means of a *pie chart* or *circle graph*. This requires the absolute numbers to be converted into relative proportions, and thus represents a gain in information in one sense and a loss in another: an idea of the numbers in the categories is lost but their relative proportions emerge more clearly. However, it is always essential to indicate the total number of observations on which a pie chart is based, otherwise it is impossible to know whether the percentages are based on 10 observations or 10,000 and this will (or should!) make a big difference to how you assess them. If a number of pie charts are being displayed together an idea of the relative sizes of the different samples can be given by making the area of the circles proportional to the sample size. In the case of the example using animal bone fragments just given, the pie chart would come out as Figure 3.2, where the angle of the appropriate sector at the centre of the circle is the corresponding percentage multiplied by 360/100. Thus, if the cattle percentage was 46 per cent, this would give 46 × 360/100 = 166 degrees.

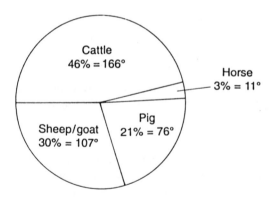

FIGURE 3.2. Pie chart of the relative proportions of bone fragments of different domestic species using the data from Figure 3.1. Number of bone fragments = 330.

The pie chart is a very helpful mode of data presentation when the aim is to illustrate relative proportions of unordered categories, especially when making comparisons, for example if you had a number of Iron Age faunal assemblages that you wished to compare. However, it can be confusing if there are numerous categories, or categories with zero or very small entries.

With an ordinal scale the ordering of our categories is fixed by reference to some criterion, so here the horizontal ordering of the bars in a bar graph does mean something; lower rank values are to the left and higher ones to the right, or vice versa. In these circumstances it is the pie chart form of presentation which can be misleading, because the last category comes round to join the first. At a higher level of ordering again not only is the ordering significant but so is the interval between the bars; an example is given in Figure 3.3, where each bar is a count of one away from those adjacent to it.

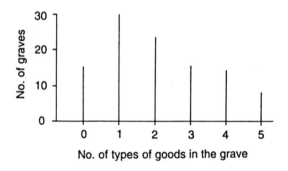

FIGURE 3.3. Bar chart of the number of graves containing different numbers of grave-good types for a hypothetical central European Bronze Age cemetery.

Here we have a bar graph summarising the number of graves in a cemetery which have particular numbers of grave goods types; thus, roughly 15 graves have no grave goods, 30 have one type, and so on. This time we are dealing with a ratio scale – zero here means lack of grave goods. But the scale shown here has one particular characteristic to which attention needs to be drawn; it can only take countable whole number or *integer* values. For a grave to contain 3.326 types of grave goods is simply impossible.

CONTINUOUS BAR CHARTS AND HISTOGRAMS

Other interval or ratio scales can take any value, and these are known as *continuous numeric* scales (often referred to as *real* values). Suppose we are measuring, for example, the heights of pots or the lengths of bones, then we might have measurements of 182.5 mm, 170.1 mm and 153.6 mm. Although the particular set of pots or bones that we measure will take a particular set of values, there is no theoretical reason why they should not take any decimal point value, the number of places after the decimal point simply being determined by the accuracy to which we are willing or able to take our measurements.

When we want to represent the frequency of different measured values of some continuous numeric variable like height, length or weight, then we are in a rather different situation from any of those looked at so far. The aim, remember, is to use the diagram to help us to pick out general patterns in the observations. If we have a scale in terms of tenths of a millimetre, the accuracy to which we have taken the measurements, we may have an observation of 182.5 mm, then another of 70.1 mm and another at 153.6 mm; probably at most one of our objects will have exactly any one of the tenth of a millimetre values. In these circumstances it is not all that easy to detect general patterns in the resulting diagram so the object of the exercise is being defeated.

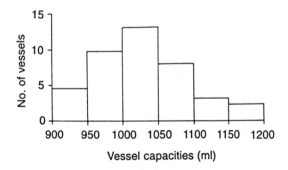

FIGURE 3.4. Bar chart of the distribution of vessel capacities for a group of 40 Bell Beakers.

What we have to do is divide our variable up into a number of intervals, whose width has been chosen by us, and then count the number of observations falling into each interval. For example, Figure 3.4 shows the frequency distribution of the capacities of a number of Bell Beaker pots. Into each of the intervals are placed all the observations which fall within it. The decision on the number of intervals to use has traditionally been an arbitrary one but it should not be made without some thought. We do not want to have so few intervals that any patterning in the distribution disappears altogether; in the case of the data in Figure 3.4 for example, it would not be all that illuminating just to have two bars, each of 150 ml width. On the other hand, if we have very narrow intervals there will be lots of gaps and holes in the distribution. This too will make it very difficult to spot any trends in the distribution when this is the most important reason for producing such diagrams in the first place. In general, it is never good to have more than twenty intervals because then the picture becomes too confusing. One rule-of-thumb which usually produces a reasonable picture is to make the number of intervals roughly equal to the square root of the number of observations; so, for example, if our data are the volumes of forty pots then we would divide volume into six intervals. In this case we can indeed see that there is a general pattern in the distribution of vessel volumes (Figure 3.4).

Because the variable is continuous it is important to be clear exactly what the bar category intervals are. First, they must be exhaustive: in other words, the range must include all the observations; this is straightforward enough. Second, they must be mutually exclusive. If one of the category intervals was 900–950 ml and the next 950–1,000 ml then there would be ambiguity, since a value of 950 would fall into both classes. We should be clear that the range for the first interval is 900–949.9 ml, and for the next 950–999.9 ml, and so on.

A diagram like Figure 3.4 almost conforms to the definition of a *histogram*. This is a bar chart of a continuous numeric distribution in which the frequency of a class is given by the *area* rather than the height of the corresponding bar and the areas of all the bars are defined to sum to one, so that each bar represents a proportion of the total. Of course, if all the intervals are the same width then the areas will correspond to the heights but if the intervals vary in width this will obviously not be the case.

Another way of expressing the information in an ordered bar graph is by means of a frequency polygon, and Figure 3.5 represents Figure 3.3 in this form.

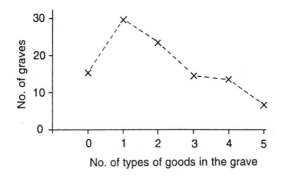

FIGURE 3.5. Frequency polygon of the data in Figure 3.3.

THE STEM-AND-LEAF DIAGRAM

The methods outlined above are the traditional means of representing the distribution of single variables in diagrammatic form. The problem with them is that the only real 'truth' in a set of observations is the scores of the observations themselves. Once we try to summarise them, even in the form of a display like those above, we start losing information. Worse still, there is no single 'correct' picture. The shape of a bar graph or histogram can vary considerably, depending on the width of the intervals and the precise starting point selected. On the other hand, as we have emphasised, we need to lose detail to gain knowledge, to see the wood for the trees. One technique which makes it possible to some extent to have your cake and eat it is the stem-and-leaf diagram, a form of bar graph which retains the individual numerical values of the raw data.

It may be illustrated by means of data on the diameters of a sample of thirty-five postholes from the late neolithic henge monument of Mount Pleasant, Dorset, England (Wainwright, 1979); these are listed in Table 3.1. To produce the stem-and-leaf the first digits of the data values (here the posthole diameters)

are separated from the other(s). These first digits are then listed
vertically down the left-hand side of the diagram in order and

TABLE 3.1. Diameters (in cm) of 35 postholes from the late neolithic
henge monument of Mount Pleasant, Dorset, England.

48	57	66	48	50	58	47
48	49	48	47	57	40	50
43	40	44	40	34	42	47
48	53	43	43	25	45	39
38	35	30	38	38	28	27

form the stem (Fig. 3.6). The remaining digit(s) for each score
is then placed in the row corresponding to its first digit, in
ascending order, to form the leaf (Figure 3.7). This gives us a
picture that loses none of the initial information.

```
2 |
3 |
4 |
5 |
6 |
```

FIGURE 3.6. The 'stem' of a stem-and-leaf diagram of the Mount
Pleasant posthole diameters listed in Table 3.1.

```
2 | 5 7 8
3 | 0 4 5 8 8 8 9
4 | 0 0 0 2 3 3 3 4 5 7 7 7 8 8 8 8 8 9
5 | 0 0 3 7 7 8
6 | 6
```

FIGURE 3.7. Stem-and-leaf diagram of the Mount Pleasant posthole
diameters listed in Table 3.1.

If, on inspection, we felt that it would be helpful to make the
intervals narrower, by making them five units wide rather than
ten, this is easily done; we simply have two rows for each digit,
one for second digits 0–4, the other for second digits 5–9
(Figure 3.8).

```
2
2 | 5 7 8
3 | 0 4
3 | 5 8 8 8 9
4 | 0 0 0 2 3 3 3 4
4 | 5 7 7 7 8 8 8 8 8 9
5 | 0 0 3
5 | 7 7 8
6
6 | 6
```

FIGURE 3.8. Stem-and-leaf diagram of the Mount Pleasant posthole diameters listed in Table 3.1 with stem intervals 5 units wide instead of 10.

KERNEL SMOOTHING[1]

In the last few years a rather different and more sophisticated approach to the problems posed by the element of arbitrariness in histogram construction has been developed. It is known as *kernel smoothing* (Wand and Jones, 1995) and is not yet widely available in statistical software (but see Baxter and Beardah, 1995). This technique does not share the problem which histograms have of the arbitrariness of the initial starting point and hence of the category boundaries all along the histogram because the *kernel density estimator* produces results corresponding to the idea of the average shifted histogram, which averages several histograms based on shifts in the category edges (Wand and Jones, 1995, p.7). Nor does it have the problem that histograms represent changing frequencies of values by a series of steps which are arbitrary and unrealistic.

The other problem, of course, is the interval width, for which some rule-of-thumb remedies were suggested above. Kernel density estimation involves moving a smoothing function, the kernel, along the observations and generating the resulting probability distribution; different patterns will result depending on the *bandwidth* of the kernel. What is involved is shown in Figure 3.9, where a simulated distribution of known shape is

---

1. This section is more complex than the rest of this chapter and can be skipped if you prefer.

estimated by kernels of different widths. It is easy to see that
the quality of the estimate depends strongly on the bandwidth
selected. Wand and Jones (1995, Chapter 3) discuss a variety of
complex ways of estimating the most appropriate bandwidth,
but trying out a variety of widths and selecting one intuitively in
terms of achieving a balance in the picture between 'rough' and
'smooth' may be just as appropriate.

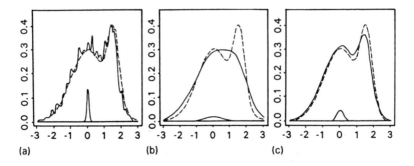

FIGURE 3.9. Kernel density estimates based on a sample of 1000
observations from a simulated mixture of normal distributions. The
solid line is the estimate, the broken line is the true density. The
bandwidths are (a) $h = 0.06$ (b) $h = 0.54$ (c) $h = 0.18$. The kernel
weight for each estimate is shown by small kernels at the base of
each figure. After Wand and Jones, 1995 (Figure 2.3).

CUMULATIVE FREQUENCY DISTRIBUTIONS

Finally, the last method of pictorial data summary to be mentioned in any detail in this chapter is the so-called cumulative
curve or cumulative frequency distribution – the word curve
being slightly misleading since it is really a series of straight
line segments joining a set of data points. Their construction is
rather more complex than that of the bar graphs, pie charts etc.
described so far.

In general, like pie charts, cumulative curves are based not on
the actual numbers of observations in our categories or intervals
but on those numbers expressed as a proportion or percentage of
the total. How they work may be illustrated once again with the
grave goods information from Figures 3.3 and 3.5 which is first
presented in the form of a table (Table 3.2).

TABLE 3.2. Number of graves containing different numbers of grave-good types from a hypothetical central European Bronze Age cemetery.

No. of types of goods	*No. of graves*	*Percentage of graves*
0	17	15.6
1	30	27.5
2	26	23.9
3	17	15.6
4	13	11.9
5	6	5.5
	109	100.0

FIGURE 3.10. Cumulative curve of the data on numbers of grave-good types presented in Table 3.2.

A new graph may now be drawn, with the horizontal scale as before indicating the number of types of grave goods in the grave but with the vertical axis a percentage scale ranging from 0 to 100. We note first that 15.6 per cent of the graves are in the zero grave goods category, so we mark that on the graph. Now when we come to the 27.5 per cent of graves in the one grave good category we add or accumulate these onto the 15.6 per cent in the zero category, so we have $15.6 + 27.5 = 43.1$ per cent as the value for the one grave good category, which can also be marked on the graph. The value tells us that 43.1 per cent of the graves have one grave good or less. We do this for all the categories in turn until the full 100 per cent of graves has been accumulated:

$$43.1 + 23.9 = 67.0$$
$$67.0 + 15.6 = 82.6$$
$$82.6 + 11.9 = 94.5$$
$$94.5 + 5.5 = 100.0$$

When the points have all been put on the graph we can join them up and the resulting line is the cumulative curve shown in Figure 3.10. This represents the shape of the cumulative distribution.

Simply as a means of representing the shape of the distribution of a single variable it may seem rather complex and unnecessary. Why not use a bar chart? The answer is that it really comes into its own in making comparisons between distributions. Bar charts, with their varying patterns of bar heights, are rather difficult to compare visually. With the continuously rising line of the cumulative curve, similarities and differences between distributions are much more readily apparent.

This form of presentation is obviously truly meaningful only if there is a real ordering on the horizontal axis, that is, if we are dealing with data measured at an ordinal scale or above. If the level of measurement is nominal, any ordering will be arbitrary, as we have already mentioned, and the shape of a cumulative curve based on any such orderings equally arbitrary; it would be possible to change the order of the categories to produce a curve of some desired shape. Nevertheless, if a fixed order of presentation of the categories is adopted when comparisons are being made, cumulative frequency distributions can and have proved helpful in the presentation of nominal data such as palaeolithic assemblages described in terms of numbers or percentages of particular artefact types; they should simply be used and viewed with caution.

The techniques described in this chapter have provided you with the basic tools for describing the distributions of single variables by pictorial means, although there is one more we will see in the next chapter. The use of the graphical summaries described here is essential prior to any further analysis, as well as giving a first insight into the patterning present in the data through the summaries these diagrams provide.

EXERCISES

3.1 The following are the figures for the number of sherds of different pottery types from the henge monument at Mount Pleasant, Dorset, England (data from Wainwright, 1979). Represent them by means of a bar graph and a pie chart and indicate which you prefer and why:

Neolithic plain bowl	391
Grooved Ware	657
Beaker	1695
Peterborough ware	6
Bronze Age	591

3.2 The sizes (in hectares) of a number of Late Uruk settlement sites in Mesopotamia (data from Johnson, 1973) are as follows:

45.0	37.0	34.8	52.0	75.0	86.0	59.7	74.0	32.0
57.7	65.0	86.0	37.0	38.4	90.5	45.0	67.0	50.0
33.0	30.0	43.2	32.0	35.2	54.5	43.1		

Use an appropriate graphical method to represent these data. Does there seem to be any pattern in the distribution of settlement sizes? Does it change if you use a different width interval?

3.3 Draw a cumulative percentage frequency distribution of the following data on the ages at death of the individuals buried in a prehistoric cemetery.

Age category	No. of burials
Infans I	10
Infans II	16
Juvenilis	10
Adultus	32
Maturus	34
Senilis	4

Four

NUMERICAL SUMMARIES OF
A SINGLE VARIABLE

The previous chapter examined methods of *graphical* representation for distributions of observations measured at different levels. This one considers *numerical* summaries of information. I would be the first to agree that this is not intrinsically a very exciting topic but there are two main reasons why it is essential. The first, and less important, is that such summaries are often an important element of published descriptions of archaeological work. Modern excavations often produce so many finds of certain categories that the only way in which the information may be presented in a form sufficiently compact to be published is in some kind of graph or tabular numerical summary. Such summaries provide the information on which inferences have been based, so that readers may have an opportunity of evaluating it. This presupposes, of course, a readership sufficiently educated to do so, a requirement which is vital for the progress of any discipline.

The second reason for a concern with numerical description is that the methods to be described later in this book, which are concerned with the much more interesting questions of identifying patterns and relationships between variables, depend on the use of the descriptive methods now to be introduced.

It is important to remember that what we were doing with our graphical methods was summarising data; we were forgetting about individuals, individual sherds, pieces of chipped stone, or whatever, and attempting to obtain some kind of overall picture of general trends in the data distribution. Although a picture or diagram of some kind may very often give us the summarised information we want, to do anything more with that summarised information it needs to be in the numerical form of *descriptive statistics* so that it can be further manipulated. However, reduction of a lot of information to one or two simple numbers can be potentially risky: there is a greater danger of being misled than when you have a graphical picture of the data in front of you. The conclusion to be drawn from this is that even if you are summarising data numerically you should always look at them graphically as well.

For nominal scale variables the matter of numerical summary is very straightforward, but no less important for that: it involves producing a table of counts of the numbers of observations in each of the relevant categories – the number of animal bones in each species category, the number of stone tools in each stone tool category, and so on; in each case we might refer to the most common – or *modal* – category. Ways in which such tables may be analysed will be considered in later chapters.

When we consider variables measured at an interval scale and above we can take the summarisation by numbers process a great deal further. To summarise the information fully, in fact, we need to measure four different aspects of the bar graphs or histograms that we have seen. These are:

1. Central tendency, or what is a typical individual?

2. Dispersion, or how much variation is there? In a picture like Figure 4.1(a) a typical individual is much more representative than in a more dispersed distribution like Figure 4.1(b).

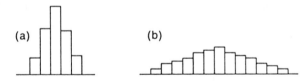

FIGURE 4.1. Two distributions in which there is (a) very little, and (b) a great deal, of dispersion round the central value.

3. Shape, which has two aspects:

3a. Is the distribution symmetrical or not? Figures 4.2 (a), (b) and (c) indicate some of the possibilities. In both the latter two cases the distribution is said to be *skew*. In (b) it is skew to the right – it has a long tail extending to the right. In (c) it is skew to the left – the tail is to the left.

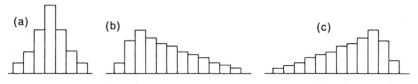

FIGURE 4.2. Examples of distributions of different shapes.

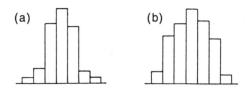

FIGURE 4.3. Examples of distributions with different length tails.

3b. The second aspect of shape concerns the length of the tails of the distribution, illustrated in Figures 4.3 (a) and (b). The degree of dispersion of these two distributions is fairly similar, but one has longer tails than the other. The length of the tails of a distribution is referred to as its degree of *kurtosis*. Distributions with long tails are *leptokurtic* and those with short tails are *platykurtic*.

In fact, the measures of shape figure much less prominently than the measures of central tendency and dispersion in most statistical applications, although the question of skewness is of great significance, usually as a problem to be overcome (see Chapter 8).

MEASURES OF CENTRAL TENDENCY

Now that these descriptive characteristics have been listed we can look at the question of central tendency in more detail. There are several ways of measuring this and the same is true for dispersion. The best known and most widely used measure of central tendency is the arithmetic mean, defined as the sum of the scores divided by the total number of cases.

Let us take as an example the diameters of seven of the Mount Pleasant postholes listed in the previous chapter:

$$48 + 57 + 66 + 48 + 50 + 58 + 47 = 374$$

There are seven postholes here so we divide 374 by 7 to give 53.4 cm as the mean diameter for this set of postholes. We are, in effect, saying here that a typical posthole is 53.4 cm in diameter. No posthole really is 53.4 cm in diameter but this value is somewhere in the middle of all of them. In fact, the arithmetic mean represents the centre of gravity of the distribution and has the specific property that the sum of the deviations of the individual scores from the mean is always zero. That is to say, if we take each of our observations, subtract the mean from each in turn and add up all the resulting differences, the answer will be zero. Thus:

$$(48-53.4) + (57-53.4) + (66-53.4) + (48-53.4) +$$
$$(50-53.4) + (58-53.4) + (47-53.4) =$$
$$-5.4 + 3.6 + 12.6 - 5.4 - 3.4 + 4.6 - 6.4$$
$$= 0.2$$

(This result is not exactly zero because of rounding error in the calculations.)

Here it is necessary to digress slightly. A verbal description has just been given of how to obtain an arithmetic mean; this description has been supplemented by a numerical example. However, if we want to specify general rules for doing operations on numbers it is much more convenient to use mathematical symbolism. Symbols are an essential part of mathematics and they are probably the single most off-putting factor for people not naturally attracted to the subject, like most archaeologists. The main thing to remember about symbols is that they are simply a form of short-hand notation which can be easily manipulated.

Let us now have a look at the symbolism that relates to the arithmetic mean, which is conventionally expressed by $\bar{x}$ (called x-bar). We can say in general that:

$$\bar{x} = \frac{x_1 + x_2 + x_3 \ldots + x_n}{n}$$

where x_1 is our first observation, x_2 the second observation, and so on. In the particular case of the postholes:

$$x_1 = 48 \qquad x_2 = 57$$
$$x_3 = 66 \qquad x_4 = 48$$
$$x_5 = 50 \qquad x_6 = 58$$
$$x_7 = 47$$

There are seven observations here, $n = 7$, and the last observation is the seventh, so here $x_n = x_7 = 47$.

But we can summarise conveniently still further and say

$$\bar{x} = \frac{x_1 + x_2 + x_3 \ldots + x_n}{n} = \frac{\sum_{i=1}^{n} x_i}{n}$$

Here x_i stands for any of our x values. Σ is the upper case Greek letter sigma and stands for summation. So we are being told to add up some x's. Which x's? The subscript and superscript of the Σ tell us which ones; they give us the range over which we are summing, from the first x to the nth x, $i = 1$ to n. In the posthole example there are seven x values which we want to add up, so we have

$$\sum_{i=1}^{7} x_i$$

When we have done the addition we divide by the number of observations n, again 7 in the example, to arrive at our value for $\bar{x}$. If the numbers which we have to add up – the range of summation - is obvious then we might leave out the subscript and superscript and simply write

$$\sum x_i$$

You will meet this notation all the time in statistics and it is very important not to be put off or intimidated by it. We can now return to the main theme, making use where necessary of this symbolic notation.

In addition to the arithmetic mean there are other measures of central tendency of a distribution to be considered. Perhaps the next most important one is the *median*, which is the half-way value in a distribution – half the values are greater than it and half less. Obviously, if we want to find such a value we have to arrange our observations in ascending or descending order of size, in other words in rank order; it is therefore possible to find the median for ordinal as well as interval and ratio data.

Let us look again at the seven posthole diameters whose mean we calculated above: 48, 57, 66, 48, 50, 58, 47 cm. The first step is to put them in order, smallest to largest (or the reverse): 47, 48, 48, 50, 57, 58, 66 cm. If we are interested in the value which has half the observations above it and half below, then obviously we want the middle value. Here we have seven observations. If we count along to the fourth one, from either end, we find 50, which is therefore the median because it has three observations above it and three below. If the number of cases is odd then the median will be the score of the middle case. If the number of cases is even then clearly there will not be a middle case, so the median is taken to be the mean of the two middle cases. Suppose there were just six posthole diameters: 48, 48, 50, 57, 58, 66 cm. In this case the median would be between 50 and 57, the mean of which is 53.5. For ordinal scale data the median rank may be obtained.

Finally, the *mode* should be mentioned. This is simply the most common or frequent value and obviously applies to nominal scale data as well as the other types, as we have noted already. It is clearly impossible for a mode to exist unless we already have a frequency distribution of some sort, a point which is particularly relevant to continuous numeric data, where two observations will hardly ever have exactly the same value.

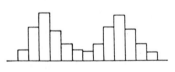

FIGURE 4.4. An example of a bimodal distribution.

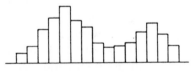

FIGURE 4.5. A distribution with a main and a subsidiary mode.

In general the mode is not of any great interest: it depends very much on the precise construction of the intervals in the frequency distribution and, unlike the mean or the median, we have no idea from the mode itself where it lies within the distribution. However, what is interesting is that it is possible for a distribution to have more than one mode (Figure 4.4) or to have a main mode and a subsidiary mode (Figure 4.5) and these are likely to be significant features of the data. It is worth emphasising that if a distribution is bimodal, or has a mode and a major subsidiary mode, then providing a single measure of central tendency is totally inappropriate. In the case of Figure 4.4 for example, the mean and the median would be in the valley between the two peaks and would thus hardly give a picture of what is a typical value in this distribution; in fact, there is no single best typical value.

In the case of the posthole diameters we might be particularly interested to see if there was more than one mode in the data since this might suggest that different thicknesses of posts were being deliberately produced for different functions. If we simply had variation around a single mode it might merely indicate the degree of success the builders had in finding timber of the right size for one single purpose, or the flexibility of their specifications.

How do these different measures of central tendency compare with one another? To some extent the one we use will depend on what we are trying to do; but in general, if we have nominal or ordinal data we do not have much choice, while for interval or ratio data the most frequently used measure of central tendency is the mean.

The mode, as noted already, simply gives us the most common value but does not tell us where it lies in relation to the other values. The mean uses more information than the median, in the sense that all the exact values of the observations are used in calculating it, whereas the median only uses the relative positions of the scores. More often than not it is desirable to make use of all the information available, so the mean is to be preferred. In fact, if the distribution is symmetrical, the mean, the median and the mode all coincide. If the distribution is very skew, however, the situation changes significantly. Suppose, for example, that in the case of the vessel capacities illustrated in Figure 3.4 one of them had a volume of 2,500 ml. Such a distribution would be skew, with one observation a long way over to the right. This would have an impact on the value of the mean capacity, which would be pulled over to the right and potentially no longer representative of the bulk of the observations. The median on the other hand would hardly be affected at all – there would just be a new largest value; it would remain much more representative of the mass of observations.

From this you can see that we cannot consider the question of central tendency – what is a typical individual – in isolation; we have to think about the shape of the distribution as well. It is always important to know what the frequency distribution of your data looks like, not least if you intend to go on to use more complex statistical methods, because if the distribution has any peculiarities of shape you need to know about them.

MEASURES OF DISPERSION

If data are widely dispersed then a simple measure of central tendency will not be such a 'typical' value as it is when data are narrowly dispersed; this point was illustrated in Figure 4.1.

There are several ways of quantifying dispersion. The simplest is the *range*, the difference between the highest and the lowest scores in the data under consideration. Its disadvantage is that it is based on only two cases and the two most extreme ones at that. Since extremes are likely to be the rare or unusual cases, almost by definition, it is usually a matter of chance if we happen to have one or two very extreme observations in our sample, so if we take a series of samples from a population the range is likely to vary a lot from one to the next.

It has been usual to take the view that the best measure of dispersion is one which makes use of all the information available in the data, in the same way as the mean does for central tendency. As we will see below, there are occasions when using all the information can give a positively misleading result. However, the natural measure of dispersion if we are using the mean as the measure of central tendency is some sort of total of the differences between the individual observations and the mean since this does indeed use all the information available. The most obvious thing to do is to take the sum of the deviations of the observations from the mean. Unfortunately, as we have already seen, this will always be zero, since the positive and negative differences cancel one another out. There are two ways round this problem: either we can ignore the sign and take the absolute value of the differences; or we can square the differences, remembering that a minus times a minus equals a plus so that all quantities become positive ones.

In fact, the second solution, squaring the differences, is the one usually adopted and the resulting measure of dispersion is known as the *standard deviation*, s:

$$s = \sqrt{\frac{\sum_{i=1}^{n} (x_i - \bar{x})^2}{n - 1}}$$

In words, we take the deviation of each score from the mean, square each difference, sum the results, divide by the number of cases minus one, and then take the square root. If we stop before taking the square root we have the variance, s^2, the average of the squared differences between the mean and the data values. Because the variance is a squared quantity it must be expressed in units which are the square of the original units of measurement. More often than not, when describing a distribution it is desirable to have the dispersion measured in the same units as the original measurements, so the standard deviation tends to be intuitively more meaningful than the variance. For instance, if we wanted to know the degree of dispersion around the mean value of the length of a set of flint blades, then if we were measuring them in millimetres we would want dispersion measured in millimetres and not square millimetres.

The variance/standard deviation plays an extremely important role in many statistical tests and for that reason is the most important measure of dispersion for sets of data for which it is an informative measure, that is to say, distributions which are unimodal and symmetric. These days the variance is normally obtained by a computer program. However, if you should have to use a calculator to obtain it, the formula given above is a bit laborious when there are a lot of observations. Below is a version which is slightly less tedious if you have to do the calculations yourself.

$$s = \sqrt{\frac{\sum_{i=1}^{n} x_i^2 - (\sum_{i=1}^{n} x_i)^2 / n}{n - 1}}$$

Let us work out the standard deviation of the seven posthole diameters, using both versions of the formula.

We have already seen that

$\bar{x} = 374/7 = 53.4$

Using the first formula the sum of the squared deviations is

$(48-53.4)^2 + (57-53.4)^2 + (66-53.4)^2 + (48-53.4)^2 +$

$(50-53.4)^2 + (58-53.4)^2 + (47-53.4)^2 = 303.71$

$$s = \sqrt{\frac{303.71}{7-1}} = 7.1$$

Before illustrating the second method, and making sure we get the same result, it is important to be clear about the difference between the terms Σx_i^2 and $(\Sigma x_i)^2$ in the formula. In the first case we are being told to take each x value, square it and sum all the squared values. In the second case we are being told to sum the x values and square the total. These give different results! Now

$$s = \sqrt{\frac{20286-(374)^2 / 7}{7-1}} = \sqrt{\frac{303.71}{6}} = 7.1$$

The precise significance of the standard deviation as a measure of dispersion will be considered in Chapter 8 when we turn to the 'normal' distribution, a special bell-shaped distribution that statisticians have found very useful; for the moment, however, we can note that, given a unimodal symmetric set of data, the standard deviation tells us what is a 'typical' deviation from the data mean. In the case of the postholes a typical deviation from the mean is 7.1 cm.

Sometimes we may want to make comparisons between sets of data in terms of their dispersion. For example, if we were studying standardisation of lithic core production in prehistoric quarries we might want to know if the sizes of cores from one quarry were more variable than those from another, perhaps to try and make inferences about different degrees of craft specialisation. Very often, the larger the mean, the larger the standard deviation, so that if one quarry produced larger cores and another smaller ones, the distribution of core sizes from the former might well have a larger standard deviation for this reason, rather than because production was less standardised. We can get rid of this effect by using the *coefficient of variation*, simply the standard deviation divided by the mean; sometimes the result is multiplied by 100 to make it a percentage. This gives us a standardised measure of dispersion.

The problem with the standard deviation as a measure of dispersion is that it is not all that robust. If there are one or two extreme values in the data set they will have a very big effect on the standard deviation because their difference from the mean is being squared, so the usefulness of the standard deviation is restricted to distributions which are unimodal and symmetrical, as we have noted already. In other circumstances a combination of the median and the *inter-quartile* range is likely to give a better indication of the value of a typical observation and the dispersion round it.

Just as we can specify the median of a distribution as that value which has 50 per cent of the observations above and 50 per cent below, so we can define the first and third *quartiles* of a distribution of data values. The first quartile (sometimes known as the *lower hinge*) is that value which has 25 per cent of the observations below and 75 per cent above it, while conversely the third quartile (or *upper hinge*) is that value which has 75 per cent of the observations below it and 25 per cent above it. The difference between the value of the first and third quartiles, the middle 50 per cent of the distribution, is known as the inter-quartile range (or midspread). Obtaining it is clearly directly analogous to obtaining the median, and its properties likewise, in the sense that only the rank order of the observations is taken into account and the existence of very large or very small values at either end of the distribution will not make any difference.

The use of the median and inter-quartile range can be extended to produce a numerical summary of a distribution consisting of the values of the median, first and third quartiles and maximum and minimum of the distribution, together with a note of the intervals between them. For the thirty-five posthole diameters it would look like this:

Min	Lower hinge	Median	Upper hinge	Max
25	38.5	44	48	66
Int	13.5	5.5	4	18

To this we can also add the distances between the minimum and the median (sometimes called the *lowspread*), between the first and third quartiles, the inter-quartile range, and between the median and the maximum (the *highspread*), thus:

Min	Lower hinge	Median	Upper hinge	Max
25	38.5	44	48	66
Int	13.5	5.5	4	18
	19		9.5	22

We can now see at a glance, for example, that the size difference between the smallest posthole (25 cm) and the first quartile (38.5 cm) is 13.5 cm, while from the first quartile to the median is only 5.5 cm, with a range from minimum to median of 19 cm.

Such tables can also be turned into the kind of visual data summary we saw in the previous chapter, in this case a *boxplot* or *box-and-whisker plot*.

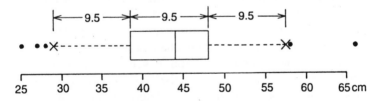

FIGURE 4.6. Box-and-whisker plot of the diameters of 35 Mount Pleasant postholes.

A boxplot for the Mount Pleasant postholes is illustrated in Figure 4.6. The left-hand side of the box is at the first quartile of the distribution, the right-hand side at the third quartile, and the line within the box marks the median. The box thus contains half the cases in the distribution. The crosses mark the cases

furthest from the box at either end but still within one inter-
quartile range of the nearest quartile. Beyond this, cases are
marked individually. In this case there are three postholes which
are extremely small and two which are extremely large in relation
to the rest of the distribution. In a real study the obvious next
step would be to identify these on the site plan and investigate
whether they appear to have any special functional role or an
unusual location.

Unlike bar graphs and stem-and-leaf displays, which give a
complete visual picture of the data, boxplots sacrifice that com-
pleteness for the sake of applying, as it were, a magnifying glass
to the distribution tails to see if they contain unusual observations.
They can be particularly useful when making comparisons
between different sets of data because it is possible to see
immediately if there is any asymmetry in the main bulk of the
observations, and whether some sets have more extreme observations than others. The reasons for the differences can then be
followed up.

DISTRIBUTION SHAPE

A combination of stem-and-leaf displays, bar charts, number
summaries and boxplots will soon reveal any peculiarities of
distribution shape. When such shape peculiarities as skewness,
multiple peaks or the presence of outliers (values very different
from the bulk of the observations) do exist, the shape of the
distribution, rather than its central tendency or dispersion, is
likely to be its most important characteristic; relying simply
on central tendency and dispersion as summary measures of a
distribution can cause you to miss the most important characteristics of a set of observations. Furthermore, if you do not know
about the distribution's shape, it is impossible to tell whether, or
in what way, the measures of central tendency or dispersion are
misleading; shape is vitally relevant to the choice of appropriate
measures for these. Although there are summary measures of
aspects of shape such as skewness, it is best perceived visually.

The importance of examining all these basic features of the
distributions of the individual variables being studied cannot be
over-emphasised. It is surprising how many people go astray by
failing to do this even when they should know better.

EXERCISES

4.1 Refer to the data on Uruk settlement sizes in Exercise 3.2. What is the shape of the frequency distribution of these data? What do you think would be the most appropriate measures of central tendency and dispersion? Calculate these measures.

4.2 Below is a list of the lengths (in metres) of some neolithic burial mounds from southern England. Analyse this distribution using the techniques described in this chapter and the preceding one and discuss your conclusions.

33	30	36	60	70	95	75	63	60
34	58	72	70	44	35	71	51	36
60	98	49	70	61	81	74	64	51
95	69	56	37	31	58	51	51	52

Five

AN INTRODUCTION TO
STATISTICAL INFERENCE

Now that we have covered some of the basics of descriptive statistics we can start looking at statistical inference and the use of statistical methods of comparison in archaeology. It should be said right at the start that statistical inference is by no means conceptually straightforward and has been a continuing source of debate at all levels, from the philosophical to everyday practice, both within mathematical statistics and in the numerous disciplines which make use of statistical methods of data analysis, including archaeology (e.g. Cowgill, 1977). A major distinction is between what are known as Bayesian and classical approaches to statistical inference. This book presents a version of the classical approach, whose nature will become apparent below. In philosophical terms the Bayesian approach is in many ways a more attractive one. It involves building statistical models of particular situations in which one's initial strength of belief in a set of alternative possibilities is expressed as a set of probabilities based on some reasonable expectation. New relevant data are then introduced, as a result of which new probabilities are calculated and consequently one's strength of belief in the different options changes. In other words, the data and the inference are closely linked together in a rigorous model ultimately expressed in the intuitively attractive idea of changing one's beliefs about a situation as new information comes in. Although the ideas of the Bayesian approach were first developed two hundred years ago it is only recently that it has become a practical proposition to apply them thanks to the availability of high-powered computers and the development of algorithms to exploit them. In the last few years Buck and Litton and a variety of colleagues have introduced their use to archaeology, especially in the context of calibrating radiocarbon dates (see

Buck et al., 1991, 1992, 1994, 1996 for examples of these and other applications) and it seems safe to suggest that their use will increase in the future. As things stand, however, the process of building Bayesian models remains a complex and situation-specific one and the circumstances in which it is possible to specify convincing prior probabilities are at the moment fairly restricted. As we will see, more traditional statistical inference techniques may also be used to change or update one's beliefs but the process is much more informal.

Within this classical framework there are two rather different contexts in which statistical inference impinges on archaeology and it is worth trying to keep them notionally separate from one another to start with, even though they are closely related.

First, and conceptually more straightforward, is the case where the archaeologist is in control, actually carrying out a selection process in the course of an archaeological project. Rarely do archaeologists have the resources to investigate everything in which they're interested, whether whole regions, complete sites or total assemblages of artefacts. Normally they can investigate only part of their population of interest and would like that part to be representative of the total if at all possible because they are interested in making inferences about the population as a whole on the basis of the sample. Provided that aims are clearly formulated, statistical theory can be extremely useful in the selection of a sample which will provide results whose reliability and precision can be assessed. There is a relatively well-defined set of problems involved here, usually included under the heading of *sampling* in archaeology, and for the most part left to be discussed below (Chapter 14).

The second main context in which statistical inference can be relevant arises from the process of comparison. Is the density of sites in area A the same as that in area B? Is the proportion of pottery type X the same at site Y as at site Z? Do rings of type S tend to occur more often in female burials than in male burials at cemetery T? Archaeological questions are quite often of this form, either comparisons between different sets of data, as in the examples just given, or comparisons between an observed set of data and the expectations derived from a theoretically-based model; for example, whether a distribution of sites suggests a preference for a particular soil type or not.

In the instances just listed it is unlikely that the two sites, regions and sexes will have exactly the same values in each case for the variable concerned. In any comparison between two cases there will almost always be some difference between them, however slight. The question which then arises is, how great does the difference have to be before we start taking it seriously and acting on the assumption that it is a 'real' one? This seems to be a perfectly valid question to ask and the discipline of statistics provides a potential way of answering it in any given case, by means of *significance testing*. In order to see how this works it will be necessary briefly to describe the theory behind it, in the abstract, before going on to an archaeological example.

SAMPLES AND POPULATIONS

Statistical inference concerns the problem of making decisions in the face of uncertainty; this uncertainty is quantified by means of probability theory. The inferences are about 'populations' and the uncertainty arises because they are made from samples of those populations. Precisely what the populations are in the case of archaeology is a matter of discussion which will be considered in some detail below but there are plenty of obvious examples in the present, for example the proportion of the UK voting-age population who intend to vote for a particular party at the next election. There are two main aspects of statistical inference: hypothesis testing and estimation. There is in fact quite a close connection between the two, but in general terms the first involves testing some idea about populations; for example, is this one the same as that one in some respect? The second involves estimating the value of some characteristic of the population on the basis of the sample data, or providing upper and lower limits within which the value may be expected to lie. The presentation of radiocarbon determinations is the classic example in archaeology of this latter procedure. In the case of both hypothesis testing and estimation what we want to do, in effect, is to say something about some aspect of a population on the basis of a sample drawn from it.

The characteristics of a population are known as *parameters*; the characteristics of a sample are known as *statistics*, and it is important to keep in mind the distinction between the two. This is aided by the fact that in the symbolic notation of statistical formulae population characteristics are generally given by Greek letters and corresponding sample statistics by ordinary lower-case letters. Thus the population mean is designated by Greek μ (mu) and the sample mean by $\bar{x}$; the population standard deviation by σ (lower-case sigma) and the sample standard deviation by s.

Parameters are *fixed* values referring to the population and are generally unknown, and sometimes even unknowable; an example might be the total number of sherds on the surface of a site at a given moment in time. Statistics, on the other hand, vary from one sample to the next and are known or can be obtained; for example, the total number of sherds in a sample of squares laid out across the site surface, collected at a particular level of detail. The problem is that *we do not know* how representative the sample is of the population, or how closely the statistic obtained approximates the corresponding unknown parameter, and our goal is to make inferences about various population parameters on the basis of known sample statistics.

The process of estimation, making inferences about the actual values that particular population parameters take, will be considered below. The account which follows will be focused on hypothesis testing. In tests of hypotheses we make assumptions about the unknown parameters and then ask how likely our sample statistics would be if these assumptions were actually true. Inasmuch as we attempt to make a rational decision as to whether or not our assumptions about the parameters are reasonable in view of the evidence at hand, hypothesis testing is a kind of decision making. The two types of questions most commonly found in hypothesis testing are:

1. What is the probability that two (or more) samples are drawn from different populations?
2. What is the probability that a given sample is drawn from a population which has certain defined characteristics?

This is clearly a rather restricted sense of the general idea of hypothesis testing. In particular, as both these questions indicate, hypotheses are statements which are defined in terms of clear expectations about the data and are therefore potentially rejectable. If the probability is low we will reject the hypothesis in question. We reject or fail to reject the hypothesis realising that since our judgement is based only on a sample we always have to admit the possibility of error due to the lack of representativeness of the sample. Probability theory enables us to evaluate the risks of error and to take these risks into consideration.

In general we start off by testing what is called the *null hypothesis*: the hypothesis of no difference. To refer back to the two questions above, we start with the assumption that our two (or more) samples are in fact drawn from the same population; or that our sample really is drawn from a population with the characteristics which we have specified. Orton (1980) presents this in the form, 'Is there a case to answer?' What is at issue is best illustrated by a straightforward if artificial example. Suppose we want to compare the densities of archaeological sites in two different areas: are they different or not? The usual procedure is to set up a null hypothesis stating that there is no difference between the two areas in their average densities of sites; one then proceeds to examine the evidence against this hypothesis of no difference.

If we imagine our two areas divided into one-kilometre squares then it is highly unlikely that every square in each of the two areas will have an identical number of sites. There are likely to be considerable differences from one square to the next, so that if one randomly picked ten squares from one of the two areas being compared and calculated the mean density of sites for those ten squares, and did the same for ten squares from the other area, the means of these two samples could be quite different from one another even if the population mean densities – the mean densities for each of the two areas as a whole – were identical. This would happen if, by chance, one picked ten squares from a thinly occupied part of one of the areas and ten squares from a densely occupied part of the other. Such chance or *stochastic* sampling effects are explicitly built into statistical tests and are therefore taken into account when we make our decision, on the basis of the test, as to whether or not the *population* mean densities, as opposed to the *sample* mean densities, really are different from one another.

The null hypothesis, H_0 as it is designated symbolically, is compared to the alternative hypothesis, H_1. For the moment we can say that this alternative hypothesis is simply the hypothesis that there is a difference; it says nothing about what size or type of difference exists, although this point will have to be qualified below. One or the other must be true. It is commonly but not invariably the case in statistical analysis that we wish to reject the null hypothesis and accept the alternative, although occasionally the null hypothesis is set up in the hope that it is true.

This may seem a rather involved way of going about things but it is necessary for two important reasons. First, it is much easier to demonstrate that some assumption is false than that it must be true. If we decide in a particular case that we cannot reject the null hypothesis but must accept it, all we are saying is that with the evidence at hand we are not in a position to reject it. Second, setting up the null hypothesis is usually the only sensible way of deriving a set of expectations with which we can compare our data. To refer to the hypothetical example above, it seems reasonable to pose the question whether the site densities are different or not, but rather odd, not to mention impractical, to test the hypothesis that the densities are 0.1 sites per sq.km. different, or 0.2, or any of the other innumerable possibilities.

If we are going to make a decision about whether or not to reject the null hypothesis, what criterion do we use as the basis for it, bearing in mind the chance effects that arise when samples are selected from populations? Essentially, we look at the values for our two samples, note the difference between them, and ask how probable it is that a difference this large could occur on the assumption that they were really two samples from the same population. If the probability is small we reject that assumption and conclude that the samples come from different populations. This probability is known as the level of significance, denoted symbolically by the Greek letter α (alpha).

It is up to the investigator to decide on the level of significance which is acceptable. This means deciding how improbable a result has to be under the assumptions of the null hypothesis before that hypothesis is rejected. Normally, before we go as far as rejecting the null hypothesis we want the probability of it being valid, given the results, to be very small, so that some confidence can be placed in our rejection of it.

By convention, the two most commonly used significance levels are $\alpha = 0.05$ and $\alpha = 0.01$. When we select a significance level of 0.05 it means that we have decided to accept the null hypothesis as true unless our data are so unusual that they would occur only 5 times in 100 or less. In other words, if we drew 100 pairs of samples from two identical populations and noted the difference between, for example, their mean values, only five of the differences, on average, would be as large as that observed. In these circumstances we would decide that the results are such that it is highly improbable that the null hypothesis is true. Similarly for the 0.01 significance level, except that this time we are asking for the results to be so unusual that they would only occur once in 100 times or less on the assumptions of the null hypothesis before we decide to reject it.

Of course, it is perfectly reasonable to use other levels of significance. If the decision is one of critical importance you may only want to take the chance of being wrong once in 1,000.

On the basis of this discussion you may think that the obvious thing to do is always to go for very conservative levels of significance – only rejecting the null hypothesis if the probability of it being valid is 1 in 1,000 or less. But there is a catch to doing this, because if you insist on only rejecting the null hypothesis under very extreme circumstances then you run a considerable risk of accepting the null hypothesis when it is in fact false, the converse error of the other.

Rejecting the null hypothesis when in fact it is true is known as a *type I error*. It means that a significant relationship or difference is being claimed when none really exists. Accepting the null hypothesis when it is false is known as a *type II error* and represents a failure to identify a significant relationship or difference where one actually does exist. In most circumstances it is more serious to make a type I error – claim a relationship or difference where none exists – than to fail to identify a significant relationship.

In setting a significance level you decide on the probability you are prepared to accept of making a type I error. It is the seriousness attached to type I error – claiming something is going on in the data when it is not – which leads statisticians to set fairly demanding standards before they are prepared to reject the null hypothesis. This presupposes, of course, that we wish to reject the null hypothesis, which is the usual case. If, on the other hand, we really hope the null hypothesis is true, we should be trying to minimise the probability of making a type II error, the probability of accepting H_0 when it is false.

In some spheres of life accepting or rejecting a null hypothesis has important practical consequences involving decision-making. For example, in quality control on an assembly line a decision may have to be taken on the basis of a sample of the items being produced as to whether there are so many defective items that some sort of action needs to be taken. Medical research may lead to decisions as to whether or not a particular drug should be licensed. Even in archaeology decisions may have to be taken on the basis of some sample investigation as to whether an area threatened by development should be excavated or preserved, or no action taken. More often than not, however, the probabilities we arrive at as a result of significance tests simply act as a guide, so we can make statements like, 'it appears to be extremely improbable that the density of settlement in area X is not different from that in area Y'.

SIGNIFICANCE TESTING IN ARCHAEOLOGY

The preceding discussion of samples and populations, null hypotheses and levels of significance has given some indication of what is involved in carrying out a significance test, but it has not considered the assumptions required if such a test is to be satisfactorily carried out, nor how archaeological data relate to those assumptions. It is now necessary to raise the various issues involved in using significance tests in an archaeological context and the best method of doing this is to follow through a hypothetical example and consider its implications.

A study is being made of a hypothetical cemetery of individual inhumation graves, some of which contain grave goods. On the basis of the distribution of grave goods in those burials identified anthropologically as belonging to females, they have been divided into two groups, labelled 'rich' and 'poor'. The question arises whether or not the anthropologically determined ages at death of these individuals tend to differ for the 'rich' and 'poor' groups. The relevant information is given in Table 5.1.

TABLE 5.1. The distribution of ages at death of a group of female burials from a hypothetical Bronze Age cemetery, for which the burials have been divided into 'rich' and 'poor' categories on the basis of their associated grave goods.

Age category at death	'Wealth' category	
	'Rich'	'Poor'
Infans I	6	23
Infans II	8	21
Juvenilis	11	25
Adultus	29	36
Maturus	19	27
Senilis	3	4
Total	76	136

The question then is of the type noted at the beginning of this chapter: are the two distributions the same or not? Given that they are not exactly the same, is the difference big enough to say that they really are different? It is Orton's question, in other words, is there a case to answer? The question is a fairly important one in the context of this particular study. If we infer that there is a real difference in this respect between the 'rich' and 'poor' graves, then we have something which needs to be accounted for. Questions immediately arise, such as did the two groups have different living conditions so that one tended to survive longer than the other? Were there social rules which led to females only being entitled to grave goods when they had reached a certain age? And so on. If, on the other hand, we infer that the difference is not large enough to be taken seriously then there is not much more to be said.

As always, the first thing to do is to set up a null hypothesis and its alternative:

H_0: there is no difference between the 'rich' and 'poor' female burials in their distribution of ages at death.

H_1: there is a difference between 'rich' and 'poor' female burials in their distribution of ages at death.

Let us suppose that in this case we will follow convention and select a significance level of 0.05; that is to say, we will reject

H_0 if, on the assumption that it holds, the results observed would only occur 5 times out of 100 or less.

In carrying out any test it is necessary to make a number of assumptions, about the population in which we are interested and also about the sampling procedures used. These assumptions can be divided into two categories: those we are willing to accept, and those we are dubious about and therefore interested in. The null hypothesis is the assumption about which we are dubious and which therefore interests us. From the point of view of the statistical test, unfortunately, all assumptions have the same logical status: if the results of the test indicate rejection of the assumptions, all we can say on the basis of the test is that at least one of the assumptions is probably false. Since the test does not indicate which of the assumptions are erroneous, it is obviously vital, if results are to be meaningful, that only one of the assumptions should be really in doubt; this can then be rejected as the invalid one. Thus, when you are selecting a test, it is important to select one that involves only a single dubious assumption, the null hypothesis.

One of the first things to be taken into account when selecting a test is the level of measurement of the data. Tests for data measured at interval or ratio level are not appropriate to data measured at a very low level. On the other hand, if we use a test appropriate for nominal level data on higher level data then we are wasting information and not using as powerful a test as we might. In the present case we can say that the age categories represent an ordinal scale – they are ordered but we are not specifying the (varying) number of years in each category.

As we will see later, many statistical tests, and statistical methods in general, require specific assumptions to be made about the form of the distribution under investigation, but this is by no means true for all of them. One test appropriate for comparing two sets of observations measured at the ordinal scale is the *Kolmogorov–Smirnov* test. The test is based on the difference between the two cumulative distributions of interest; for the version described here both the samples should be greater than forty in size (there is also a one sample version of this test, not described here).

The first step is to convert the original counts into proportions of their category total. Thus, for example, there are 76 burials in the 'rich' category; 6 of the 76 belong in the *Infans I* age category, which proportionally is 6/76 = 0.079 on a scale from 0 to 1, or 7.9 per cent on a scale from 0 to 100. In the 'poor' category 23/136 burials are in the *Infans I* age group, 0.169, or 16.9 per cent. This operation is performed on each of the age categories in each of the wealth classes, to give Table 5.2

TABLE 5.2. Numbers and proportions of burials by wealth and age categories.

Age	'Wealth' category			
category	'Rich'		'Poor'	
Infans I	6	0.079	23	0.169
Infans II	8	0.105	21	0.154
Juvenilis	11	0.145	25	0.184
Adultus	29	0.382	36	0.265
Maturus	19	0.250	27	0.199
Senilis	3	0.039	4	0.029
Total	76	1.000	136	1.000

The proportions are then accumulated for each age category within each of the 'wealth' classes, in the way we have already seen when producing a cumulative distribution (see pp. 30–2 above). Thus, the proportion of 'rich' burials in the category *Infans II* or younger is 0.079 + 0.105 = 0.184; in the category *Juvenilis* or younger it is 0.184 + 0.145 = 0.329; and so on. The result of this operation is given in Table 5.3.

TABLE 5.3. Cumulative proportions of burials by wealth and age categories.

Age category at death	'Wealth' category	
	'Rich'	'Poor'
Infans I	0.079	0.169
Infans II	0.184	0.323
Juvenilis	0.329	0.507
Adultus	0.711	0.772
Maturus	0.961	0.971
Senilis	1.000	1.000

The test is based on an assessment of the largest difference between these two distributions of cumulative proportions, so the next step is to calculate the differences between them for each age category and to note which is the largest (without regard to whether the difference is positive or negative); see Table 5.4.

TABLE 5.4. Cumulative proportions of burials by wealth and age categories and differences between them.

Age category	'Wealth' category		Difference
	'Rich'	'Poor'	
Infans I	0.079	0.169	0.090
Infans II	0.184	0.323	0.139
Juvenilis	0.329	0.507	0.178
Adultus	0.711	0.772	0.061
Maturus	0.961	0.971	0.010
Senilis	1.000	1.000	1.000

The distributions can also, of course, be presented graphically to obtain an intuitive feeling of what they look like and what the difference between them represents; the two distributions are shown in Figure 5.1, with the largest difference marked.

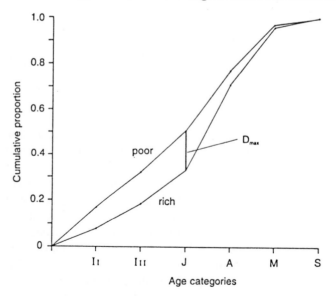

FIGURE 5.1. Plot of the cumulative age distributions of 'rich' and 'poor' burials using the data from Table 5.1.

On the basis of this we can see that the largest difference lies in the *Juvenilis* category and is 0.178 or 17.8 per cent: by the end of the *Juvenilis* age category 50.7 per cent of the 'poor' individuals are dead but only 32.9 per cent of the 'rich' ones.

The question is: do we regard this as an unusually large difference between the two distributions on the null hypothesis assumption that they both represent samples from identical populations whose differences arise as a result of chance variation. To find this out, the observed difference is compared with an expected distribution of differences derived theoretically. Such distributions are often presented in the form of statistical tables, and we will see an example of this later. The Kolmogorov–Smirnov test is slightly different in that the minimum difference between two cumulative distributions which will be significant at a given level is obtained by evaluating a formula. If the observed difference is equal to or greater than this, it is statistically significant at the set level. In this case we have set the significance level at 0.05 and the appropriate formula is

$$1.36 \sqrt{\frac{n_1 + n_2}{n_1 n_2}}$$

where n_1 = the number of individuals in sample 1 and n_2 = the number of individuals in sample 2. Here

$$1.36 \sqrt{\frac{76 + 136}{(76)(136)}} = 0.195$$

1.36 is the theoretically derived multiplication factor appropriate to the 0.05 significance level. If the 0.01 level is required, the coefficient is 1.63; if 0.001 it is 1.95.

Having obtained the minimum required difference for H_0 to be rejected at the given significance level, we see that the observed maximum difference ($D_{max_{obs}}$) of 0.178 is not as great as the minimum required to reject the null hypothesis at the 0.05 level ($D_{max_{0.05}}$), which is 0.195. Since the observed difference is less than the minimum required, we cannot reject the null hypothesis. There is not a significant difference in the distribution of ages at death between the 'rich' and 'poor' categories.

It is important to note that *this does not mean that the*

distributions are the same. It simply means that there is insufficient evidence to suggest that they are different; there does not appear to be a 'case to answer'. We cannot be very sure that there is anything going on here that needs to be accounted for, so to go on to try and offer reasons for the difference is completely beside the point; indeed, it is positively misleading.

SIGNIFICANCE TESTING: IMPLICATIONS

At this point, however, we need to stop and take stock. In carrying out the test just described we have begged an important question and have failed to mention a key assumption of all significance tests. Let us look a bit more closely at what we have just done.

Using a significance test to answer the question, *are these two distributions different from one another?*, presupposes the rephrasing of the question to read, do the two sets of sample data we have come from identical populations? As we have seen, statistical inference is all about making inferences about populations on the basis of samples. But what is the population of which our data can be regarded as a sample?

This brings us on to the key assumption of all significance tests referred to above. They presuppose that we have a sample or samples from a population and that there is independence of selection within the sample: in other words, that the selection of one individual has no effect on the choice of another individual to be included in the sample. The method usually adopted to try to meet this requirement is *random sampling*. A random sample has the property not only of giving each individual an equal chance of being selected but of giving each combination of individuals an equal chance of selection.

It is obvious that no archaeological sample can be considered a random sample of what was once present. It is true, as we noted at the beginning of this chapter, that sometimes archaeologists are in a position to select random samples of the archaeological record; the problems of this are considered below in Chapter 14. However, in most cases, and certainly in that considered in our example, we are dealing with a set of data which has not been collected in this way, and indeed, it is hard to imagine how it could have been. Furthermore, if the hypothetical cemetery from which the burials of our example are derived has been totally excavated, then in one sense at least we are dealing with a population and not a sample at all. If we are dealing with a population, where does the sampling variation come from which is supposed to account for the differences between the samples?

In fact, this is a problem which arises in most non-experimental disciplines. One answer is to say that there is indeed no sampling variation, so in the case of our example we state, correctly, that there is a difference (of 0.178) between the two cumulative distributions and go on to discuss the reasons for it. More commonly, however, it is argued that even in contexts like this it is appropriate to have a concept of random or chance variation against which we can evaluate our results, so the question of where such chance variation could come from, and how it might be correctly generated for the purposes of a test, must be addressed.

There are two slightly different ways of making sense of the idea of sampling variation in such a context. The first is through the concept of randomisation (see for example Manly, 1991). In the case we have just considered, the null hypothesis implies that the relative number of 'rich' and 'poor' burials in a given age category is a matter of chance. Overall, in the cemetery as a whole, 36 per cent of the burials are 'rich' and 64 per cent are 'poor'. In the *Infans I* category, for example, there are 29 burials so on the null hypothesis we would expect 64 per cent (roughly 19) of these to be 'poor' and 36 per cent (roughly 10) to be 'rich'. Imagine now a procedure in which a computer is used to generate 29 random numbers, between 0.0 and 1.0, one for each burial. If the number falls between 0.0 and 0.36 we assign that burial to the 'rich' category, if it falls between 0.37 and 1.0 we assign it to the 'poor' category. Over a very large number of repetitions of this procedure we would indeed get a 36 per cent to 64 per cent split in the assignment of burials to the two categories. In any given set of 29 random numbers, however, it is quite likely that we would not get exactly the 10:19 split that we expect, in the same way that if you toss a coin 10 times only occasionally will you get 5 heads and 5 tails even though the two are equally likely.

If you repeat the operation of selecting 29 random numbers and assigning graves to the two categories a large number of times, say 100, then most of the time the result will not be that far away from 10:19 'rich' : 'poor'. Nevertheless, occasionally you might get 5:24 or 19:10. At all events, you generate a *distribution* of splits between the two categories under the assumption of the null hypothesis. If the actually observed split (which is 6:23) falls somewhere within the main body of the distribution of random splits then it does not contradict the null hypothesis. If it is one which is so extreme that it never occurs in the random distribution then it represents an event which would occur less than one time in 100 under the null hypothesis so we are likely to take that as strong evidence against the null hypothesis. Or, of course, it may fall somewhere between these two extremes, for example, it may be a split which occurs four times in our 100 randomly generated splits.

Placing our actual result in the context of a lot of results randomly generated on the basis that the null hypothesis is true seems an intuitively plausible and convincing way of deciding whether to take our actual result seriously as providing evidence against the null hypothesis – in this case against the view that the numbers of 'rich' and 'poor' burials in a given age category are exactly what you would expect given that the cemetery is made up of 36 per cent 'rich' burials and 64 per cent 'poor' ones. It is the randomisation process which generates the sampling variation that we need.

Of course, the Kolmogorov–Smirnov test carried out above was based not simply on comparisons within a single category but on comparing the two cumulative distributions. However, you can see that the principle just illustrated can be easily extended. We could generate a random 'rich' : 'poor' split for each of our age categories, produce the cumulative distributions for 'rich' and 'poor' and note the biggest difference between them. We could then repeat this operation 100 or 1000 times, each time noting the biggest difference; we could then see whether the difference in our real data set was unusual or not.

It is easy to see that, although in principle it is possible to do all this, in practice it is likely to be moderately laborious and to demand a certain level of technical expertise in programming; furthermore, each randomisation test must be set up anew for each particular problem and data set. In the example above we simply used a standard test and the question obviously arises whether this can in fact be regarded as equivalent, in terms of giving the same result as the randomisation process would.

Manly (1991, p. 17) notes that good agreement is not unusual when the two procedures are based on equivalent measures (here the maximum difference between two cumulative distributions); so long as the data meet the assumptions of the standard test the two will give more or less the same result. He also endorses the point that this discussion has been trying to make:

> An interesting apect of the general agreement between classical and randomisation tests with 'good' data is that it gives some justification for using classical statistical methods on non-random samples since the classical tests can be thought of as approximations for randomisation tests. (Manly, 1991, p. 17)

In some circumstances, then, we can indeed use standard tests, while in others it will be necessary to generate a randomisation distribution. Noreen (1989) argues that it is always preferable to use the randomisation approach and provides extensive program listings for this purpose.

Randomising the data values in the way described is probably the most straightforward and generally satisfactory way of conceptualising the idea of significance testing in an archaeological context. A slightly different, or rather, more general, way is through the use (or at least the concept) of *Monte Carlo* tests:

> With a Monte Carlo test the significance of an observed test statistic is assessed by comparing it with a sample of test statistics obtained by generating random samples using some assumed model. (Manly, 1991, p. 21)

In an archaeological context such as that dealt with in this example we might conceive of the evidence as one specific empirical outcome of a system of behaviour based on social rules. Any given act or example of behaviour producing archaeological evidence will be based on the rules but is likely to be affected by all sorts of contingent circumstances, so that variation is introduced which is in fact random or chance variation, in the sense that it is not systematically related to the rules generating the behaviour. The argument is clearly more appropriate to some archaeological circumstances than others, and in particular to cases where we know we are dealing with the results of intentional behaviour, and that our observations are not being biased in some way by recovery factors (although these will introduce their own random variation).

In order to use such an approach in the case of our burial example we would have to be aware of two limitations. First, the results only apply to the burials in this particular cemetery; they do not take into account the fact that 'rich' and 'poor' individuals in any or all of the different age categories may have been buried elsewhere, or may not have been buried at all in an archaeologically recognisable fashion. Second, it would have to be shown that any relationship between 'wealth' category and age distribution was not the result of some other factor, such as variation in preservation conditions. With these stipulations it could be argued that any patterning in the relation between age at death and 'wealth' category was the result of rule-bound social behaviour, but that for all sorts of reasons there will have been variation in the closeness with which rules were followed, producing a distribution of behaviour with a mean value and variation around it. Where such behaviour has an archaeological outcome the particular set of actions whose evidence we recover will be just one of a range of possibilities.

It is important to remember this discussion of the nature of significance testing in the chapters which follow, and of course if you are undertaking such tests in your own work.

OTHER TESTS FOR DIFFERENCE BETWEEN TWO ORDINAL SCALE DISTRIBUTIONS

The main intention of describing the Kolmogorov–Smirnov test in this chapter was to give an idea of what is involved in statistical inference, but it is worth noting that this is by no means the only technique for testing whether two ordinal scale distributions are different from one another. The *Mann–Whitney test* and the *runs test* may also be used in such circumstances. These are not described in detail here but may be found in many statistics textbooks (e.g. Fletcher and Lock, 1991). However, a brief indication of what is involved in these tests will be presented, to give an idea of when they are appropriate.

Imagine that we have survey data for the sizes of twenty early neolithic sites on two different soil types in southern Italy.

Estimating site size from survey data can be problematical and is very often imprecise. In this case we do not feel justified in stating the precise area of each site but we do feel that we can rank them according to size. Do larger or smaller sites tend to be on one soil type rather than the other?

We can rank the sites in order of size, indicating for each site the soil type (A or B) on which it lies (largest to smallest, left to right). We might obtain an ordering like this:

AABABBBABAAABBABBAAB

or like this:

BBBBBABBBABBAAAAAAAA

In the first case there are very short runs of sites on the same soil type mixed in with short runs of sites on the other soil type; i.e., sites on the two soil types are intermixed in terms of size. In the second case the number of runs is much smaller: there is a predominance of sites on soil B at one end of the size range and of soil A on the other. The runs test will tell us whether the number of runs we have in a particular case is less than what we would expect if the two distributions were randomly intermixed.

Thus, in the first case above we have twelve runs and in the second we have six, and there are ten sites on each soil type. In a situation such as this, where there are twenty observations or less in each of our two categories, we can find out whether our result is significant at the 0.05 level by consulting a table (see Table A in the Appendix at the back of the book). This involves looking in the body of the table for the number of runs corresponding to the number of observations. In this case N_1 (the number of sites on soil type A) is ten, as is N_2 (the number of sites on soil type B). The corresponding number of runs is six. In other words, for these sample sizes, if the number of runs observed is six or less, it is statistically significant at the 0.05 level.

In the second of the two cases above, then, we can reject the null hypothesis that the sites on the two soil types are randomly intermixed in terms of size and conclude that there is a significant difference between the two soil types with respect to the rank order of site sizes – there is a tendency for larger sites to be on soil type B.

The Mann–Whitney test is very similar and to illustrate what is involved we can stay with the same example. Again we rank the sites in order of size. We can now focus on all the sites on one of the soil types. Here it doesn't matter which since there are ten of each, but if the numbers weren't equally balanced we would choose the soil type with the smaller number of sites. We then note for each of our sites, say those on soil type B, how many of the sites on soil A rank lower than it. Thus, for the first of the two orders given above we see that the highest ranked soil-type B site is third, with eight soil-type A sites below it. The next highest ranked soil B site is fifth, with seven type A sites below it, and so on. In the second case above, each of the first five soil B sites has ten soil A sites below it. We add up the number of A sites below B sites for all the B sites; this sum total represents the U statistic. If in general the B sites are smaller than the A sites they will have very few A sites below them; if they are larger they will have very many below them; while if the site sizes on the two soil types are randomly intermixed the number of A sites below B sites will be somewhere in the middle. We use the Mann–Whitney test to find out if the numbers in our particular case do differ significantly from random intermixing.

In the first example above the U statistic (the total number of A sites below B sites) is as follows:

$$U = 8 + 7 + 7 + 7 + 6 + 3 + 3 + 2 + 2 = 45$$

Of course, we could also have calculated the converse of this – the number of B sites below A sites. In fact, there is a shortcut to doing this:

$$U' = N_1 N_2 - U$$

In this case,

$$U' = 100 - 45 = 55$$

In fact, the relevant statistical tables have actually been set up to make use of the smaller of the two numbers.

In the second data set above, the total number of A sites below B sites is

$$U = 10 + 10 + 10 + 10 + 10 + 9 + 9 + 9 + 8 + 8 = 93$$
$$U' = 100 - 93 = 7$$

So it is the smaller of these that we use in the test.

Once again, we can compare our result with a statistical table to find out whether or not it is statistically significant. Table B in the appendix shows the values of the U statistic for the 0.05 significance level, for sample sizes between one and twenty. If we look in the body of the table for the value corresponding to samples of ten and ten we see that it is twenty-three. In other words, an observed value of twenty-three or less for the U statistic will be significant at the 0.05 level. Thus, in the case of our first example, with a U value of forty-five, we have to accept the null hypothesis that sites of different sizes are intermixed with respect to soil type whereas in the second case, with an observed U value of seven, we can reject the null hypothesis and conclude, as with the runs test, that there is a significant difference between the two soil types with respect to the rank order of site sizes. In fact, for a given data set it is usually easier to obtain a significant result with the Mann–Whitney test than the runs test and in this sense the Mann–Whitney test is said to be *more powerful*. Of course, in the case of both tests, if you are carrying them out using a computer statistical package, then you will not need to worry about the statistical tables because you will be given the exact probability of your result.

CONCLUSION

This chapter has attempted to deal with the significance test aspect of statistical inference; the subject of estimation will be considered below. The aim has been to discuss the issues involved in using such tests in the context of a specific example. As I have already emphasised, however, significance tests are by no means the only, or most important, reason for the use of quantitative methods in archaeology. In fact, as we will see in later chapters, *statistical significance* and *substantive significance in archaeological terms* are not necessarily the same thing.

EXERCISES

5.1 On one side of a prehistoric settlement is a cemetery of megalithic tombs. Among other aspects, interest is focused on the significance of the spatial distribution of the tombs, and it occurs to the investigator that the proximity of the tombs to the settlement may be relevant in some way. The tombs and their contents vary in a number of different respects and in particular it has proved possible to divide them on the basis of their morphology into an 'elaborate' category and a 'simple' category. The cemetery has been divided into a number of bands of approximately 200 m width, although varying somewhat as a result of the local topography. Band A is the closest to the settlement and the distances of the bands increase up to band F, which is the furthest. Given the information below, is there any indication that distance from the settlement and tomb elaboration are related? Discuss the assumptions that you are making in your analysis.

Band	No. of elaborate tombs	No. of simple tombs
A	12	6
B	8	6
C	17	10
D	7	16
E	13	19
F	14	18

5.2 In a study of social patterns at a hypothetical Formative site in Mexico an investigation of the burials was carried out. Some of them were in ordinary graves whereas others were in built tombs. The question arose whether any biological characteristics of the individuals in the cemetery were associated with the difference in burial mode.

Below is information on the number of individuals in each of a series of age categories, divided according to whether they were buried in ordinary graves or built tombs. Are the age distributions of the buried populations different for the two burial types?

	Age Group					
	1	2	3	4	5	6
Graves	25	18	29	14	24	9
Tombs	8	4	6	18	40	5

5.3 Below is information on the length of bone fragments from two pleistocene caves in southern England. Do you think that the length distributions of the fragments at the two sites are different from one another?

Length category (mm)	No. of frags in Cave 1	No. of frags in Cave 2
0–9	1	0
10–19	21	6
20–29	15	11
30–39	5	11
40–49	7	6
50–59	1	6
60–69	2	6
70–79	3	4
80–89	3	2
90–99	0	5
100–109	2	9

Six

ESTIMATION AND TESTING WITH THE NORMAL DISTRIBUTION

The preceding chapter has illustrated the role of statistical significance testing in archaeology and shown how to carry out some tests relevant to rank order data. In this chapter we will look at the other aspect of statistical inference – estimation – and in connection with this, at significance tests which are appropriate when we have data measured at an interval or ratio scale. This involves a consideration of the so-called *normal distribution.*

Even if you have no idea what a normal distribution is, the odds are that you have heard of it and believe it to be important in some way. In this you would be largely correct, both because a large number of observed distributions are found to be approximately normal, and because of the theoretical significance of this distribution, in inductive/inferential statistics and as the basis for many statistical methods. We will begin by looking at it from a descriptive point of view, and in particular at how the standard deviation (see above, p. 42) relates to it.

THE NORMAL DISTRIBUTION

In considering the use of bar charts to display the frequency distributions of continuous numeric variables in Chapter 3 it was noted that the width of the intervals is important. In particular, if the intervals of the distribution become narrower and narrower for a given sample size, the distribution starts to look very irregular, with gaps and holes in it. If we increased the number of cases, however, and kept increasing it as we made our intervals narrower, then the distribution would become increasingly fine in its subdivisions but still retain the same shape. Thus in Figure 6.1, it would be possible to go from (a) to (b).

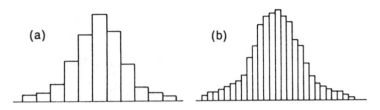

FIGURE 6.1. (a) Histogram with wide intervals; (b) Histogram with very narrow intervals, based on a very large number of observations.

Assuming that the distribution has the shape shown in Figure 6.1, if we imagine the intervals becoming infinitely narrow and the number of observations correspondingly large, we end up with a smooth bell-shaped curve (Fig. 6.2).

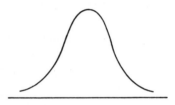

FIGURE 6.2. A normal distribution

Just as the area within a bar chart can be calculated by summing the areas of the individual rectangles, so the area under the smooth curve can be calculated by summing the infinitely large number of rectangles under the smooth curve; this is the calculus operation of integration.

The normal curve is a symmetrical smooth bell-shaped curve defined by a particular equation; one feature of it is that the two tails extend infinitely in either direction without reaching the horizontal axis. At the level of this text the equation itself is not of any interest. What is important is that regardless of what particular mean and standard deviation a given normal curve may have, there will be a constant proportion of the area under the curve, or a constant proportion of the cases in a frequency distribution of this form, between the mean and a given distance from the mean, expressed in standard deviation units (Fig. 6.3).

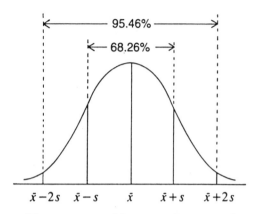

FIGURE 6.3. The percentage of the area under a normal curve within one and two standard deviations of the mean.

It is worth giving several examples of this to make it clear. Thus, the area under the curve between the mean and a point one standard deviation either greater or smaller than the mean will be 34.13 per cent of the total area under the curve. Between one standard deviation less than the mean and one standard deviation more than the mean there will be twice 34.13 per cent, or 68.26 per cent of the area under the curve. The corresponding figures for two standard deviations are 47.73 per cent and 95.46 per cent, and for three standard deviations 49.86 per cent and 99.73 per cent.

Although these figures are based on the theoretically defined normal curve, many empirically obtained frequency distributions of data are sufficiently close to it for these rules about the proportion of the distribution within particular standard deviation distances from the mean to be applicable. Furthermore, as we will see below, even when the distributions themselves are not normal, there are still many circumstances in which we are entitled to use normal-based theory.

The fact that many real frequency distributions are quite close to normality, so that the theoretical results can be used, is not accidental. If the value of some variable is the result of the cumulative effect of a large number of other variables which are independent of one another, then it can be proved mathematically that the distribution of the values of that variable will be approximately normal. An example of such a variable in the field of biology, where the normal distribution saw early application, is body height. This is mainly determined by a large number of genetic factors, but also by such factors as nutrition and environment. These different factors will tend to act in different directions. The result is that the distribution of heights in a population will be a normal one, as indeed it is. There are many archaeological instances of ratio scale variables, particularly physical measurements such as lengths, breadths, weights, volumes and so on, which are likewise affected by a large number of different factors acting in different directions, with the result that the distribution of the variable values is a normal one, or at least not far from it.

It is now necessary to show how these constant proportionalities characteristic of the normal distribution may be used and interpreted in a specific archaeological case. This will inevitably be somewhat artificial since they are generally used as a means to an end rather than being an end in themselves, which is how we will have to treat them here. Let us suppose then that we are dealing with a large set of projectile points, whose lengths are normally distributed, with a mean of 110 mm and a standard deviation of 20 mm (see Fig. 6.4). Initially we want to find out the proportion of their lengths which lies between 110 and 140 mm.

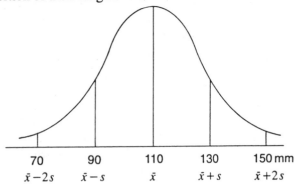

FIGURE 6.4. The distribution of lengths of a large number of projectile points from the south-western United States.

It is first necessary to work out how many standard deviations 140 is from 110; in millimetres it is 30 and the standard deviation is 20. If we divide the difference between the mean and the

value in which we are interested by the standard deviation, we
obtain the figure we want: 30/20 = 1.5. The value 140 is 1.5
standard deviations away from the mean. When a quantity is
presented in the form of a number of standard deviations away
from the mean of its distribution it is said to be in the form of a
Z score (or standard score), where Z represents the deviation
from the mean in standard deviation units. The general expression is

$$Z = \frac{x - \bar{x}}{s}$$

where $\bar{x}$ is the mean, s is the value of the standard deviation, and
x is the value of the boundary of the interval in which we are
interested.

How do we get from a value for Z to a value for the proportion of cases within that interval? The answer is that tables have
been constructed to do this for what is known as the standard
form of the normal curve, expressed in terms of Z scores (see
Table C in the Appendix). The table assumes that the area under
the normal curve sums to 1.0, with 0.5 to the left of the mean
and 0.5 to the right. The values of Z are given down the margins
of the table and along the top. The first two digits of Z are
obtained by reading down and the third by reading across. There
are many minor variations in the way these tables are set up but
in the version presented here the left-hand page of the table is
for negative Z values, i.e. values less than the mean, and the
right-hand page for positive values, those greater than the mean.
In this case we are interested in a Z value of +1.50, so we look
down the left-hand column of the right-hand page for Z = 1.5
and across to the first column right, corresponding to Z = 1.50.
Figures within the body of the table indicate the proportion of
the total area under the curve which lies between the Z value and
the extreme right-hand end of the curve. In this case we see that
the value is 0.06681, or c.6.7 per cent. But we want to find the
area not between Z = 1.5 and the right-hand end of the curve,
but between the mean and Z = 1.5. We know that the proportion
between the mean and the right-hand end is 0.5, so the proportion between the mean and Z = 1.5 must be 0.5 − .06681 =
0.43319. Rounding the two last figures we have 0.433 or 43.3
per cent of the area under the curve lying between the mean and

a line at $Z = 1.5$. Translating back into our example, we can say that 43.3 per cent of the projectile-point lengths will be between 110 and 140 mm (see Figure 6.5).

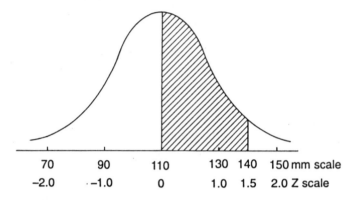

70	90	110		130	140	150 mm scale
-2.0	-1.0	0		1.0	1.5	2.0 Z scale

FIGURE 6.5. Distribution of projectile-point lengths with Z-scores corresponding to actual standard deviation values.

If we had been asked to find the proportion of lengths between 110 and 80 mm, or 1.5 standard deviations less than the mean, we would find the value in the table corresponding to $Z = -1.50$, which is 0.93319; that is to say, 93.3 per cent of the total area under the curve is between a line at $Z = -1.50$ and the extreme right-hand end of the curve. We want the area between $Z = -1.50$ and the mean, so we have to subtract 0.5, to give 0.43319; unsurprisingly, exactly the same as between the mean and $Z = +1.50$. If the question had referred to the proportion of lengths between 80 and 140 mm, or within 1.5 standard deviations either side of the mean, we would simply double the answer for one half: $0.433 + 0.433 = 0.866$. Obviously, the proportion or percentage can easily be translated into real numbers if necessary so long as we know the total number of observations in our distribution.

If we had been asked to find the proportion of projectile points with lengths greater than 140 mm then the problem would have been less complicated. We would simply need to know the area between $Z = +1.50$ and the extreme right-hand end of the curve. We obtain this simply by reading off the value for $Z = 1.50$ in the table, as we already have done to work out the first question: 6.7 per cent of the area under the curve is between $Z = 1.50$ and the extreme right of the curve, so that 6.7 per cent of the points have a length greater than 140 mm.

For points less than 80 mm the procedure is similar to the first two cases we looked at. The area under the curve corresponding to $Z = -1.50$ is 0.93319, as we have seen already, so we have $1.0 - 0.93319 = 0.06681$, or 6.7 per cent of points with length less than 80 mm.

As noted above, not all tables of the standard normal distribution are set up precisely as in Table C, but they are all very similar and it should not be difficult to work out what to do.

In effect, what we are doing when we perform these operations is carrying out a standardisation of our original data. We start off with a particular normal distribution with a mean and standard deviation expressed in terms of the units in which the observations were made, millimetres in the examples just given. We then re-express the observations in terms of standard deviation units either side of the mean. The mean becomes zero and the observations less than the mean are negative quantities; those greater than the mean are positive, thus the new distribution has a mean of zero and a standard deviation of one. No matter what the original units of measurement, we can convert any normal distribution to this standard deviation unit form and it will have the properties which we have seen to characterise the normal distribution, in terms of the proportion of the area under the curve, or cases within the distribution, within a given interval, the information given in the Z table.

ESTIMATION AND CONFIDENCE INTERVALS

Now that we have seen the characteristics of the normal distribution it is time to turn to the topic of estimation, the second aspect of statistical inference referred to in the previous chapter. There we saw that population parameters were fixed and unknown but that sample statistics could be collected to estimate their corresponding population parameters. Since we do not know the population parameters, and would not need to take a sample if we did, we can never know how close our estimates are to the parameter value. Accordingly, if we are going to make estimates and want to have some confidence that they are reasonable ones, they have to be based on a method of sample selection which has secure theoretical foundations. The most straightforward way of doing this is by selecting a *simple random sample*. As we saw in Chapter 5, such a sample has the characteristic that any individual, and any combination of individuals, has an equal chance of occurring in it. Such a sample can be selected by drawing members from the population one at a time *without replacement*; this means that once an item has been selected it is withdrawn from the selection pool and does not have a second chance of being chosen. The mechanism of choice is normally a computer's random number generator, or published tables of numbers derived from such generators.

Usually, we are interested in estimating a population mean, or some quantity closely related to it. Thus, we might be interested in estimating the mean density of sites in a region, the total number of sites in a region, the total number of houses on a site, the proportion of some type in a site pottery assemblage, the mean capacity of a particular vessel type, and so on.

If we want an estimate of a population mean from a simple random sample, the sample mean will be perfectly satisfactory since it is unbiased. Unfortunately, but unsurprisingly, this does not mean that any simple random sample mean will always correspond to the mean of the population from which it is drawn. Rather, if we take a series of simple random samples from a population and obtain the mean of each of those samples, then each of those means will be slightly different – there will be a distribution of means. It is the mean of the distribution of sample means which will correspond to the unknown population parameter.

The upshot of all this is that while obtaining a specific sample mean is fine as far as it goes, we have no basis at the moment for knowing whether the particular one we have obtained from a given sample is a good estimate or not. If we are dealing with the mean of a continuous variable – for example, the mean length in millimetres of a sample of projectile points, calculated to three places of decimals – then the probability that this corresponds exactly to the population mean is almost infinitely small.

If we want to have some degree of confidence in our estimate of the population mean we must take into account the dispersion of the distribution of sample means to which we have referred above. But how do we do this when in at least nine cases out of ten all we will have is a single sample?

The answer is that we start from the dispersion of the sample itself – the sample standard deviation. We are not interested in this estimate of the dispersion of the population for its own sake, however, but in the dispersion of the distribution of sample means. Nevertheless, the more variable the population is, the more variable are likely to be the means of a series of samples drawn from it. Statistical theory which it is not possible to go into here enables us to go from the sample-based estimate of the population standard deviation to an estimate of the standard deviation of the notional distribution of sample means – known as the *standard error of the mean*. The formula is

$$s_{\bar{x}} = \frac{s}{\sqrt{n}}$$

In words, we can obtain an estimate of the standard error of the mean by dividing an estimate of the population standard deviation by the square root of the number of observations in the sample. It makes sense intuitively that the dispersion of a distribution of means will not be as great as the dispersion of the individual population values, and that as the sample gets larger and therefore increasingly representative of the range of population variability, the standard error should decrease.

But how does having an estimate of the standard error of the mean help us to arrive at an estimate of the population mean in which we can have some specified degree of confidence? The answer to this is that it depends on the properties of the normal distribution.

At this point you may want to object that this is fine if the distribution of observations in the sample we are dealing with is normal, but what about the many circumstances in which it is not? In fact, it can be shown that so long as the sample size is reasonably large, greater than, say, fifty or so, the shape of the hypothetical distribution of means, which is the one that matters for our estimate, will be normal, even when the shape of the *population distribution* is quite far from this.

This may seem rather surprising and the best way of obtaining some intuitive feel for why it is not is to try some experiments yourself. The easiest way to do this is by means of dice-throwing. Assuming that the dice is fair, if you throw it a large number of times you will end up with only slight variations from what is known as a *uniform* distribution. Each number, from one to six, will occur more or less the same number of times. If you do the same with a second dice you will get the same result. Now try throwing both dice together and noting the total, which you can divide by two to give the mean. The result will be as shown in Figure 6.6.

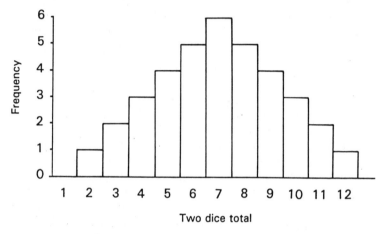

FIGURE 6.6. Expected frequency distribution resulting from the tossing of two dice.

In other words, even with a sample of two from a uniform distribution the distribution of means will start to look normal because there are more ways of getting seven and adjacent numbers than of getting two or twelve.

As we have just seen, it is characteristic of the normal distribution that there will be a constant proportion of the observations within a given number of standard deviations either side of the mean. Thus, if we have a normal distribution of sample means we can say, for example, that 68.2 per cent of the means will fall within one standard error either side of the overall mean; or that 95 per cent of the means will fall within 1.96 standard errors either side.

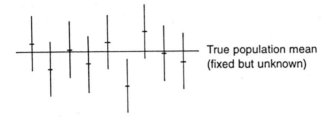

FIGURE 6.7. Relationship between population mean and a series of sample means; each bar shows a sample mean and the range covered by a fixed number of standard errors.

Since this overall mean is the population mean in which we are interested, we can say, for example, that the means of 95 per cent of the simple random samples which we select from this population will fall within 1.96 standard errors of the population mean. However, since we don't know the population mean we have to work this the other way round: for 95 per cent of the simple random samples drawn from the population a distance of 1.96 standard errors either side of the sample mean will include the true population mean; for 5 per cent of the samples it will not. Of course, we can change the percentages by changing the number of standard errors. What is involved may usefully be illustrated by a diagram (Fig. 6.7). The procedure enables us to produce a confidence interval: a range within which our parameter should lie, with a specified level of probability, the range being expressed in terms of the number of standard errors associated with the level of probability in which we are interested.

It's now about time that this theoretical discussion was illustrated by means of a simple example. Let us suppose that we have selected a simple random sample of fifty arrowheads from a collection for the purpose of obtaining an interval estimate of the mean length of the collection as a whole, and that we want our estimate to have a 95 per cent probability of being correct. We will suppose that our measurements have produced a mean length for our sample of 22.6 mm, with a standard deviation of 4.2 mm. The first step is to obtain the standard error of the mean, using the formula given above.

$$s_{\bar{x}} = \frac{4.2}{\sqrt{50}} = 0.594$$

The sample mean, as we have seen, is 22.6 mm. In order to obtain an interval which will have a 95 per cent probability of including the population mean and assuming that the notional distribution of sample means is normal, we know that we have to take an interval of 1.96 standard errors either side of the sample mean. Thus, our interval is defined by the sample mean ± 1.96 standard errors. Here

$$22.6 \pm (1.96)(0.594) = 22.6 \pm 1.16$$

and we can say that there is a 95 per cent probability that the mean length of the collection of arrowheads as a whole lies in the interval 21.44 – 23.76 mm. We may, of course, have been unlucky and the simple random sample we have selected may be one of the 5 per cent which does not include the true population mean. If we are worried about this we can decide to increase our probability of being correct, but only at the expense of widening the interval within which the population mean is estimated to lie. Thus, if we want a probability of 99 per cent of being correct, then to include 99 per cent of a distribution we have to go out 2.58 standard errors either side of our sample mean. In this case

$$22.6 \pm (2.58)(0.594) = 22.6 \pm 1.53$$

so there is a 99 per cent probability that the mean length of the population of arrowheads lies between 21.07 and 24.13 mm.

For constructing a confidence interval in general we can write

$$\bar{x} \pm Z_\alpha \frac{s}{\sqrt{n}}$$

where Z_α is the Z score, or number of standard deviations, associated with a particular probability level.

Here we must interject a minor complication which will come to play a more important role below. Using the Z score, as we have done throughout our example, is perfectly satisfactory if our sample size is larger than say forty or so, but if it is smaller then we have to take account of the fact that s, our estimate of the population standard deviation, is itself of course based on a sample and that different samples will produce different values for it. Small samples will in general be more variable from one to the next and we have to take account of this by using in our estimates not the normal distribution but Student's *t* distribution. This distribution is flatter and more dispersed than the normal distribution and becomes increasingly flat as sample sizes get smaller, converging on the normal distribution as the sample size gets larger. Thus, instead of the formula above we have

$$\bar{x} \pm t_{\alpha, d.f.} \frac{s}{\sqrt{n}}$$

where $t_{\alpha, d.f.}$ is the *t* value for a given number of degrees of freedom ($= n - 1$, where n is the sample size) associated with a particular probability level (see Table D; note that for the boundaries of the confidence interval you need to use *t* for the 2-sided test, i.e. the 2α row at the top of the table). That is to say, if we want a 95 per cent confidence interval, we want to know the range for the central 95 per cent of the distribution. But the *t* values are given in terms of the tails. If we are interested in 95 per cent it means that 2.5 per cent in each tail, 5 per cent altogether, is outside the range. So to find the right *t* value for a given number of degrees of freedom we need to find the two-tailed 5 per cent value. This will give us the right number of standard errors for a 95 per cent confidence interval.

Of course, the specification of confidence intervals in this way presupposes that you have a simple random sample – this is what in effect guarantees the validity of the procedure. However, it is possible in some circumstances to obtain confidence intervals using randomisation techniques (see, for example, Manly, 1991, pp. 18–20, 28–30).

THE *t*-TEST

We have just seen that it is possible to obtain confidence intervals for the mean of a distribution (and by extension for such quantities as totals and proportions, see Chapter 14). However, we can also ask significance test questions about means. Examples might be: is the mean size of burial mounds different in this cemetery from that one? Do burials with swords have more of other types of grave goods than those without? Is the mean age of cattle at death different in this bone assemblage from that one?

The idea, of course, is essentially the same as that we have seen already in the context of the Kolmogorov–Smirnov and other tests in the previous chapter and we can likewise make use of the randomisation assumption as a justification for carrying out the test even if we do not have a random sample. That is to say, so long as the data meet the assumptions of the classical test then this will produce a very similar result to the corresponding randomisation test and be more straightforward to carry out.

In fact, we cannot carry out a test for the difference between two means without also taking into account the degree of dispersion of the values in the two samples. Let us take as an example some data concerning the lengths of lithic scrapers from a cave site in Zimbabwe (derived from Walker, 1995, but with alterations). Is there any evidence that scrapers from layers III and IV at the site are different in length? The two distributions are shown in Figure 6.8 and it can be seen that they are reasonably normal in shape.

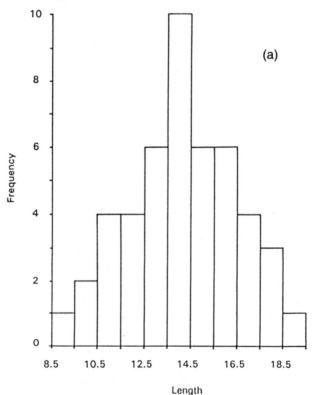

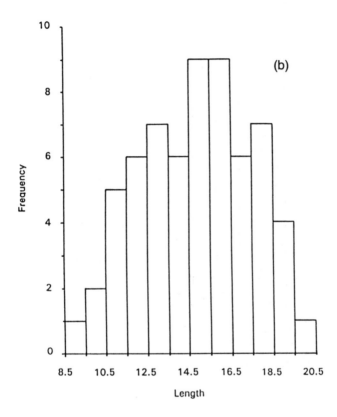

FIGURE 6.8. (a) Histogram of scraper lengths from layer III of a cave in Zimbabwe. (b) Histogram of scraper lengths from layer IV in the same cave.

The question may be rephrased to ask: is the mean length of scrapers in layer III different from that in layer IV? Or, in other words, is the difference in mean length between the two groups of scrapers different from zero? We can get an intuitive idea from Figure 6.9 but we need to be more rigorous than this.

We may imagine two populations of scrapers from which we successively draw random samples and compare the means of the samples with one another. If the two populations have the same mean length then the distribution of differences we generate will be centred on zero. Sometimes the mean of one sample will

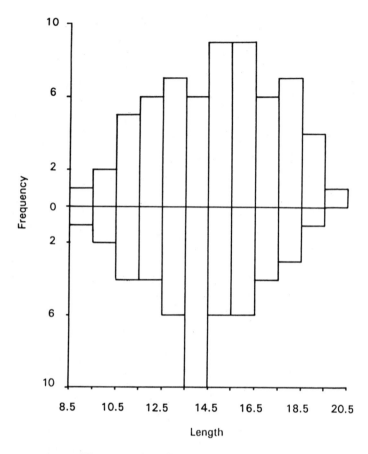

FIGURE 6.9. Histograms from Figure 6.8 placed back to back; top is layer IV, bottom is layer III.

be bigger and sometimes the other but the majority of differences in either direction will be fairly small. The same is true if we apply the randomisation argument. Given that there are forty-seven scrapers from one layer and sixty-three from the other, we could randomly assign our scrapers to the two groups, calculate their means and then the difference between them. Again, we would expect the distribution of differences to centre on zero because membership of one group or the other was assigned purely at random. In fact, as we saw above when discussing confidence intervals, in just the same way as the notional distribution of sample means is normally distributed, so is the distribution of differences between the two means, and this holds even when the populations themselves are not normally distributed so long as the samples are larger than about fifty.

When we want to compare two sample means in this way we make use of the 2-sample *t*-test. In the case we are examining the null hypothesis is that the mean length of scrapers from layer IV is not different from that of layer III. What other assumptions do we have to make? First, that we are dealing with interval or ratio scale measurements; here we are dealing with lengths. The second general assumption is that the two populations are normally distributed. The bar charts in Figure 6.8 suggest that this is the case but in fact our samples are sufficiently large that this assumption can be relaxed. Third, we have to assume (in this version of the *t*-test) that selection of items for inclusion in one sample did not affect selection for the other sample. This is true in the present case – the selection of scrapers from layer IV was not conditioned by the selection for layer III; if it had been we would have had to use a version of the *t*-test appropriate for matched samples (see for example Blalock 1972, Chapter 13). The assumption of random sampling we have already dealt with: even though we do not have random samples we can justify the significance test on the basis of randomisation. As usual we will assume the 0.05 significance level.

The final assumption which needs to be addressed concerns the variances of the two populations. We saw earlier when we were looking at confidence intervals that we had to calculate the standard error of the mean – to give us the dispersion of the distribution of means which we needed. In the case of the 2-sample *t*-test, where the object is to decide whether a particular difference between two means is big enough to be genuinely different from zero, we need to know how dispersed the distribution of differences is. In other words, we need to know the standard error of this distribution of differences. This, in turn, depends on the standard error of the mean for the two separate samples, which in turn depends on their standard deviations or variances. If these are equal then we can obtain a pooled estimate of their common variance, which is preferable for the *t*-test. If the two variances are not equal then we cannot form a pooled estimate and have to use the two sample variances separately.

This produces complications, for example in calculating the number of degrees of freedom associated with the test, although these days statistical computer packages can cope with these.

We can test whether the variances are equal by using the F-test. The assumptions are essentially the same as for the 2-sample t-test in that it presupposes independent random samples from populations with a normal distribution, but of course in this case the null hypothesis is that the two variances are equal. If the two variances are equal then if we divide one by the other the answer will be one. If we adopt the practice of putting the larger variance on top then any departure from equality will produce an answer greater than one. The question then is: is the departure great enough to indicate a significant difference? This involves comparing the calculated result with a value in a statistical table of the F distribution (although, of course, statistical programs will provide the probability for you). Let us follow through the procedure in relation to our scraper length example.

H_0: the variances of the populations of scraper length from which the samples are derived are equal.
H_1: the variances are not equal.
Significance level 0.05

Other assumptions as above, which the scraper data meet.

Variance of sample 1 $(s_1^2) = 7.05$
Variance of sample 2 $(s_2^2) = 5.49$

$$F = \frac{s_1^2}{s_2^2} = \frac{7.05}{5.49} = 1.28$$

To find the value of F with which to compare this figure we need to know the degrees of freedom associated with the two samples. In each case it is the sample size minus one; in this case sixty-two and forty-six. Because the value of F depends on both sample sizes there are separate sub-tables of F for each significance value. The table for a significance level of 0.05 is given as Table E. If we look this up we see that the critical value for sixty-two and forty-six degrees of freedom at the 0.05 significance level is 1.51. Our calculated value, 1.28, is less than

1.51 so we must accept the null hypothesis and conclude that we have no evidence that the variances are different.

On this basis we can now proceed to the *t*-test using a pooled estimate of the variance, because it can be regarded as the same for both samples.

H_0: the mean length of scrapers from layer III is not different from that of scrapers from layer IV.

H_1: the mean length of layer III scrapers is different from layer IV scrapers.

Significance level = 0.05

Assumptions: ratio scale data

independent random samples

normal populations

equal variances

The calculations for the *t*-test are actually quite laborious, which is why it is just as well that they're all done by computer these days.

$$t = \frac{\bar{x}_1 - \bar{x}_2}{s_{\bar{x}_1 - \bar{x}_2}}$$

The top line is quite straightforward; we simply subtract one sample mean from the other. But we need to see how big this difference is in relation to the standard error of the distribution of differences between the means, because this is what will tell us whether it's an unusually large difference or not. We can now carry out the calculations. The quantities we need are as follows:

$$\bar{x}_1 = 14.83 \qquad \bar{x}_2 = 14.17$$
$$s_1^2 = 7.05 \qquad s_2^2 = 5.49$$
$$n_1 = 63 \qquad n_2 = 47$$

The formula for the standard error of the difference between the means is

$$s_{\bar{x}_1 - \bar{x}_2} = \sqrt{\frac{(n_1-1)\, s_1^2 + (n_2-1)\, s_2^2}{n_1 + n_2 - 2}} \sqrt{\frac{n_1 + n_2}{n_1 n_2}}$$

In this case we have

$$s_{\bar{x}_1 - \bar{x}_2} = \sqrt{\frac{(62 \times 7.05) + (46 \times 5.49)}{(63 + 47) - 2}} \sqrt{\frac{63 + 47}{63 \times 47}}$$

$$= \sqrt{\frac{437.1 + 252.54}{108}} \sqrt{\frac{110}{2961}}$$

$$= \sqrt{6.39} \sqrt{0.0371}$$

$$= (2.53)(0.193) = 0.489$$

$$t = \frac{14.83 - 14.17}{0.489} = 1.35$$

In order to compare this result with the t-table we need, as before, to know the number of degrees of freedom. In this case it is $n_1 + n_2 - 2$. The relevant numbers are

$$63 + 47 - 2 = 108$$

If we look at the t-table (Table D), we see that we need to know whether our test is 1- or 2-tailed before we can establish whether or not the result is significant. In the present case we are interested in a 2-tailed test because our null hypothesis is that there is no difference between the means and the alternative is that there is. Looking in the table for the 2-tailed 0.05 level of significance with 108 degrees of freedom, we see that the tabulated value is approximately 1.98. Our calculated value of t is only 1.35, so we have to accept the null hypothesis and conclude that there is no evidence that the scrapers from the two layers are different in length.

But suppose our question had not been are the scraper lengths from the two layers the same or different, but are the scrapers from layer IV (mean length 14.83 mm) *greater* in length than those from layer III (mean length 14.17 mm). The only evidence in favour of this would be finding that layer IV scrapers were larger than layer III ones; if it turned out that layer IV scrapers were significantly *smaller* than those from layer III, this would still be evidence in favour of the null hypothesis that layer IV scrapers are not greater in length than those from layer III. In these circumstances we are only interested in whether our observed t value lies in the extreme right-hand tail of the distribution; the left-hand tail is irrelevant.

In other words, if H_0 is that the mean of one sample is not greater than the mean of the other, and H_l is that it is greater, then we have a 1-tailed test. The same would apply if we had a hypothesis involving 'less than'. If we have a 1-tailed test, i.e. we are only interested in either the left-hand or right-hand tail of the distribution, then it is easier to obtain a significant result at a given significance level; for example, the value which is significant at the 0.05 level for a 2-tailed test will be significant at the 0.025 level on a 1-tailed test. In the present case, however, if we check the t value required for a 1-tailed 0.05 level of significance, we find that it is approximately 1.66, so our calculated value is still not significant.

It may be helpful at this point to compare the result of our conventional t-test of the difference in mean length between the scrapers from the two levels with that we obtain from making the same comparison using the randomisation procedure described in the previous chapter; in other words, we want to see where our observed difference in mean scraper length lies in a distribution of randomly generated differences. This is obtained by randomly selecting two samples of scrapers without regard to which layer they come from and noting the difference between the means of the two samples. In this case the operation has been repeated 100 times.

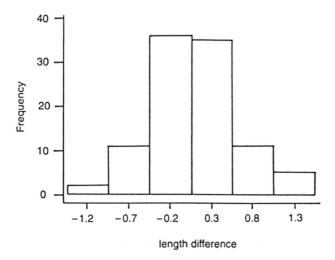

FIGURE 6.10. Histogram of differences between the means of two randomly selected samples of scrapers.

The resulting histogram is shown in Figure 6.10. We can see from this that the mean of the distribution of differences is around zero, as we would expect; in fact, it is 0.076 mm. The observed difference in mean scraper length between the two layers is 0.66 mm. If we look at the histogram we see that while a difference of ± 0.66 is not in the centre of the distribution it is certainly not far enough into the tails to be statistically significant. The standard deviation of the randomised distribution of difference is 0.497 mm, compared with 0.492 mm obtained by conventional means. If we divide the observed difference by this we have $0.66/0.497 = 1.33$. That is to say, our observed difference is 1.33 standard errors away from the mean of the randomised distribution, compared with our conventional t-test result of 1.34. In this case then, as we would expect, the conventional test and the randomisation test give the same result.

WHAT IF THE DATA ARE NOT NORMALLY DISTRIBUTED?

We have seen above that for at least some statistical purposes it does not matter if the population is not normally distributed so long as the sampling distribution of sample means is. Nevertheless, certain methods do presuppose a normal distribution and the question naturally arises whether a particular data set is normally distributed or not. The best way to find out is to plot the cumulative frequency distribution of the data on special graph paper known as *arithmetic probability paper*, or, more usually these days, use a computer statistics program to carry out the corresponding operation. As you can see from Figure 6.11, the horizontal axis is plotted in regular equal units for the range of the variable concerned, but the vertical scale records the cumulative distribution of observations (divided into 1,000 parts) on a variable scale so that, for instance, the vertical distance from 50–60 per cent (500–600 on this scale) is similar to the vertical distance from 1–2 per cent. Note that the vertical scale is drawn from 0.1 to 999.9. This is because the normal curve is *asymptotic* as we have already noted: it approaches zero at both ends without ever actually reaching it, thus 0 per cent and 100 per cent (0 and 1,000) are infinitely distant. The constant horizontal and variable vertical scale have the effect of turning the cumulative curve of a normal distribution into a straight line and any departures of the data values from that line will be easily visible.

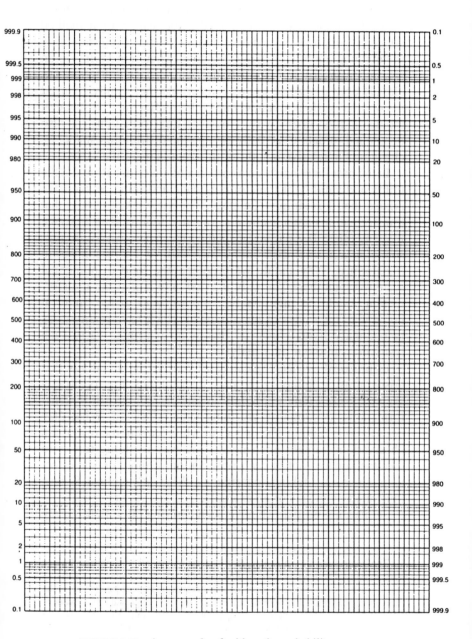

FIGURE 6.11. An example of arithmetic probability paper.

What happens if the data are not normal and we want them to be so for some reason, such as the application of a method which presupposes normal distributions? Can we and should we do anything about it? There is no doubt about our ability to do so, by means of transformations. The Z standardisation has already been described in this chapter, but that simply changed the original scale into a new one without affecting the shape of the distribution in any way. However, transformations can also be applied to data to actually change the distribution shape, by changing the relative lengths of different parts of the scale.

In the past there has been a certain amount of debate about the utility and validity of transforming data, and some people have argued that it is simply 'fudging'. The view taken here is that transformations are a useful and valuable tool for data analysis, like any other. If a particular method that you wish to use presupposes a normal distribution then there is no reason not to transform it. Why should we privilege one form of numerical scale over another? The only proviso here is that the transformation should be interpretable, and we tend to feel more at home with the scales of measurement which have reality to us in our daily lives. However, that is no reason to carry such restrictions into our data analysis.

In practical archaeological cases one of the situations that arises most commonly is that distributions are positively skewed, with a long upper tail. In this case the possible transformations to normality are quite straightforward. What they need to do is 'pull in' the upper tail while leaving the rest of the observations largely unchanged. One way of doing this is to take the square root of each observation; a more drastic effect is produced by taking logarithms.[1] What is involved is best illustrated by means of an example.

Let us suppose that we have been carrying out a field survey

---

1. The logarithm of a number is that number expressed as a power of some other number. There are two well-known systems: common logarithms and natural logarithms. In the latter case numbers are expressed as powers of e, the exponential constant; in common logarithms they are expressed as powers of 10. Thus, 10 is 1 (10^1), 100 is 2 (10^2), 1,000 is 3 (10^3) and so on. Numbers in between can be expressed as fractional powers; e.g. 50 is $10^{1.6989}$, so 50 expressed as a common logarithm is 1.6989.

and have been collecting lithic artefacts over an area using a grid system. As a result of this we have information about the number of lithic artefacts per square for each grid square. We want to carry out a correlation analysis in these data (see below, Chapter 8) and to do this it is preferable for the data to be normally distributed. We have plotted a bar chart of the data and found that the distribution is positively skewed so we want to carry out a transformation of the type just described. Rather than transform each observation we will transform the midpoint of each class interval; this is less laborious and easier to demonstrate. The untransformed distribution is given in Figure 6.12.

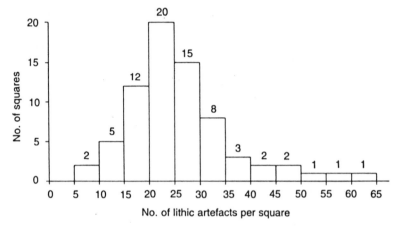

FIGURE 6.12. Distribution of numbers of grid squares containing different numbers of lithic artefacts: data from a hypothetical field survey.

If we try a square root transformation we need a new horizontal scale in units of root *x*. To obtain this we look at the value of the class midpoints in the original bar chart, take their square roots and then put the cases from each original class into the correct square root class. As you can see from Figure 6.13, the data now show a much closer approximation to normality.

If we were trying a log transformation we would need a new scale in units of log *x* (here log to the base 10). By analogy with the square root example we take the log of each class midpoint, work out our scale and plot the bar chart (Figure 6.14).

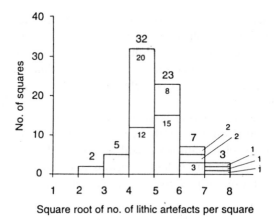

FIGURE 6.13. Distribution of numbers of grid squares containing different numbers of lithic artefacts: number of artefacts per square transformed to the square root of the original value.

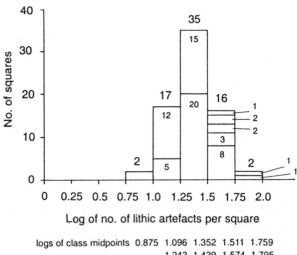

logs of class midpoints 0.875 1.096 1.352 1.511 1.759
                                 1.243 1.439 1.574 1.795
                                                1.628
                                                1.676
                                                1.720

FIGURE 6.14. Distribution of numbers of grid squares containing different numbers of lithic artefacts: number of artefacts per square transformed to the common logarithm of the original value.

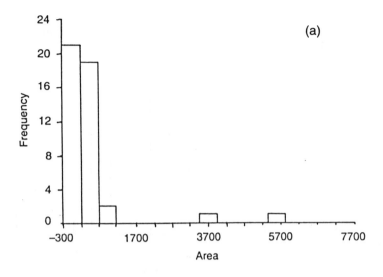

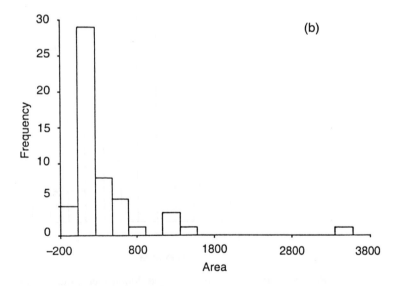

FIGURE 6.15. (a) Histogram of areas of *marae* enclosures from the island of Moorea. (b) Histogram of areas of *marae* enclosures from the island of Tahiti.

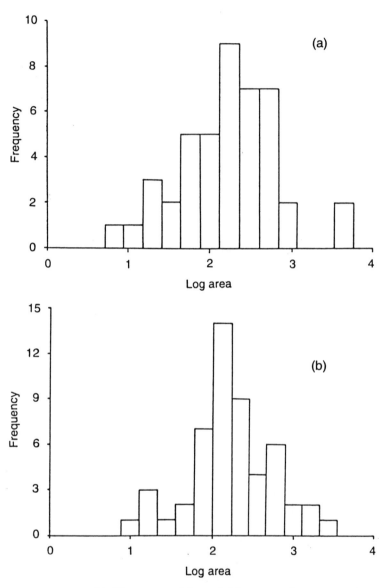

FIGURE 6.16. (a) Histogram of logged Moorea enclosure areas.
(b) Histogram of logged Tahiti enclosure areas.

In fact, as you can see, in this case the result comes out very
similar for both transformations, the square root and the log.
This is because the positive tail in this case is not very long.

Suppose the highest observation had been 1,000,000. The square root of this number is 1,000 but its logarithm is 6, so in this case the difference between the two is considerable. As a general guide, logarithms are appropriate for inherently positive data in which the values go close to zero (e.g. densities), while square roots are often used to transform frequency-count data.

Let us briefly look at an example where this sort of procedure is useful (based on data from Wallin, 1993). We are studying the *marae*, or ceremonial enclosures, of the Society Islands in the Pacific, and the question arises whether those on the main island of Tahiti tend to be *larger than* those on the neighbouring island of Moorea in the same group. The enclosures are rectangular and the measure of size is taken to be their area. In principle, this is clearly a case where we could use a 1-tailed *t*-test, but as Figure 6.15 shows, the distributions are extremely skewed, especially that for Moorea. In these circumstances it seems sensible to log the values to see if that improves things. The result is shown in Figure 6.16 and it is clear that we have in fact succeeded in producing distributions which are now reasonably close to normality.

The relevant information is given in Table 6.1 below

TABLE 6.1. Summary information on logged *marae* areas for Tahiti and Moorea.

	Tahiti	*Moorea*
Sample size	52	44
Mean log area	2.24	2.21
Variance log area	0.275	0.368

The variances are not significantly different from one another so we can use a pooled estimate of the standard error.

H_0: The mean size (in terms of logged area) of Tahiti *marae* is not greater than that of Moorea *marae*.
H_1: the mean size is greater.
Significance level = 0.05
Test is 1-tailed.

Number of degrees of freedom = 52 + 44 − 2 = 94

$$t = \frac{2.24 - 2.21}{0.116} = 0.26$$

The required value for *t* to be significant at the 0.05 level with 94 degrees of freedom for a 1-tailed test is approximately 1.66 so we must accept the null hypothesis and conclude that there is no evidence that the *marae* of Tahiti are larger.

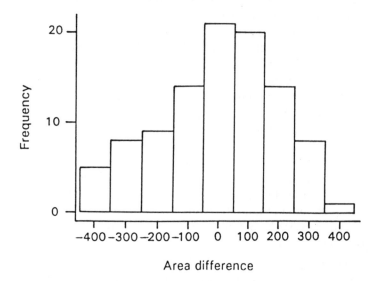

Area difference

FIGURE 6.17. Histogram of differences between the means of two randomly selected samples of unlogged enclosure areas.

We can again compare this result with that achieved by a randomisation test. In fact, we can go a step further back and carry out a randomisation test on the unlogged values. The histogram of differences between the means of the unlogged *marae* sizes from the two islands, based on 100 repetitions, is shown in Figure 6.17. It can be seen that the distribution of differences is close to normality despite the extreme skewness of the original distributions. The observed difference of 91.1 sq.m can be seen to be very close to the mean, so that it is clearly not statistically significant. In comparing the result with that we would have obtained from a standard *t*-test the key figure is the standard error of the difference between the means. The value produced by the conventional technique is 166 sq.m, compared with 190 sq.m produced by randomisation. In other words, the conventional method underestimates the real dispersion in the distribution of differences. The result is a conventional *t* value of 0.55, compared with the equivalent value of 0.47 obtained by randomisation; i.e. a slight overestimate of the significance by the conventional method, although in fact both results are nowhere near significant.

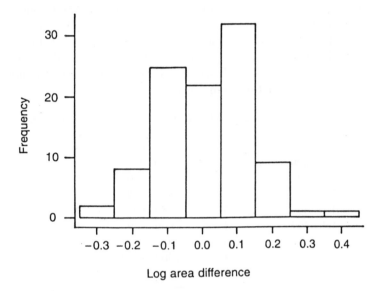

FIGURE 6.18. Histogram of differences between the means of two randomly selected samples of logged enclosure areas.

The randomised distribution of differences for the logged data is shown in Figure 6.18. The observed difference in log area of 0.03 can be seen to be very close to the mean of the randomised distribution and thus not remotely significant. As we saw above, the result produced by the conventional *t*-test was a value of 0.26, based on a pooled standard error of 0.116. The corresponding randomised values are 0.23, based on a standard error of 0.13, and close to the conventional result.

EXERCISES

6.1 A group of pots is found to have a mean capacity of 950 ml, with a standard deviation of 56 ml. The shape of the distribution of volumes is normal. (a) What proportion of the pots have a cubic capacity greater than 1050 ml? (b) What proportion have a capacity less than 800 ml? (c) What proportion of the capacities lie between 900 and 1000 ml?

6.2 In the course of a study of a group of handaxes it is decided to investigate the relationship between handaxe weight and a number of other variables. The methods it is required to use presuppose that the handaxe weights are normally distributed. Compilation of a frequency distribution of weights produces the information below. Check whether it is normal and if it is not take appropriate action to make it so.

Interval (g)	No. of handaxes	Interval (g)	No. of handaxes
200–249	5	650–699	3
250–299	10	700–749	3
300–349	13	750–799	2
350–399	17	800–849	2
400–449	13	850–899	2
450–499	8	900–949	1
500–549	5	950–999	1
550–599	4	1000–1049	1
600–649	4		

6.3 An archaeologist has been carrying out a study of the *marae* ceremonial enclosures of the Society Islands in the Pacific. In the course of the investigation data have been collected on several aspects of the *marae* and the *ahu* platforms found within them. Relevant variables and values are listed below.

Site: merely an identifying number.

Valley: a code identifying the valley in which the particular *marae* occur.

Enclosure size: measured in square metres; a preliminary check indicated that this variable was very skewed so it has been logged.

Ahu volume: based on length, breadth and height measurements in metres; this too turned out to be skewed so it has been logged.

Site	Valley	Log enclosure size	log Ahu volume
1	1	2.871	2.025
2	1	2.517	0.386
3	1	2.346	1.687
4	1	1.483	0.414
5	1	1.924	0.380
6	1	1.988	0.980
7	1	1.845	−0.553
8	1	2.009	−0.631
9	1	2.158	0.380
10	1	2.556	0.021
11	1	1.954	−0.398
12	1	2.003	0.715
13	1	2.353	−0.063
14	1	1.870	−0.004
15	2	1.942	−0.421
16	2	2.168	0.225
17	2	2.046	−0.423
18	2	2.221	−0.125
19	2	2.311	−0.058
20	2	2.141	0.017
21	2	1.950	−0.155
22	2	2.401	2.431
23	2	2.807	2.431
24	2	2.740	0.641

Is there any indication that the enclosures tend to be of different sizes in the two valleys?

6.4 Obtain 95 per cent confidence intervals for the logged *Ahu* volumes listed above for each of the two valleys.

Seven

THE CHI-SQUARED TEST AND MEASURES OF ASSOCIATION

The previous two chapters have been concerned with cases where the level of measurement of the data is ordinal or higher. This chapter examines the chi-squared test, which is used for data measured at the nominal scale, in other words, simply classified into categories; it is also easy to calculate, although that is less important these days. It can be used to assess the correspondence between distributions in a wide variety of different situations and as a result is applied very extensively.

There are two slightly different versions of the chi-squared test, although obviously the principle in both is the same. The first, perhaps less familiar to archaeologists, is the 1-sample test, in which a sample is compared to a specified theoretical population and a test is made of how good the correspondence or 'fit' is between these two distributions; the idea is clearly important when we are testing theoretically derived models.

In describing the test it is easiest to begin with an example. A question frequently of interest is the distribution of settlement in relation to soil differences: were certain areas more attractive than others to early settlement?

Suppose we have an area in eastern France with three different soil types: rendzina, alluvium and brown earth. There are fifty-three late Neolithic settlements in the area and a look at the map suggests the possibility that the rendzinas may have been preferred. The question is whether or not it is possible that the distribution of settlements with regard to soil could be a matter of chance. If all three soil types were equally attractive to settlement then it would be reasonable to assume that we should find approximately the same density of settlement in each. In other words, the distribution of settlements would be roughly evenly spread over the landscape and variations would not relate to soil but to such factors as small local differences in topography, or the whims of the founding settlers. In this context we can use the chi-squared test.

TABLE 7.1 Numbers of late neolithic settlements on different soil types in eastern France.

Soil type	No. of settlements
Rendzina	26
Alluvium	9
Brown earth	18
	53

The first thing we can do is to note the number of settlements on each of the soil types (Table 7.1). How do we calculate the theoretically derived expected frequencies to compare with these? We have already seen that if we postulate that all three zones were equally attractive to settlement, we should expect the same density of settlements in each. This represents our theoretically-derived null hypothesis for calculating expected frequencies. Thus, it is reasonable to assume that if rendzinas make up 32 per cent of the area, as we will suppose they do, then 32 per cent of all the settlements should be on rendzinas; similarly, if we suppose 43 per cent of the area to be brown earth and 25 per cent to be alluvium. In other words, we calculate the expected number of settlements for each soil type by allotting the same proportion of the total number of settlements to that soil type as it occupies of the total area (Table 7.2).

TABLE 7.2 Observed and expected numbers of late neolithic settlements on different soil types in eastern France.

Soil type	Observed no. of settlements	% of area	Expected no. of settlements
Rendzina	26	32	17.0
Alluvium	9	25	13.2
Brown earth	18	43	22.8
	53	100	53.0

If we compare the observed and expected values in this table for the number of settlements on each of the soil types, there are

some obvious differences between the distribution anticipated
if all areas were equally attractive to settlement and what we
actually observe. The question is, are the differences so great
that the probability of their being the result of chance variation
is acceptably low? This is where the chi-squared test has its role.

The 1-sample chi-squared test presupposes a set of observations divided up into a number of mutually exclusive categories.
A comparison is then made between the distribution of observations across the categories and the distribution to be anticipated
under some theoretically derived expectation, specified by the
null hypothesis. The differences between the two distributions
for each category are noted and a chi-squared value is calculated,
based on the sum of the differences. The calculated value is then
compared with the minimum value required to reject the null
hypothesis at the level of significance which has been set.

Carrying out the test requires a number of assumptions. As
always, it is necessary to specify a null hypothesis and set a
significance level, and either to have a random sample from a
population or be able to justify the test as corresponding to its
randomisation equivalent in the way discussed in the previous
chapters. The level of measurement is not at all demanding,
simply a nominal scale with at least two mutually exclusive
categories into which the observations have been divided; the
observations themselves must be *counts*, not percentages or other
forms of ratio.

The formula for chi-squared is given by

$$\chi^2 = \sum_{i=1}^{k} \frac{(O_i - E_i)^2}{E_i}$$

where k is the number of categories,
   O_i is the observed number of cases in category i,
   E_i is the expected number of cases in category i,
   and χ^2 is the symbol representing chi-squared, using the
   Greek letter 'chi'.

In words this formula reads as follows: for each category
subtract the expected value from the observed value, square this
difference, and divide this result by the expected value; once
this has been done for each category, sum the results for all
categories. The result is a calculated chi-squared value.

Once we have computed a value for chi-squared we need to test it for statistical significance. As with the *t*-test, we do this, if a computer has not done it for us, by comparing our result with the values in a table (Table F in the Appendix). In order to find the relevant value in the table with which to make the comparison we need to know two things: the level of significance which has been decided – straightforward enough – and the number of degrees of freedom associated with the sample.

In the case of chi-squared the basis for the degrees of freedom is rather different from the *t*-test. Essentially, the form of the theoretical chi-squared distribution, which is tabulated in the chi-squared table, varies according to the number of categories into which the observations are divided. The greater the number of categories, the larger the value of the chi-squared statistic obtained from the data needs to be, in order to reach a given level of significance. In the case of the 1-sample test, however, the number of degrees of freedom is not equal to the number of categories but to the number of categories minus one; in symbols

$$v = k-1$$

where v (Greek letter 'nu') is the number of degrees of freedom and k is the number of categories.

Why should this be the case? This is best illustrated by referring to our example, where there are fifty-three observations (settlements) divided into three categories (soil types). Given that there is a total of fifty-three observations altogether, and that $26 + 9 = 35$ are in the first two categories, then the value in the third category *has to be* $53 - 35 = 18$. In other words, the values in the first two categories are free to vary but the value in the last category is not; it is fixed by the requirement that the sum over all three categories should equal the total number of observations with which we started.

When you know the relevant number of degrees of freedom and the level of significance it is possible to find the appropriate value in the table with which to compare the calculated value. In a chi-squared table the number of degrees of freedom is given down the left-hand side and the significance level across the top. Thus, if you have two degrees of freedom and are using the 0.05 significance level, then you find the row for $v = 2$, go across it until you reach the column for the 0.05 significance level and read off the number, in this case 5.99. This is the tabulated chi-squared value with which the calculated value must be compared:

If $\chi^2_{calc} \geq \chi^2_a$, reject H_0

If $\chi^2_{calc} < \chi^2_a$, accept H_0

Before turning to our example, however, one more point needs to be noted. If the test has only one degree of freedom then no category should have an *expected* value less than five; with larger numbers of categories this restriction can be relaxed considerably but there should never be any expected values of zero because this will mean that the corresponding term in the equation for calculating chi-squared will be infinity. Where samples are very small, alternatives, such as Fisher's Exact Test (e.g. Blalock, 1972, pp. 287–91), are available.

Now that the general procedure for carrying out a chi-squared test has been described, it is possible to show its use in our example, which must first be set up in the appropriate form for a significance test:

H_0: settlements are equally distributed across all three soil types.

H_1: settlements are not equally distributed across all three soil types.

Selected significance level: $\alpha = 0.05$

There is no need to be extremely conservative in selecting the level. We are interested in whether or not we have an indication of a divergence from equality of distribution.

The data are measured at a nominal scale only, they are counts divided into categories and the categories are mutually exclusive. None of the expected values calculated above is less than five. Use of a 1-sample chi-squared test is therefore appropriate. The expected values under H_0 have already been generated (Table 7.2) so it is now possible to carry out the necessary calculations.

$$\chi^2 = \sum_{i=1}^{k} \frac{(O_i - E_i)^2}{E_i}$$

$$= \frac{(26-17.0)^2}{17.0} + \frac{(9-13.2)^2}{13.2} + \frac{(18-22.8)^2}{22.8}$$

$$= 4.76 + 1.34 + 1.01$$

$$= 7.11$$

This must now be compared with the appropriate tabulated value. Degrees of freedom are $k-1$, where k is the number of categories: here $3-1=2$. From the table the critical chi-squared value for two degrees of freedom and the 0.05 level of significance is 5.99. If $\chi^2_{calc} \geq \chi^2_{\alpha}$, reject H_0: here $7.11 > 5.99$, and therefore we reject the null hypothesis in this case.

But it is important not just to stop at this point. It is necessary to relate the result of the test to the archaeological problem. Here we have to accept the alternative hypothesis that settlements are not equally distributed across all three soil types. In terms of randomisation we can say that if we carried out a large number of experiments randomly allocating fifty-three settlements to these three soil types on the assumption of an equal distribution, the distribution we have actually observed would be a very unusual one, and at the 0.05 level would require us to reject the assumption of an equal distribution. There may be many reasons for this, and we will consider the problems of moving from statistically significant associations and correlations to inferences about causation below.

THE CHI-SQUARED TEST FOR CROSS-CLASSIFIED DATA

Having looked at the case in which a sample is compared to a specified theoretical population, let us now turn to the use of the chi-squared test to test for independence of classification in cases where data have been classified in terms of two different criteria, again beginning with an example.

Suppose we are studying an inhumation cemetery where the burials are in a crouched position and we suspect there is a relationship between the sex of the individual lying in the grave (anthropologically determined) and the side on which they are lying. We have the information given in Table 7.3 in which the burials are categorised according to their values on the two variables concerned – sex and side-lying; thus, there are twenty-nine males on their right-hand-side and so on. Tables like this are often referred to as *contingency tables*. This one is a 2 × 2 (2 by 2) contingency table since there are two rows – right-hand-side and left-hand-side – and two columns – male and female. The individual entries in the table, e.g. that for female, right-hand-side, are referred to as the cells. The numbers at the end of each row are the row totals and at the bottom of each column, the column totals. In the bottom right-hand position is the total number of observations, here eighty-seven.

TABLE 7.3 Side on which individuals were placed in the grave cross-tabulated against their sex, for a Bronze Age inhumation cemetery.

	M	F	
RHS	29	14	43
LHS	11	33	44
	40	47	87

Basically, the test for such tables is very similar to the one we have just seen, in that the data are counts divided into mutually exclusive categories. This time, however, instead of comparing the distribution of an observed sample with that of a theoretically specified population, we are asking whether two classifications of our data are independent of one another, in the sense that membership of a particular category of one classification is unrelated to membership of a particular category of the other. Nevertheless, in both cases we are testing for what statisticians call 'goodness-of-fit'.

The assumptions required in this test are again very similar to those for the 1-sample test: nominal scale or higher level of measurement and no expected frequency less than five in the case of one degree of freedom (see p. 112 below for degrees of freedom in contingency tables). Now, however, we have two distinct classification criteria, divided into at least two mutually exclusive categories. Thus, to refer to our examples, for the 1-sample chi-squared test our settlements were categorised according to one variable alone, their soil type; for the contingency table our burials are categorised or classified in terms of two variables: their biological sex and the side on which they are lying in the grave.

The calculation of chi-squared, as before, is based on the difference between the observed and expected values for each category. The number of categories is the number of cells in the table: in our example there are two anthropologically identified sex categories and two side categories, so the number of cells, as you can see from Table 7.3, is $2 \times 2 = 4$.

For the 1-sample chi-squared test the expected values were generated by the theoretical population postulated by the null hypothesis. The idea is very similar here, in that we are asking whether male and female burials have the same proportional division into left-hand-side and right-hand-side burials. Thus, if there are altogether forty-three right-hand-side burials and forty-four left-hand-side burials then we would expect the forty-seven female burials and the forty male burials to be divided into the right-hand-side and left-hand-side categories according to the 43:44 ratio. We can obtain the appropriate expected values for a given cell in the table by multiplying the row sum corresponding to the cell by the column sum corresponding to the cell and dividing the result by the total number of observations. Thus, for the top left-hand cell of the table given above the expected value is $(40 \times 43)/87 = 19.8$.

It is possible to work out the expected values for the other cells in the table in the same way. However, since we know the marginal totals of the table and the expected value for the top left-hand cell, we can obtain the expected values for the other three cells by subtraction.

$43 - 19.8 = 23.2$
$40 - 19.8 = 20.2$
$44 - 20.2 = 23.8$

We then make out a table including the expected values in parentheses (Table 7.4) and we are now in a position to set up the significance test for the burial data.

H_0: the distribution of male and female burials across the two burial position categories, left-hand-side and right-hand-side, is not different.

H_1: the distribution of male and female burials across the two categories is different.

Selected significance level $= 0.05$

TABLE 7.4. Side on which individuals were placed in the grave cross-tabulated against their sex, with the expected values for each category shown in parentheses.

	M	F	
RHS	29	14	43
	(19.8)	(23.2)	
LHS	11	33	44
	(20.2)	(23.8)	
	40	47	87

The data meet the required assumptions for a chi-squared test on cross-classified data, so the next step is to calculate the chi-squared value for the data, using the formula given above. The results are shown in Table 7.5.

TABLE 7.5. Calculation table for obtaining chi-squared value from data in Table 7.4.

Category	O_i	E_i	$(O_i - E_i)$	$(O_i - E_i)^2$	$\dfrac{(O_i - E_i)^2}{E_i}$
1	29	19.8	9.2	84.64	4.27
2	14	23.2	−9.2	84.64	3.65
3	11	20.2	−9.2	84.64	4.19
4	33	23.8	9.2	84.64	3.56
					$\chi^2 = 15.67$

The process of testing this calculated value for significance is the same as before, in that it is compared to the value in the chi-squared table which corresponds to the required level of significance and the appropriate number of degrees of freedom. For the test on cross-classified data, however, the number of degrees of freedom has to be calculated differently and is given by $v =$ (the number of rows in the table − 1)(the number of columns in the table − 1). For our example we have $(2-1)(2-1) = 1$.

This may be related to the observation above that once we had worked out the expected value for the top left-hand cell of the table, the expected values for the other cells were fixed and could be obtained by subtraction. If we now look up the tabulated value of chi-squared for one degree of freedom and the 0.05 level of significance we find that it is 3.84. $\chi^2_{calc} = 15.67$,

15.67 > 3.84, and accordingly we reject H_0. We can note incidentally that a value of 15.67 for chi-squared would even be significant at the 0.001 level.It thus appears that male and female burials are not distributed in the same way over the two position categories.

One final calculation note. The method described above is the general way of calculating chi-squared, however many rows and columns there are in the table. In fact, for the case of a 2 × 2 table, with two rows and two columns, there is an alternative more convenient formula if you should have to do the calculations by hand or with a calculator:

$$\chi^2 = \frac{n(ad-bc)^2}{(a+b)(c+d)(a+c)(b+d)}$$

where n is the sample size and a, b, c, d refer to the cells of a table labelled as follows:

a   b
c   d

HOW USEFUL IS THE CHI-SQUARED TEST?

It should be clear from what has been said about the chi-squared test that it can be extremely useful and informative, but it is important to be fully aware what the result of a chi-squared test can and cannot tell us.

First, the chi-squared test does not tell us anything about the way in which the variables are related; it simply measures departures of expected from observed values. Second, but more important, chi-squared does not tell us about the strength of a relationship; it simply tells us about the probability that a relationship exists. For a relationship to be statistically significant it is not necessary for it to be significant in the sense of being strong; it is possible for a relationship to be statistically significant yet quite weak. This is because statistical significance arises from the combined effect of two different factors: the strength of the relationship and the size of the sample. Consequently, we *cannot* use the value of chi-squared or its associated probability level as a measure of strength of relationship and say, for example, that a result significant at the 0.001 level indicates a stronger relationship than one significant at the 0.05 level.

The effect of sample size on the chi-squared value and significance level may be illustrated by looking again at the burial example discussed above, altered slightly for the purposes of this illustration so that all the numbers are even ones (Table 7.6). Here chi-squared = 18.33 with one degree of freedom, significant at much more than the 0.001 level. If we halve the numbers but keep the same proportional distribution across the categories, we have Table 7.7. Here chi-squared = 9.16 with one degree of freedom, significant at the 0.01 level. Similarly, if we doubled the original numbers, we would obtain a chi-squared value of 36.66. Thus, in general, if we keep the proportions in the cells constant and simply multiply the numbers by some factor, k, then we multiply the resulting chi-squared by k.

TABLE 7.6. Side on which individuals were placed in the grave cross-tabulated against their sex.

	M	F	
RHS	30	14	44
LHS	10	34	44
	40	48	88

TABLE 7.7. Side on which individuals were placed in the grave cross-tabulated against their sex. Numbers in each category are half those in Table 7.6.

	M	F	
RHS	15	7	22
LHS	5	17	22
	20	24	44

All this makes sense. If we are asking the significance test question – does a relationship exist or not? – we will have more confidence in our answer if it is based on a large number of observations. If the number of observations is very large, then even if only a very weak relationship exists between our variables, or only some slight difference between our samples, we can have some confidence that it is 'real'. Conversely, if the number of observations is very small then for any difference or relationship to be regarded as 'real' it will have to be very marked indeed. Such marked differences or strong relationships are almost bound to be of interest to us, but the same is not necessarily true of weak ones: a very slight relationship or difference may be 'real', but does it matter?

MEASURING ASSOCIATION

The foregoing discussion shows that we need to measure strength of relationship separately from statistical significance, and that chi-squared at least is not an appropriate way of doing this, except perhaps in those rare instances where our aim simply involves the making of comparisons across samples which are identical in size.

This question of comparisons is an important one. Generally, we are not interested in a given single case where the strength of relationship is being measured. More often than not, comparisons are being made, for example with the same measure on other data sets. For this reason such measures need to be standardised. It is also convenient for such measures to have a well-defined upper and lower limit, conventionally 1.0 as the upper limit and either 0.0 or -1.0 as the lower limit. Most measures take a value of 1.0 or -1.0 when the relationship is a perfect one and a value of 0 when there is no relationship between the variables.

Given that chi-squared is dependent on sample size one obvious thing to do is to divide the value of chi-squared by n, the number in the sample; this means that we will get the same result when the proportions in the cells are the same, regardless of the absolute numbers. The coefficient obtained by dividing chi-squared by n is known as ϕ^2 (phi-squared); its value is 0 when there is no relationship between the two variables. With 2×2 (or $2 \times k$) tables ϕ^2 has an upper limit of 1.0 which is reached when the relationship between the two variables is perfect, as shown in Table 7.8. In this case $\chi^2 = 100$ and $\phi^2 = 100/100 = 1.0$.

TABLE 7.8. An example of a perfect relationship or association in a 2×2 table.

	M	F	
RHS	50	0	50
LHS	0	50	50
	50	50	100

In a 2×2 table, whenever two diagonally opposite cells are empty the chi-squared value for the table will be equal to the number of observations and ϕ^2 will therefore be 1.0; this is sometimes referred to as *absolute* association. Referring to this substantive case we could say that variation in the side on which individuals are lying in the grave is completely accounted for by their sex, or associated with their sex.

As noted above, ϕ^2 has the convenient upper limit of 1.0 only when the table has two rows and/or two columns. This will hold true, for example, in a table of two rows and twenty columns, or two columns and twenty rows, but not in a table of 3×20, or even 3×3. For tables where the number of rows and columns is greater than two, ϕ^2 will have a higher upper limit than 1.0. In order to scale it down to have this limit for larger tables, ϕ^2 itself must be standardised. The best-known of these standardisations is Cramer's V^2:

$$V^2 = \frac{\phi^2}{\min(r-1, c-1)}$$

where $\min(r-1, c-1)$ refers to either (the number of rows -1) or (the number of columns -1), whichever is the smaller. This takes a maximum value of 1.0 even when numbers of rows and columns are not equal, and for tables larger than 2×2 or $2 \times k$; in these latter two cases V^2 obviously reduces to ϕ^2.

Yule's Q is another measure of association or relationship quite frequently used, although it is only applicable to the 2×2 table:

$$Q = \frac{ad - bc}{ad + bc}$$

where a, b, c, d refer to the cell frequencies of a table labelled as follows:

a   b

c   d

Imagine a 2×2 table in which we plot the presence/absence of something, for example a particular grave good type in a grave, against the presence/absence of something else, say another grave good type. We can label the table thus:

	+	−
+	+ + (a)	+−(b)
−	−+(c)	−−(d)

The top left cell indicates joint presence, the bottom right joint absence, and the other two the cases where one is present and the other is absent. The a and d cells are the cases where our two attributes *covary* positively: when one is present so is the other, when one is absent the other is too. Thus, multiplying together the number of instances of joint presence (a) and joint absence (d) gives us a measure of the *positive covariation* between our two attributes. On the other hand, multiplying the number of instances where one is present and the other is absent (b), and where one is absent and the other is present (c), gives us a measure of the *negative covariation* between our two attributes: the extent to which the presence of one implies the absence of the other. If, when one is present, the other is sometimes present and sometimes absent then there is no systematic relationship between the two. The definitive example of no relationship is when ad (the positive covariation) is equal to bc (the negative covariation), and thus $Q = 0.0$. On the other hand, Q will have a limit of $+1.0$ for perfect positive covariation or association and $−1.0$ for perfect negative association. Thus, while ϕ^2 can only be positive Q can also take negative values. However, the major difference between these two measures lies in the way they treat association, a point best illustrated by an example.

In both Tables 7.9 and 7.10 the value of one of the cells is 0. It is a result of the formula for Q that it takes a value of 1.0 in both of them, and indeed in any 2×2 table with a 0 entry. In this case we can see that it reflects the perfect association between the male category and one of the side-lying categories – the right-hand side. By contrast, in the first table female burials are equally split between the two sides, while in the second they tend towards the left, the opposite pattern to the males. In neither case are females exclusively associated with the left-hand-side, which would be required for ϕ^2 to take a value of 1.0, but of course ϕ^2 does increase from the first table to the second as the distribution of females becomes more asymmetrical.

TABLE 7.9. Comparison between Q and ϕ^2, example 1. Here $Q = 1.0$ and $\phi^2 = 0.375$.

	M	F	
RHS	60	20	80
LHS	0	20	20
	60	40	100

TABLE 7.10. Comparison between Q and ϕ^2, example 2. Here $Q = 1.0$ and $\phi^2 = 0.643$.

	M	F	
RHS	60	10	70
LHS	0	30	30
	60	40	100

Q is a good coefficient for picking out partial associations, like that between males and the right-hand-side position in the example above, but once it has reached its limit it can obviously go no further. It has therefore been criticised because it cannot make the distinction between what is sometimes called 'complete' association, when one cell takes a zero value, and 'absolute' association, referred to above, when two diagonally opposite cells take zero values and ϕ^2 reaches its upper limit. Nevertheless, Q can be very useful so long as this point is borne in mind.

OTHER MEASURES OF ASSOCIATION

Phi-squared, Cramer's V^2 and Yule's Q are by no means the only measures of association for variables measured at a nominal scale. A number of others are also available but most are not described here in any detail. The aim is not to be comprehensive but to present a number of coefficients that are useful in themselves and, more importantly, to give an idea of what is involved in measuring association. Nevertheless, it is worth mentioning Goodman and Kruskal's τ (tau) and λ (lambda), which are computed by many statistics packages, and illustrating the use of the τ coefficient.

Both these statistics relate association between variables to reducing the number of errors we will make in guessing the value of one variable if we use the values of the other to help us in our guess. Thus, to take the data from Table 7.10, we know that there are 100 graves, seventy with right-hand-side and thirty with left-hand-side burials. Suppose we have to guess for each grave whether it is left-hand-side or right-hand-side. If we made seventy right-hand-side guesses and thirty left-hand-side guesses, many of them would be wrong. If, on the other hand, we know the sex of the individual buried, we can improve our guesswork considerably because the individual's sex and the side on which they are lying in the grave are related to one another. Thus, if we know that a grave contains a male we must guess that the burial is right-hand-side, because there are no left-hand-side male burials. If we know that the grave contains a female our best guess is that it will be a left-hand-side burial, although we won't always be right. The stronger the relationship between the two variables, the more successful we will be in using the value of a case on one to predict its value on the other. If there is no relationship between them, using one to predict the other won't help.

Goodman and Kruskal's τ and λ use this general idea in slightly different ways, but both of them are asymmetrical. This is worth thinking about! To refer to our example in Table 7.10 again: if we know that a grave contains a male we can predict with 100 per cent success that the individual will be on his right-hand side; however, if we know that an individual is on its right-hand side we cannot predict with 100 per cent success that it will be a male, because ten of the seventy are female.

We can use the data from Table 7.10 to show how the τ coefficient actually works (see Blalock, 1972, pp. 300–1). If we assume that we don't know the sex of the individuals then we have to assign 70 of them at random to the RHS category, but since 30 out of the 100 don't belong in this category on average we can expect to make $70 \times 30/100 = 21$ errors when we make our assignments to the RHS category. Similarly, we must assign 30 individuals to the LHS category but since 70 out of 100 don't belong there we will make on average $30 \times 70/100 = 21$ errors again. So in total we are likely to make 42 errors when we assign our 100 individuals to these two categories.

We can now look at what happens when we know the individual's sex. Given that an individual is male, we must place all 60 of them in the RHS category. Since all the males belong in the RHS category and none in the LHS category, we can expect to make $60 \times 0/60 = 0$ errors in this case. Similarly, when we place no males in the LHS category we will again not be making any errors. If we now turn to the female burials it's slightly different. We need to assign 10 female burials to the RHS category but since 30 out of the 40 do not belong in this category we can expect on average to make $10 \times 30/40 = 7.5$ errors in assigning females to the RHS category. Similarly again, when we assign females to the LHS category, 10 out of the 40 do not belong here so we can expect $30 \times 10/40 = 7.5$ errors again.

In total, if we know the sex of the individual we can expect to make $0 + 0 + 7.5 + 7.5 = 15$ errors in assigning individuals to side-lying categories, instead of 42. The τ coefficient gives us the proportional reduction of errors (Blalock, 1972, p. 301):

$\tau =$ (number of errors not knowing sex – number of errors knowing sex)/number of errors not knowing sex.

In this case

$\tau = (42 - 15)/42 = 0.643$

In other words, by knowing the sex of the individual we make 64 per cent fewer mistakes in assigning individuals to side-lying categories. This could only be the case if the two things – sex and side-lying – were strongly associated with one another.

We noted above that τ was asymmetrical – here, if we know a burial is male we can be certain that it's RHS but if it is on its right-hand-side we cannot be certain it's male. Nevertheless, for a 2×2 table such as this one the τ value will be the same whichever way round you take it, because the categories are in a sense the converse of one another. Thus, in this case, if we know a burial is female we cannot be certain it's LHS, but if we know it is LHS then it must be female.

We can further note (see for example Blalock, 1972, p. 301) that in the case of a 2×2 table the value of τ will be the same as the value for ϕ^2, as the values for Table 7.10 confirm.

ASSOCIATION AND CAUSAL INFERENCE

Often, when we are looking at association in the way indicated above, we are thinking, as we have already implied, in terms of an *independent* and a *dependent* variable. Thus, in the case of the individual's sex and the side on which they are lying in the grave, it is possible to visualise the side on which the individual was deposited in the grave as *dependent* on their sex, but not their sex as being dependent on the side on which they are lying. This is satisfactory as far as it goes. However, although we have talked in a statistical sense about one variable accounting for another or being associated with another, we cannot necessarily infer a causal relationship between the two. All statistics books warn of the danger of inferring causation from association, because of the possibility of spurious correlation.

Of course, causal relationships can never be disentangled by mere statistical analysis, but in the process of disentangling them statistical methods can be either extremely useful or positively misleading. If we simply take the first statistic we obtain at its face value we can easily be misled. It is important to be sure that any connection we infer between objects, events or processes is 'real', and it is generally suggested that the acid test of a 'real' relationship is that it should not change regardless of the conditions under which it is observed; in other words, does the relationship between two variables persist or disappear when we introduce a third?

The process of investigating relationships among variables under a variety of different conditions is a very general and important one if valid inferences about those relationships are going to be made. We will see it occurring again and again. The idea will be introduced here in terms of contingency tables and the various statistics we have seen used as an aid to understanding them. If we start off with a simple 2×2 table, we can ask what happens when we introduce a third variable, so that we have a $2 \times 2 \times 2$ table. We will use examples to illustrate some of the possibilities.

TABLE 7.11. Volume of grave cist tabulated against the sex of the individual buried.

	Volume of grave pit	
	<1.5 m³	>1.5 m³
M	22	47
F	33	26

$\chi^2 = $ 7.51, significant at 0.01
$\phi^2 = $ 0.059
$Q = -0.461$

In Table 7.11 we have a statistically significant relationship between the sex of the individual buried and the volume of the grave pit in which they have been found. There is a tendency for females to be found in the smaller grave pits and males to be found in the larger ones. In terms of some of the standard arguments about burial practice and social status we might conclude that we have evidence here for a lower status for women, less energy being put into digging their grave pits. What happens though if we take into account the height of the individuals in the graves, using estimates derived from long bone measurements? If we want to introduce an extra variable like this we have to split our original table into two (Table 7.12).

TABLE 7.12. Volume of grave pit tabulated against the sex and estimated height of the individual buried.

		Volume of grave pit		
		<1.5 m³	>1.5 m³	
Est height	M	17	4	$\chi^2 = $ 0.032
<1.55 m	F	29	6	$\phi^2 = $ 0.0006
				$Q = -0.064$
Est height	M	5	43	$\chi^2 = $ 0.57
>1.55 m	F	4	20	$\phi^2 = $ 0.008
				$Q = -0.26$

What has happened, now that we have introduced a consideration of individuals' estimated height into the situation? The answer is that the χ^2 values are no longer significant – indeed they have decreased much more than would be expected from the decrease in sample size – and the two association coefficients, for both tables, are much closer to zero than they were in the combined table. In other words, when we introduce (or control for) height the relationship between grave pit volume and sex largely disappears. We can conclude from this that it was spurious: it actually resulted from the fact that there is a relationship between the height of individuals and the volume of their grave pit, and that women tend to be smaller than men. The situation may be represented as in Figure 7.1.

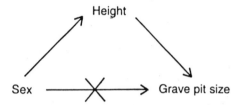

FIGURE 7.1. Factors affecting grave pit size and the relationships between them.

But the example we have just seen is not the only way in which a third variable can change the picture presented by an initial two-variable relationship and one more important example will be illustrated here.

TABLE 7.13. Presence/absence of beads tabulated against the rank of the individuals buried with them.

		Beads in grave		
		Present	*Absent*	
Rank	High	53	39	$\chi^2 = 3.31$
	Low	44	55	$\phi^2 = 0.09$
				$Q = 0.25$

Staying on the cemetery analysis theme, let us suppose that on some reasonable criterion we have divided the burials into 'high rank' and 'low rank' groups. The criterion did not involve consideration of presence or absence of beads in the grave and we now wish to see if this is related to rank. From Table 7.13 we have no evidence of a statistically significant relationship; the χ^2 value is not significant at the 0.05 level. Let us now try controlling for the sex of the individual buried (Table 7.14).

TABLE 7.14. Presence/absence of beads tabulated against the rank of the individuals buried with them, subdivided by sex.

		Beads in grave				
		Present	Absent			
Male	High rank	5	33	$\chi^2 =$		7.71
	Low rank	19	28	$\phi^2 =$		0.09
				$Q =$		−0.64
Female	High rank	42	6	$\chi^2 =$		15.22
	Low rank	29	27	$\phi^2 =$		0.15
				$Q =$		0.73

Whereas initially we did not have a statistically significant relationship between the presence of beads and rank we now have two highly significant ones in each of the separate sub-tables. Furthermore, if we look at the Q coefficients we see that the value for males is fairly strongly negative while that for females is fairly strongly positive. If we look at the two sub-tables to see what is going on we find that 'high-ranking' males tend not to have beads whereas 'high-ranking' females do tend to have them. That is to say there are two very different relationships between rank and beads in each of the separate subtables and the initial table was a kind of average of these two opposites and hence did not give a significant result. This outcome is known as *interaction*: the values of the third variable interact with the relationship between the other two variables. Further progress can only be made by dividing our observations into two groups on the basis of the interacting variable (here the individual's sex) and continuing the search for connections within each group separately.

It should be apparent from the above that when we have cross-classified data we need to examine them in considerable detail; simply carrying out a chi-squared test is insufficient and may be positively misleading; furthermore, often you can be pretty sure ahead of time that the chi-squared result is going to be significant, so by relying solely on this you gain little new information. Nevertheless, it should be equally apparent that sorting out what is going on when you have several variables is a complex task. We will look at some more tools for dealing with these problems below (Chapter 10) but in general it is helpful if you have some clear idea at the beginning about how the variables are related, which you can then test. In addition, it is a good idea to bring other possibly relevant variables into the analysis even if an initial association between two variables appears to be a strong one: it may be spurious. On the other hand, a relationship that initially appears weak may be masked by something else.

EXERCISES

7.1 In an excavated cemetery of single inhumation burials 35 per cent of the skeletons have been found to have bronze rings as grave goods. A group of fifteen graves has just been found, adjacent to but separate from the rest, and 10 of them contain bronze rings. Is this group of graves different from the rest of the cemetery with regard to the deposition of rings?

7.2 In an analysis of spatial patterns in local exchange in Mesopotamia a particular type of centrally produced pottery is examined (data from Johnson, 1973). Examination suggests that the width of the painted lines used in decoration differs between the two centres of manufacture; study of a bar graph of line widths of the pottery suggests that the lines can be divided into two categories, heavy and fine. Settlements in the study area divide into two groups, eastern and western. Is the pottery with the two line types differentially distributed with regard to the east–west division, given the information below?

	Eastern area	*Western area*	
Heavy line	42	10	52
Fine line	17	21	38
	59	31	90

7.3 We are studying a cemetery in which there are three different grave types: simple earth pits, graves with wooden chambers, and graves with stone chambers. We suspect there may be a relationship between the type of grave in which individuals were buried and their age at death: we can define three age categories for the skeletons: less than 21, 21–40, over 40. Individuals are distributed as shown in the table below. Is there a significant relationship between age and grave type?

	<21	21–40	>40
Simple pit	23	19	11
Wooden chamber	12	17	13
Stone chamber	10	16	15

7.4 An analysis is being carried out of the association between two different motifs occurring on a particular set of ceramic vessels, based on the following data:

		Motif 1	
		Present	Absent
Motif 2	Present	29	17
	Absent	23	32

Do your conclusions about the relationship between the two motifs change when independent evidence of the chronology of the vessels is used to assign them to two phases:

		Motif 1	
		Present	Absent
	Early		
Motif 2	Present	15	7
	Absent	9	11
	Late		
Motif 2	Present	14	10
	Absent	14	21

Eight

RELATIONSHIPS BETWEEN TWO NUMERIC VARIABLES: CORRELATION AND REGRESSION

METHODS OF VISUAL DISPLAY: SCATTERGRAMS

The investigation of relationships between two numeric variables has one great advantage over the study of relationships between nominal scale variables: it is much easier to present the relationships in the form of a visual display, in this case a *scatter diagram* or *scattergram*, where one variable is plotted against another. As always, such pictures can convey a great deal of information and prevent us from being misled, which can happen all too easily if we consider only numerical summaries of relationships.

For each observation we have a value for one variable and a value for another. Thus, suppose we are interested in how much pottery from the Romano–British kilns of the New Forest, in southern England, reaches sites at varying distances from the source. We might have the information shown in Table 8.1. We can then produce a scattergram and plot in the points, with distance as the horizontal axis and pottery quantity as the vertical axis. Each site is placed at the appropriate point above the horizontal axis and opposite the vertical axis corresponding to its values on the variables (Fig. 8.1).

TABLE 8.1. Quantities of New Forest pottery recovered from sites at varying distances from the kilns.

Site	Distance (km)	Quantity (sherds per m³ of earth)
1	4	98
2	20	60
3	32	41
4	34	47
5	24	62

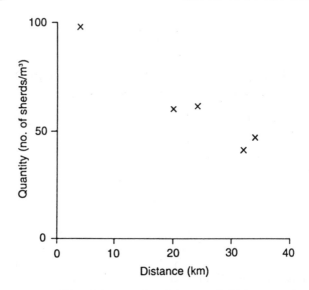

FIGURE 8.1. Plot of the quantity of Romano-British pottery from the New Forest kilns reaching various sites, in relation to the distance of the sites from the kilns.

This scattergram simply as it stands is extremely informative. We can see that the quantity of pottery decreases as distance from the source increases. We can also see that the relationship is roughly in the form of a straight line: an appropriately positioned straight line would pass very close to all the points. In other words, for a given increase in distance, there is a given decrease in pottery quantity, all along the distance scale, and all the sites more or less follow this relationship.

In this case we can say that one of these variables is an independent and the other a dependent. Pottery quantity is in some way affected by distance and therefore dependent on it, but the converse, that distance of the sites from the source is affected by pottery quantity, does not hold. In such circumstances it is conventional to make the independent variable the horizontal axis, or x axis of the graph, and the dependent the vertical or y axis.

It need not always be the case that we can specify dependent and independent variables. Suppose we are studying the dimensions of a group of neolithic beakers in order to characterise the main aspects of variation in their shape (cf. Whallon, 1982, for a study of Swiss neolithic vessels); we might plot height against rim diameter (Fig. 8.2). We can see that they match one another quite closely, so that the rim diameter and height are in a fairly constant proportion to one another. In this example we can still plot the scattergram and it plays the same kind of role as the previous one in showing us the relationship between the two variables; however, there is no intrinsic reason why one of them should be regarded as dependent on the other.

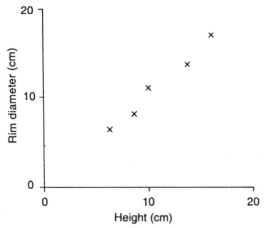

FIGURE 8.2. Rim diameter plotted against height for a hypothetical group of neolithic beakers from Hungary.

Scattergrams are the most important means of studying the relationships between pairs of variables. From them we can gain an idea first of the *direction* of a relationship: is it positive or negative? The height *v.* rim diameter plot is an example of the first: as heights become larger rims become larger. The pottery and distance plot is an example of the second: as distance increases, pottery quantity decreases.

The scattergram will also tell us about the shape of the relationship. Both those illustrated have clearly been straight line or *linear* relationships. By no means all relations between variables are of this kind. In fact, graphs of the decrease in quantity of some material or product with distance from its source are more commonly of the type shown in Figure 8.3. This relationship is curvilinear, but it is still *monotonic*, i.e. goes in the same direction; thus here, throughout the range, as distance gets larger quantity gets smaller; it is not the case anywhere that for part of the distance scale pottery quantity decreases and then for the next part increases.

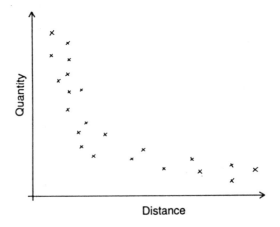

FIGURE 8.3. Plot of hypothetical quantities of a commodity reaching certain sites against the distance of these sites from the source, showing a curvilinear relationship.

An example of a *non-monotonic* relationship would be Figure 8.4, which would be of interest to archaeologists trying to esti- mate the ages at death of the animals whose bones they are studying. In this case the tooth increases in height as it grows after eruption and the animal's age increases, but as the tooth starts being used it is gradually ground down and its height starts decreasing.

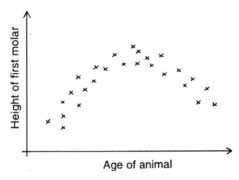

FIGURE 8.4. Plot of height of first molar against age at death for a number of sheep jawbones of known age at death.

The scattergram will also give us an idea of the strength of the relationship. Compare the two scattergrams of the relationship between weight and number of flake scars for two hypothetical groups of handaxes (Figure 8.5). In one case the relationship is clearly much stronger than in the other because the points are much more narrowly concentrated together in a long thin band: they are generally much closer to any straight line we might draw through the scatter of points.

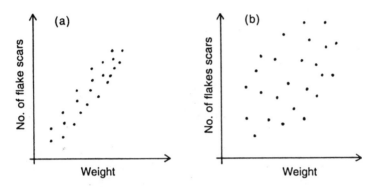

FIGURE 8.5. Scattergram of weight against number of flake scars for two groups of handaxes.

In any study of relationships between interval scale variables it is always essential as a first step to plot the scattergram and see what it looks like. But we may want to do more than this. We may want to describe the relationship mathematically, perhaps for the purpose of comparison with other similar data sets. Similarly, we may well want to define the strength of relationship mathematically: how good is the fit of the data to the proposed relationship? Nevertheless, the appropriate way to do this can only be decided by looking at the scattergram first, a point which will become more apparent below.

DESCRIBING RELATIONSHIPS BY NUMBERS

The Form of the Relationship

The process of describing the form of the relationship is known as *regression* and that of measuring how well the data fit the relation is *correlation*.

Regression differs from other techniques we have looked at so far in that it is concerned not just with whether or not a relationship exists, or the strength of that relationship, but with its nature. In regression analysis we use an independent variable to estimate (or predict) the values of a dependent variable.

The most general way of stating a hypothesised relationship mathematically is $y = f(x)$. This does not tell us a great deal: simply that the value of y (the dependent variable) at a particular point is a function of the value of x (the independent variable) at that point. It does not say anything about the specific nature of that relationship although it would be easy enough to put in some figures, e.g.

$$y = x \quad \text{(a)}$$
$$y = 2x \quad \text{(b)}$$
$$y = x^2 \quad \text{(c)}$$

These may be worth spelling out. Thus, (a) tells us that the y value at a given point is the same as the x value of the point; (b) tells us that the y value is twice the x value of the point; (c) states that the y value of a given point is the square of the x value at that point. Such equations can be represented by lines on a graph; those for the three simple equations above are shown in Figure 8.6.

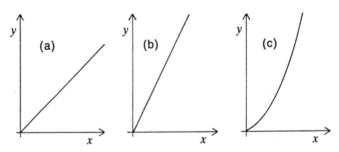

FIGURE 8.6. Graphs of the equations (a) $y = x$; (b) $y = 2x$; (c) $y = x^2$.

If our specification of the relationship between two variables by one of these functions is perfect, then from a knowledge of x at a given point we can predict the value of y for that point with certainty. For example, if there was a perfect relationship in a particular case between the density of obsidian at a site and the distance of the site from the obsidian source, then from a knowledge of the distance of the site from the obsidian source we could predict exactly its obsidian density; or if there was a perfect relationship between height and rim diameter for a group of vessels, then from a knowledge of rim diameter we could predict height exactly (and vice versa in this case).

Of course, things are never completely predictable. In some cases this may be simply because of imperfections in our measurement procedures; in most cases it is because effects are usually the result of a variety of causes operating together, many of which are themselves subject to more or less random influences. What we therefore have to do is look for general trends in our data, estimating the relationship between x and y and also the accuracy with which values of y can be derived from this estimated relationship.

The situation where there is a relationship may be contrasted with that which obtains when x and y are statistically independent. In this case we cannot predict y from x, or rather, knowledge of x does not improve our prediction of y; the stronger the dependence the more accurate our prediction will be.

It is the graph which provides the link between the scattergrams we saw at the beginning of the chapter and the mathematical equations just described. If we think of one of the best-known kinds of examples of regression analysis in archaeology, fall-off in the quantities of a particular type of material from a source with distance from that source – a situation illustrated already in Figure 8.1 – we can imagine that for every fixed distance from the source there will be a range of quantities; not all sites at a given distance from the source will have the same amount. Nevertheless, for each range of quantity values at a given distance we can calculate a mean and we can plot the position of these means for all the distances. The line traced out by following these means of y's (quantities) for fixed x's (distances) is known as the *regression equation* of y on x. In practice it is rarely the case that there will be a number of y values for a given x value; this generally occurs only in designed experiments, where it can be arranged to do so. Nevertheless, the method does not depend on this; the assumptions on which it does depend will be considered below.

The line itself can take any form but we will only consider the simplest case, when the regression equation is a linear one and the relationship is a straight line. This is not such a restriction as might be imagined, because many empirical relationships do take this form and because it is often possible, as we will see, to transform variables so that the relationship between them becomes linear. Such linear relationships have the virtue of being easier to understand at an intuitive level. We can write an equation for a general linear relationship, as follows:

$$y = a + bx$$

where y is the dependent variable, x is the independent variable, and the coefficients a and b are constants, i.e. they are fixed for a given set of data.

If $x = 0$ then the equation reduces to $y = a$, so a represents the point where the regression line crosses the y axis (see Fig. 8.7); this is generally known as the *intercept*. The b constant defines the slope or gradient of the regression line, the amount of change in a vertical direction (along the y axis) for a given horizontal distance (along the x axis). Thus, for the pottery quantity in relation to distance from source example illustrated above, the b value represents the amount of decrease in pottery quantity for a given increase in distance from the source (it is calculated below, p. 138); for the height and rim diameter example it is the amount of increase in rim diameter associated with a given increase in height. Figure 8.7 illustrates what is involved.

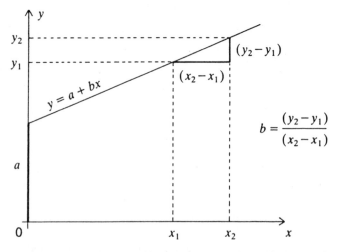

FIGURE 8.7. The slope and intercept (*a* and *b* coefficients) of a regression line.

As the slope becomes steeper so the amount of change in *y* for a given change in *x* becomes greater. When the line is horizontal, on the other hand, *b*, the slope, is obviously zero, indicating that changing values of *x* do not make any difference to *y*. It is clear that this means that there is no relationship between the two variables concerned; or, looked at from another point of view, knowing the *x* values of a set of observations does not help to predict their *y* values. But we have to qualify this. If *b* is zero it means that there is no *linear* relationship between the two variables; certain forms of non-linear relationship, like that shown in Figure 8.4, can produce a slope (*b*) value of zero even when the relationship is a strong one. Finally, it should be noted that if *y* decreases as *x* increases, in other words the relation between the two is an inverse one, then the sign of the *b* coefficient will be negative. How all this works out we will now see with our pottery example.

Having produced the scattergram of the relationship between quantity and distance from the source (Fig. 8.1) on the basis of the information in Table 8.1, we now want to describe the relationship mathematically. This means finding the appropriate intercept and slope values (*a* and *b* coefficients) for this particular set of data, to put in the equation $y = a + bx$. However, a glance at the scattergram (Fig. 8.1) soon shows that although the relationship is good it is not perfect: there is no straight line which will go exactly through all the data points. What we want to do is find the straight line which gives the *best fit* to the data points. How do we do this?

One intuitively appealing way is to plot the scattergram of the observations and then simply draw in by eye a best-fitting straight line through the dots; we could then work out the slope and intercept values for the line. Unsurprisingly, this is not entirely satisfactory since there are no definite criteria of what is a best fit. The most common method of fitting an unambiguous best-fit line through a set of data points is known as the method of *least-squares*. This requires a bit of explanation.

For each data point we can note its actual *y* value. For any *y* value that does not actually lie on the regression line there will be a discrepancy between that actual *y* value and the *y* value for that point predicted by the regression. What is involved for a

particular data point is illustrated in Figure 8.8, which looks at
one particular segment of a regression line.

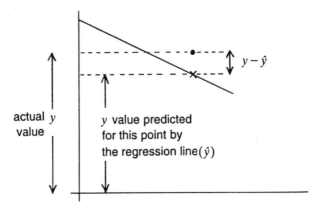

FIGURE 8.8. The difference between the actual y value of a data
point and the value predicted by a regression.

The least-squares method finds the straight line which minimises

$$\sum_{i=1}^{n} (y_i - \hat{y}_i)^2$$

where n = the number of data points, y_i = the actual y value of
point i, and $\hat{y}_i$ = the value of point i predicted by the regression.
Let's go through what this means in words.

For each data point we can obtain the difference between its
actual and predicted y values (in our example the difference
between the actual quantity of New Forest pottery at a site and
the quantity predicted by the regression line); this is the $y_i - \hat{y}_i$
term. We are then told to square this difference, to repeat the
whole operation for each of our data points, then add up all the
resulting quantities. This total must be minimised. In other
words, we must as it were 'juggle around' the exact position of
the regression line until we find the line which produces the
smallest possible sum of squared differences between actual and
predicted values.

We use the squared deviations for the same reason as we use
squared differences from the mean to define dispersion in calculating the variance and standard deviation of a single variable:

if we simply took the differences without squaring them the positive and negative differences would cancel one another out and they would sum to zero. Inevitably, however, the result of the procedure is that the slope and position of the regression line are most influenced by the points with the largest deviations from the mean, and this is one of the sources of weakness of least-squares regression, because one or two extreme values can have a big effect on the results.

It is important to note here that it is the sum of the squared *vertical* distances which are being minimised, since we are interested in the regression of y on x, that is to say, the effect of x on y. If we wanted to regress x on y we would use the horizontal distances (or more likely switch the axes around). In later chapters we will see some methods which involve using the distances perpendicular to a best-fit line.

In fact, we don't actually need to do any juggling round to find the position of the best-fit regression line satisfying the least-squares criterion. Equations have been obtained which enable the appropriate a and b coefficients for any given set of data to be calculated. For b we have:

$$b = \frac{\sum_{i=1}^{n}(x_i-\bar{x})(y_i-\bar{y})}{\sum_{i=1}^{n}(x_i-\bar{x})^2}$$

In words, starting with the top line: we take the x value of a given data point and subtract the mean of the xs. We then take the y value of that data point and subtract the mean of the ys. Having done that we multiply the two x and y quantities together. We carry out this operation for each of our data points and add up all the results. This quantity, known as the *covariation* between x and y, is then divided by the denominator. For the latter we take the x value of each data point in turn, subtract the mean of the x's from it, square the resulting difference, repeat the operation for all data points, and again add up all the results; this quantity is the variation in x. It is used to divide the sum on the top line to give the b value, the slope of the regression line; another way of looking at it is that we standardise the covariation between x and y in terms of the variation in x.

For the a coefficient we have

$$a = \frac{\sum\limits_{i=1}^{n} y_i - b \sum\limits_{i=1}^{n} x_i}{n} = \bar{y} - b\bar{x}$$

As you can see, this is much more straightforward.

For b there is also another version of the formula which is less laborious from the point of view of hand calculation with a calculator, although this is a consideration of relatively minor importance these days when virtually all such work is done with computer packages:

$$b = \frac{n\sum\limits_{i=1}^{n} x_i y_i - (\sum\limits_{i=1}^{n} x_i)(\sum\limits_{i=1}^{n} y_i)}{n\sum\limits_{i=1}^{n} x_i^2 - (\sum\limits_{i=1}^{n} x_i)^2}$$

where n is the number of data points; $\sum\limits_{i=1}^{n} x_i y_i$ means for each data point multiply the x value by the y value and add them all up; $(\sum\limits_{i=1}^{n} x_i)(\sum\limits_{i=1}^{n} y_i)$ means sum all the x values of the data points, then sum all the y values and multiply the two totals. There is a similar distinction in the denominator between $\sum\limits_{i=1}^{n} x_i^2$ and $(\sum\limits_{i=1}^{n} x_i)^2$.

We can now calculate the actual a and b values to describe the relationship between pottery quantity and distance from the source kilns in our example; see Table 8.1. Using the computing formula above for b, the various quantities relevant to its calculation are as follows: $n = 5$; $\sum y_i = 308$;

$$\sum x_i = 114; \sum\limits_{i=1}^{n} x_i y_i = 5990; \text{ and } \sum\limits_{i=1}^{n} x_i^2 = 3172. \text{ Then}$$

$$b = \frac{(5 \times 5990) - (114 \times 308)}{(5 \times 3172) - 12996} = -\frac{5162}{2864} = -1.80$$

Having obtained the b coefficient we need the intercept value:

$$a = \frac{\sum y_i - b\sum x_i}{n} = \frac{308 - (-1.8 \times 114)}{5}$$

$$= \frac{513.2}{5} = 102.64$$

On the basis of this information we can now write the regression equation as

$$\hat{y}_i = 102.64 - 1.8x$$

which says that at the source there should be 102.64 sherds of the pottery type/m³ of earth according to the regression line, and that this quantity declines by 1.8 sherds/m³ for every kilometre of distance from the source. The resulting line is shown in Figure 8.9.

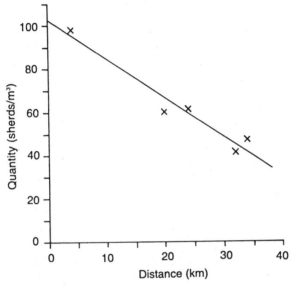

FIGURE 8.9. Graph of the regression equation $\hat{y} = 102.64 - 1.8x$.

The Strength of the Relationship: Correlation

So far we have seen how to establish the two parameters of a regression equation, *a* and *b*, and thus indicate the form of the relationship between *x* and *y*. But this does not tell us anything about the accuracy of the estimates of *y* that are given by the regression line. To find out how good the fit of the line to the data is we need to use the correlation coefficient, which measures the strength of the relationship between two variables. Strength of a relationship is a topic with which we are already familiar in the case of nominal scale variables from the previous chapter.

With interval scale variables the general idea of measuring the strength of relationship is the same but the specific details of going about it are different.

Considered in graphical terms, the correlation coefficient is a measure of the extent to which data points are scattered more or less widely around the regression line. When they are all close to it, it means that correlation is strong and that a prediction of the y value at a given point based on the x values will be very good. If the points are widely scattered around the line, it means that correlation is weak and prediction of y based on x will be poor. The point may be demonstrated with reference to Figure 8.5 above. The correlation coefficient would be higher for the scattergram on the left than on the right: the data points in (a) are obviously much more closely bunched around the regression line which would go through this scatter of points. It is also obvious from these scattergrams that predictions of y based on x will be much better for (a). If we look at (b) we can see that for a given x value there is a wide range of possible y values. If the scatter of points is circular, correlation will be zero and knowledge of x will be no help in predicting y. Thus, the correlation coefficient is a measure of the extent to which two variables *covary*, although it is important to remember that it is a measure of *linear* or straight line correlation. As we have noted already in relation to the slope, certain kinds of curvilinear relationship could produce a correlation value of zero even for perfect relationships, a point which demonstrates again the importance of looking at the scattergram before you go ahead with any further analysis (cf. Fig. 8.4). Indeed, all this discussion is very similar to that for the b or slope coefficient, which is no surprise when we look at the formula for the correlation coefficient (r):

$$r = \frac{\sum(x_i - \bar{x})(y_i - \bar{y})}{\sqrt{\sum(x_i - \bar{x})^2 \; \sum(y_i - \bar{y})^2}}$$

A hand computation version is:

$$r = \frac{n\sum x_i \, y_i - (\sum x_i)(\sum y_i)}{\sqrt{[n\sum x_i^2 - (\sum x_i)^2][n\sum y_i^2 - (\sum y_i)^2]}}$$

As you can see, the numerator of the expressions for r and b is the same, the covariation between x and y.

The difference between the two lies in the denominator: for the correlation coefficient the covariation is standardised in terms of the variation in both x and y. The maximum possible value that the covariation can reach is equal to the denominator, the square root of the product of the variation in x and y. Thus the maximum value that r can take is 1.0, which will be positive when the covariation term is positive and negative when it is negative. The maximum value will be reached when all the points are on the straight line (Fig. 8.10). As we have already noted in passing, when x and y are independent of one another, the correlation coefficient, like the slope (because it has the same numerator), will be 0.

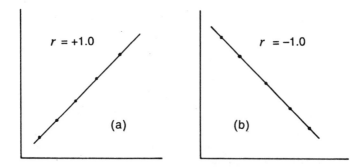

FIGURE 8.10. Scattergram and regression line for which there is (a) perfect positive correlation, (b) perfect negative correlation.

There are, however, two important differences between r and b which arise from the difference in their denominator. First, because the correlation coefficient is standardised in terms of the variation in both the variables, it is symmetrical: it does not matter which of the variables is taken to be independent, nor indeed if neither of them is; the correlation between x and y is the same as that between y and x. The slope of the regression of y on x, however, is not the same as the slope of the regression of x on y, unless the angle of the regression line is forty-five degrees and the scales of the axes are identical. You can see this by looking at Figure 8.9, which shows the regression line for the regression of pottery quantity on distance from source. If you turn it on its side for a moment and imagine that pottery quantity is the horizontal axis, you can see that the slope with reference to this axis is much steeper than the slope in relation to the real x axis. In addition, it is obvious that a rate of change in pottery quantity per kilometre increase in distance from source is something different from a rate of change in distance per sherd decrease in pottery quantity. Second, whereas slope is measured in the units of the original variables (for example, the amount of change in pottery quantity for a given increase in distance), correlation is a unitless quantity which can thus be used as a basis for comparison in a wide variety of different circumstances.

Before we leave the correlation coefficient we need to consider its squared value (r^2). This is known as the coefficient of determination and has its own interesting properties, which must now be examined.

We saw above that one way of looking at a regression analysis is to see it as improving our estimates of the y value of particular points by using information we have about their x values. If knowledge of x does improve our predictions of y it means that the two variables are in some way related, although we have to bear in mind the *caveats* from the previous chapter that association does not necessarily, or even very often, mean explanation of one in terms of the other.

The coefficient of determination provides a means of quantifying the improvement, in a way not unlike the τ coefficient we saw in the previous chapter. If knowledge of x does not help us to predict y then our best estimate of any particular y value is the mean of y ($\bar{y}$). As we saw in Chapter 4, how far this mean is a typical value depends on the degree of dispersion of the distribution around the mean (assuming for the moment the distribution is symmetrical). Thus, one way of assessing how good our prediction of y based on $\bar{y}$ is likely to be is to note the dispersion around the mean, given by $\sum(y_i-\bar{y})^2$. This is, of course, the sum of squares, or variation, in $\bar{y}$, the first stage of calculating the standard deviation.

If we then carry out the regression of y on x to improve our prediction of y, we can assess the general quality of our predictions by looking at the dispersion of the observations not around the mean of y now but around the regression line, given by $\Sigma(y_i - \hat{y}_i)^2$. This is the quantity already referred to earlier in this chapter as that which least squares regression tries to minimise. It is known as the *residual variation* around the regression line. To the extent that this is smaller than the variation round the mean of the y values, $\bar{y}$, we achieve an improvement in prediction by using the regression line (i.e. our knowledge of the x values of the data points) as a basis for prediction rather than the mean of the y values. Thus the amount of improvement = $\Sigma(y_i - \bar{y})^2 - \Sigma(y_i - \hat{y}_i)^2$. Or alternatively, in words: variation accounted for by the regression equals the original variation minus the residual variation. This 'improvement' quantity, the amount of variation 'accounted for' by the regression is sometimes referred to as the 'explained' variation, but it is really rather misleading to use that word in this context.

If we divide the variation accounted for by the regression $(\Sigma(y_i - \bar{y})^2 - \Sigma(y_i - \hat{y}_i)^2)$ by the variation around the mean of the y's, we obtain the proportion of the total variation in the data accounted for by the regression and it is this which is known as r^2, the coefficient of determination, the square of the correlation coefficient; in many ways it is more intuitively meaningful than the latter quantity. Its value is often multiplied by 100 to put it on a percentage scale and it is then sometimes known as the 'percentage level of explanation'.

It is now time to illustrate these two coefficients with reference to the pottery and distance example for which the regression equation was obtained above. Using the computation formula for r,

$$r = \frac{(5 \times 5990) - (114 \times 308)}{\sqrt{[(5 \times 3172) - 12996][(5 - 20938) - 94864]}}$$

$$= \frac{-5162}{\sqrt{(2864 \times 9826)}} = -0.973$$

This tells us that the relationship between pottery quantity and distance from the source is a virtually perfect negative linear one, as we would indeed expect from the scattergram. If we now square the value to obtain the coefficient of determination we have

$$r^2 = -0.97^2 = 0.94 = 94\%$$

This tells us that by using distance to estimate pottery quantity at our sites we reduce the original variation in the data (the variation around the mean value of quantity) by nearly 95 per cent; i.e., nearly 95 per cent of the variation in pottery quantity is related to distance, only 5 per cent or so is left over as variation around the regression line. Whether distance itself 'explains' the variation in pottery quantity is another matter, but any explanation must obviously take this strong relationship into account.

To be told that 95 per cent of the variation in quantity of this New Forest pottery at different sites relates to the distance of the site from the source kilns may seem to be attaching an unnecessary number to something which was already obvious from the scattergram and its regression line, since it is clear from this that the relationship between quantity and distance is very close. To some extent such a comment would be justified at this point. The pay-off comes in two areas. First, if we are making comparisons, for example, of the relationship between quantity of a material and distance from source for a range of different materials, comparing a series of definite numbers is much more satisfactory than comparing one's visual impressions of a series of scattergrams. Second, once we get on to investigating the relationships between larger numbers of variables than two we again need numbers, both to compare and to manipulate them further, as we will see.

We can finish this section by noting that r^2 generally provides a more realistic assessment of the strength of a relationship than r when we come to considering what the numbers mean for interpretation purposes. Thus, an r value of 0.4 suggests at least a moderate relationship between two variables. When we square it, however, we see that it means that only 0.16 (or 16 per cent) of the variation in the one variable is related to the other, not a very high proportion.

RANK CORRELATION

The previous chapter looked at ways of examining relations between nominal scale variables, but methods also exist that are appropriate for ordinal scale, or rank-order, data. Probably the best-known of these is Spearman's coefficient of rank correlation, which is simply the product moment correlation (r) applied to the ranks of the observations rather than their actual values; but Kendall's τ_b and τ_c are better if there are large numbers of ties, that is to say if large numbers of observations have the same rank. Like the standard correlation coefficient we have seen above, all of them vary between +1.0 and −1.0, which represent perfect positive and negative correlation respectively, while the 0.0 value corresponds to a complete lack of relationship. Details of the techniques may be found in such texts as Blalock (1972), or Fletcher and Lock (1991).

An example of the use of rank correlation is given in Shennan (1985). As part of a study of field survey methods an investigation was made of the abilities of different fieldwalkers to spot different kinds of material on the field surface. By a rather complex series of methods it was possible to rank each walker in terms of their abilities at picking up pottery and lithics. The rank order of ability at picking up pottery could then be compared with that of picking up lithic artefacts, to see if, in general, high or low ability in one was related to high or low ability in the other. In fact, they weren't related: someone who is good at seeing pottery on the surface won't necessarily be especially good with lithic artefacts, and vice versa.

In this example there were no tied ranks, i.e. no ties between several people for, say, third place in the rank order. In other cases there often are. Let us suppose, again on the basis of survey data, that we can divide the sites of a particular period in an area into the rough size categories large, medium and small; as in the example of the Mann–Whitney and runs tests above (Chapter 5) this is something we might feel able to do even if we do not feel justified in estimating exact site sizes. Let us suppose also that a categorisation of the soils in the region exists in terms of whether they are excellent, average or poor in quality for the purposes of arable agriculture, and that we know which sites are on which of these soil categories. All the sites in a particular rank category, whether for size or soil quality, may be said to be tied for that category. To what extent is site size related to soil quality?

TABLE 8.2. Site size category tabulated against soil quality category.

		Soil quality		
	Excellent	Average	Poor	Total
Large	15	7	2	24
Medium	6	11	4	21
Small	7	7	8	22
Total	28	25	14	67

We can construct a table of our observations (Table 8.2). Kendall's τ (not to be confused with Goodman and Kruskal's τ referred to in the previous chapter) can then be obtained to find out whether there is indeed any correlation between the size category of the site and the arable agricultural potential of the soil on which it is located.

In this case, for the purpose of easy hand calculation, we can use the τ_c version of the formula, for data grouped into a small number of categories. The basis of this coefficient is as follows. If the ranks on the two variables were perfectly correlated, all the large sites would be on excellent soils, all the medium ones on average soils and all the small ones on poor soils. As you can see from the table, this is not the case. Nevertheless, if we take the category of large sites on excellent soils (fifteen sites), we can see that all four entries in the table below and to the right of this are lower in rank on both variables. Similarly, for medium sites on excellent soils the two entries below and to the right are again lower in rank on both variables. We can do the same thing for large and medium sites in the average soil quality column. All these together represent *concordant* ranks (C) and we can sum them:

$$C = 15(11+4+7+8) + 6(7+8) + 7(4+8) + 11(8) = 712$$

But we can also note pairs of categories with *discordant* ranks. Thus, if we take the category of large sites on average soils and look below and to the left, we can see that there are entries on excellent soils but with medium and small sites. Similarly again, below and to the left of the medium sites on average soils category there are a number of small sites on excellent soils, which there wouldn't be if the correlations between the two variables were very good. We can also count up the entries below and to the left of the two upper entries in the poor soil category. Altogether the number of discordant values (D) is:

$$D = 7(6+7) + 11(7) + 2(6+7+11+7) + 4(7+7) = 286$$

The τ statistic is based on subtracting the number of discordant values from the concordant values and standardising the result:

$$\tau_c = \frac{C-D}{\frac{1}{2}n^2\frac{(m-1)}{m}}$$

where m = the number of rows or the number of columns, whichever is the smaller.
n = the total number of observations.

Here

$$\tau_c = \frac{712-286}{\frac{1}{2}(67^2)\frac{3-1}{3}} = \frac{426}{1496.3} = 0.285$$

So in this case we have evidence for a moderate correlation between site size and soil quality, both categorised as rank-order variables.

CONCLUSION

We have now extended the idea of looking at relationships between variables beyond the nominal scale variables we saw in the previous chapter to rank-order and in particular interval and ratio scale variables. In the case of the latter we saw that the most important part of the whole process was looking at the scattergram but that methods were available not just to describe the strength of the relationship, in terms of the goodness-of-fit of the data to the regression line, but also to specify the form of the relationship in terms of the equation of the regression line. These methods are important in themselves but they also form the basis for the more complex and advanced techniques described in Chapters 10 and 12.

EXERCISES

8.1 A study is being carried out of the degree to which the effects of trampling are recognisable in ceramic assemblages from settlements. After some experimental studies the investigator postulates that there is a relationship between the mean size of the sherds in the assemblage (based on measurements of maximum sherd length) and the standard deviation of the sherd size values for the assemblage, which holds only for trampled assemblages and not for untrampled ones. Given the information below, is the investigator correct? Is it possible to distinguish trampled from untrampled assemblages?

Standard deviation (mm)	Mean size (mm)	Before/After trampling
5	18	After
7	23	After
9	24	After
11	27	After
9	29	After
12	31	After
15	35	After
12	37	After
16	37	After
13	39	After
12	30	Before
9	34	Before
19	41	Before
20	41	Before
22	41	Before
26	42	Before
25	45	Before
25	59	Before
14	54	Before

8.2 A study investigating the origins of agriculture postulates that if ground stone artefacts were being used in various ways for cereal processing, there should be a relationship between the quantity of cereal grains recovered and the number of ground stone tools. Information from a number of early neolithic sites gives the following results. Do they provide evidence for such a relationship and if so, what is it? Discuss any complications you see in drawing archaeological conclusions from such an analysis.

Site	No. of ground stone tools	No. of cereal grains
1	3	180
2	5	260
3	7	250
4	4	380
5	6	400
6	8	370
7	6	460
8	8	450
9	11	400
10	8	580
11	11	580
12	13	650
13	12	700

8.3 As part of an investigation of palaeolithic stone technology and its complexity a study is being carried out of the factors affecting the number of flake scars on handaxes. One suggestion is that it is simply a result of overall handaxe size, which can be measured in terms of weight. Given the information below, what is the relationship between weight and number of flake scars? Is it a good one?

No. of flake scars	Weight (g)	No. of flake scars	Weight (g)
18	210	37	620
19	300	72	510
33	195	57	565
28	285	53	650
24	410	46	740
36	375	78	690
45	295	68	710
56	415	63	840
47	500	82	900

8.4 An archaeological survey has been carried out in southern England. Its approach has been to collect information on artefact densities in terms of one-hectare quadrats. Below are the Iron Age and Romano–British pottery counts for a number of quadrats. Investigate the relationship between them.

Iron Age	Roman	Iron Age	Roman
4	5	12	55
3	20	9	61
7	20	7	62
6	33	13	79
6	46	9	81
9	45	14	98

Nine

WHEN THE REGRESSION DOESN'T FIT

In the previous chapter we saw the basics of regression and correlation analysis but were very careful to avoid any complications. It was noted, however, that we were only concerned with straight line regression and that we should always look at the scattergram to check whether the scatter of data points really does show a linear trend, rather than some kind of non-linear pattern. This point leads on to the general question of the assumptions required to carry out a valid regression analysis; obviously a very important topic which we have not yet examined.

Problems about the relationship between the data and the assumptions required by regression analysis can be seen particularly clearly in the *residuals* from the regression: where the regression doesn't fit, the difference between the actual y values of our data points and those predicted by the regression. But the residuals are also important from another point of view. In fact, they may be more interesting archaeologically than the regression itself, but it requires the regression analysis for the interest to emerge.

As an example, let us suppose again that we are dealing with the fall-off in quantity of a material with increasing distance from its source. We might note that at a particular distance the majority of sites have only a small quantity of the material, but a small number have much more. The question naturally arises why this should be the case. We can then find out which sites these are and see what features they share, not shared with the others, which could explain the phenomenon. They might all be close to a particular main transport route for example. Hodder and Orton (1976, pp. 115–17), in an analysis of the distribution of Romano–British pottery from the Oxfordshire kilns, were able to show that the sites which had more of this pottery than expected given their distance from the source were those where water transport could have been involved. In another study Shennan (1985) used regression methods to pick out flint scatters with exceptionally large and exceptionally small numbers of retouched pieces. Plotting the distribution of these on the map it was apparent that they were characteristic of certain types of location.

For both substantive and methodological reasons then, it is necessary to look carefully at the residuals from a regression.

RESIDUALS

In the same way as we used $\Sigma(y_i - \bar{y})^2$ in the calculation of the variance or standard deviation of a single variable, so we can use the deviations of the y values from the regression, $\Sigma(y_i - \hat{y}_i)^2$, to calculate the variance or standard deviation around the regression line:[1]

$$s^2_{y_i-\hat{y}_i} = \frac{\Sigma(y_i-\hat{y}_i)^2}{n}$$

where $s^2_{y_i-\hat{y}_i}$ is the variance of the distribution of y values around the regression line, y_i is the actual y value of the ith data point, $\hat{y}_i$ is the estimated y of the ith point according to the regression, and n is the number of observations.

TABLE 9.1. Information for calculating the standard error of the regression for the Romano–British pottery quantity data from Table 8.1.

y_i	$\hat{y}_i$ *	$(y_i - \hat{y}_i)^2$
98	95.44	6.55
60	66.64	44.09
41	45.04	16.32
47	41.44	30.91
62	59.44	6.55
		104.42

* Calculated from $y = 102.64 - 1.8x$

1. The denominator in this version of the formula is n, which presupposes that we are only interested in the variation around the regression for the particular data set analysed. If we wanted to estimate the variance around the regression line for a population of which this was a sample, the divisor would be $n - 2$, since two degrees of freedom are lost in calculating the regression. It is worth checking which version is used by your computer package.

The square root of this is the standard deviation of the distribution, known as the *standard error of the regression*. For the pottery quantity example we have the information in Table 9.1. Applying the formula above we have

$$s_{y-\hat{y}}^2 = \frac{104.42}{5} = 20.88$$

$$s_{y-\hat{y}} = \sqrt{20.88} = 4.57$$

The standard error of the regression of pottery quantity against distance is 4.57.

As we will see shortly below, one of the stipulations of the regression model is that the distribution of the residuals around the line should be normal. This being so, we can note that if we put standard error bands around the regression line, then these bands will include approximately 68 per cent of all the observations, while bands at ± 2 standard errors will include 95 per cent of all observations; the point is illustrated in Figure 9.1 (although it is important to note that the process of statistical inference about the regression is more complex than simply taking note of these error bands; see below, pp. 173–5).

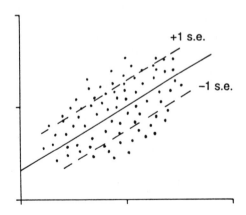

FIGURE 9.1. One-standard-error band around a regression line.

In fact, as well as using r or r^2 as a general indication of the fit of the regression, we can also use the standard error of the regression as an indicator of the precision of the estimates, in the same way as we use the standard deviation as a measure of the dispersion for a single variable. We can put an extra term into the regression equation to recognise this:

$$\hat{y}_i = a + bx_i \pm s_{y_i - \hat{y}_i}$$

where $\hat{y}_i$ is the estimated value of y_i, a and b are the intercept and slope, x_i is the x value of the relevant point, and $s_{y_i \cdot \hat{y}_i}$ is the standard error of the regression. In the pottery quantity example the specific figures in the formula are

$$\hat{y}_i = 102.64 - 1.8x_i \pm 4.57$$

When the distribution of residuals is normal then we can say that about 68 per cent of the residuals will fall within this range. Assuming a normal distribution for the pottery example, approximately 68 per cent of them will fall within the range $\pm$ 4.57; or alternatively, an estimate that any given real y value is in the range $\pm$ 4.57 around the regression line will have about a 68 per cent probability of being correct. In actual fact, for these particular data three out of the five observations fall within one standard error of the regression line and all of them within two standard errors; given the very small number of observations the correspondence with these expectations is about as close as it could be. However, it is important to emphasise again that these figures only refer to the dispersion around this particular regression line; they do not by themselves represent a confidence interval for a population estimate of the kind that we saw in Chapter 6; to obtain such estimates involves further complications (see below pp. 173–5).

One other useful property follows from the normal distribution of residuals. We saw in Chapter 7 that any observation in a distribution could be transformed into a Z score by expressing the observation in terms of numbers of standard deviation units away from its mean, where

$$Z = \frac{x - \bar{x}}{s}$$

For a normal distribution the score can then be looked up in the normal table to find the proportion of the distribution which lies between the mean and a point that distance away from it.

In the same way, if we take any given residual term $(y_i - \hat{y}_i)$ from the regression and divide it by the standard error of the distribution of residuals around the regression, we produce a quantity analogous to the Z score called the standardised residual:

$$Z_{y_i - \hat{y}_i} = \frac{y_i - \hat{y}_i}{s_{y - \hat{y}}}$$

The standardised residual from the regression has the same properties as the Z score and can be linked to the standard normal distribution in the same way by using the normal table, assuming, of course, that the residuals are normally distributed.

For the second observation in the pottery quantity and distance example we have

$$Z_{y_i - \hat{y}_i} = \frac{60 - 66.64}{4.57} = -1.45$$

This y value is 1.45 standard errors less than the value estimated by the regression.

As we will see in the following section, the standardised residual, with its link to the normal distribution, has properties which make it extremely useful for investigating whether the regression assumptions really are met or not, and indeed more generally for picking out interesting patterns in regression results.[1]

THE REGRESSION MODEL

Everything we have done so far in relation to regression is valid only insofar as certain assumptions are satisfied. These assumptions are of a variety of types but failure to meet them is always

---

1. You should always check what version of the regression residuals is provided by a particular statistical package as this varies considerably and may not be exactly as described here.

reflected in the residuals. For this reason it is very important to use graphs, not just to look at the original data but also to look at the structure of the residuals. Analyses based simply on an examination of summary statistics are insufficient. Least-squares regression is quite robust with regard to minor violations of the assumptions but gross violations can seriously distort conclusions. In this section we will go through the assumptions then indicate how violations of them can be detected and what can be done about them.

Assumptions

1. In the version of regression considered here it is presupposed that the independent variable as well as the dependent are measured at an interval scale or above.

2. It has been noted already that we are concerned only with simple linear regression, where the relationship between the two variables takes the form of a straight line. Obviously, if the trend is not linear then an analysis which assumes that it is will not be very satisfactory; an example is shown in Figure 9.2.

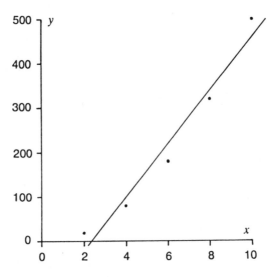

FIGURE 9.2. Scattergram of a non-linear relationship between x and y.

In this example y does increase with increasing x but at different rates in different parts of the x scale. Simply calculating the linear regression and its associated correlation coefficient would in fact suggest that there was a strong linear trend. It is examination of the graph which shows that the straight line represents an unsatisfactory description of the relationship since it underpredicts at the beginning and end of the line and overpredicts in the middle.

3. The distribution of the residuals around the regression line must be normal. This is particularly important if we want to use the regression to obtain interval estimates for y in the way discussed in the previous section, or if we want to carry out significance tests; see Figure 9.3 for exaggerated examples of normal and non-normal distributions of residuals.

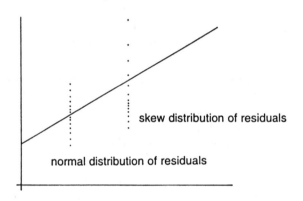

FIGURE 9.3. Distribution of residuals around a regression line.

4. The mean of the distribution of residuals must be zero for every x value; in other words, the distributions of residuals must be centred on the regression line. If they are not it usually comes down either to a violation of the linearity assumption described above, or to the presence of autocorrelation (see below).

5. One of the most important assumptions of regression analysis is that variation around the line is *homoscedastic*. In other words, the amount of variation around the line is the same at all points along it. If it is not then the variation is said to be

heteroscedastic. There is a variety of ways in which heteroscedasticity can arise. Two of the most common ones are illustrated
in Figure 9.4. In Figure 9.4 (a) observations with small x values
tend to be fairly close to the line while those with large x values
are much more dispersed. In (b) there is only a small number of
cases with very large values of x, the bulk of the values being
small.

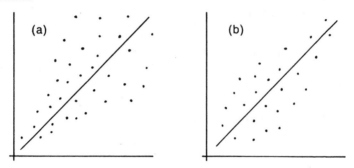

FIGURE 9.4.   Heteroscedastic distribution of residuals.

6.   Autocorrelation refers to the assumption that the error terms
associated with particular observations must be uncorrelated with
one another. In other words, the residual in y for one x value
should not be related to that for other x values. An example of
what this may look like is shown in Figure 9.5.

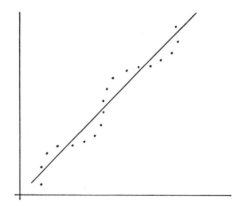

FIGURE 9.5.   An example of autocorrelation in the residuals from a
regression.

Here when a residual is positive it is very likely that adjacent residuals will also be positive, and the same for negative ones. In other words, the error values of adjacent terms are correlated with one another. As with the other regression assumptions, failure to take autocorrelation into account is likely to produce misleading results. In the case illustrated the value of the correlation coefficient for a linear relationship would be very high, implying that for any given increase in x there is a corresponding increase in y; in fact, depending on precisely where we are on the x axis, the increase in y for a given x will vary considerably.

The regression model is fairly robust with regard to minor violations of the assumptions. The most important ones are linearity (which, as we have seen, subsumes several of the others), homoscedasticity and uncorrelated errors.

Detection and Remedy of Violations of the Regression Assumptions

As has already been suggested, one of the best and simplest ways of detecting discrepancies between model and data is through examination of the regression residuals. As we saw above, the standardised residuals are like Z scores in that they have zero mean and unit standard deviation. With a moderately large sample these residuals should be distributed approximately normally. Graphing the residuals will reveal whether or not this is the case; if it is not, then problems of some sort exist.

The most commonly used plots are those in which the standardised residuals are plotted as the ordinate (or y axis) against either the independent variable, x, or the estimated value of y, i.e. $\hat{y}$. Examples of both are illustrated in Figure 9.6. There is really nothing to choose between them for bivariate regression although the first plot, against the independent variable, probably makes interpretation rather more straightforward. As we will see in the next chapter, however, in multiple regression there is no option but to plot the residuals against $\hat{y}$.

If the model is correct, the standardised residuals tend to fall between $+2.0$ and -2.0 in value and are randomly distributed (see Figure 9.6); they should not show a distinct pattern of variation. When the assumptions do not hold there is patterning. Not only does this tell us that we have to take action to make the data fit the assumptions if we are going to use the technique, it also often has substantive insights to give us, in terms of revealing unsuspected structures in the data. As we have seen above, the residuals can often be more interesting than the regression itself since frequently the regression line only systematises what we thought we knew already. It is when that systematisation reveals that the patterning in the data is more complex than we thought that new knowledge may potentially be gained. In such cases the mathematically defined regression provides a secure baseline for comparison and the detection of irregularities. A good example of the patterning which can emerge has already been referred to above: Hodder and Orton's demonstration that in a regression analysis of the quantity of a certain type of Romano–British pottery against distance from source, high positive residuals were obtained in areas accessible by water transport (Hodder and Orton, 1976). It is always possible in bivariate regression to obtain an idea whether problems exist simply by looking at the scattergram of the raw data, but the residual plots are much more effective – they act like a magnifying glass on the errors. When we come to multiple regression in the next chapter, dealing with more than two variables, then residual plots are the only available option.

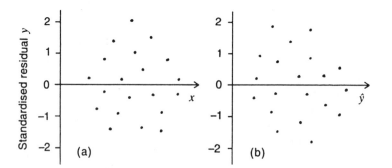

FIGURE 9.6. Examples of standardised residual values of data points (vertical axis) plotted against (a) their x values, (b) the $\hat{y}$ values predicted for them by the regression.

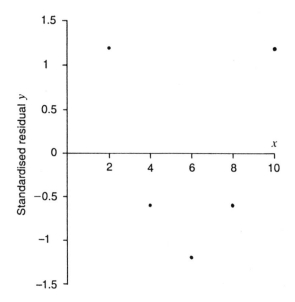

FIGURE 9.7. Plot of the standardised residuals from the regression line of Figure 9.2 against their *x* values.

We can now turn to the detection and remedying of failure to meet assumptions of the linear regression model.

1. *Non-linearity.* It has already been noted that non-linearity in the relationship between two variables can arise in a number of different ways. An example has been shown in Figure 9.2, and although the lack of linearity emerges clearly enough in the scattergram, Figure 9.7 shows how it is even clearer in the corresponding residual plot, which certainly does not show a random scatter of points.

Very often such relationships can be made linear by means of a straightforward transformation of the kind we have seen in Chapter 6; generally this involves logging both the *x* and *y* axes or just the *y* axis alone. In the first case you take the logarithms of both the *x* and *y* values of your data and use these, first as the axes of a new scattergram and second for calculating a regression equation and correlation coefficient. Figure 9.8 shows the result of transforming the data values in Figure 9.2 in this way. As you can see, they now form a straight line.

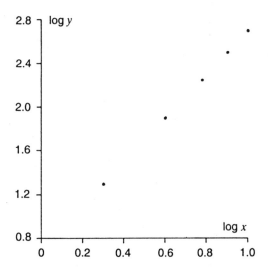

FIGURE 9.8. Data from Figure 9.2 with the x and y values transformed to the logarithms of their original values.

Changing the data values in this way also changes the form of the regression equation. The basic equation we saw in Chapter 8 was $y = a + bx$. Now we have

$$\log y = \log a + b\log x$$

The other alternative is to take logarithms of the y values only and to produce a new scattergram in which the vertical axis is in units of log y but the x axis stays the same; the regression and correlation can then be calculated with the transformed y values. This time the regression equation takes the form

$$\log y = \log a + \log bx$$

It is the fact that the y axis is logged that results in the logged exponents, a and b, because both of these are expressed in terms of y: a is the point where the regression line cuts the y axis and b is the amount of change in y for a given change in x. The x values, of course, do not change.

What is involved in these procedures is best seen by means of a worked example. Once again let us consider a hypothetical distance fall-off study, this time of the quantity of a certain type of Mesoamerican obsidian at sites at various distances from the

TABLE 9.2. Density of a certain type of Mesoamerican obsidian for sites at varying distances from the source.

Distance (km)	Density (g/m³)	Distance (km)	Density (g/m³)
5	5.01	44	0.447
12	1.91	49	0.347
17	1.91	56	0.239
25	2.24	63	0.186
31	1.20	75	0.126
36	1.10		

source, where quantity at a site is measured in terms of weight (g)/m³ of excavated earth. The figures are shown in Table 9.2. The first stage of the analysis will be to calculate the regression and correlation for these data.

$$n = 11 \quad \sum x_i y_i = 284.463$$
$$\sum x_i = 413 \quad \sum y_i = 14.715$$
$$(\sum x_i)^2 = 170569 \quad (\sum y_i)^2 = 216.531$$
$$\sum x_i^2 = 20407 \quad \sum y_i^2 = 40.492$$

$$b = \frac{(11 \times 284.463) - (413 \times 14.715)}{(11 \times 20407) - 170569}$$
$$= \frac{-2948.2}{53908} = -0.055$$

$$a = \frac{14.715 - (-0.055 \times 413)}{11} = 3.403$$

Thus the regression equation is:

$$\hat{y} = 3.403 - 0.055x$$

$$r = \frac{(11 \times 284.463) - (413 \times 14.715)}{\sqrt{[(11 \times 20407) - 170569][(11 \times 40.492) - 216.531]}}$$
$$= \frac{-2948.2}{\sqrt{(53908 \times 228.88)}} = -0.839$$

$$r^2 = -0.839^2 = 0.704$$

The correlation coefficient has the value of -0.839 and the r^2 value of 0.704 indicates that just over 70 per cent of the variation in lithic quantity is related to distance from the source.

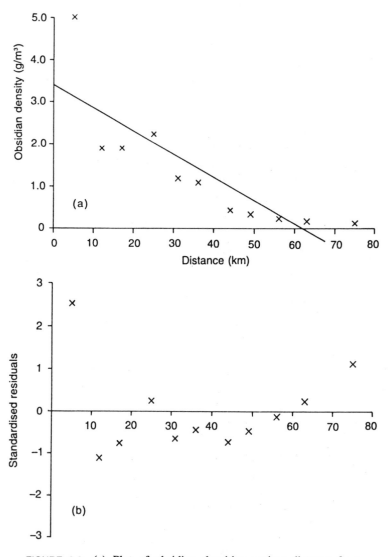

FIGURE 9.9. (a) Plot of obsidian densities against distance from source with the regression line $y = 3.403 - 0.055x$ superimposed. (b) Plot of the standardised residual obsidian densities against distance from source.

These values indicate a strong linear relationship between the two variables, and if we simply examined the numbers calculated above we might take the investigation no further. If we look at the scattergram (Figure 9.9a), however, we see that the distribution of points is not in a straight line so that the linear regression does not describe the relationship correctly: it underpredicts at the beginning and end of the line and overpredicts in the middle; consequently, the linear correlation associated with it is also incorrect. The problems are brought out even more clearly by the standardised residual plot (Figure 9.9b).

Since the regression does not fit some action must be taken. Inspection of the raw data scattergram suggests that a linear relationship would fit all the data points except the first one quite well. This first point could therefore be regarded as an 'outlier' and the analysis re-run without it. It may well be legitimate in certain circumstances to exclude observations in this way, but the procedure obviously has considerable dangers; at the worst, any data points which do not fit the analyst's model could simply be thrown out. There must therefore be a good reason for doing it; for example, reasons why that particular observation may not be a valid one, perhaps poor excavation procedure or a very small excavated sample.

In this case we will suppose that there is no reason to reject the first data point; it is therefore necessary to find a model which fits all the data, obviously in this case some sort of curvilinear relationship. Since it is much more straightforward to fit the regression in a linear form than in the original curvilinear one, a transformation must be carried out. Knowledge of other similar cases (cf. Hodder and Orton, 1976; Renfrew, 1977) suggests that it would be appropriate to log the y axis, in other words to work with the logarithms of the original y values (see Table 9.3).

TABLE 9.3. Density and logged density of a certain type of Meso-american obsidian for sites at varying distances from the source.

Density (y)	Logged density (log y)	Density (y)	Logged density (log y)
5.01	0.6998	0.447	−0.3497
1.91	0.2810	0.347	−0.4597
1.91	0.2810	0.239	−0.6216
2.24	0.3502	0.186	−0.7305
1.20	0.0792	0.126	−0.8996
1.10	0.0414		

We can now calculate the regression using the transformed y values:

$$n = 11 \qquad \sum x_i y_i = -161.865$$
$$\sum x_i = 413 \qquad \sum y_i = -1.3285$$
$$(\sum x_i)^2 = 170569 \qquad (\sum y_i)^2 = 1.7649$$
$$\sum x_i^2 = 20407 \qquad \sum y_i^2 = 2.8412$$

$$b = \frac{[11 \times (-161.865)] - [413 \times (-1.3285)]}{(11 \times 20407) - 170569}$$

$$= \frac{-1231.68}{53908} = -0.0229$$

$$a = \frac{-1.3285 - (-0.0229 \times 413)}{11} = 0.739$$

Thus the regression equation is:

$$\log \hat{y} = 0.739 - 0.0229x$$

$$r = \frac{[11 \times (-161.865)] - [413 \times (-1.3285)]}{\sqrt{[(11.20407) - 170569][(11 \times 2.8412) - 1.7649]}}$$

$$= \frac{-1231.6795}{\sqrt{(53908 \times 29.488)}} = -0.9769$$

$$r^2 = -0.9769^2 = 0.9543$$

It is obvious that this relationship fits the data far better than the original one. The r^2 value indicates that over 95 per cent of the variation in *logged* obsidian density is related to *untransformed* distance from the source; in fact, no other relationship fits as well. Obviously though, we should now look at the scattergram for the transformed relationship and the associated residual plot (see Figures 9.10 and 9.11).

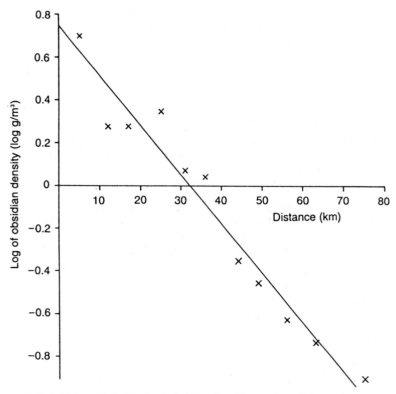

FIGURE 9.10. Plot of logged obsidian densities against distance from source with the regression line log $\hat{y} = 0.739 - 0.0229x$ superimposed.

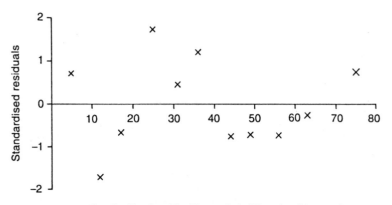

FIGURE 9.11. Standardised residual logged obsidian densities against distance from source.

It is clear from the examination of these plots that the fit of the line to the data along its length is much better. The previous under- and over-prediction have been removed and the distribution of the residuals is much closer to the amorphous scatter to be expected when the regression assumptions are met. There remains, however, a slight suggestion of heteroscedasticity and autocorrelation in the residuals; they would probably deserve further investigation in a real study. It is worth noting that this slight indication was completely swamped in the first version of the regression by the non-linearity.

The main potential problem with this or any other transformation is in interpretation. The regression equation log y = $0.739 - 0.0229x$ means that there is a decrease of 0.0229 in log y for a unit increase in x. It is all too easy to forget that the transformation has been carried out and to discuss the results as if it had not. By taking antilogs it is possible to put the best fit regression line back on the original scattergram as the appropriate curve (see Fig. 9.12) and it can be seen that it fits very well, showing clearly that near the source fall-off in quantity is fairly rapid but thereafter is very slow indeed.

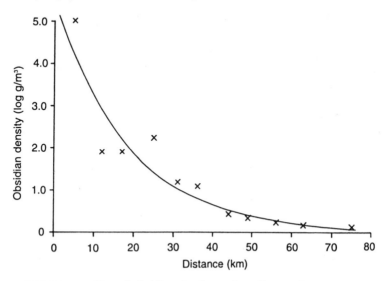

FIGURE 9.12. Plot of obsidian density against distance from source with the anti-logged version of the regression line log $\hat{y}$ = $0.739 - 0.0229x$ superimposed.

2. *Heteroscedasticity*. It is now necessary to turn to the problems which arise when the amount of variation around the regression line varies at different points along it. Like non-linearity, this too will emerge clearly from examination of raw data scattergrams and residual plots. The two ways in which it most often arises were shown in Figure 9.4(a) and (b). In the second case, where there are small numbers of observations with large *x* values, we might again want to consider whether any of them are outliers which it might be appropriate to remove from the analysis. If not, then logging one or both variables will have the effect of 'pulling back' the extreme observations so that they are closer to the rest, and as a result it is very likely that the variances along the line will be equalised.

The first case, where the variation around the line increases as the *x* values become larger, is more problematical and is likely to require the use of so-called *weighted least-squares* regression techniques which are beyond the scope of this text.

3. *Autocorrelation*. The presence of correlation between the residuals from a regression should emerge quite clearly from study of the relevant scattergram and residual plot, but a test for it may also be carried out, using the Durbin–Watson statistic (see, for example, Chatterjee and Price, 1977). Consideration of this statistic, however, is really only meaningful if the data represent something like a time sequence.

Often the presence of correlated errors suggests that there is some other variable having an effect on the dependent, *y*, in addition to the independent variable already being considered. Investigating this will involve adding other independent variables to the regression which your knowledge of the situation suggests might be relevant; the regression will then be a multiple one (see next chapter). However, more often than not autocorrelation is related to the distribution in time or space of the observations and is intrinsic to the spatial or temporal pattern. It is then necessary to find ways round it. The example which follows illustrates one possibility in this respect.

An intensive investigation of an area of the south-western United States has produced information on the density of settlement sites per km^2 for a succession of chronological phases (Table 9.4). The questions that arise are, how does site density

change with time and how good is the fit of the data to this
proposed relationship?

TABLE 9.4. Number of settlement sites per square kilometre for the
succession of chronological phases in an area of the south-western
United States (data from Plog, 1974).

Time period (years)	Sites per km²	Time period (years)	Sites per km²
0–50	0.25	300–350	1.05
50–100	0.25	350–400	1.00
100–150	0.55	400–450	1.15
150–200	0.60	450–500	1.30
200–250	0.95	500–550	1.65
250–300	1.00		

Before starting the analysis it should be noted that our
chronology variable is in terms of intervals rather than fixed
points so that it contains some measurement error. The standard
regression model presupposes that there is no measurement
error in the x variable and we would normally have to use a
rather different regression technique to cope with this (reduced
major axis regression; see for example Davis, 1986). For the
purpose of this example, however, I propose to assume that all
the sites of a given phase were in occupation at the midpoint of
that phase so that we can take the midpoint as a fixed value.

The scattergram of these data with the regression line superimposed is shown in Figure 9.13. The equation for the line is

$$\hat{y}_i = 0.191 + 0.0025x$$

It tells us that the site density increases by 0.25 sites/km²
every 100 years. The coefficient of determination, or r^2 value is
0.932, indicating that 93.2 per cent of the variation in site
density is associated with the time trend, and thus that the fit of
the data to the regression relationship is extremely close.

But can we accept this at its face value or is it misleading?
The distribution of the points around the regression line suggests
the possibility of autocorrelation in the residuals, although it
is not great enough to produce a significant value for the

Durbin–Watson statistic. However, a glance at the relation between the points and the line suggests that there is some variation in the difference between adjacent points, despite the extremely high r^2 value and its indication of a very close fit between regression and data. How does this arise?

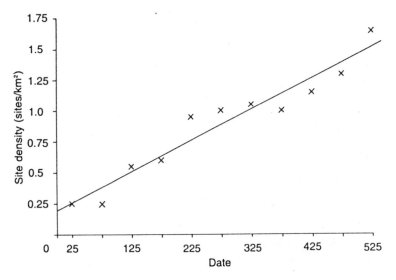

FIGURE 9.13. Scattergram of site densities against date.

It is highly likely that in cases such as this one many of the sites occupied in one period will also be occupied in the subsequent one, and quite probably the one after as well. Thus, the observations are not independent of one another because that for one period will be related to that for the previous one. The result of this process of accumulation is that when the regression tells us that there is a constant rate of increase of 0.25 sites/km² every 100 years, with an r^2 value of 93.2 per cent, it may be giving a very misleading impression of the rate of change over time, how constant it is and the goodness-of-fit of the data to it.

To remove this accumulation effect, instead of regressing the original density values against the time sequence we can look at the time differences between pairs of phases and the density differences associated with these: that is to say, we measure the time difference and the site density difference between all

possible pairs of points and plot one against the other. The
scattergram is shown in Figure 9.14 with the regression line
superimposed.

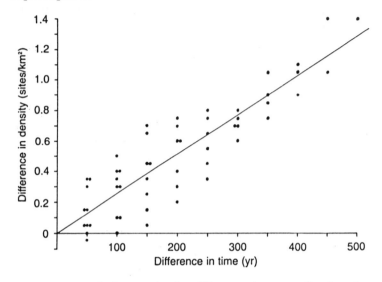

FIGURE 9.14. Settlement density differences between all pairs of
phases plotted against the time difference between the two phases.

The slope is almost identical to that of the original regression,
as indeed it should be, but we now have a much less misleading
picture of the goodness-of-fit of the data to the relationship. The
variation in density differences between adjacent phases is
shown in the range of y values for $x = 50$; the range of variation
in density differences for phases 150 years apart is even greater.
All this is reflected in an r^2 value of 78.9 per cent compared with
the 93.2 per cent of the original regression. Thus it appears that
the rate of change in settlement density in this area varied considerably during the period in question and was not the constant
that it first appeared. This result raises a further set of archaeological questions concerning the reasons behind these varying
growth rates. Even here care is necessary, however; for example,
there are now signs of heteroścedasticity in the variance around
the regression line. Moreover, it should not be thought that
this procedure of taking differences is a universally appropriate
recipe for overcoming problems of the kind described, when

temporal autocorrelation arises, even though it is very illuminating in this particular case.

STATISTICAL INFERENCE

The aim of the preceding discussion of some of the problems of regression analysis and ways in which they may be overcome has been to show that the object of using the technique is not mechanically to calculate two or three coefficients which simply put a number on what we know already, but to obtain information about patterning in our data which would not otherwise be apparent. In this, modern approaches to normal-theory-based regression are similar to the exploratory data analysis approach, with its emphasis on distinguishing the 'rough' from the 'smooth' in a relationship.

It is, of course, possible to use statistical inference in a regression context, when our data are a genuine random sample of some population or can be conceived of in terms of a randomisation experiment, by randomly permuting (mixing up) the x and y values, as we have seen in Chapters 5 and 6. It will then be meaningful to make statements to the effect, for example, that a particular value for the correlation coefficient is significantly different from zero. Such tests are always included in the regression programs of statistics packages and do not require further attention here. However, there is one aspect of regression statistical inference which does deserve a mention: the estimation of confidence intervals for the regression. These too are provided by most programs and an example is shown in Figure 9.15. The inner pair of lines represents the confidence interval for the regression line itself; that is to say, in 95 per cent of cases the regression line will lie within this interval. However, as we saw at the beginning of the chapter, if we are using the regression line to make predictions we have to take into account the dispersion of the observations around the regression line. In order to obtain a valid population interval estimate, or prediction interval, of the y value for a given x value, we need to take into account *both* the dispersion around the line *and* the variation in the line itself which will occur from sample to sample. The other pair of bands represents the 95 per cent prediction interval taking into account both these sources of variation. The question which arises is, why are these bands relatively narrow in the middle but wider as you move away towards either end of the regression line?

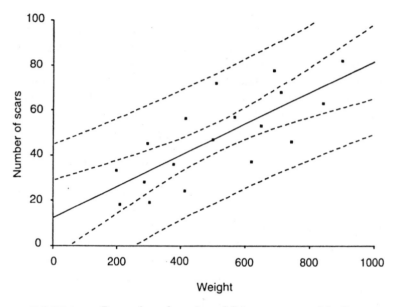

FIGURE 9.15. Regression of number of flake scars on weight for a group of handaxes, showing confidence interval bands around the regression.

The main reason is as follows. If you imagine taking a large number of samples of x and y values from a population and carrying out a regression analysis each time, then the value of the regression slope, b, will vary from sample to sample; sometimes it will be rather smaller than others, sometimes it will be rather larger. There will be a distribution of different values with the mean corresponding to the slope for the population as a whole. Now the regression line, by definition, must go through the point marking the joint mean of the x and y values and this acts like the fulcrum of a see-saw. What is involved is shown in Figure 9.16. A sample with a slightly flatter slope will produce a line which is in exactly the same position as the line produced by a sample with a steeper slope at the position of the joint mean, but as you go further away in either direction the two lines will diverge from one another by an ever increasing amount. Since the confidence intervals around a regression must always take into account the sampling variation in the slope, they will always diverge in this way.

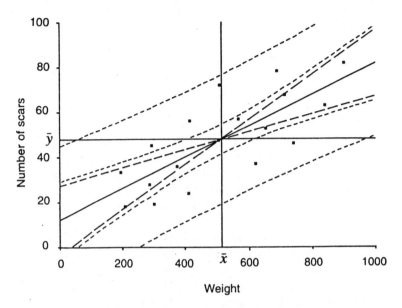

FIGURE 9.16. Regression of number of flake scars on weight for a group of handaxes. In addition to the regression line and confidence interval bands, the scattergram shows the means of the two variables and the slope of regression lines two standard errors greater than and less than the central mean regression slope.

ROBUST REGRESSION:
THE EXPLORATORY DATA ANALYSIS APPROACH

The EDA approach rejects the standard forms of regression for the same reason as it rejects the use of the mean and standard deviation in describing the distribution of single variables: they are both unduly affected by the values of extreme cases in the data set. The argument is that the description of the relationship between two variables should be *robust* and not influenced by extremes, which, as we have noted before, are almost bound to be atypical. This is a good argument as far as it goes but it is worth noting that the various transformations discussed above can reduce the influence of extreme observations on least-squares regression and also make the data conform more closely to the specifications of the regression model. To resort to the use of EDA methods at the first sign that the data do not meet the assumptions of standard regression analysis may actually result in loss of information; or rather, not all the information present in the data may emerge. In the autocorrelation case-study above it would have been positively misleading not to consider the substantive implications of the suggestion of autocorrelation which merged from the first analysis.

Nevertheless, where robust description of a relationship is required, as it often will be, then the EDA alternative to least-squares regression known as the *Tukey line* may be used. Like the EDA approach to single variable description it is based on the median rather than the mean because the median is a resistant measure; compared with least-squares regression it also has the virtue of simplicity.

The first step is to divide the observations into three roughly equal sized groups, based on their values on the x axis; in effect, those with small, medium and large x values. Once this has been done the median of the x values and the median of the y values in the first and last groups are obtained. From this point on there are two different ways of arriving at the Tukey line. The first method is a direct graphical one and involves establishing the position of the median x and y values of the first and last groups of observations on the scattergram, joining them up with a straightedge, and then moving the straightedge up or down parallel to the line until half the data points are above the line and half below (Hartwig and Dearing, 1979, p. 35).

The alternative is to use arithmetical methods to calculate the slope and intercept of the line, where the equation for the line is the same as in least-squares regression, $\hat{y} = a + bx$, but the basis of calculating the coefficients is different:

$$b = \frac{(\text{median } y_3 - \text{median } y_1)}{(\text{median } x_3 - \text{median } x_1)}$$

where median y_3 means the median y value in the third group of observations, that with the largest x values; median y_1 means the median y value in the first group of observations, that with the smallest x values; median x_3 means the median x value in the third group of observations; median x_1 means the median x value in the first group of observations.

a = the median of the values d_i, where $d_i = y_i - bx_i$

Once the coefficients have been calculated the equation can be written and the line plotted in the usual way.

It is helpful to illustrate the procedure with an example (see Fig. 9.17), a hypothetical study from Mesoamerica of the relation between settlement sizes and the quantity of imported obsidian at those settlements. It is fairly characteristic of the type of situation where a Tukey line might be employed, in that the data do not appear to meet the requirements of least-squares regression especially well; in particular, there are a couple of outlying observations, only to be expected in a study involving settlement sizes, which would be likely to have an excessive influence on the coefficients of an ordinary regression; in other words, the regression relationship defined would not really be relevant to the bulk of the observations.

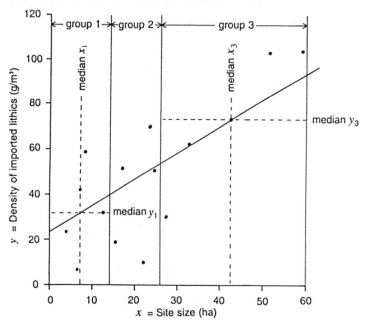

FIGURE 9.17. Calculation of a Tukey line for a scatterplot of densities of imported lithics at a series of sites in Mesoamerica, against the size of the sites where they occur.

The application of the graphical method of obtaining the Tukey
line is illustrated on the scattergram (Fig. 9.17). There are five
data points in each of the three groups; in the third group the
same point has both the median x and median y value, in the first
group this is not the case. In this particular example the line
joining the two medians does itself have half the data points
below it and half above it so there is no need to move the
straightedge to any other position; the line joining the two
medians is the Tukey line required.

For the arithmetic method we have

$$b = \frac{(73.0-32.0)}{(42.5-7.0)} = \frac{41}{35.5} = 1.15$$

Finding the intercept value is more tedious, since we must use
the formula

$$d_i = y_i - 1.15x_i$$

to obtain the d values of all the points before we can find the
median d value. As an example, for the point with the lowest y
value

$$d = 7 - (1.15 \times 6.5) = -0.48$$

For that with the highest y value

$$d = 104 - (1.15 \times 59) = 36.15$$

The median d value is 23.9 and a glance at the scattergram
confirms the correctness of this as the intercept value. Thus the
equation for the Tukey line is

$$\hat{y}_i = 23.9 + 1.15x_i$$

This tells us that from a starting point of 23.9 there is an
increase in lithic density of 1.15g/m^3 of earth for each one
hectare increase in site size.

This line will be considerably more robust than the corresponding least-squares regression in that removal of the top two
or three cases from consideration will have a much less drastic
effect on the form of the relationship for the data set as a whole.
That is to say, in the case under consideration the rate of
increase in lithic density indicated by the Tukey line equation

applies to the bulk of the cases and is not just a result of the difference between the biggest sites and the rest. Even if the largest sites are removed it has little effect on the rate of increase in lithic density with increasing site size indicated by the Tukey line. This is seen in Figure 9.18, where the Tukey line for all the data and that which applies to the data with the three largest sites removed are both shown. In contrast, the effect of removing the largest sites on the slope of the least-squares regression line is considerable, as a comparison of the different regression lines also shown in Figure 9.18 makes clear.

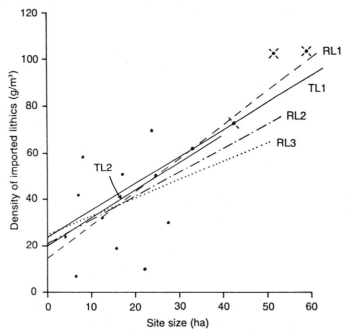

FIGURE 9.18. Comparison of Tukey lines and least-squares regression lines for all the data and with large observations deleted: TL1 is the Tukey line for all data; TL2 is the Tukey line for data with the 3 largest observations deleted; RL1 is the least-squares regression line for all data; RL2 is the least-squares regression line with the 2 largest observations deleted; and RL3 is the least-squares regression line with the 3 largest observations deleted.

As Hartwig and Dearing (1979, p. 35) point out, in many cases the basic idea of carrying out such forms of analysis as fitting a line is to define general patterns (the smooth) and distinguish them from deviations from the patterns (the rough); a resistant characterisation of the smooth is likely to keep the distinction between the smooth and the rough as clear as possible. More recent methods of doing this in the case of bivariate relationships include the kernel smoothing methods mentioned in Chapter 4 (see for example Wand and Jones, 1995, Chapter 5).

EXERCISES

9.1 Investigate the relationship between obsidian percentage and distance from source for the following lithic assemblages, using regression techniques to specify its form and strength.

Distance	per cent obsidian	Distance	per cent obsidian	Distance	per cent obsidian
12	98	85	21	210	8
25	92	82	44	233	16
67	77	112	56	300	10
30	67	150	33	329	5
42	39	154	15	381	8

9.2 Shaft length and the number of tooth marks are recorded on a set of ten animal bones from a palaeolithic cave assemblage:

Shaft length (mm)	40	40	50	60	70	80	90	110	130	140
No. of tooth marks	0	0	1	2	0	5	0	2	7	0

(a) Plot the data and fit a Tukey line, superimposing it on the plot. (b) Calculate the regression line for these data. Explain your choice of dependent variable. Plot the regression line on the graph from part (a). Are the regression assumptions satisfied? (c) Comment on the interpretation of the two lines drawn in parts (a) and (b).

9.3 On sites in Mesoamerica the presence of plazas and pyramids is an indication of the carrying out of important political/ritual activities implying the presence of local élites. Does the scale of plaza building appear to be related to that of pyramid building and are either of these related to the overall size of the sites concerned?

Site	Plazas	Pyramids	Site size (ha)
1	4	5	0.8
2	3	2	1.04
3	3	4	1.40
4	5	9	1.92
5	2	2	0.40
6	2	1	0.24
7	4	6	4.10
8	3	5	2.85
9	1	2	0.48
10	7	13	3.90
11	10	17	3.21
12	3	5	0.58
13	2	2	0.29

Ten

FACING UP TO COMPLEXITY: MULTIPLE REGRESSION AND CORRELATION

By the end of the previous chapter, considerable complexities had been introduced into the basic concepts of regression and correlation with which we began. Nevertheless, the treatment considered only the relationship between two variables, in general one dependent and one independent variable.

As we saw in Chapter 7, it is very often necessary to deal with more variables than this if we wish to obtain any real understanding of a given situation. Thus, to take a topic from the previous chapter, we may be interested in why the quantities of some imported material vary between a number of different settlements. Most of the examples presented concerned themselves only with distance from the source as the reason for the variation. The last example, however, was a hypothetical investigation of the way in which imported material quantity on a settlement might relate to the settlement's size. Any real study, of course, would want to take into account both distance and settlement size. As we will see, this cannot be done by simply carrying out two separate bivariate regression analyses; all three variables must be included in a *multiple regression analysis*, in which there will be a single dependent variable – material quantity – and two independents. In multiple regression analysis there will always be only a single dependent variable but there may be any number of independents – variables which we think may have some effect on the dependent, on the basis of some hypothesis we have developed.

This added complexity has an effect on our analyses. Whereas virtually all the techniques which have been presented up to now can be carried out quite straightforwardly, albeit a bit tediously, with a calculator, multiple regression and the majority of the other techniques to be described in the next few chapters *require* the use of a computer to carry them out, except in the simplest and most trivial cases, because of the complexity of the calculations involved. This complexity is associated with a significantly higher order of mathematical difficulty, in particular involving the use of matrix algebra.

It seemed inappropriate in a text such as this to present an introduction to matrix algebra and then to go through the mathematics of the techniques in detail. It would have taken up a large amount of space and moved the text up to a level of mathematical sophistication unsuitable for most of the intended audience. Nevertheless, there is a price to be paid for this. Whereas, up to now, we have seen the detailed workings of virtually all the methods described, in much of what follows the detailed workings will remain a 'black box'. This obviously has its dangers and pitfalls, into which archaeologists have fallen in the past; for those who intend to be serious practitioners of these techniques there is no alternative to acquiring the detailed knowledge and seeking advice from professional statisticians. However, the view taken here is that it is possible to obtain an understanding of the theoretical structure of the techniques without a detailed knowledge of the mathematics involved, and thus to gain a valid intuitive insight into them and their role.

The chapter begins with a brief introduction to the basics of the multiple regression model. A more detailed examination of various aspects of multiple correlation and regression then follows; this is done with reference to an archaeological example, so that the discussion does not become too theoretical and the implications of the techniques for archaeological data analysis become apparent. Finally, some important extensions of these techniques are considered which have come to have particular importance as a result of the growth of predictive modelling in archaeology in the context of geographic information systems.

THE MULTIPLE REGRESSION MODEL

The principles of multiple regression are the same as for simple regression. In general, we want to estimate a regression equation by fitting it to some empirical data. It will be assumed that the relationship is linear (the assumptions of the technique will be discussed below) and we will be using the least-squares criterion to obtain the best fit of the regression to the data. Whereas in the simple regression case the equation was $y = a + bx$, now it is

$$y = a + b_1 x_1 + b_2 x_2 + ... + b_k x_k$$

In the simple regression case we were fitting a line to our two-dimensional scatter of points (Figure 10.1a). If, for the sake of visualisation, we take the simplest multiple regression case, when we have two independent variables, we can see that what we are trying to fit is a plane rather than a line – a plane is a line's two-dimensional equivalent (Figure 10.1b). Once we move beyond three variables the situation becomes very difficult to visualise but the principle remains exactly the same and mathematically it is perfectly feasible: we will be trying to fit a plane not of two dimensions, as in the case illustrated, but of as many dimensions as there are independent variables.

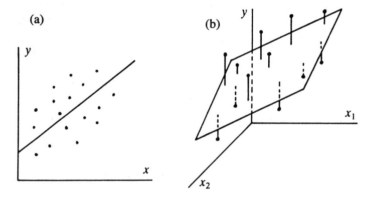

FIGURE 10.1. (*a*) Scattergram of the relationship between a dependent variable (*y*) and an independent (*x*), with the regression line drawn in. (*b*) Scattergram of the relationship between a dependent variable (*y*) and two independents (x_1 and x_2): the regression line has become a regression plane (after Blalock, 1972).

To return to our three-variable case. Where $x_1 = x_2 = 0$ we have $y = a$, which is the height at which the regression plane crosses the *y* axis. The slope, or *b*, coefficients work as follows. Imagine a vertical plane perpendicular to the x_2 axis, projected so that it intersects with the regression plane (Figure 10.2).

Where it intersects with the regression plane this vertical plane is simply a straight line on the regression plane surface. Because the vertical plane, and therefore the line of intersection, is perpendicular to the x_2 axis, all the points on it have the same value for the x_2 variable. The slope of this line is b_1 in the multiple regression equation; that is to say, it is the slope of the regression of y on x_1 alone, since for this particular line all the x_2 values are constant. In the same way, if we construct a vertical plane perpendicular to the x_1 axis, then the line along which it intersects the regression plane will have slope b_2 and will represent the regression of y on x_2, with x_1 held constant. In multiple regression the aim is to find the a, b_1 ...b_n coefficients which produce the regression plane giving the best fit to our data on the least-squares criterion. We will see below the way in which the overall goodness-of-fit of this plane to the data may be measured using the multiple correlation coefficient.

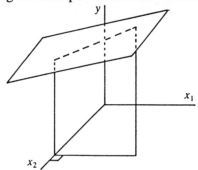

FIGURE 10.2. A vertical plane at right angles to x_2 projected upwards until it intersects the regression plane: the line of intersection represents the regression of y on x_1.

But multiple regression and correlation are not just about finding the overall effect of a set of variables on a dependent variable. As has been implied already, we are also interested in the effect of our independent variables taken one at a time, with the others held constant. The laboratory experimenter can achieve this situation in reality by manipulating the conditions of the experiment. Archaeologists obviously cannot do this; we have to control the situations we're investigating, insofar as this is possible, during the analysis phase. To control in this way we have to use partial correlation and regression coefficients.

PARTIAL CORRELATION

We will start with partial correlation, which is the more important of the two, and illustrate what is involved with an example. We will suppose that a programme of fieldwork has given us information on the sizes (in terms of area) of a number of settlements in a region of Mexico. We are interested in the reasons for the variation and suspect that they may have something to do with the available agricultural resources in the vicinity (cf. Brumfiel, 1976). Information is therefore collected on the area of available agricultural land around each of these sites, and on the productivity of the land (see Table 10.1).

TABLE 10.1. Information about site size, area of available agricultural land and land productivity (in arbitrary units) for 28 hypothetical Formative Period sites in Mexico.

	Site size (ha)	Available agricultural land (km²)	Relative productivity index
1	30.0	17.9	0.75
2	33.0	12.7	0.87
3	37.0	17.6	0.71
4	42.0	6.0	0.85
5	42.0	21.6	0.83
6	44.9	29.4	0.73
7	47.0	19.6	0.89
8	53.2	29.0	0.87
9	55.0	21.4	0.72
10	55.0	50.8	0.89
11	55.2	31.8	0.90
12	60.0	24.8	0.81
13	62.0	26.4	0.92
14	63.1	34.0	0.94
15	64.5	39.1	0.99
16	65.0	35.4	0.82
17	67.7	34.8	0.96
18	69.7	53.0	0.91
19	74.0	54.2	0.94
20	75.0	73.3	1.01
21	76.0	95.9	1.09
22	77.0	66.8	1.05
23	80.5	51.0	1.23
24	86.0	61.2	1.06
25	88.0	72.5	1.29
26	90.0	54.7	1.22
27	95.3	89.9	1.00
28	99.0	89.9	1.26

In terms of a regression analysis:

> Dependent (y) variable = site size
> First independent (x_1) variable = area of available agricultural land
> Second independent (x_2) variable = relative productivity

We can start by carrying out a simple regression of site size on available agricultural land, and obtain the following results:

$$\hat{y} = 35.4 + 0.656x_1$$
$$r_{yx_1} = 0.864$$
$$r_{yx_1}^2 = 0.746$$

The corresponding scattergram is shown in Figure 10.3. In words, this result states that where there is no available land, site size is estimated to be 35.4 ha; and that for every increase in available land of 1 km², site size increases by 0.656 ha. The correlation between the two variables is 0.864. Given that available land is the independent variable and site size the dependent, we can say that variation in the area of available agricultural land accounts for 74.6 per cent of the variation in site size.

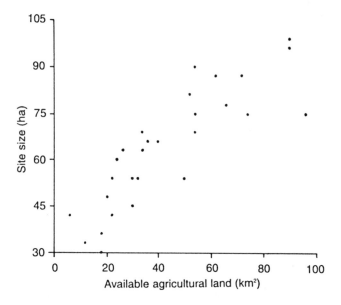

FIGURE 10.3. Scattergram of site size against area of available land, from the data in Table 10.1.

Similarly, if we carry out a regression of site size on land productivity we have:

$$\hat{y} = -28.9 + 97.9x_2$$
$$r_{yx_2} = 0.832$$
$$r_{yx_2}^2 = 0.693$$

The scattergram is shown in Figure 10.4, and the result suggests that for every increase in the productivity index of 1.0 there is an increase of 97.9 ha in site size. Correlation is 0.832 and variation in productivity accounts for 69.3 per cent of the variation in site size.

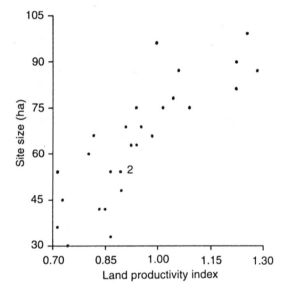

FIGURE 10.4. Scattergram of site size against productivity index of available land, from the data in Table 10.1.

Together the two r^2 figures we have just seen appear to suggest that our two independents – area of available land and land productivity – account for $74.6 + 69.3 = 143.9$ per cent of the variation in site size. Clearly this gives us grounds for suspicion! But what is actually wrong with the procedure?

Suppose we ask whether land productivity and available land area are related to each other. They might be, if, for example, the geomorphological conditions in which larger areas of soil were produced were diffferent from those in which smaller areas originated; the contrast between large alluvial plains and small colluvium-filled basins might be an instance of this. The point may be investigated by regressing x_2 (productivity) on x_1 (available land area):

$$\hat{x}_2 = 0.74 + 0.0048x_1$$
$$r_{x_2x_1} = 0.738$$
$$r_{x_2x_1}^2 = 0.545$$

A scattergram (with productivity as the vertical axis) is shown in Figure 10.5 and it appears from this result that 54.5 per cent of the variation in productivity is in fact accounted for by variation in the area of land concerned.

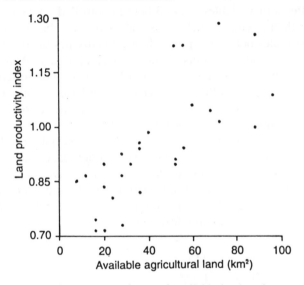

FIGURE 10.5. Scattergram of area of available land against productivity index of land, from the data in Table 10.1.

This poses problems for the initial two regressions we carried out since it means that they were not independent of one another. The second regression, y on x_2 (site size on productivity), was partly also a regression of y on x_1 (site size on area of land), because x_2 and x_1 are both related to each other. This situation raises two difficulties. First, we cannot tell how much of the variation in site size is related to available land area, how much to land productivity, and how much to the two of them together. Second, it means, as we suspected, that the conclusion that the two independents together account for about 144 per cent of the variation in site size was indeed incorrect: because it included an element of double counting. We cannot simply add the two separate r^2 values together because the two overlap with one another as a result of the relationship between x_1 (available land area) and x_2 (land productivity). It is in the solution of these problems that partial and multiple correlation have their role.

It is convenient here to make a slight change in notation and to designate our independent variable, y, as x_0. Our partial correlation coefficient can then be expressed as, for example, $r_{01.23}$, which reads as 'the correlation between variables 0 and 1 with the effects of variables 2 and 3 being controlled'. This is much neater than having to include xs and ys in the subscript. Of the two variables before the point, the first is usually the dependent and the second the independent variable currently of interest. Any number of independent variables can be controlled; the number being controlled is known as the order of correlation, so with two controls it is a second-order correlation coefficient, with no controls it is a zero-order coefficient.

It is important to note that with the partial correlation coefficient, e.g. $r_{01.2}$, we remove the effect not just of the relation between x_0 and x_2, but also of the relationship between x_1 and x_2.

The first-order partial correlation coefficients, i.e. those holding only one other variable under control, can be obtained by means of the following formula:

$$r_{ij.k} = \frac{r_{ij} - (r_{ik})(r_{jk})}{\sqrt{1-r_{ik}^2}\,\sqrt{1-r_{jk}^2}}$$

e.g.

$$r_{01.2} = \frac{r_{01} - (r_{02})(r_{12})}{\sqrt{1-r_{02}^2}\,\sqrt{1-r_{12}^2}}$$

It is easy to see that computation of these would become very tedious if you had to do it by hand, because of the large number of coefficients which have to be calculated, but of course they are produced by all relevant statistics packages.

At this point it is important to return to our example, to see how the partial coefficients are obtained and how they differ from the zero-order coefficients seen above.

We need to investigate the relationship between site size and area of available land, holding land productivity constant; and between site size and land productivity holding area of available land constant. To do this we simply put the relevant numbers in the expression for the first-order partial:

$$r_{01.2} = \frac{r_{01} - (r_{02})(r_{12})}{\sqrt{1 - r_{02}^2}\ \sqrt{1 - r_{12}^2}}$$

$$= \frac{0.864 - (0.832)(0.738)}{\sqrt{1 - 0.832^2}\ \sqrt{1 - 0.738^2}}$$

$$= 0.6678$$

$$r_{01.2}^2 = 0.6678^2 = 0.446$$

The final figure tells us that just over 44 per cent of the remaining (or residual) variation in site size is accounted for by variation in the area of available land, once variation in productivity has been taken into account. It is important to note that this is *not* 44 per cent of the total variation in site size but 44 per cent of the variation in site size not accounted for by productivity. To see how this relates to the total variation in site size we will have to wait a little longer.

The corresponding operation can now be carried out for the relationship between site size and productivity with available land area held constant. From the usual expression for first-order partials we have:

$$r_{02.1} = \frac{r_{02} - (r_{01})(r_{21})}{\sqrt{1 - r_{01}^2}\ \sqrt{1 - r_{21}^2}}$$

$$= \frac{0.832 - (0.864)(0.738)}{\sqrt{1 - 0.864^2}\ \sqrt{1 - 0.738^2}} = 0.572$$

$$r_{02.1}^2 = 0.572^2 = 0.327$$

Thus, it can be seen that just over 32 per cent of the residual variation in site size not accounted for by area of available land is accounted for by variation in land productivity when the effect of area of available land on this is controlled.

It should be obvious from this example that any serious investigation of the relationships between variables cannot be left at the level of zero-order coefficients. Nevertheless, the analysis and understanding of the relations between large numbers of zero-order and partial correlation coefficients is a complex business. It is necessary to examine the differences in sign and magnitude between partials and zero-orders, to see whether the control variables are suppressing, explaining or having no effect on the relations between the variables of interest.

MULTIPLE CORRELATION

The previous section of this chapter concentrated on how to isolate the effect of individual variables in the context of a regression analysis with a number of independent variables. What we have not yet considered, however, is how we assess the overall effect of all the independents taken together on variation in the dependent. The multiple correlation coefficient (R) measures the goodness-of-fit of the least-squares regression surface as a whole to the dependent variable values. The square of the multiple correlation coefficient (R^2) indicates the percentage of the variation in the dependent variable accounted for by the least-squares surface.

This is all very well as a matter of definition, but how is the quantity, or its square, actually found, in the light of the problems we have seen about adding together zero-order coefficients and the need to calculate partials. Clearly, as our example showed, the percentage of variation in the dependent accounted for by the regression overall cannot simply be the sum of the zero-order r^2 values, for the same reason – that of double counting.

On the other hand, summing the partials is also incorrect. Whereas summing the zero-order values involves double-counting, summing the partials has the converse problem that it is not sufficient. This is because each partial only gives us the effect of an individual variable by itself on the residual part of the dependent, with no influence from the other independent variables; so summing them only gives the total effect of all the individual variables taken alone on that part of the variation in the dependent which doesn't relate to any of the other independent variables. What is missing is that we don't know how the residual variation in the dependent relates to its total variation and also that when independents are correlated with one another they will not only each have an individual effect on the dependent; there will also be an effect of the joint action of the relevant variables. Accordingly, we need something different from any of the co-efficients we have seen so far.

The formula for multiple R^2 for the three-variable case is:

$$R^2_{0.12} = r^2_{01} + r^2_{02.1}(1 - r^2_{01})$$

where $R^2_{0.12}$ is the multiple coefficient of determination between x_0 and both x_1 and x_2. It is the proportion of the total variation in x_0 accounted for by the two independents both separately and together.

To obtain it we first let one of the independents do all the 'explaining' it can. This is the meaning of the r^2_{01} term: it is the proportion of the variation in the dependent accounted for by the first independent. If the total variation in the independent is defined as 1.0, then after the first independent has accounted for its share of the variation, the proportion remaining to be accounted for is $(1 - r^2_{01})$. Now we see how much of the remaining variation in the dependent can be accounted for by the second independent and add this to the variation accounted for by the first, to obtain the overall effect of the two together. Why then is the second part of the formula $r^2_{02.1}(1 - r^2_{01})$ and not simply $r^2_{02}(1 - r^2_{01})$?

It is because by including the term r^2_{01} we already have in the equation all the effect of the first variable. If x_1 and x_2, our independents, are correlated then there will be some effect of x_1 expressed in r^2_{02}, so if we used this in the equation we would again be making the mistake of double counting. We must remove any effect of x_1 on r^2_{02} and we do this, of course, by controlling for it, and taking the partial $r^2_{02.1}$. To make the argument more concrete it will be helpful at this point to return to our example and obtain the multiple R^2 value, i.e. establish the proportion of the variation in site size accounted for by the overall effect of area of available land and land productivity, acting both separately and together. In the course of this chapter we have already calculated the relevant quantities:

$$r_{01}^2 = 0.746$$

$$1 - r_{01}^2 = 0.254$$

$$r_{02.1}^2 = 0.327$$

$$R_{0.12}^2 = 0.746 + (0.327)(0.254)$$

$$= 0.746 + 0.083 = 0.829$$

That is to say, area of available land and land productivity altogether account for 82.9 per cent of the variation in site size for this set of data, made up by letting area of available land account for all the variation it can – 74.6 per cent – and letting land productivity 'explain' what it can of the remainder – 8.3 per cent.

But we can break this down further, since as it stands we do not yet know how much of the 74.6 per cent is the effect of area of available land alone and how much is the joint effect of this and land productivity together. The partial $r_{01.2}^2 = 0.446$ tells us that 44.6 per cent of the variation in site size (x_0) not accounted for by land productivity (x_2) is accounted for by variation in area of available land alone, i.e. 44.6 per cent of the $(1 - r_{02}^2)$ value of 30.7 per cent. To find out what proportion of the total variation in site size is accounted for by variation in available land alone we therefore calculate:

$$r_{01.2}^2 (1 - r_{02}^2) = (0.446)(1 - 0.693) = 0.137$$

That is to say, 13.7 per cent of the variation in site size is accounted for by variation in available land alone.

The corresponding quantity for land productivity has already been calculated in the course of obtaining the multiple R^2 value:

$$r_{02.1}^2 (1 - r_{01}^2) = (0.327)(1 - 0.746) = 0.083$$

Thus, 8.3 per cent of the variation in site size is accounted for by productivity alone.

Given that the overall multiple R^2 was 82.9 per cent and only 8.3 + 13.7 = 22 per cent is attributable to the separate effects of available land and land productivity, it appears that 60.9 per cent of the variation in site size is accounted for by the joint effect of the two independent variables, in that larger areas of available land tend to have greater fertility.

In this case then, as in many empirical situations, there is a not inconsiderable degree of overlap in the effects of the two variables, so that the multiple R^2 is not very much larger than the largest single value. The opposite extreme, of course, is when the independent variables are actually uncorrelated with one another, and then the R^2 formula reduces to

$$R^2_{0.12} = r^2_{01} + r^2_{02}$$

i.e. the variance accounted for is simply the sum of the two zero-order r^2 values. R^2 is obviously at its maximum in this situation, which is clearly preferable since it means that the two independents are accounting for *different parts* of the variation in the dependent. When they are correlated, on the other hand, they are accounting for the same variation and thus ambiguity is introduced into our interpretations. This problem, which can have complex technical ramifications in regression analysis (see for example Chatterjee and Price, 1977), is known as *collinearity* or *multicollinearity*.

One obvious way of recognising collinearity is by comparing the simple and multiple correlation coefficients. Suppose we have two independent variables, x_1 and x_2, and one dependent x_0. If we compare the zero-order r^2_{01} with the multiple $R^2_{0.12}$, the difference is the improvement in 'statistical explanation' achieved by adding in the second independent variable. If this improvement is very small, it suggests that the second variable is strongly correlated with the first, or that it is simply having no effect on the dependent. Which of these two possibilities is the case may be established by looking at the value of r^2_{12}, the coefficient of determination between the two independents themselves; if this is large it confirms that collinearity exists.

One way of getting round this problem is simply to drop one of the independent variables from the analysis; another way is to make the independent variables uncorrelated, for example by means of principal components analysis (see below), and then to regress the dependent variable against the principal components. On the other hand, we do not necessarily want to neglect or re-define the various relationships among the independents out of existence since they may themselves be quite informative, as in our site-size example.

THE MULTIPLE REGRESSION COEFFICIENT

Having examined the correlation issues we must now return to the multiple regression equation, which we looked at briefly at the beginning of the chapter. It was stated then that the slope coefficients of the equation (the bs) referred to the amount of change in the dependent for a given change in a specific independent, with the other independents held constant. The idea is clearly very similar to that involved in partial correlation and in fact the slope coefficients are known as *partial regression coefficients*. The notation is also very similar, so that we have:

$$\hat{x}_{0.1...k} = a_{0.1...k} + b_{01.2...k}\, x_1 + b_{02.1,3...k}\, x_2 + ... + b_{0k.1...k-1} x_k$$

Or in the three variable case:

$$\hat{x}_{0.12} = a_{0.12} + b_{01.2}\, x_1 + b_{02.1}\, x_2$$

a represents the intercept value, when the values of all the independent variables are zero.

The formulae for the a and b coefficients are:

$$a_{0.12} = \bar{x}_0 - b_{01.2}\bar{x}_1 - b_{02.1}\bar{x}_2$$

$$b_{01.2} = \frac{b_{01} - (b_{02})(b_{21})}{1 - (b_{12})(b_{21})}$$

It is easy to see that the formula for b is really very similar to that for partial r.

We now have a partial regression coefficient which indicates the absolute increase in our dependent variable associated with a unit increase in our first independent variable, the other independents being held constant, and, of course, we can do the same for all our independents.

The multiple regression equation for our example of site size regressed on area of available land and land productivity is:

$$\hat{x}_0 = -1.87 + 0.416x_1 + 50.3x_2$$

If, for illustrative purposes, we calculate the coefficient for x_1 using the formula given above and the results of the bivariate regressions calculated earlier in the chapter for these variables, we have:

$$b_{01.2} = \frac{0.656 - (97.9)(0.0048)}{1 - (114.0)(0.0048)} = \frac{0.1861}{0.4528} = 0.411$$

Rounding error is responsible for the slight difference between this and the coefficient of 0.416 above.

The equation tells us that the value of site size is best predicted by assuming that when area of available land and land productivity are 0, site size is -1.87 ha, and that it increases thereafter by 0.416 ha for each 1 km² increase in area of available land and by another 50.3 ha for each unit increase in the productivity index.

Suppose, however, that we want to compare our slope coefficients with one another so that we have a measure of the amount of increase/decrease in the dependent associated with a unit increase in each independent variable, in terms which are comparable from one variable to the next. This is likely to cause problems because the independent variables will almost certainly be measured on different scales; in the example given above, for instance, available land was measured in square kilometres and productivity on an arbitrary scale with a much smaller range. In these circumstances it is meaningless to compare a unit change in one variable with a unit change in another.

If we are interested in such relative rates of change what we have to do is transform our b coefficients into what are known as *beta coefficients*, or *beta weights*, standardised partial regression coefficients. To do this we standardise each variable by dividing it by its standard deviation, in other words we obtain its Z score, and on the basis of this we obtain adjusted slopes which are comparable from one variable to the next. In mathematical symbols we obtain

$$Z_{x_i} = \frac{(x_i - \bar{x}_i)}{s_{x_i}}$$

This, of course, gives us a variable with mean $\bar{x} = 0.0$ and

$s = 1.0$. We then have a transformed regression equation, which for the two-variable case is

$$\hat{Z}_{x\,0.12} = \beta_{01.2}Z_{x_1} + \beta_{02.1}Z_{x_2}$$

As we are dealing with Z scores, the mean of every variable is zero so that the a coefficient is also zero and therefore drops out of the equation.

Our standardised partial regression coefficients, or beta weights, thus indicate relative changes in variables on a standard scale. They are actually obtained through standardising the b coefficient by the ratio of the standard deviation of the two variables:

$$\beta_{01.2} = b_{01.2}\,\frac{s_{x_1}}{s_{x_0}}$$

or, more generally,

$$\beta_{ij.k} = b_{ij.k}\,\frac{s_j}{s_i}$$

Or alternatively by using the following formula based on the relevant correlation coefficients:

$$\beta_{01.2} = \frac{r_{01}-(r_{02})(r_{12})}{1-r_{12}^2}$$

The result of evaluating these formulae tells us the amount of change in the dependent produced by a *standardised* change in one of the independents when the others are controlled. Clearly, whether you use the ordinary b coefficient or the beta weight depends on whether you are interested in relative or absolute changes.

We can complete this section by calculating the multiple regression equation for our example using beta weights:

$$\beta_{01.2} = \frac{0.864-(0.832)(0.738)}{1-0.545} = 0.549$$

$$\beta_{02.1} = \frac{0.832-(0.864)(0.738)}{1-0.545} = 0.427$$

Thus we have

$$\hat{Z}_{x\,0.12} = 0.549\,Z_{x_1} + 0.427\,Z_{x_2}$$

That is to say, according to the equation, for each increase of one standard deviation in area of available land there is a corresponding increase of 0.549 standard deviations in site size; and for each one standard deviation increase in productivity there is an increase of 0.427 standard deviations in site size. The sum of these two effects gives our best prediction of site size, measured in terms of standard deviations from its mean, on the basis of the least-squares criterion. Comparison of the coefficients of each of the two independent variables indicates that a given increase in area of available agricultural land has a greater effect on site size than a given increase in land productivity, a comparison which may now be made in a valid fashion because the scales of the two variables have both been converted into the same units – units of standard deviation from the mean of their distribution.

An interesting example of an analysis using such multiple regression techniques models the income of English manors given in Domesday Book in terms of the various resources of the manors, for which data are also given (McDonald and Snooks, 1985).

ASSUMPTIONS

Now that we have described the basic procedures of multiple regression it is necessary to consider the assumptions behind it. The first point to emphasise here is that all the assumptions outlined in the previous chapter for simple bivariate regression also hold for multiple regression, with the extra ramification that in the latter they must hold for the relationship between the dependent and each of the independents. Furthermore, as we have seen already, the independent variables themselves should not be too strongly inter-correlated.

It will be obvious from this that the process of investigating whether the assumptions do indeed hold for a particular multiple regression analysis can be a complex one if there are many independent variables. Moreover, it is quite likely that for at least one or two of the relationships the assumptions will not be perfectly met, and the question then arises of the extent to which they may be ignored before the analysis becomes a meaningless one, a question to which there is not a straightforward answer.

The previous chapter provided guidance on the detection of problems and the solution of them and what was said there applies equally to multiple regression. The first step should always be to study the distributions of the individual variables to see that they are approximately normal; then to investigate the scattergrams of the various bivariate relationships to see that they are linear. Finally, the residuals from the multiple regression itself should be examined for patterning in their distribution.

Again to reiterate what was stated in the previous chapter, if the assumptions are not met it does not mean that a regression analysis cannot be carried out, but that appropriate action must be taken first. Very often this will raise complexities which require the involvement of a professional statistician.

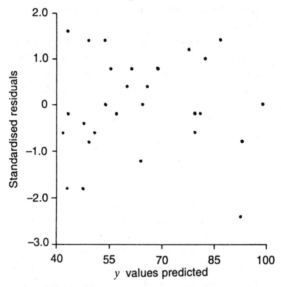

FIGURE 10.6. Scattergram of standardised residuals from multiple regression of site size on area of available land and land productivity, plotted against the site size values predicted by the multiple regression, from the data in Table 10.1.

As far as the example followed through in this chapter is concerned, it was noted above that some collinearity is present, leading to ambiguity in assessing the separate effects of area of available land and land productivity, but the extent of it is not so great as to cause the drastic problems illustrated by Johnston (1978, pp. 74–7). The variables for our example were constructed so as to have reasonably normal distributions, while the scattergrams shown earlier in this chapter (Figures 10.3–10.5) indicate that the various bivariate relationships are approximately linear. Finally, the scatterplot of the standardised residuals from the multiple regression against the *y* values predicted by it (Figure 10.6) shows no very obvious patterning to indicate that the assumptions have been violated.

LOG-LINEAR MODELLING

What has been described in the previous section is the standard version of multiple regression, in which it is assumed that dependent and independent variables are measured at an interval or ratio level. In fact, this is just one version of what is known as the *generalised linear model* (Lindsey, 1995; Everett and Dunn, 1983), in which variation in data values is accounted for in terms of the *additive* effects of a number of variables; in the example in the previous section variation in site size was accounted for in terms of the additive effects of area of available land and land productivity.

It is actually quite straightforward to extend the idea to cases where the independent variables are not numeric but are categorical ones; however, things are rather more complex if it is the dependent that is a nominal or ordinal scale variable. Archaeologists have encountered situations involving nominal scale dependent variables increasingly in recent years as a result of the growth of predictive modelling in the context of geographic information systems. In such studies information is available for each of a set of defined land units concerning the presence or absence of a site within the unit (the dependent variable) and various other attributes of the unit, such as its soil type, aspect and topographical position (independent variables). The object of the exercise is to use the landscape information to predict the probability that a particular land unit will contain a site. This is clearly of interest for management purposes but will also give us an idea of the kinds of factors that past people took into account when making their site location decisions. The relevant technique is known as *logistic modelling* or *logistic regression* if it involves quantitative as well as categorical independent variables. It has now been described and illustrated extensively in an archaeological geographical information systems context (e.g. Parker, 1985, Warren, 1990, Maschner and Stein, 1995) so it will not be described here. What we will look at is a technique which may be seen as an extension or generalisation of logistic modelling through which we can explore all the relationships between a set of categorical variables. The method is known as *log-linear modelling*.

The essence of the technique is to build models of the possible relationships between variables in the data set, to derive expected values for these different models, and to decide which model best fits the data by comparing the expected values produced by the models with the observed data values, with the stipulation that the model selected should be the simplest which shows a reasonable fit between observed and expected.

The log-linear bit comes into the building of the models; the following discussion of what this involves is influenced by Lewis (1986). The simplest possible model is the null hypothesis of independence; in other words, variation in any one variable is not related to that in any of the others. In the chapter on the chi-squared test we saw that in order to find the expected value for a given cell of the table we multiplied the row sum by the column sum and divided by the total number of observations.

$$\text{expected value} = \frac{(\text{row sum})(\text{column sum})}{\text{total number of observations}}$$

We obtained the expected value by a process of multiplication and division. If, however, we wanted the log of the expected value we could change this as follows:

log (expected value) = log (row sum) + log (column sum) − log (total number of observations)

Because with logarithms addition corresponds to normal multiplication and subtraction to normal division, we now add and subtract instead of multiplying and dividing. As our expression for the expected value now only involves addition and subtraction it is said to be *additive*, or *linear*, in the logarithms of the original values. As we have seen, such linear models are more straightforward to handle.

Suppose that, having worked out the log of the expected value in the way illustrated, it is considerably different from the log of the observed value. What this means is that modelling the expected value in terms of the row sum, the column sum and the total number of observations is insufficient. Something is missing. If we now postulate that our two variables are related and *add* an extra term to our equation to take account of this relationship then, if we're only dealing with two variables, we will find that our new model fits perfectly. If we're dealing with *more than* two variables we can successively add extra terms to the equation, trying to improve the fit between expected and observed. Our choice between the various possible models will be determined by the goodness of the fit and the criterion of simplicity.

TABLE 10.2. Volume of grave cist tabulated against the sex of the individual buried and against the individual's estimated height.

| | | Volume of grave cist | |
		≤ 1.5 m³	> 1.5 m³
Est. height	M	18	4
≤ 155 cm	F	30	6
Est. height	M	4	43
> 155 cm	F	3	20

As usual, what is involved is best illustrated by means of an example. Let us consider again the example from Chapter 7 where we were trying to understand the relationship between the volume of the grave pits, and the height and sex of the individuals buried in them, in an analysis of a hypothetical cemetery of single inhumation burials (see Table 10.2). The simplest model to test for this table is that the three variables are unrelated to one another, the most basic null hypothesis in other words. We can write out this model as follows, for the top left cell in Table 10.2, using the approach described above:

log (expected number of small males in small grave pits) =
  log (total number of males) +

log (total number of small grave pits) +
log (total number of small individuals) –
log (total number of observations)

What it says is that the total number of small males in small grave pits is simply a function of the total number of males, small grave pits and small individuals, taking into account the total number of observations.

TABLE 10.3. Expected values added to the data in Table 10.2.

		Volume of grave cist	
		≤ 1.5 m³	> 1.5 m³
Est. height	M	18(13.4)	4(17.8)
≤ 155 cm	F	30(11.5)	6(15.3)
Est. height	M	4(16.2)	43(21.5)
> 155 cm	F	3(13.9)	20(18.4)

If this is a good model then the expected number of small males in small grave pits which it produces will be very close to the actual number. If it's not, then of course there will be a discrepancy. We can model the expected numbers for all the cells of the table in this way, and if there are a lot of discrepancies between observed and expected values the resulting chi-squared value will be statistically significant. The expected and observed values for the example are shown in Table 10.3 and the test for the difference between them can now be carried out. In fact, for reasons which will become apparent below, the chi-squared statistic is not used, but a statistic which is equivalent to it, known as G^2.

$$G^2 = 2\sum[(\text{observed})\log_e \frac{\text{observed}}{\text{expected}}]$$

where summation is over all the cells in the table. For the example considered here we have

$$G^2 = 2[18\log_e(18/13.4)+4\log_e(4/17.8)+30\log_e(30/11.5)$$

$$+6\log_e(6/15.3)+4\log_e(4/16.2)+43\log_e(43/21.5)$$

$$+3\log_e(3/13.9)+20\log_e(20/18.4)] = 87.54$$

The statistical significance of the G^2 value may be obtained from the chi-squared table, but of course this requires us to know the correct number of degrees of freedom for our example: degrees of freedom = (number of cells) − (number of quantities estimated from the data). There are eight cells and we have had to obtain four quantities from the data (number of males, number of small grave pits, number of small individuals and the total number of observations), so here the number of degrees of freedom is four. With four degrees of freedom the G^2 value is very highly significant. The null hypothesis that the three variables are independent of one another must be rejected.

The next step is to try to improve our model. Since independence doesn't hold there must be relationships between sex, grave-pit size and individual height which we haven't taken into account. The possibilities here are quite considerable. First, any single pair of these variables may be related:

> sex and grave-pit size
> sex and individual height
> individual height and grave-pit size

At a more complex level any two pairs may be related:

> sex and grave-pit size, and at the same time sex and height
> grave-pit size and sex, and grave-pit size and height
> height and sex, and at the same time height and grave-pit size

More complex again, all three pairs may be related:

> sex and grave-pit size, and sex and height, and grave-pit size and height

Finally, all three variables may be simultaneously related to one another: thus sex may be related to grave-pit size not just directly, or pairwise, but indirectly via height as well, and this may be true of all three variables.

It is possible to see that as you work through the levels of complexity, each one includes the one below, so that if two pairs of variables are related this obviously implies that one pair was related at the previous step; similarly, for three pairs to be related two pairs must be at the level before.

The idea is to start at the simplest level and work up the hierarchy of complexity, stopping with the simplest model that fits the data. At each successive level of complexity a degree of freedom is lost, since the data are being used to estimate the association between each pair of variables. Thus, on our model of independence, or no association, that we started with there were four degrees of freedom. By the time we get to the highest level of complexity, where all three variables are simultaneously related to one another, there are no degrees of freedom left at all. The expected numbers would correspond to the observed numbers and we would simply be reproducing the data we started with, so this final model, which is said in the jargon to be *saturated*, does not have much interest!

The discussion above is summarised in Table 10.4 (based on Fienberg, 1980), which lists the various models, the number of degrees of freedom associated with them and their descriptions in terms of mathematical symbols, using Fienberg's notation. You should note that for models 2 and 3 only one of the three possible options is listed.

TABLE 10.4. Possible log-linear models for the relationships between three variables.

Model	d.f.	Abbreviation	Symbolic description
1. No association	4	[1][2][3]	$\log E_{ijk} = u + u_1 + u_2 + u_3$
2. Association of 1 pair of variables	3	[12][3]	$\log E_{ijk} = u + u_1 + u_2 + u_3 + u_{12}$
3. Association of 2 pairs of variables	2	[12][23]	$\log E_{ijk} = u + u_1 + u_2 + u_3 + u_{12} + u_{23}$
4. Association of 3 pairs of variables	1	[12][23]]13]	$\log E_{ijk} = u + u_1 + u_2 + u_3 + u_{12} + u_{23} + u_{13}$
5. Interaction between all 3	0	[123]	$\log E_{ijk} = u + u_1 + u_2 + u_3 + u_{12} + u_{23} + u_{13} + u_{123}$

To illustrate how the equations are to be read, let us take that for model 3 in relation to our example, assuming that, as when we were testing for independence, we want the expected value for the number of small males in small grave-pits, but now postulating that there is a relationship between sex and grave-pit size, and between grave-pit size and height.

log (expected number of small males in small grave pits) $[\log E_{ijk}] =$

log (total number of observations) $[u]$ +
log (total number of males) $[u_1]$ +
log (total number of small grave pits) $[u_2]$ +
log (total number of small individuals) $[u_3]$ +
log (interaction between sex and grave-pit size) $[u_{12}]$ +
log (interaction between grave-pit size and height) $[u_{23}]$

Having already rejected the model of no association for our example we can now set up and test the various possible level-2 models, postulating an association between any one of the pairs:

2(a) sex and grave-pit size
2(b) individual height and grave-pit size
2(c) sex and individual height

TABLE 10.5. Expected values for model 2a added to the data in Table 10.2.

		Volume of grave cist	
		≤ 1.5 m³	> 1.5 m³
Est. height	M	18(10.0)	4(21.3)
≤ 155 cm	F	30(15.0)	6(11.8)
Est. height	M	4 (12.0)	43(25.7)
> 155 cm	F	3 (18.0)	20(14.2)

TABLE 10.6. Expected values for model 2b added to the data in Table 10.2.

		Volume of grave cist	
		≤ 1.5 m³	> 1.5 m³
M	≤ 155 cm	18(25.9)	4 (5.4)
	> 155 cm	4 (3.8)	43(34.0)
F	≤ 155 cm	30(22.1)	6 (4.6)
	> 155 cm	3 (3.2)	20(29.0)

TABLE 10.7. Expected values for model 2c added to the data in Table 10.2.

		Sex	
		M	F
≤ 1.5 m³	≤ 155 cm	18 (9.5)	30(15.5)
	> 155 cm	4(20.2)	3 (9.9)
> 1.5 m³	≤ 155 cm	4(12.6)	6(20.5)
	> 155 cm	43(26.8)	20(13.1)

Tables 10.5–10.7 show the observed values for the data, together with the expected values under each of these models. The G^2 (chi-squared equivalent) values for these different models, and for the initial test of independence, are shown in Table 10.8, where variable 1 = sex, 2 = volume and 3 = height.

TABLE 10.8. Summary of fit of log-linear models of relationships between sex, height and grave-pit volume.

Model	Abbreviation	G^2	d.f.
1. No association	[1][2][3]	87.54	4
2. Association of 1 pair of variables:			
a)	[12][3]	79.70	3
b)	[1][23]	11.38	3
c)	[13][2]	76.17	3

All these G^2 values are significant at least at the 0.01 level, which means that it is highly improbable that any of these models fit the data values: the differences between the observed values and the values expected under the model are too great. Nevertheless, it is clear that model 2b, presupposing a relationship between height and volume, produces a marked drop in the G^2 value and provides the best fit of any of the models tried so far.

Let us move up to the next level, and models which presuppose relationships between two pairs of variables.

3(a) sex and height are related and so are height and grave-pit size; sex and grave-pit size are not related.

3(b) sex and height are related and so are sex and grave-pit size; height and grave-pit size are not related.

3(c) sex and grave-pit size are related, height and grave-pit size are related, but sex and height are not related.

TABLE 10.9. Expected values for model 3a added to the data in Table 10.2.

| | | *Volume of grave cist* | |
		≤ 1.5 m³	*> 1.5 m³*
Est. height	M	18(18.2)	4 (3.8)
≤ 155 cm	F	30(29.8)	6 (6.2)
Est. height	M	4 (4.7)	43(42.3)
> 155 cm	F	3 (2.3)	20(20.7)

TABLE 10.10. Expected values for model 3b added to the data in Table 10.2.

| | | *Volume of grave cist* | |
		≤ 1.5 m³	*> 1.5 m³*
M	≤ 155 cm	18 (7.0)	4(15.0)
	> 155 cm	4(15.0)	43(32.0)
F	≤ 155 cm	30(20.1)	6 (15.9)
	> 155 cm	3(12.9)	20(10.1)

TABLE 10.11. Expected values for model 3c added to the data in Table 10.2.

| | | *Sex* | |
		M	*F*
≤ 1.5 m³	≤ 155 cm	18(19.2)	30(28.8)
	> 155 cm	4 (2.8)	3 (4.2)
> 1.5 m³	≤ 155 cm	4 (6.5)	6 (3.5)
	> 155 cm	43(40.5)	20(22.5)

Tables 10.9–10.11 show the observed values for the data again, but now with the expected values for each of the three

level-3 models. A look at these indicates immediately that the fit of model 3(a) is excellent, that of 3(b) is very poor while that of 3(c) is also good. The G^2 goodness-of-fit values for these three models and all the others we have looked at are presented together in Table 10.12, with all results which are statistically significant at the 0.05 level marked by an asterisk.

TABLE 10.12. Summary of fit of log-linear models of relationships between sex, height and grave-pit volume.

Model	Abbreviation	G^2	d.f.
1. No association	[1][2][3]	87.54*	4
2. Association of 1 pair of variables:			
a)	[12][3]	79.70*	3
b)	[1][23]	11.38*	3
c)	[13][2]	76.17*	3
3. Association of 2 pairs of variables:			
a)	[13][23]	0.36	2
b)	[12][13]	69.17*	2
c)	[12][23]	3.98	2

It is when we come to comparing the results in a table like this that the use of G^2 rather than chi-squared becomes important. If we take, for example, the G^2 value for a level-2 model, say model 2(b), and subtract it from the G^2 value for the level-1 model of independence, the difference between them is a measure of the improvement in goodness-of-fit. In this case $87.54 - 11.38 = 76.16$. Such comparisons can be carried out between models at any two different levels. We could, for example, obtain the difference between the level-1 G^2 and that for model 3(a): $87.54 - 0.36 = 87.18$, the improvement obtained by predicting the cell values not on the assumption of independence but on the assumption of a relationship between variables 1 and 3 (sex and height) and 2 and 3 (height and grave-pit size).

Furthermore, the differences may be tested for statistical significance, using the number of degrees of freedom obtained by subtracting the number of degrees of freedom for the higher level model from the number for the lower level. Thus, for our second example above, the number of degrees of freedom for the level-1 model of no association is four, the number for model 3(a) is two, so we have a G^2 difference of 87.18 with two degrees of freedom, which we can look up in the chi-squared table to establish its statistical significance. If the more complex model produces a statistically significant decrease in G^2 then we can adopt it.

When we look at the results for the level-3 models we see that two of the three G^2 values represent a considerable improvement over those of level 2. The one which does not, model 3(b), has a worse fit than model 2(b), and this occasions no surprise because it leaves out the relationship between variables 2 and 3, pit size and individual height, which model 2(b) established as very important.

Clearly, the best-fitting model is model 3(a), with a G^2 value of almost zero, indicating a virtually perfect fit between the expectations of this model and the data values. Is it significantly better than model 2(b)? Let us compare the G^2 values: 11.38 $- 0.36 = 11.02$ with one degree of freedom, which is highly significant. The appropriate model, following the formulation of Table 10.4 is:

$$u + u_1 + u_2 + u_3 + u_{23} + u_{13}$$

Again, if we want to relate this to the predicted value for a particular cell, and take as usual the cell representing small males in small grave pits, we have

log (expected number of small males in small grave pits) =
    log (total number of observations) +
    log (total number of males) +
    log (total number of small grave pits) +
    log (total number of small individuals) +
    log (interaction between grave-pit size and height) +
    log (interaction between sex and height)

In other words, the grave-pit size is related to the individual's height and the individual's height is related to their sex, but sex and grave-pit size are not directly related. These relationships, which make intuitive sense, account for what is going on in the data, and there is no need to move to a higher level of complexity.

By now the kinship between the log-linear modelling

technique and the standard multiple regression described in the main part of this chapter should be readily apparent. In both cases the logic of the approach is fairly straightforward and since in practice they are always carried out by computer-based statistics programs, the details of the calculations, for example those involved in obtaining the expected values for the different models, do not present any problems.

A recent study by Maschner and Stein (1995) analysed site locations on the north-west coast of North America using both logistic regression and log-linear modelling. The logistic regression indicated that using four variables – climatic exposure, beach quality, solar exposure and island size – an accurate prediction of site presence was possible for 84 per cent of the sites in the sample. However, they felt that this analysis did not go far enough because it failed to address the potential inter-relationships between the four site location variables; they therefore explored these using log-linear modelling.

In this case they found that they needed to include not just pairwise interactions between variables, as in the example presented above, but a three-way interaction, between island size, beach quality and solar exposure. That is to say, sites on the large island tended to have good beaches and southerly exposures while medium-sized and smaller islands tended to have sites that were more often northerly exposed, with poorer beach quality. Climatic exposure, on the other hand, was completely independent of the other three variables, implying that sheltered locations were preferred regardless of island size, quality of beach or solar exposure (Maschner and Stein, 1995, p. 70).

Distance to water, as an ordinal scale variable, was then added to the model to see what effect this would have. In fact, it did not alter any of the results of the first model but did show a relationship to island size, in that sites on large and medium-sized islands tended to be chosen close to a source of water but on the small islands water was not a significant determinant of site location because of its scarcity. Finally, site area, again measured on an ordinal scale, was added to the model and found to be completely independent of the locational variables. In other words, given that beach quality, solar exposure, island size and climatic exposure were always relevant to site location there was no further differentiation in terms of locational variables for sites of different sizes. Insofar as site size relates to scale and/or duration of occupation, these seem to relate to factors other than those considered in this study. As Maschner and Stein (1995, p. 72) point out, this negative conclusion is still a very important one.

In summary then, the facilities which log-linear modelling (of which logistic modelling may be seen as a special case, cf. Lindsey, 1995, pp. 55–7) provides to dissect the relationships between nominal and ordinal scale variables can be enormously useful in teasing out the connections, and their absence, between complex sets of factors.

EXERCISES

10.1 In an archaeological study of factors affecting the density of obsidian at a series of large early Classic sites in Mesoamerica it is hypothesised that distance from the source and site size, reflecting functional importance, are the important variables. Given the information below (data from Sidrys, 1977), is this the case? Use multiple regression and multiple and partial correlation methods to assist you in drawing your conclusion.

Obsidian density *(g/m³ earth)*	*Distance from source* *(km)*	*Site size* *(ha)*
38	70	32
32	105	16
35	110	24
23	110	14
18	145	33
23	160	30
27	150	29
30	165	40
14	195	65
22	205	44
16	240	37
21	260	48
7	280	59

10.2 In a study of the relationship between the economies of Roman villas and adjacent towns, the proportions of cattle in the faunal assemblages at a number of villas are noted, together with the distances of the villas from the nearest town and the dates at which they were occupied. The correlations are as follows:

Distance from town-proportion of cattle $r = 0.72$
Date-proportion of cattle $r = 0.55$
Date-distance from town $r = 0.60$

Discuss the relationship between these variables.

10.3 A study has been carried out of the material culture at a number of nineteenth-century frontier forts in Canada to investigate whether known ethnic differences in the people present at the forts are reflected in patterns of personal consumption of material items. The analysis is based on material from two sets of forts: one set occupied by French Canadian men, the other by men from Orkney. Clearly, ethnicity may not be the only relevant factor and three other variables have also been considered: assemblage size, length of site occupation and the region where the fort is situated. The specific question is, to what extent do these different variables, and ethnic identity in particular, affect artefact diversity, i.e. the number of different types of artefacts present at the forts.

Below are the results of a multiple regression analysis carried out to investigate the extent to which these factors do affect assemblage diversity. What conclusions do you draw?

$R^2 = 0.974$

	Beta weight value	SE of this value
Assemblage size	0.007	0.002
Occupation length	− 0.07	0.142
Ethnicity	24.74	3.62
Region	− 1.32	1.64

10.4 An analysis is being carried out of the formation processes affecting the archaeological deposits found in the rooms of Pueblo structures in the south-western United States. A question of particular interest is the relation between the activities going on in the rooms when they were in normal use, believed to be represented by deposits from the floors of the rooms, and subsequent activities, believed to include rubbish-dumping and 'squatting' in abandoned rooms, and to be represented by deposits from the room fills as opposed to the floor. The main body of data available for investigating this issue is the pottery from the various deposits. The tables below show the results of correlation analyses based on thirty rooms, in which the three variables are:

1. The floor area of the room in which the pottery was found
2. The density of pottery on the floor of the room
3. The density of pottery in the fill of the room

Discuss the results from a statistical and an archaeological point of view, with special reference to the question of the relationship between the pottery from the fill deposits and the other two variables.

Multiple regression with fill sherds as dependent:
$R^2 = 0.22$
Floor area contribution (r_{01}^2): 0.19
Floor sherd density contribution ($r_{02.1}^2 (1-r_{01}^2)$): 0.03

Zero order correlations

	Floor area	*Fill sherds*	*Floor sherds*
Floor area	1.00	0.44	0.80
Fill sherds	0.44	1.00	0.45
Floor sherds	0.80	0.45	1.00

Partial correlations

	Floor area	*Fill sherds*	*Floor sherds*
Floor area	1.00	0.15	0.75
Fill sherds	0.15	1.00	0.18
Floor sherds	0.75	0.18	1.00

Eleven

CLASSIFICATION AND CLUSTER ANALYSIS

The previous chapter represented an increase in the level of complexity compared with earlier ones because it involved the analysis of multiple variables. However, it was largely concerned with the case where one variable could be considered a dependent, affected by a set of independents whose links had to be taken into account to obtain a satisfactory analysis of their effect on the dependent. In the next two chapters we will look at techniques for analysing data described in terms of many variables, where we make no stipulations or assumptions about dependents and independents. The items may be graves described in terms of counts of different types of grave goods present; lithic assemblages described in terms of counts of different lithic types; ceramic compositions described in terms of proportions of different elements; ceramics described in terms of the presence/absence of particular decorative motifs; or handaxes whose shapes are characterised by a set of measurements. The range of possibilities is endless.

Faced with trying to get a grip on such complexity we may have a number of aims: to look for archaeologically significant groupings in the items, to look for archaeologically significant patterns of association between the variables, and to relate these patterns to some other factor(s) believed to be relevant to accounting for them. For example, we might want to relate our ceramic compositions to the use of different clays, or changing handaxe shapes to a chronological trend in the manufacture of different forms.

These are tasks which archaeologists have always carried out, since long before the application of quantitative methods to their subject. Classification in particular, as with biology, was important to archaeology from the start, since it provided the basis for bringing order to the mass of material being recovered from the ground. The main aim of such work was to create so-called 'space-time systematics' – to define coherent patterns in space and time. Thus, artefact types and styles were defined and their chronological range and spatial distribution were identified. On the basis of consistent patterns of co-occurrence between different types in specific places and times archaeological cultures were defined and taken as evidence of the social traditions of human groups. All this was done essentially intuitively by people who had acquired expertise as a result of training and exposure to the material. Clarke (1968) referred to it as an 'intuitive manipulative dexterity learned by rote'. Much of the inspiration for the approach came from art history and one of the classic examples of its use was Beazley's definition of particular examples of Classical Greek Black Figure and Red Figure pottery as the products of particular vase painters (Beazley, 1963).

From the 1950s onwards certain people began to argue that such patterns were best defined mathematically since mathematical methods eliminated the subjectivity inherent in the intuitive approaches and were repeatable, so that two different people working on the same material would get the same result. In the 1960s the advent of processual archaeology led to an interest in new goals, such as social reconstruction, the definition of exchange patterns and the specification of lithic toolkits, which again depended on grouping items together and specifying links between variables, thus providing a new set of reasons for using mathematical methods by archaeologists who were temperamentally and ideologically inclined to do so as part of their espousal of a new approach.

Although much theoretical water has gone under the bridge since then, the justification for the use of multivariate analysis techniques remains the fact that they provide a set of extremely useful tools for grouping items together and specifying links between variables. First, their use helps to make the basis of any groupings of items or variables more explicit. Second, given the frequent need to seek order in large numbers of items described in terms of large numbers of variables – what Read (1989) refers to as the complexity threshold – they can reveal patterning present in the data which would otherwise fail to emerge. Of course, they aren't the only way of doing this – sometimes more traditional and more intuitive methods are perfectly appropriate.

The use of multivariate methods obviously presupposes that we have an appropriate description of the objects of interest we are analysing, as we emphasised in Chapter 1. We describe with a purpose in mind, implicit or explicit, and it is far better that it should be explicit, so that we give active thought to the descriptive variables we select, and the way in which we construct them, in relation to that purpose, whether it is the definition of spatial and chronological variation or any other. Read (1994; Read and Russell, 1996) has pointed out that there is sometimes a tendency to create and throw in as many variables as we can think of when carrying out a multivariate analysis in the belief that 'it will all come out in the wash', that is to say, any meaningful patterns will emerge. But in fact such meaningful patterns in some variables can potentially be obscured by including variables which aren't relevant to those particular distinctions, as he demonstrates. Once again, the importance of the hard *archaeological* work of thinking through our description cannot be over-emphasised.

Furthermore, different multivariate methods have different properties, which produce different results. They are objective in the sense that once the choices are made they can be carried through consistently and mechanically by means of a computer. Nevertheless, the choices must be made in the light of the particular problem and data in question: they should not be arbitrary, nor can they be regarded as objective, but they should be reasoned, on both archaeological and methodological grounds. Some of the methodological issues will be discussed below.

This discussion does not mean that in our description of the data and our use of analytical methods we are simply *imposing* order on the world. The view taken here is that structure and order in our data may or may not exist, but their existence and form, if any, are waiting to be *discovered*. Any structure will be with respect to our description, and our methods of analysis may hide it, distort it or reveal it, but the very possibility of these alternatives indicates the contingent reality of its existence.

This approach is very similar to that of Wright (1989), who

sees multivariate analysis as the analysis of tables of data to search for latent structure, where structure depends on the strength and pattern of associations between variables. If you have a large data table:

> The task of intuitively discovering the degree of structure by eye is a hopeless one. This means that we are acknowledging that structure can be latent. Latent structure, like the latent image on an exposed photographic film, needs developing. A multivariate method, using the photographic analogy, is a developer of structure. It is only a developer – it cannot create structure where none is already latent. In fact, we can extend the photographic analogy further. Just as we may use the developer on our film and find no image, so may we use our multivariate method on our table and find no structure (or find only a 'fog', too insubstantial to attribute to anything other than chance). (Wright, 1989, pp. 10–11)

In what follows the object will be to demonstrate the validity of these assertions, describe some of the main techniques and look at some of the complications and difficulties which arise in their use and interpretation. But while it is important not to underestimate these, that is not at all the same as rejecting the use of such methods in principle.

SOME PRELIMINARY DEFINITIONS AND DISTINCTIONS

The multivariate methods to be described in detail in this chapter and the next two may be divided into two groups: those which operate on a table or matrix of items described in terms of a set of variables, and those which operate on a table of similarities or distances between each item and every other derived from the initial table of items and variables. The former are arguably more useful and productive in many circumstances (the issues will be examined below) and to some extent, as they have developed, they have come to take over some of the role previously filled by the similarity-based methods, which developed earlier; they are treated in the next chapter. However, similarity- and distance-based methods still have an important role, as Krzanowski (1988, pp. 88–9) points out. These are described first, in the current chapter, not least because they are close in many respects to more traditional non-numerical approaches to archaeological classification. Before doing this, however, we need to make a further set of distinctions.

Broadly speaking, *classification proper* is concerned with the definition of groupings in a set of data, based on some idea that the members of a group should be more similar to one another than they are to non-members; within-group similarity should be in some sense greater than between-group similarity; alternatively expressed, groups should exhibit internal cohesion and external isolation (Cormack, 1971). The aim in classification studies is generally to *discover* the pattern of groupings in a set of data, with as few assumptions as possible about the nature of the grouping (cf. Gordon, 1981, p. 5). This is generally done by means of *cluster analysis*.

This may be contrasted with the procedure of *discrimination*, which presupposes the existence of a given number of known groups and is concerned with the allocation of individual items to those groups to which they belong most appropriately. It might be used, for example, to allocate a new find to the most appropriate of the categories in an existing classification. Alternatively, it can be employed to investigate the way in which a categorisation relates to another set of variables. For example, we may have a number of ceramic vessels from different sites and the vessels may be characterised in terms of a series of measurements describing their shape: do the vessel shapes differ from site to site? The problem becomes: given the division of vessels between sites, is that division reproduced when we attempt to divide up the vessels on the basis of the variables defining their shape (cf. Read, 1982)? Answering such a question involves discrimination and not classification; the basic ideas behind the method are briefly described in Chapter 14.

Another procedure again is *dissection*. In some cases we may know that our data are not divisible into groups which exhibit internal cohesion and external isolation: there is simply a continuous scatter of points in which no natural division can be made. Nevertheless, it might be that for some purpose we would wish to divide them up; such a more or less arbitrary division would be a dissection (cf. Gordon, 1981, p. 5).

A much more important set of procedures goes under the

general heading of *ordination*. We saw when we were looking at regression analysis that if we have information about a number of items in terms of their values on two variables we can represent the relations between the items by means of a scattergram, the axes of which are defined by the two variables in question. In the chapter on multiple regression we saw that such a representation was impossible with more than three variables. Clearly then, looking visually for groups of similar items when they are described in terms of a large number of variables is impossible: there are too many dimensions. The aim of ordination methods is, among other things, to represent and display the relationships between items in a low-dimensional space – generally of two or at most three dimensions – while still retaining as much as possible of the information contained in all the descriptive variables. A visual check of the scattergram will indicate whether groups – defined as areas of relatively high point density – are present. Ordination methods are the subject of the next chapter and are usually based on the direct analysis of the items and their descriptive variables but they do not have to be; they can also be used on tables of similarities or distances. They are generally regarded as the most informative multivariate techniques. The results of such analyses can be used as input to methods of clustering, or classification proper, as described above.

Within classification proper we can usefully make some further distinctions, in terms of the different ways in which it is possible to go about group formation, or clustering. One category is known as *partitioning* methods (Gordon, 1981, pp. 9–10). The use of these involves making a decision about the number of groups in which we are interested (this point will be qualified below), but unlike discrimination does not require any specification of the sizes of the different groups. Individuals are grouped together with those with which they are in some sense most similar, so that the specified number of groups is formed.

The other main category is that of *hierarchical* methods, which can themselves be subdivided into *agglomerative* and *divisive* groups. Hierarchical agglomerative methods start with all the items under consideration separate and then build up groups from these, starting by grouping the most similar items together, then grouping the groups at increasingly low levels of similarity until finally all the items are linked together in one large group, usually at a very low level of similarity. Divisive methods start with all the items in a single group and then proceed to divide the groups up successively according to some criterion. In both types of hierarchical method the relationships between the items and the groups may be represented in the form of a tree diagram or *dendrogram*.

All these cluster analysis methods, but perhaps particularly the divisive ones, to some extent impose their own patterning on the data, as we will see. A divisive method, for example, will impose a series of divisions on a set of data regardless of whether the resulting groups represent genuine distinctions or an arbitrary dissection. Thus, the results of cluster analysis have to be treated with care.

SIMILARITY AND DISTANCE MEASURES

It has already been said that prior to the use of any cluster analysis method (except the divisive ones) it is necessary to have some measure which expresses the relationships between the individuals in the analysis. We have generally talked about assessing the similarity between items but we can also talk about distances rather than similarities, and in general terms one can be regarded as the converse of the other (cf. Späth, 1980, pp. 15–16).

TABLE 11.1. Matrix of similarities between four hypothetical ceramic assemblages, using the Robinson coefficient of agreement.

	1	2	3	4
1	200	14	11	9
2	14	200	147	163
3	11	147	200	157
4	9	163	157	200

As already noted above, methods of numerical classification are based on an $n \times n$ matrix of similarities or distances between the n objects being studied, so the first step in an analysis is to compute this matrix. An example of such a matrix of the similarities between four items, in this case hypothetical ceramic assemblages, is shown in Table 11.1. Down the *principal diagonal* of the matrix run the similarities of each object with itself, obviously the maximum possible, in this case 200 (see below pp. 233–4 for an explanation of this coefficient). In fact, of course, we don't need all the matrix because the two halves, above and below the principal diagonal, are mirror images of one another. Thus, s_{12}, the similarity between items 1 and 2, is the same as s_{21}, that between items 2 and 1, in this case 14. A matrix such as this is said to be a *symmetric* matrix and only one or other half is needed for analysis. Most distance or similarity matrices are symmetric in this way.

The similarity or distance coefficients which it is possible to enter into such a matrix are many and varied (see for example Sneath and Sokal, 1973; Wishart, 1987). They have different properties and some are appropriate for quantitative numeric data while others are based on qualitative presence/absence data; choices should not be made without thought. Here it will only be possible to examine a few of the most important ones.

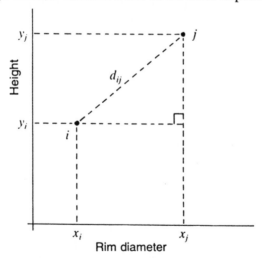

FIGURE 11.1. Scattergram of height against rim diameter for four ceramic vessels, showing the definition of Euclidean distance between vessels *i* and *j*.

The measure most commonly used with interval or ratio scale data is the *Euclidean distance coefficient*. Given two variables,

i and j, measured in terms of a number of variables, p, the Euclidean distance coefficient, d_{ij} is defined as

$$d_{ij} = \sqrt{\sum_{k=1}^{p} (x_{ik} - x_{jk})^2}$$

This is simply the straight line distance between two points and what its calculation involves, of course, is Pythagoras' theorem. It is best illustrated with a two-dimensional example. Suppose we want to measure the straight line distance between a number of vessels in terms of their height and rim diameter (Figure 11.1). We take the distance between each pair of objects, i and j, on the x axis, $(x_i - x_j)$, that between them on their y axis, $(y_i - y_j)$, square these two distances, add them together and take the square root. Thus, in this case

$$d_{ij} = \sqrt{(x_i - x_j)^2 + (y_i - y_j)^2}$$

Carrying out this operation for every pair of points gives a matrix of distances between them, like the tables of distances between towns that one finds in road atlases.

If there are more than two variables then we have to add in extra $(x_{ik} - x_{jk})^2$ terms so that there is one for every descriptive variable, before taking the square root, and that is what the general formula tells us to do.

When two points are in the same place – the items are identical in other words – d_{ij} is zero; the opposite possible extreme value is in principle infinity – the two points are infinitely far apart – but in practice the maximum distance in any given case will be that between the two most dissimilar items in the data set.

A problem arises with this measure concerning the scale of the axes. This is particularly the case when the measurements of the items under study are all to the same scale but range within different limits. Such a problem would arise if, for example, we were interested in classifying bronze swords in terms of measurements of their length, breadth and thickness. Clearly, length is likely to vary over a much greater range than thickness and accordingly will have a much greater effect on the classification.

If we want to counteract effects of this kind it is necessary to standardise the measurement scales, and the convention most commonly used is to give each variable equal weight by transforming the observed values into standard scores, as described in Chapter 6.

There is, however, another problem in the use of the Euclidean distance measure since it presupposes that the axes of the space defined by the variables in the analysis are at right-angles to one another, so that we have a rectangular coordinate system. This point will become clearer to you when you have read the next chapter, but we can say now that the axes will only be at right angles to one another (or *orthogonal* to use the jargon term) when the variables are completely independent of one another, which in practice will never be the case. If the variables are intercorrelated and therefore the axes are not at right angles, then the d_{ij}s will be over- or under-estimated by an amount depending on the size of the correlation and whether it is positive or negative.

The most common solution to this problem is to make sure the axes are at right angles by defining the distance measure not on the original variables but on the axes defined by the principal components derived from the variables, as we will see in the following chapter; but alternative methods are also available (see for example Johnston, 1978, pp. 217–19; Mather, 1976, pp. 313–14; Everitt, 1980, p. 57). The issues are extensively discussed by Baxter (1994, pp. 167–70).

Although a variety of other similarity/distance measures in addition to Euclidean distance are available for use with interval- and ratio-scale data, only one more will be mentioned here, a measure based on summing the absolute differences rather than the squared differences between the points, for each variable, thus:

$$d_{ij} = \sum_{k=1}^{p} | x_{ik} - x_{jk} |$$

This tells us to take the difference between points i and j in terms of their values on each variable in turn, for as many variables as there are in the analysis, and to add the differences together, without squaring them and without regard as to whether they are positive or negative (the modulus symbol – the vertical lines – tells us to ignore the sign of the differences). This distance measure is known as a *city-block metric*; why this is so may be shown by a two-dimensional example, illustrated in Figure 11.2. The formula in this case requires us to take the difference between i and j on the first variable $|x_i - x_j|$ and the difference between them on the second variable $|y_i - y_j|$ and add the two together. This gives us a distance measure made up of two straight lines turning a corner.

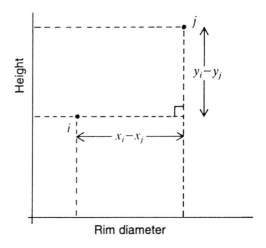

FIGURE 11.2. Scattergram of height against rim diameter for two ceramic vessels (i and j), showing the definition of city-block distance between the two.

If we now turn to appropriate measures of similarity between items for use with presence/absence (or dichotomous) data we find an enormous variety of coefficients, all of which do slightly different things. The major difference between them is in the question of whether or not they take *negative matches* into account, a negative match being the situation where neither of the units or individuals under consideration possesses the attribute in question. The point may be illustrated by means of an example. Suppose we have two graves scored in terms of whether or not they possess certain grave good types, as in Table 11.2.

TABLE 11.2. Two graves scored in terms of the presence/absence of ten different grave-goods types.

	Goods types									
	1	*2*	*3*	*4*	*5*	*6*	*7*	*8*	*9*	*10*
Grave 1	1	0	1	1	0	0	0	1	1	0
Grave 2	1	0	0	1	1	0	0	1	0	0

In this example we have assumed that there are ten different grave goods types present in our data set as a whole, but that types 2, 6, 7 and 10 are not actually present in either of these two hypothetical graves. It is arguable that in a case such as this absence of a particular type does not have the same status as its presence, and that in particular one would not wish to give joint absence of a type from a pair of graves the same weight as joint presence. This would be especially the case if some of the types occurred only very infrequently. Such a situation, where zero and one have a different status, may be contrasted with that which would arise if, for example, we were coding the sex of the individual in the grave as zero for male and one for female, where the two values have the same status and are simply labelled arbitrarily.

Of the range of coefficients appropriate for presence/absence data, only two of the most important are described here. These take contrasting positions with regard to their treatment of negative matches. What sort of treatment is appropriate in a given case should be considered carefully at the beginning of an analysis.

The Simple Matching Coefficient

For each pair of items their scores for each attribute are compared and it is noted whether they match (i.e. are the same) or not. The number of matches is then expressed as a proportion of the total number of attributes. What this involves can usefully be illustrated by looking at the comparison between any two individuals in the form of a 2 × 2 table (Table 11.3). For each pair of individuals we count the number of attributes present in both (a); the number present in j but not i (b); the number present in *i* but not *j* (*c*); and the number absent from both (*d*). Putting in the data for our example of the two graves from Table 11.2 gives us Table 11.4.

TABLE 11.3. General table for the comparison of two items in terms of the presence/absence of a series of attributes.

| | | Individual *i* | |
		Attribute +	Attribute −
Individual *j*	Attribute +	*a*	*b*
	Attribute −	*c*	*d*

TABLE 11.4. Comparison of graves coded in Table 11.2 with regard to presence/absence of the ten coded attributes.

| | | Grave 1 | |
		+	−
Grave 2	+	3	1
	−	2	4

For the simple matching coefficient then

$$S = \frac{a+d}{a+b+c+d}$$

In words: positive matches plus negative matches, divided by the total number of attributes. In the case of our two graves:

$$S = \frac{3+4}{3+1+2+4} = \frac{7}{10} = 0.7$$

The Jaccard Coefficient

This takes the opposing principle with regard to negative matches: they are disregarded altogether. If two items are the same in the sense of not possessing some attribute, this is not counted either as a match or in the total number of attributes which forms the divisor for the coefficient; for any given pair of items the divisor is the number of attributes actually present in one or other of the items in the pair. In terms of our general 2×2 table (Table 11.3):

$$S = \frac{a}{a+b+c}$$

With regard to our example we have:

$$S = \frac{3}{3+1+2} = \frac{3}{6} = 0.5$$

As we have noted above, it would obviously be preferable to use the Jaccard coefficient if you had a data set in which there was a large number of attributes which occurred only rarely, so that a given individual or case possessed only a small proportion of the total range. In this situation, if the simple matching coefficient was used, all the cases would be defined as more or less identical to one another.

So long as they are chosen appropriately, these coefficients and the many others available will provide a satisfactory definition of the similarity between two items; but suppose we want a measure of association between two *variables*, in the same way as the correlation coefficient provides such a measure for numeric variables? For example, if we are analysing the grave goods within a cemetery on the basis of which graves they are present in, to find out if there are specific sets of goods which tend to be associated with one another. If they are true dichotomous variables, in which the one and zero values are equally important (i.e. the sort of cases for which the simple matching coefficient is appropriate) then there is no problem.

However, it is not satisfactory when we are dealing with comparisons where we do not want the negative matches – the joint absences – to count. Do we want the strength of association between, let us say, bracelets and belt-plates in the burials to be affected, or even determined, by their joint absence from the majority of the graves?

Using the Jaccard coefficient to measure the association between variables is one answer and this is the approach adopted by Hodson (1977, 1990) in his analysis of the grave goods from the Hallstatt cemetery; but it is not entirely satisfactory. As an example, let us take the data in Table 11.5, which shows the presence or absence of two different grave goods types in a set of nine graves. The value of the Jaccard coefficient in this case is $S = 3/6 = 0.5$. But there are two ways of looking at this question, of which the Jaccard coefficient represents only one. It tells us that half the occurrences of type 1 are associated with type 2. However, if we look at this from the point of view of the less common attribute 2, we can think of it in a different way: we could say that it has a perfect association with type 1 since every time it occurs type 1 is present as well.

TABLE 11.5. Two grave-good types scored in terms of whether or not they are present in a series of graves.

| | Grave numbers | | | | | | | | |
	1	2	3	4	5	6	7	8	9
Grave goods type 1	1	1	0	1	0	0	1	1	1
Grave goods type 2	1	0	0	0	0	0	1	0	1

An alternative to the Jaccard is to use the following coefficient:

$$S = \frac{1}{2} \left(\frac{a}{a+c} + \frac{a}{a+b} \right)$$

where the letters refer to the general 2×2 table presented in Table 11.3.

This coefficient takes the positive matches as a proportion of the total occurrences of the first attribute (here grave goods type 1) under consideration, then as a proportion of the second attribute, and finally averages the two. It is clear that with this coefficient the less frequent attribute receives much more weight than with the Jaccard coefficient, although it might still be argued that the average is rather spurious.

The matrix of coefficients produced by this technique, like all the coefficient matrices we have seen so far, is symmetric: the half below the principal diagonal is a mirror-image of that above the diagonal. Another approach to the problems posed by such cases as that just outlined is to produce an asymmetric matrix, in which the two halves are different from one another; thus, one half of the matrix will be made up of terms of the form $a/(a+c)$ and the other half of terms $a/(a+b)$. Methods of analysing such matrices are discussed by Krzanowski (1988, pp. 120–3) but have found very little if any use in archaeology. Carr (1985) discusses the issues raised by such type frequency asymmetries in the context of intra-site spatial analysis, where the object is to identify spatial association between different types.

In fact, the technique of correspondence analysis, discussed in Chapter 13, provides a means of analysing patterned associations in both items or units and variables at the same time which is appropriate for situations where we have counts or presence/ absence data for nominal variables (at least for cases where the simple matching coefficient would be an acceptable measure of similarity).

Up to now the contrast has been drawn between numeric variables on the one hand and binary variables on the other, but archaeological data are sometimes characterised by neither of these; *multistate* attributes occur very frequently. An example from the field of pottery studies might be *rim type*. This is the attribute or variable and it will have a series of attribute states; for example, simple rim, notched rim, rolled rim, everted rim, etc., which are mutually exclusive – only one state can occur on any one vessel – and exhaustive – they cover all the different varieties of rim form which occur in the data set under consideration.

The obvious way to treat these is as single variables with a variety of possible nominal values but in standard software this facility is not always available and an alternative (albeit slightly less satisfactory) is to record them as a series of binary variables. To take our rim form example, we can have four variables, one for each rim type; the one occurring in any given case is coded as present and the other three as absent. Nevertheless, it is important to be careful over the choice of similarity coefficient in these circumstances: ones which exclude negative matches from consideration are satisfactory but those which include them are not, because the variables are logically inter-connected so that negative matches are bound to occur simply because of the way the variables are defined. For the same reason correspondence analysis is also inappropriate here, and indeed for analysing such qualitative data generally. Here there is no alternative to working with the similarity/distance matrix either by means of clustering or ordination.

Often a given archaeological data set may be described in terms of both quantitative, dichotomous and multistate variables and sometimes we may want to calculate a similarity measure using variables of all these different kinds at once. This is possible by using Gower's general coefficient of similarity (Gower, 1971; Krzanowski, 1988, pp. 28–9). The formula is:

$$S = \frac{\sum\limits_{k=1}^{p} s_{ijk}}{\sum\limits_{k=1}^{p} w_{ijk}}$$

Here two individuals, i and j, are being compared over a series of variables, p, the similarity s_{ijk} being evaluated for each variable in turn and all the s_{ijk}s being summed at the end. The sum of all these values, however, is standardised by division by the sum of the 'weights', w_{ijk}, associated with each variable in the comparison of any pair of individuals, i and j.

The idea of weights is the intuitive one of using some means of varying the importance attached to particular variables in any given comparison. In the context of Gower's coefficient the weights are generally used in a very simple manner; thus, the weight is set at 1 when comparison between objects i and j for the kth variable is possible, and 0 when the value of the variable is unknown for either or both objects i and j.

When presence/absence variables are involved, s_{ijk} is set to 1 for a positive match and 0 for a mismatch. Since in these circumstances the weight attached to the variable will be 1, the result of this comparison will be fully taken into account in the evaluation of the final similarity coefficient. If the match is negative, i.e. both i and j do not possess the particular attribute in question, then we have again to make the choice whether we want to count it in or not. If we do not, the weight for that particular variable is set at zero, so that the treatment corresponds to the Jaccard coefficient; otherwise, the weight is set at 1.

For qualitative or multistate variables $s_{ijk} = 1$ if the attribute states for the two units are the same, and 0 if they differ; w_{ijk} is generally set at 1 unless the attribute is non-applicable, although again there is no reason in principle why it should not be varied to reflect any ideas the analyst may have about the relative importance of the different states.

For quantitative variables

$$S = 1 - \frac{\left|x_{ik} - x_{jk}\right|}{R_k}$$

where R_k is the range for variable k. In other words, we take the value of variable k for object j and subtract it from the value for object i, ignoring the sign of the result. We then divide the result by the range of the variable, i.e. the difference between its highest and lowest values, before subtracting the result from 1. Obviously, in the specific case where objects i and j are those with the highest and lowest values, the result of evaluating this $S = \frac{\left|x_{ik} - x_{jk}\right|}{R_k}$ term will be 1, which when subtracted from 1 will produce a similarity of 0 for the comparison on this particular variable.

Baxter (1994, p. 153) observes that despite its apparent promise and some early applications Gower's coefficient has never come into general archaeological use.

To complete this discussion of measuring similarity, a final coefficient worth mentioning, despite its undoubted drawbacks (Doran and Hodson, 1975), is the Robinson coefficient (Robinson, 1951), specifically devised for the archaeological purpose of measuring similarity between pottery assemblages described in terms of percentages of different types. This coefficient is one kind of city-block metric. It totals the percentage differences between defined categories for pairs of archaeological assemblages. The maximum possible difference between any two units is 200 per cent. By subtracting any calculated difference from 200 an equivalent measure of similarity or agreement is obtained. The formula is:

$$S = 200 - \sum_{k=1}^{p} \left| P_{ik} - P_{jk} \right|$$

where P is the percentage representation of attribute or type k in assemblages i and j.

It may be useful to demonstrate the two extreme possibilities with simple examples:

a)	Type 1	Type 2
Assemblage 1	50%	50%
Assemblage 2	50%	50%

$$\sum |P_{ik} - P_{jk}| = |50 - 50| + |50 - 50| = 0$$

$$S = 200 - 0 = 200$$

b)	Type 1	Type 2
Assemblage 1	100%	0%
Assemblage 2	0%	100%

$$\sum |P_{ik} - P_{jk}| = |100 - 0| + |0 - 100| = 200$$

$$S = 200 - 200 = 0$$

It is worth concluding this section by re-emphasising the point that the growth of new methods for multivariate analysis of the original data matrix of objects and variables, particularly correspondence analysis, has not superseded the kind of analysis based on distances and similarities, since for certain kinds of nominal variables turning the original data matrix into a similarity matrix provides the only possibility of analysis (Krzanowski, 1988, pp. 88–9). Furthermore, as we have noted in passing, they can also be used to extend the analysis of the results of ordination procedures based on the data matrix.

SEARCHING FOR PATTERNING IN SIMILARITY AND DISTANCE MATRICES: CLUSTER ANALYSIS

In this chapter we have followed through a path on which we have used the values of our cases on their variables to create a measure of similarity or distance between those cases, as opposed to using the values of the cases on their variables directly. The issues involved in this have already been discussed in general terms and the techniques relevant to the latter approach will be described in detail in the next chapter. But in both approaches we have the problem of how we find patterning in what may well be a very large table of numbers, in this case a symmetric matrix of similarity or distance coefficients. As usual the easiest way is to produce some kind of picture or representation. One way is to adopt what we have already referred to as the *ordination* approach, involving the display of the similarities in some form of scattergram; this must be left to the next chapter because the techniques involve consideration of some issues which have not yet been addressed. Another way is to use the methods of cluster analysis.

Hierarchical Methods

We have already seen that behind this group of techniques lies the idea that objects can be similar to one another at different levels, so that the results can be represented in the form of a dendrogram: a tree diagram representing the relationships between individuals and groups. These techniques, like those of numerical taxonomy generally, came to archaeology from biology, where the hierarchy of relationships depicted could be seen as relating to evolutionary trees. In archaeological data there is no such obvious hierarchy of inter-relationships between items and groups to which a hierarchical representation of similarities corresponds and this has occasionally been seen as a reason for rejecting the use of such hierarchical techniques in archaeology. The view taken here is that the notion of similarity in some respects and not others, and of greater and lesser similarity, is an entirely familiar one in archaeology which it may be both helpful and legitimate to conceptualise and represent in a hierarchical fashion.

Agglomerative Techniques

As we have seen, these start with a series of individuals and then build up groups from these. First the most similar items are grouped together, then individuals are added to these groups and the groups themselves are linked together until finally they are all joined in a single group.

The task which the agglomerative methods perform is to carry out the operation in the best possible way, according to some defined criterion. A variety of such methods exist because a variety of criteria exist in terms of which the similarity between a given individual and a group, or between two groups, may be evaluated.

a) *Nearest Neighbour or Single Link Cluster Analysis.* This is probably the simplest clustering method and for that reason is very useful for illustrating the procedures involved. The criterion of linkage in this case is that to join a group a given individual must have a specified level of similarity with any member of the group; for two groups to join any member of the one group must have a specified level of similarity with any member of the other. In other words, similarities or distances between individuals and groups, or between groups and other groups, are defined as those between their nearest neighbours.

TABLE 11.6. Matrix of similarities between five ceramic vessels, on the basis of their decorative motifs (after Everitt, 1980).

	1	*2*	*3*	*4*	*5*
1	1.0	0.8	0.4	0.0	0.1
2	0.8	1.0	0.5	0.1	0.2
3	0.4	0.5	1.0	0.6	0.5
4	0.0	0.1	0.6	1.0	0.7
5	0.1	0.2	0.5	0.7	1.0

The procedure is best illustrated by actually carrying out an analysis of a small similarity matrix of the relationships between five ceramic vessels on the basis of their decorative motifs (see Table 11.6; figures derived from Everitt, 1980, pp. 9–10). The highest similarity is that between vessels 1 and 2, so the first step in the procedure is to join these two together. These no longer have separate identities in the matrix; they are a group and the similarities between this group and the other individuals in the matrix must be evaluated according to the nearest-neighbour criterion, as the basis for producing a revised similarity matrix.

As an example, to find the similarity between the group and vessel 3, you look at the similarity between vessels 1 and 3, and between 2 and 3, and whichever is the larger counts as the similarity between the group, of vessels 1 and 2, and vessel 3. Here the similarity between 1 and 3 is 0.4 and between 2 and 3 it is 0.5, so the latter is chosen. The same procedure is carried out for the group and vessels 4 and 5, and the matrix produced is shown in Table 11.7.

TABLE 11.7. Reduced matrix of similarities between five ceramic vessels, after first stage of nearest-neighbour cluster analysis which has grouped vessels 1 and 2 together (after Everitt, 1980).

	(12)	*3*	*4*	*5*
(12)	1.0	0.5	0.1	0.2
3	0.5	1.0	0.6	0.5
4	0.1	0.6	1.0	0.7
5	0.2	0.5	0.7	1.0

This matrix in turn is examined for its largest value, the similarity between vessels 4 and 5 of 0.7, so these two now become another group, whose similarity with the first group and the remaining individual vessel must be established so that a third matrix may be produced. The procedure is as before. The similarity between the first group (vessels 1 and 2) and vessel 3 is unchanged at 0.5. To find the similarity between the first group and the second group on our nearest-neighbour criterion we look for the larger of the two similarities between group 1 and vessel 4 and group 1 and vessel 5, and see that it is 0.2 for the latter. The remaining entry for the matrix is found in similar fashion, to give Table 11.8.

TABLE 11.8. Reduced matrix of similarities between five ceramic vessels, after second stage of nearest-neighbour cluster analysis which has grouped together vessels 4 and 5, in addition to 1 and 2 (after Everitt, 1980).

	(12)	*3*	*(45)*
(12)	1.0	0.5	0.2
3	0.5	1.0	0.6
(45)	0.2	0.6	1.0

The next stage is for vessel 3 to join the second group at a similarity level of 0.6, while the final step is to join the two groups, on the same criterion, at a similarity of 0.5. The sequence of links may now be represented as a dendrogram, with a similarity scale down the side (Fig. 11.3).

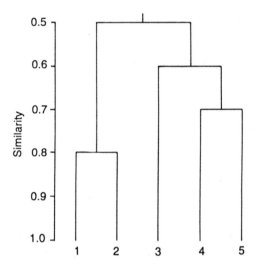

FIGURE 11.3. Dendrogram of results of single-link cluster analysis of the matrix of similarities between five ceramic vessels shown in Table 11.6 (after Everitt, 1980).

Although useful for illustrative purposes this is not generally considered a particularly good technique for looking for clusters in data since the nearest-neighbour criterion for group member-ship tends to produce a phenomenon known as 'chaining', where groups are successively linked to one another by single intermediate individuals.

b) *Furthest neighbour or Complete Linkage Analysis.* The crite-rion specified by this method is that to join a group a given individual must have a specified degree of similarity with the member of the group from which it is most dissimilar; for two groups to join, the two individuals, one from each group, which are most dissimilar from one another must have a specified degree of similarity. Once again then we are looking for the highest similarity values in the succession of matrices, but defined on the basis of furthest rather than nearest neighbours.

The dendrogram resulting from furthest-neighbour cluster

analysis of the matrix used in the nearest-neighbour example is shown in Figure 11.4. In this case the relative similarities have changed but the actual configuration of the dendrogram is identical to that for single linkage. This is unusual; more often than not the configurations are very different.

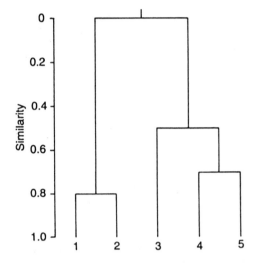

FIGURE 11.4. Dendrogram of results of furthest-neighbour cluster analysis of the matrix of similarities between five ceramic vessels shown in Table 11.6 (after Everitt, 1980).

Again, furthest neighbour is a technique better taken as a straightforward illustration of the way different results arise rather than for practical use since the results it produces are generally agreed to be misleading and unhelpful.

c) *Group Average or Average-Link Cluster Analysis.* This is also sometimes known as the unweighted pair group method. Here the similarity or dissimilarity between groups is defined as the arithmetic average of the similarities between pairs of members, i.e. as

$$\frac{\sum_{i=1}^{n} \sum_{j=1}^{n} S_{ij}}{n_i \, n_j}$$

where S_{ij} is the similarity between a member of group i and a member of group j, n_i is the number of individuals in group i, and n_j the number of individuals in group j. The formula tells us to take the first individual of group i, obtain the similarity between it and all members of group j, sum these similarities, then go on to the second member of group i and repeat the process, and so on until all members of group i have been accounted for. The resulting overall sum of similarities is then divided by the product of the number of individuals in each of the two groups. What this involves may be illustrated diagrammatically (Fig. 11.5).

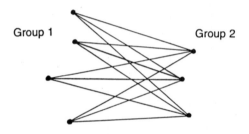

FIGURE 11.5. Diagram illustrating the calculation of average similarity between two groups.

Here there are two existing groups, 1 and 2. The lines linking the members of the two groups are the S_{ij}s (or d_{ij}s in this case), of which there are twelve. These are summed and then divided by $n_1 \times n_2$, the number of items in each of the two groups; here $4 \times 3 = 12$. At each stage of the average link cluster analysis the similarities/distances between the groups and/or individuals are calculated, following the group-average criterion where groups are involved, and the pair of groups and/or individuals with the greatest similarity or smallest distance at each step are linked together.

This is certainly the most widely used technique in archaeology and has an intuitive attraction compared with the two described above. As Baxter (1994, p. 158) points out, it also consistently produces results which archaeologists seem to find satisfactory; however, the issue of the validity of cluster analysis results is a complex one to which we will have to return below.

d) *Ward's Method.* There is a variety of other hierarchical agglomerative methods, although a number of them can be shown to be variations of a more general procedure (Everitt, 1980, pp. 16–17; Gordon, 1981, pp. 46–9). Only one more will be described here, Ward's method, which has had a considerable amount of use within archaeology for the analysis of continuous numeric data such as the results of trace element analyses, but also by Whallon (1984) for intra-site spatial analysis.

The idea behind it is that satisfactory clusters should be as homogeneous as possible. One way to define homogeneity is in terms of the distance of the members of a cluster from the mean of that cluster. In Ward's method the distance is the *error sum of squares* (ESS): the total sum of squared deviations or distances of all points from the means of the clusters to which they belong. The aim of the method is to join individuals and groups successively in such a way that at each step in the fusion process the error sum of squares is the minimum possible; in other words, the clusters remain as homogeneous as possible. The method is best understood by means of an example (data derived from Everitt, 1980, pp. 16–17).

TABLE 11.9. Matrix of squared Euclidean distances between five projectile points, based on measurements describing their shape.

	1	2	3	4	5
1	0.0	1.0	36.0	64.0	121.0
2	1.0	0.0	25.0	49.0	100.0
3	36.0	25.0	0.0	4.0	25.0
4	64.0	49.0	4.0	0.0	9.0
5	121.0	100.0	25.0	9.0	0.0

A matrix of squared distances between five projectile points based on quantitative measurements of variables describing their shape is shown in Table 11.9. At the beginning, when all the individuals are separate from one another, the total ESS has a value of 0. Then those two individuals with the smallest distance between them, i.e. those whose fusion will produce the minimum increase in ESS, are linked, here individuals 1 and 2, separated by a squared distance of 1.0. In the case where we are dealing with only two individuals the increase in ESS is given (Gordon, 1981, p. 42) by

$$I = \frac{1}{2} \, d_{ij}$$

Here

$$I_{(12)} = \frac{1}{2} \, (1.0) = 0.5$$

As with our single-link cluster analysis example we now need to calculate a new reduced matrix, giving the distances between the group mean and the other items in the analysis. A general formula for obtaining the new distances is given by Gordon (1981, p. 42):

$$d_{k(ij)} = \frac{n_k + n_i}{n_k + n_i + n_j} \, d_{ki} + \frac{n_k + n_j}{n_k + n_i + n_j} \, d_{kj} - \frac{n_i}{n_k + n_i + n_j} \, d_{ij}$$

where $d_{k(ij)}$ is the distance between group or items k and the new group made up of groups or items i and j, n_i is the number of items in group i, n_j is the number of items in group j, n_k is the number of items in group k, d_{ki} is the distance between group/ item k and group/item i, d_{kj} is the distance between group/item k and group/item j, and d_{ij} is the distance between group/item i and group/item j. In the present example the calculations are as follows (in practice, of course, such calculations are always carried out by computer):

$$d_{3(12)} = \frac{1+1}{1+1+1} \, 36 + \frac{1+1}{1+1+1} \, 25 - \frac{1}{1+1+1} \, 1$$
$$= 24.0 + 16.66 - 0.33 = 40.33$$

$$d_{4(12)} = \frac{2}{3} \, 64 + \frac{2}{3} \, 49 - \frac{1}{3} \, 1$$
$$= 42.66 + 32.66 - 0.33 = 75.0$$

$$d_{5(12)} = \frac{2}{3} \, 121 + \frac{2}{3} \, 100 - \frac{1}{3} \, 1$$
$$= 80.66 + 66.66 - 0.33 = 147.0$$

The other distances in the new matrix are as before, so the result is Table 11.10.

TABLE 11.10. Reduced distance matrix between five projectile points after the first stage of a Ward's method cluster analysis which has linked together items 1 and 2.

	(12)	*3*	*4*	*5*
(12)	0.0	40.333	75.0	147.0
3	40.333	0.0	4.0	25.0
4	75.0	4.0	0.0	9.0
5	147.0	25.0	9.0	0.0

The smallest distance is now that between individuals 3 and 4, a distance of 4.0. Again we need to find the increase in ESS resulting from the formation of the new group, in the same way as before:

$$I = \frac{1}{2} 4 = 2.0$$

and once more we need to produce a new matrix (Table 11.11):

$$d_{(12)(34)} = \frac{2+1}{2+1+1} 40.33 + \frac{2+1}{2+1+1} 75.0 - \frac{2}{2+1+1} 4$$

$$= 30.25 + 56.25 - 2 = 84.5$$

$$d_{5(34)} = 16.66 + 6 - 1.33 = 21.33$$

TABLE 11.11. Reduced distance matrix between five projectile points after the second stage of a Ward's method cluster analysis which has linked items 3 and 4, in addition to 1 and 2.

	(12)	*(34)*	*5*
(12)	0.0	84.5	147.0
(34)	84.5	0.0	21.333
5	147.0	21.333	0.0

Looking at the new matrix we can see that the smallest distance is that between the group of 3 and 4 and individual 5 of 21.33. As before, the increase in ESS resulting from including a new individual is equal to half the distance between them. In this case $21.33/2 = 10.66$.

It remains to evaluate the single entry in the final matrix (Table 11.12), the distance between group (12) and group (345):

$$d_{(12)(345)} = \frac{2+2}{2+2+1}\ 84.5 + \frac{2+1}{2+2+1}\ 147.0 - \frac{2}{2+2+1}\ 21.33$$

$$= 67.6 + 88.2 - 8.53 = 147.27$$

TABLE 11.12. Reduced distance matrix between five projectile points after the final stage of a Ward's method cluster analysis.

	(12)	*(345)*
(12)	0.0	147.268
(345)	147.268	0.0

Again the increase in ESS is half the distance, giving a value of 73.65. The results may be summarised in the form of a table (11.13) and the links represented in the form of a dendrogram (Fig. 11.6). In contrast to the other examples we have seen, there is a much bigger jump in distance between the joining of the lower-level clusters and the final coming together of the two groups. This is because the technique is working with *squared* distances so that the larger distances between individual and groups are exaggerated.

TABLE 11.13. Increase in error sum of squares (ESS) associated with successive linkages in the Ward's method cluster analysis of the matrix in Table 11.9.

Fusion	*ESS increase*	*Cumulative ESS*
1 2	0.5	0.5
3 4	2.0	2.5
(34) 5	10.7	13.2
(12) (345)	73.7	86.9

Ward's method has been widely used in analyses of such real numeric data as trace-element concentrations but also forms the basis of Whallon's technique of unconstrained clustering (Whallon, 1984).

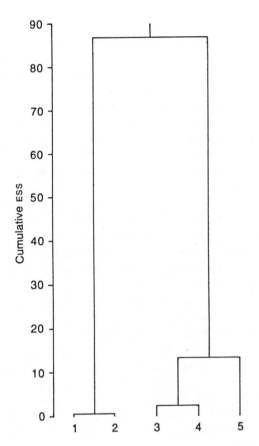

FIGURE 11.6. Dendrogram resulting from analysis by Ward's method of the distance matrix in Table 11.9.

Divisive Techniques

Divisive methods of cluster analysis start off with all the units or individuals together in a single group which is then successively sub-divided. There are two main groups of divisive methods, polythetic and monothetic; the former are based on the consideration of the values of all the variables in the analysis at any given division step, the latter on the values of a single variable (cf. Everitt, 1980). Only the monothetic approach is considered here since it is the only one which has had any impact on archaeology (e.g. Tainter, 1975; Peebles, 1972; O'Shea, 1984).

Its use in practice has largely been restricted to cases where the data are dichotomous: all those with a 1 value go in one group, all those with a 0 value in the other. When there is a series of successive division steps, producing smaller and smaller subdivisions, the result once again is a hierarchy. Divisive methods have been particularly used by ecologists, for classifying areas of land by the species present, or species in terms of their presence in particular areas, and the main method is generally known as *association analysis*.

Having said that the series of divisions is made in terms of the presence or absence of a single attribute at any given time, the question arises as to the means of selecting the best attribute for making such a division: what is meant by 'best'? The basic idea is that the two groups produced at any given division step should be as dissimilar as possible from each other, not just in terms of their value on the variable used to make the division but overall, in terms of all the variables in the analysis. In other words, presence/absence of the attribute used for division should be related to the presence/absence values of the other attributes; the attribute whose presence/absence is most closely related to the values of the other variables in the data set being split will be the one to choose. Even so, there is still a variety of ways in which this general criterion may be defined. The one chosen to illustrate the method is not particularly satisfactory for reasons to be indicated below but it is very convenient and straightforward in terms of showing what the technique involves.

TABLE 11.14. Data matrix for ten graves scored in terms of the presence/absence of four grave-goods types.

	Grave goods types			
Grave	*1*	*2*	*3*	*4*
1	0	0	1	1
2	0	0	1	1
3	1	1	1	0
4	1	1	1	0
5	0	1	1	1
6	1	1	0	0
7	1	1	1	1
8	1	0	0	0
9	0	0	0	1
10	0	0	0	1

Suppose we have ten graves scored in terms of the presence/absence of four grave goods types (Table 11.14). One way of seeing whether the values on one variable are related to the values on another is to calculate the chi-squared statistic for the association between those two variables. The idea behind the approach is that the chi-squared values actually measure strength of association in this context, because sample size is a constant for all the comparisons. If a particular variable is strongly related to other variables, it means that for a given case its value on the first variable will be a good predictor of its value on the others. The result is that a group defined on the presence/absence of the first variable will be relatively homogeneous since the state of that variable will specify the particular states taken by the other attributes, for the members of that group. The variable most closely related to the others, and therefore most appropriate for making the division, will be the one with the highest chi-squared values for its relations with the others. Thus, we have to calculate the chi-squared value for each attribute's association with every other and then sum the results for each variable to see which is the highest, as shown in Table 11.15.

We now sum the chi-squared values for each variable:

Goods type $1 = \chi^2_{12} + \chi^2_{13} + \chi^2_{14} = 3.6 + 0.0 + 6.66 = 10.26$

Goods type $2 = \chi^2_{21} + \chi^2_{23} + \chi^2_{24} = 3.6 + 1.66 + 1.66 = 6.93$

Goods type $3 = \chi^2_{31} + \chi^2_{32} + \chi^2_{34} = 0.0 + 1.66 + 0.28 = 1.94$

Goods type $4 = \chi^2_{41} + \chi^2_{42} + \chi^2_{43} = 6.66 + 1.66 + 0.28 = 8.61$

It appears from this that variable 1 is overall more closely associated with the other variables; that is to say, presence or absence of the other grave goods types is most closely related to the presence or absence of type 1. The result of this is that the best division of the graves is into those where type 1 is present and those where it is absent. It is not possible to obtain two more dissimilar groups on the criterion we have used. In Table 11.16 the graves are arranged in their two groups. It can be seen that types 2 and 4 are markedly differently distributed in the two subdivisions, although type 3 is identically distributed in both and its presence/absence is obviously not related to that of type 1, as the relevant chi-squared statistic indicated.

TABLE 11.15. Contingency tables showing associations between each pair of grave-goods types for the data presented in Table 11.14.

(a) Type 1		+	−		
Type 2	+	4	1	5	$\chi^2_{12} = 3.6$
	−	1	4	5	
		5	5	10	

(b) Type 1		+	−		
Type 3	+	3	3	6	$\chi^2_{13} = 0$
	−	2	2	4	
		5	5	10	

(c) Type 1		+	−		
Type 4	+	1	5	6	$\chi^2_{14} = 6.666$
	−	4	0	4	
		5	5	10	

(d) Type 2		+	−		
Type 3	+	4	2	6	$\chi^2_{23} = 1.666$
	−	1	3	4	
		5	5	10	

(e) Type 2		+	−		
Type 4	+	2	4	6	$\chi^2_{24} = 1.666$
	−	3	1	4	
		5	5	10	

(f) Type 3		+	−		
Type 4	+	4	2	6	$\chi^2_{34} = 0.278$
	−	2	2	4	
		6	4	10	

TABLE 11.16. Graves listed in Table 11.14 sorted so that all those in which goods type 1 is present and all those in which it is absent are grouped together.

		Grave goods types		
	Grave	2	3	4
Type 1 present	3	1	1	0
	4	1	1	0
	6	1	0	0
	7	1	1	1
	8	1	0	0
Type 1 absent	1	0	1	1
	2	0	1	1
	5	1	1	1
	9	0	0	1
	10	0	0	1

Only one division step has been illustrated in this example but in association analysis a succession of subdivisions of this type is carried out.

There are undeniable problems in using chi-squared in this way (see Cormack, 1971; Baxter, 1994, p. 173); one obvious one is the question already discussed above of how seriously one takes the *d* cell of the contingency table, the joint absences or negative matches. As noted above, the chi-squared method has been presented here for illustrative purposes rather than as a recommendation of its suitability. Other division criteria are available, in particular one known as the *information statistic*. It gives a measure of the disorder in a group. It has a value of zero when all members of a cluster are identical and increases as the group becomes more diverse (see Sneath and Sokal, 1973, pp. 141–4, 241–4; Baxter, 1994, pp. 151–2). It has been used by Peebles (1972), Tainter (1975) and O'Shea (1984), among others.

Partitioning Methods

All the cluster analysis methods we have seen so far have been hierarchical, but it is now time to turn to the partitioning methods, to which reference has already been made. Instead of there being multiple levels of grouping at different levels of similarity, a decision is made as to an appropriate number of clusters and then individuals are assigned to the one to which they are closest. This process of assignment is not a trivial one because as new individuals are added to a cluster the definition of the cluster changes. The methods which have been devised to carry out this task are not analytical techniques which can be guaranteed to produce a single correct answer, since the number of possible variations in the assignment of items to groups quickly becomes enormous as the number of items in the analysis increases; they are techniques which use the speed of computers in carrying out large numbers of calculations to search through the data, assigning individuals to groups according to a set of rules based on some criterion. The assignment that results should be as close as possible to the optimum but this cannot be guaranteed.

The first decision that has to be made concerns the number of clusters to be started, although in practice, as will be explained below, it is possible to operate in a more or less hierarchical manner, successively reducing the number of clusters of interest. Once the initial number has been decided it is necessary to provide a basis for starting the clusters. Procedures suggested for defining the starting points include random selection of a specified number of individual cases, corresponding to the number of clusters required, and the use of the results of some other clustering method for the relevant number of groups. When the starting cluster centres have been chosen individuals are allocated to the cluster to whose centre they are nearest.

The idea of allocating individuals to the groups to whose centre they are nearest is clearly the same as that in Ward's method, and very often an error sum of squares based on squared Euclidean distance is used in partitioning methods as well. In Ward's method the best fusion of individuals into groups is achieved by the hierarchical pattern of linkage, but as with all the hierarchical methods of cluster analysis, a cluster, once formed, can never be broken and its members redistributed to another group or groups. This can lead to anomalous situations, in that an individual's membership may be appropriate when it joins, but as other items join the group and its definition changes, the initial item may become peripheral to it, to such an extent that it should really now join a different group with which initially it did not have much in common. The idea of reassessing a grouping process at any stage and, if appropriate, reallocating individuals to other groups is intuitively attractive.

This is precisely what the partitioning methods known as *iterative relocation* or *k-means* techniques do. As individuals are added to the cluster the centre of each cluster is recalculated, either every time a new individual is added to it or at the end of the process of allocating items to clusters. At this point the question arises whether all items are in the most appropriate cluster, so each is considered in turn to see if it should be reassigned to a different one. A variety of criteria have been proposed for making these decisions but the basic idea behind them all is that the dispersion of the different clusters should be reduced and the distinctions between them maximised, again a concept similar to the idea of minimising ESS in Ward's method.

Of course, once one item is moved then the centre of the cluster it comes from and the one it moves to both need recalculating, so the process of relocation is a laborious one for which efficient computer algorithms are required. It continues until any further moves fail to cause an improvement in the criterion being used. A very much simplified version of the procedure is illustrated in Figure 11.7, in which only two clusters are considered.

As noted above, the solution achieved at the end of the relocation process on any particular occasion may or may not represent the best possible overall allocation (or *global optimum* as it is sometimes known in the jargon). This is normally checked by repeating the process using different random starting points for the clusters.

As pointed out above, although the procedure is carried out for a specific number of clusters, it can also be carried out in a quasi-hierarchical fashion. Thus, once the best-fit solution for a given number of clusters is found, the two nearest ones can be joined and the relocation procedure repeated. When this has been done, the number of clusters may be reduced again and the whole process repeated for as many clusters as are required. It is important to note that this process is not hierarchical in the sense of the hierarchical methods we've seen above. They produced clusters whose members were unchanging except that new members were added as the number of clusters decreased. With the iterative relocation methods described in this section clusters can also change their membership as their number is reduced.

1. Two individuals are selected as starting points for the two clusters; a third individual is introduced and allocated to its nearest cluster:

2. The position of the centre of cluster 2 is recalculated; another case is introduced and allocated:

3. Position of centre of cluster 1 is recalculated; another case is introduced and allocated:

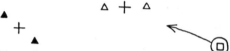

4. Position of centre of cluster 2 is recalculated; another case is introduced and allocated:

5. Position of centre of cluster 1 is recalculated; another case is introduced and allocated:

6. Position of centre of cluster 2 is recalculated; another case is introduced and allocated:

7. Position of centre of cluster 1 is recalculated; left-most individual of cluster 2 is now closer to the centre of cluster 1, so is allocated to it:

8. Centres of both clusters finally recalculated;

FIGURE 11.7. Successive stages of an iterative relocation partitioning procedure for two clusters.

This process of gradually reducing the number of clusters and obtaining the result at each stage can also be used to gain insight into the likely number of 'real' clusters in the data, since the error sum of squares (or usually some function of this) can be compared for solutions involving different numbers of clusters. If there is no real set of reasonably distinct clusters in the data then as their number decreases the ESS value will simply gradually increase. However, if there is a level of real clustering then, when the number of clusters is reduced by one below this, the ESS value should rise markedly. If we plot the ESS value (or usually its log) against the number of clusters then a sudden upward kink in the curve, where the ESS value goes sharply up, will be indicative of a level at which there are likely to be real clusters (i.e. the number of clusters at the bottom of the kink). Of course, there may be more than one of these levels. The results for a real data set may also be compared with those for a randomised version of it (see below).

Among other things, this technique has been used to define spatial clustering on occupation sites, where the data to be clustered are the spatial coordinates of individual artefacts or ecofacts. Gregg et al. (1991) report an extensive case-study of the use of this method and unconstrained clustering to characterise the spatial patterning recorded for a !Kung occupation site.

Evaluating the Results of Cluster Analysis

As Baxter (1994) points out, it is clear from the literature that archaeologists in many different sub-areas of the discipline have felt the need to use cluster analysis, for the sorts of reasons outlined in the introduction to this chapter. Why they have tended to use cluster analysis rather than the ordination methods described in the next chapter is not entirely clear but we may suggest a couple of possible reasons. First, there is a good fit between the kinds of classification tasks archaeologists have always carried out and the kinds of things cluster analysis does, producing groups on the basis of assessments of similarity; this is familiar ground. Second, cluster analysis does not involve the rather complex-seeming transformations of the data which are involved in ordination. The question is: do they do what we want them to do in terms of revealing meaningful structure in the data, or are the clusters merely a product of the methods used? And what basis do we have for preferring the results of one clustering method to another?

The answers to these questions are by no means unequivocal, because it is not simply a matter of distinguishing between right and wrong methods but of considering the criteria by which a particular technique defines good clustering – whether these are appropriate to the structure of the data at hand. However, cluster analysis is generally used in precisely those situations where we know very little about the structure of our data, while the theoretical foundation of many of the methods is itself uncertain. A great deal of literature has been generated by these problems which it is impossible to go into here; an extensive and up-to-date review is provided by Baxter (1994, Chapter 8). However, the issues cannot be ignored even in an introduction such as this.

First, both Baxter (1994) and Wright (1989) tend to suggest that, in general, group average (average link) is the best of the hierarchical methods, although it is certainly not guaranteed to find structure in the data which is known to be present. Wright (1989) argues that Ward's method tends to violate the natural structure of data when we are in a position to see that structure in a scattergram. Both also emphasise the virtues of the k-means method with its relocation facility and lack of a hierarchical assumption, but it should be pointed out that it is only suitable for data where Euclidean distance is an appropriate similarity measure.

Nevertheless, we should not forget Read's (1989, p. 46) point that clustering procedures may on the one hand fail to distinguish groups that would be recognised by any archaeologist and on the other find groups which cross-cut the known structure of simulated data. As Read puts it:

> Cluster procedures do not 'work' in general. This is not to say that there are no cases where the results are valid; rather, there are no statistical means to assess whether or not the results are correct, just a partial, or even incorrect delineation of structure for the data being explored. (Read, 1989, p. 46)

In fact, a variety of means have been suggested for evaluating cluster analysis results and while individually they have their problems (see Baxter, 1994, Chapter 8) and do not have the strong theoretical foundation Read is looking for, together they provide a useful set of tools (see for example Aldenderfer, 1982). There is certainly no excuse for simply carrying out a single cluster analysis and accepting the results as of archaeological significance.

First, histograms of individual variables and scatterplots of pairs of variables can be obtained to see whether there are indications of multimodality and clustering.

Second, scattergrams can be plotted of the data not in terms of their values on the original variables but on their scores on the transformed axes produced by the ordination methods described in the next chapter.

Third, in the case of hierarchical methods of clustering stopping rules can be used to try and define a significant number of clusters (see Baxter, 1994, pp. 162–3).

Fourth, discriminant analysis and associated statistics can be used. This attempts to maximise the separation between existing groups and provides an indication of the extent to which this is possible (see Chapter 13 and Baxter, 1994, Chapters 9 and 10).

Another approach to validation considers the extent to which the grouping of the individual items into clusters distorts the patterning of similarities or distances between the individual items; it can also be used to compare the amount of distortion between clustering methods. The CLUSTAN suite of programs has two such measures: Jardine and Sibson's Δ (Jardine and Sibson, 1968) and the so-called cophenetic correlation coefficient for use with hierarchical methods. The second of these will be illustrated with an example to show what is involved; the similarity matrix used in the single-link cluster analysis example presented above will be compared with the grouping of similarities resulting from that analysis.

The original similarity matrix (Table 11.6) is reproduced here for ease of reference (Table 11.17); these similarities will be designated s_{ij}. The next stage is to derive the patterning of similarities produced by the cluster analysis; these similarities will be designated s^*_{ij}. The s^*_{ij} values between each pair of units may be read from the single-link dendrogram (reproduced as Fig. 11.8) by noting the coefficient values at which the units become linked. Thus, units 1 and 2 become linked at 0.8, 4 and 5 at 0.7, 3 to 4 and 5 at 0.6, 1 and 2 to 3, 4 and 5 at 0.5. From these figures we can produce the new matrix S^*_{ij} (Table 11.18) and we can plot corresponding elements of these two matrices against one another on a scattergram; thus, for example, the real similarity between 1 and 5 is 0.1 whereas according to the dendrogram it is 0.5; the scattergram is shown as Figure 11.9.

TABLE 11.17. Matrix of similarities (s_{ij}) between five ceramic vessels, on the basis of their decorative motifs.

	1	2	3	4	5
1	1.0	0.8	0.4	0.0	0.1
2	0.8	1.0	0.5	0.1	0.2
3	0.4	0.5	1.0	0.6	0.5
4	0.0	0.1	0.6	1.0	0.7
5	0.1	0.2	0.5	0.7	1.0

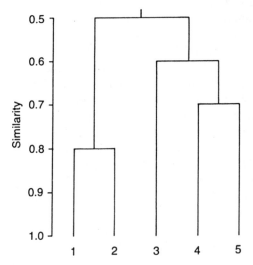

FIGURE 11.8. Dendrogram of results of single-link cluster analysis of the matrix of similarities between five ceramic vessels shown in Table 11.17.

We can also obtain the correlation coefficient between the matrices on the basis of their corresponding elements; it is calculated in exactly the same way as a normal correlation coefficient and is known in this context as the cophenetic correlation coefficient. In this case its value is 0.44. As noted already, the technique can also be used to compare the S^*_{ij} matrices resulting from different clustering methods. Baxter (1994, pp. 166–7) has pointed out that the value of this correlation is likely to be determined by what happens at the higher levels of the tree, which may be well beyond the clusters which have been defined as of interest. The scattergram (Fig. 11.9) shows how the distortion increases very markedly at the final join. The scattergram itself could be used to indicate an appropriate level of clustering and the coefficient calculated for this and levels below only.

TABLE 11.18. Matrix of similarities (s^*_{ij})between five ceramic vessels, derived from the dendrogram linkages in Figure 11.8.

	1	2	3	4	5
1	1.0	0.8	0.5	0.5	0.5
2	0.8	1.0	0.5	0.5	0.5
3	0.5	0.5	1.0	0.6	0.6
4	0.5	0.5	0.6	1.0	0.7
5	0.5	0.5	0.6	0.7	1.0

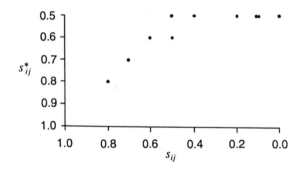

FIGURE 11.9. Scattergram of s^*_{ij} similarities against s_{ij} similarities, based on the matrices in Tables 11.18 and 11.17 respectively.

Another way of investigating the validity of clustering results is to analyse a particular data set by a variety of different methods. If they all give very similar results in terms of cluster structure and membership then it suggests that there is strong clustering in the data; ways of systematising this idea are discussed by Gordon (1981, pp. 132–6). On the other hand, if different methods do not give the same result it does not necessarily mean that there is not real patterning to be found, or that one of them is not representing it correctly. It may be that the cluster structure is successfully identified by one method based on one set of assumptions but not on another based on a different set. Krzanowski (1988, pp. 94–5) is rather sceptical about this way of proceeding.

Finally, a number of variations on the theme of randomisation which has been emphasised throughout this book may also be used in the evaluation process. For example, a data set may be randomly divided into two subsets and analyses carried out on each of these to see if they match each other. A more radical approach is to randomly permute the values of the variables across the different cases, thus destroying any structure of association or similarity which may exist, and to compare the results with those of the real data, either visually and intuitively, for example in terms of dendrogram structure, or perhaps using the measures for measuring common membership of clusters discussed by Gordon (1981, pp. 132–6). Wright (1989) advocates this approach and provides facilities for carrying it out.

BEYOND STANDARD CLUSTER ANALYSIS

It will be clear by now that when using cluster analysis perhaps even more than in other areas of the application of quantitative methods to archaeology, clear thought about aims, the nature of the data, the properties of the numerical description and its analysis, and the appropriate means of evaluating the results are essential.

However, an alternative way of improving things, in some cases at least, is to make as much use as possible of prior knowledge. There may not be much of this available at the beginning of a particular study but if we carry out our analysis in stages then the earlier stages can illuminate and inform the later ones. Thus, to take a straightforward example, Hodson's (1990) analysis of the burials from the Hallstatt cemetery was pursued separately for the male and female burials when it was apparent that their grave inventories were very different. In effect, this is a more controlled application of the principles behind the divisive methods of cluster analysis discussed above.

A more subtle and complex example has been presented by Read (1994; Read and Russell, 1996) in his development of a typology for a set of utilised lithic flakes. As he points out, in many cases we do not know which of the variables we have measured will be relevant to the patterning in a data set so we take many different measurements to be on the safe side. However, the presence of irrelevant variables can actually hide structure present in other variables if their distributions are independent of the distributions of the significant ones and they are all analysed together, for example in a cluster analysis. As Read and Russell put it (1996, p. 667), we need methods 'sensitive to the embeddedness of lower dimensional structure in a higher dimensional measurement space'. Furthermore, we may find that different variables are relevant at different levels, and to only some subsets of the data. Thus, in Read's case-study there was a distinction in the small flakes between narrow ones and wide ones which was not apparent in the large flakes, which could, however, be divided into thick ones and thin ones. But if the distinction between large and small had not been made first and the analyses of the two groups pursued separately then the further distinctions would not have become apparent because they would have been submerged in the complex patterns of variation all being considered at the same time.

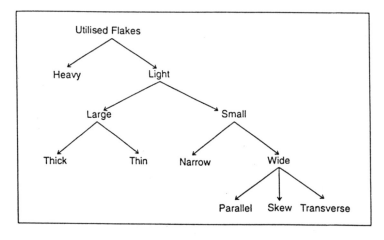

FIGURE 11.10. A taxonomy of utilised flakes based on a sequential multivariate analysis (after Read and Russell, 1996).

Once the variables have been defined and measured, the first step in the analysis is to look for a criterion to subdivide the data, which may involve looking at individual distributions, bivariate variable plots or plots of the results of ordination methods (see next chapter). The data set is then split on the basis of the relevant variable and the subsets searched for further distinctions. The process of subdivision is repeated until it can go no further. The results are shown in Figure 11.10. The distinctions correspond to distinctions made in practice by flake makers and users even if not recognised explicitly by them. Their significance is confirmed by the way the frequencies of the different types vary between sites. The groupings were not intuitively obvious without the use of quantitative methods nor were they discovered by a standard method of cluster analysis in which all the variables were included at the same time. They were found by means of a sequential analysis involving the careful use of cluster analysis and ordination methods, in which the earlier stages of analysis directed the later ones.

EXERCISES

11.1 Below is a series of measurements (on p. 262) describing the shape of a number of bevel rim bowls of the Uruk period in Mesopotamia. The diagram below shows what the different measurements refer to (information from Johnson, 1973). Carry out a cluster analysis of these data to try to establish groupings within them. Try more than one technique and think how you might validate your results. Can you see any problems with this analysis?

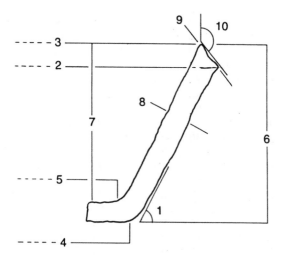

Key: 1 Base angle; 2 Rim diameter (estimated to 0.5 cm); 3 Interior rim diameter (to 0.5 cm); 4 Base diameter (to 0.5 cm); 5 Interior base diameter (to 0.5 cm); 6 Side height (measured to 0.1 cm); 7 Interior side height (to 0.1 cm); 8 Side thickness; 9 Rim thickness; 10 Rim angle.

base angle	rim diam.	inter. rim diam.	base diam.	inter. base diam.	side hgt.	inter. side hgt.	side thick.	rim thick.	rim angle
58	160	150	80	70	73	65	108	145	128
57	140	130	70	65	67	62	94	111	137
55	175	155	70	70	71	61	107	110	137
58	180	170	70	65	84	80	106	121	154
62	195	180	80	70	86	72	108	135	150
60	165	160	70	65	85	78	111	130	159
53	180	170	80	65	85	75	120	123	148
68	130	120	60	50	71	65	108	104	150
48	150	140	70	60	70	55	133	129	165
58	200	190	80	75	96	84	159	141	147
47	210	200	85	75	79	74	114	135	163
60	160	150	80	70	87	80	110	121	136
55	180	170	80	80	88	83	109	118	160
65	190	165	80	75	91	79	132	169	150
63	190	170	75	70	89	85	137	129	155
67	220	210	80	75	118	105	145	138	170
44	170	150	80	70	58	44	103	123	154
63	185	170	75	80	80	74	117	139	148
52	160	150	60	55	75	69	109	126	148
62	215	200	90	85	97	81	138	128	133
41	175	160	65	60	70	62	110	137	151
47	190	170	75	80	69	58	120	129	148
50	185	160	70	65	94	80	126	143	152
55	195	180	70	65	85	80	130	129	151
49	195	180	70	65	77	69	124	102	148
58	140	120	65	60	66	54	113	143	130
62	170	160	65	60	90	70	94	131	137
55	135	120	70	65	73	64	109	102	136
53	170	160	70	65	78	64	123	124	135
60	175	160	70	60	83	70	112	142	155
52	140	120	70	65	73	62	116	126	145
59	150	140	75	70	88	76	101	126	135
61	140	130	70	60	92	85	116	103	152
56	145	130	65	60	72	65	125	134	136
60	175	160	75	65	93	78	111	160	130
53	165	160	70	60	74	65	111	62	160
49	165	150	80	75	75	62	129	147	154
60	160	140	70	65	78	66	114	146	143
59	170	160	70	60	91	77	138	119	146
57	165	160	80	63	77	60	91	124	170
55	170	160	80	65	70	66	140	121	149

11.2   The excavator of a series of Andean sites is interested in the factors affecting the occurrence of different plant species at those sites: possibilities are site location, the period to which the sites belong, and the status of the parts of the site from which the plant remains come. The table below shows the site name, phase and social status (élite versus commoner) for ten different site areas. For each area the frequency of four different plant species is recorded, in terms of the percentage presence of each type, i.e. the percentage of excavated units in each site area in which it occurred.

A cluster analysis of the ten site areas was carried out, using Euclidean distance as the similarity measure, and Group Average and Ward's Method as the clustering techniques. The figure below (on p. 264) shows the results for Group Average (that for Ward's Method was identical). What are the characteristics of the different clusters in terms of the plant species composition of the site areas? What factor(s) appear to relate most strongly to the plant species profiles?

Site	Phase	Status	Maize	Solanum	Chenopo-dium	Legumes
Tun	1	com	8	17	31	0
Tun	1	élite	22	28	59	19
Ump	1	com	43	25	66	13
Ump	1	élite	44	47	78	6
Hat	1	com	0	0	20	0
Hat	1	mixed	67	6	67	0
Hat	2	com	63	13	83	0
Hat	2	élite	62	33	74	7
Marc	2	com	60	20	52	8
Marc	2	élite	71	7	43	0

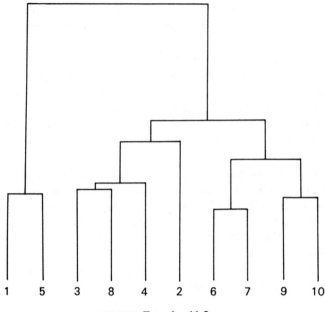

FIGURE Exercise 11.2

Twelve

MULTIDIMENSIONAL SPACES AND PRINCIPAL COMPONENTS ANALYSIS

In the previous chapter we saw that descriptions of objects of interest in terms of large numbers of variables could be turned into tables of inter-individual similarities and distances, and that items could be grouped together on the basis of these. The resulting groups, it is hoped and intended, have archaeological significance. Their existence and nature may be explicable in terms of other archaeologically interesting factors and in any event it is much easier to deal with and understand a small number of groups than what may be hundreds of separate individuals.

However, in the introduction to the last chapter we also mentioned the idea of analysing directly tables of scores of objects on variables, rather than tables of similarities, as well as procedures for *ordination* – the representation of relationships between items and between variables in a space of a small number of dimensions which still retains most of the information in the original descriptive variables. This chapter is concerned with these topics, and in particular with what may be seen as the foundational technique in this area, principal components analysis.

Let us begin by looking at what is intended in the contrast between basing an analysis on similarities between items and basing it directly on the values of the objects on the variables. Of course, in a similarity-based analysis the similarities are themselves based on the values of the objects on the variables but it is the similarities which are analysed and searched for patterning. The first problem with this approach is that the process of creating similarities/distances involves a loss of information. We may know, for example, that two ceramic vessels have a certain degree of similarity with one another but this is summarised in a single number which no longer provides the information about which variables are the ones in which they resemble one another and which are those in which they differ. The second problem, arising from this, is that we lose the relationship between the objects and the variables which describe them (Wright, 1989). We can carry out an analysis of the similarities between the objects and the associations between the variables but we can't directly link the two. We can link them indirectly by, for example, looking at a defined group of items and seeing what values of the variables appear to characterise this group as opposed to others, but this can be rather vague and subjective, as well as involving a great deal of work.

So long as it is appropriate for the data concerned, a mode of analysis which considers objects and variables together is likely to be more informative because we can see more directly how the two are related. The main methods to be described in this and the following chapter – principal components analysis and correspondence analysis – provide this capability. They analyse a table of values of objects on variables directly, without the intervening step of creating a similarity or distance matrix.

PCA and CA are ordination methods. Understanding these involves ideas from both regression and cluster analysis. In the context of simple bivariate regression we used scattergrams to see if any trends were present in the distribution of the obser-vations – the existence of strong trends indicated that variation in one variable could be accounted for in terms of another. But we could also have used the scattergrams to see which points were similar to one another and which were not by looking at the distances between them; and indeed, if we had wished, we could also have noted whether there was any indication that the objects fell into distinct groups. The axes of the scattergrams were formed by the variables so we could see directly which cases had which values. However, our examination of multiple regression showed, among other things, that with more than three variables, at most, representing our data by means of scattergrams in this way is simply impossible. If we want to do this we have to plot them two or at most three at a time. This is certainly worth doing for its own sake but obviously does not give us an overall picture: we cannot look visually for overall trends or groupings when we have large numbers of variables.

The aim of ordination methods is to compress the information contained in a large number of variables into a much smaller number of new variables, ideally only two or three, while losing as little as possible. We can then produce scattergrams of our data, expressed in terms of these new variables, which will allow visual appreciation of a large amount of information. The scattergrams will inform us on whether there are any trends or groupings within the data. Furthermore, as we shall see, the process of obtaining the new variables itself produces interesting information, and in some cases forms the main object of the exercise, since it can show whether there are latent patterns common to the variation in whole groups of variables. However, it is worth noting that although the best known, most widely used and arguably most important ordination methods operate on a table of scores of objects on variables, there are also techniques which carry out the same sort of analysis on similarity/distance tables where these are unavoidable (see Chapter 13).

An archaeological example of the general ideas involved may be helpful at this juncture, before we get on to the specifics of the method and its application. Let us suppose that we are analysing a group of lithics collected from a survey where each item has been described in terms of a series of measurements. We can imagine trying to represent the items as points in a space. There are as many dimensions to this space as there are variables and each lithic is represented by a point in the space whose position is defined by its values on the variables. We can further imagine that within this space the points will not necessarily be equally scattered in all directions; they may be distributed over a relatively short range in some directions and a considerably longer one in others. Assuming that the variables have been standardised (see below, p. 270), the directions of longest scatter will represent the major trends of variation in the data, indicating that some of the variables are correlated with one another. It is possible to define the orientation of these different directions or axes and also the lengths over which the points are distributed along them.

We start by defining the orientation of the longest axis and its length because this will represent the most important pattern of correlation among the variables. Once this has been established we can define the line or axis which goes through the next longest part of the point scatter, subject to the proviso that it must be at right angles to the first (see below), and we can obtain its length too. It is possible to go on doing this for as many independent dimensions of our space as exist, but given that our aim is to reduce the dimensionality of the data the hope – often a reasonable one – is that only a small number of these will be important. These axes often have a substantive interpretation in terms of the data from which they are derived. In the case of our lithics it may be that the axis along which they are most widely scattered represents a general correlation between a whole series of measurements which vary predominantly in relation to flake size; the second axis might represent a series of correlations between variables which relate to their length:breadth ratio.

We can establish a set of coordinates for the points (here lithics) in relation to these axes and use these new coordinates to produce scattergrams, which may be interpreted in terms of both the clustering of lithics, which are closest or most similar to which, and also in terms of the nature of the axes, referred to above. Instead of relying on a visual assessment of the scattergrams, a cluster analysis could be carried out using the coordinates of the objects on the new axes as input, rather than the original raw data, as we noted in the previous chapter.

This example brings out the twin aspects of ordination. The concern with similarities or distances and patterning within them is common to cluster analysis. The idea of looking for trends in the variation is something we have seen in regression. Nevertheless, there are some significant differences between ordination and regression and it is worth drawing attention here to one in particular. In regression analysis the aim is to model and account for the variation in a dependent variable in terms of the effect of one or more independents. Here we do not make any assumptions about which variables are dependent or independent. We simply obtain a measure of correlation or covariation between each variable and every other and analyse the matrix which results.

The application of procedures such as this to the analysis of all kinds of archaeological data has proved helpful in a large number of cases because it is a way of disentangling complex patterns of variation which are otherwise not easily assimilated.

The techniques of ordination come within an area of statistics known as *multivariate analysis*. They differ from the techniques used in cluster analysis in that whereas the latter is in many respects a group of *ad hoc* heuristic techniques without a secure theoretical foundation, most areas of multivariate analysis have a secure basis in mathematics and statistical theory. As we have had occasion to remark already, the mathematics behind these methods is complex and for this reason they have often been regarded as very deep and mysterious, and avoided by some as a result. While care and knowledge are essential for their use, the aim of this chapter is to show that conceptually they are readily comprehensible, certainly to the extent that it should be possible for anybody to understand and evaluate properly published analyses.

This chapter will provide a detailed account of the method of principal components analysis, together with a discussion of the related method of *factor analysis*. In the next chapter correspondence analysis will be described in some detail and much briefer accounts given of some other multivariate methods.

AN OUTLINE OF PRINCIPAL COMPONENTS ANALYSIS

It has already been stated that the mathematics involved are too complex for this to be an appropriate place to present a rigorous account of principal components analysis (see, for example, Morrison, 1967; Krzanowski, 1988). In these circumstances the best way of presenting an intuitively comprehensible account is by means of pictures and geometry. That which follows relies heavily on the very lucid presentation of Johnston (1978), designed for a fairly similar level of readership; a very good alternative is presented by Davis (1986) and also by Krzanowski (1988), who combines a mathematical and a geometrical account. In an archaeological context it is described by Baxter (1994, Chapters 3 and 4) and briefly but informatively by Madsen (1988, pp. 15–20).

The starting point for principal components analysis is the covariation between the variables. If a set of variables can be summarised by a smaller number of variables, the implication is that the values of the original variables are correlated with one another – they are closely related to one another. Such a new summary variable can be seen in some sense as the average of a group of variables; the more closely related they are the better the summary will be, and the more meaningful on its own as a replacement for the original variables.

To see how principal components arise we need to look again at how the covariation between variables is measured. We saw in Chapter 8 that covariation in its technical sense was given by $\sum(x_i - \bar{x})(y_i - \bar{y})$; this could be divided by the sample size to give an average covariation or covariance. If the variables we are dealing with have been standardised, i.e. transformed to Z scores in which the values are expressed as numbers of standard deviation units away from the mean (see Chapter 7), then the value of the covariance between any two variables will also be automatically standardised and will correspond to the correlation coefficient between the two variables; it follows from this transformation that the variances of the individual variables are also standardised, to a value of 1.0. In the remainder of this chapter we will assume that the relationships between variables are expressed as correlation coefficients (rather than covariances), although such a standardisation is not necessarily something which we would wish to adopt in a real analysis; this point is discussed further below (see also Baxter, 1994, pp. 65–6; Wright, 1989; Krzanowski, 1988, pp. 68–70).

To develop a geometrical presentation of principal components then, we first need a geometrical method of representing correlations. If we imagine our variables as vectors of equal length emanating from a common origin, then one way of representing their relations with one another is in terms of the angular distance between them. This is best illustrated visually (Figure 12.1). Here we have four variables each represented as a line with a direction, starting from a common origin. In terms of our pictorial representation and our convention for its interpretation, x_1 and x_2 are closely interrelated and neither is very closely related to x_3, although x_2 is closer to it than x_1; finally, x_4 is more or less diametrically opposed to x_1 and x_2, and more or less unrelated to x_3.

The reason that this is a very useful representation is that the sizes of the angles can be directly related to the values of the correlation coefficients, since these correspond to the cosines of the angles concerned. Thus, in our pictorial convention, when two variables are perfectly correlated, the angle between them is 0: they are superimposed (Figure 12.2). Obviously, in such a case the value of the correlation coefficient is 1.0; similarly, the cosine of an angle of 0 degrees is 1.0.

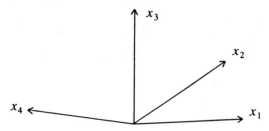

FIGURE 12.1. Geometric representation of the correlations between four variables.

FIGURE 12.2. Geometric representation of two perfectly correlated variables.

FIGURE 12.3. Geometric representation of two variables showing perfect inverse correlation between them.

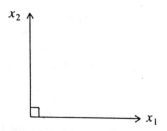

FIGURE 12.4. Geometric representation of two uncorrelated variables.

Again, when two variables are diametrically opposed we represent the angle between them as 180 degrees (Figure 12.3). The value of the correlation coefficient here would be -1.0; the cosine of an angle of 180 degrees is -1.0.

Unsurprisingly, an angle of 90 degrees has a cosine of 0.0 (Figure 12.4). In these circumstances the correlation between x_1 and x_2 is also 0, so we can represent two variables which are completely unrelated to one another by two vectors at right angles; in statistical jargon the two variables are *orthogonal*.

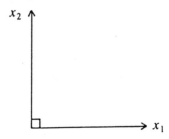

FIGURE 12.5. Two uncorrelated variables.

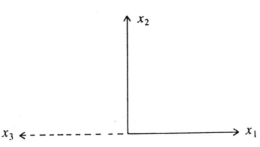

FIGURE 12.6. A failed attempt to represent a third uncorrelated variable on a two-dimensional surface.

When dealing with two variables we can always represent the correlation between them in terms of angular distance correctly on a flat piece of paper, i.e. in two dimensions. Above, in Figure 12.1, we also saw a diagram which represented the correlations between four variables in two dimensions, but this is by no means always possible. Imagine a case in which the four variables were uncorrelated with one another; in other words, each has a correlation of 0 with every other. We can draw the first two correctly (Figure 12.5), but try putting in the third (Figure 12.6):

this is obviously incorrect; although x_3 has a correlation of 0 and an angle of 90 degrees with x_2, it is at 180 degrees to x_1, with a perfect negative correlation of -1.0. The only way to put in the third vector correctly is to have it coming up vertically out of the paper, although a distorted representation can be given (Figure 12.7). If we add in the fourth uncorrelated and therefore orthogonal variable even this becomes impossible; the relations between all the variables can only be represented correctly in a four-dimensional space.

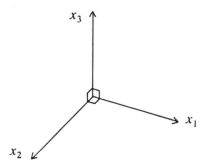

FIGURE 12.7. Geometric representation of three uncorrelated variables.

In general, the maximum number of dimensions required to represent the correlations between a specified number of variables is given by the number of variables, but it may be less. In the extreme case that all of them were perfectly correlated with each other then only one dimension would be required.

In principal components analysis we start with the matrix of correlation coefficients (or covariances) between our variables and the aim is to produce from these a new set of variables which are uncorrelated with one another. Precisely how this relates to our aim of defining summary variables, and thus being able to present scattergrams in two dimensions which effectively summarise the information from ten variables, will become clearer below. Nevertheless, we can note here that if it is possible to represent the relations between ten variables correctly in two dimensions then we can replace the ten by two new ones at right angles *which contain all the original information.*

The idea is not dissimilar from the kinds of statistical summary which we have already seen. We may have a large number of values of some variable, which together make up a normal distribution. Given its shape, once we know its mean and its standard deviation there is an enormous amount we can say about it just on the basis of the two summary numbers, without needing to worry about the original data values.

In the present case, rather than obtaining a mean number we want to start by obtaining a mean variable. This will be a new, synthetic variable, in the same way that a mean rarely coincides exactly with any of the numbers in a distribution. It will also be the variable which is overall closest to all the original variables in the analysis, again a similar concept to that behind the mean of distribution. In the present context we can define closeness in terms of angular distance. The variable which is overall closest to all the original ones will be in such a position that the sum of the angles between it and all the others is the smallest possible.

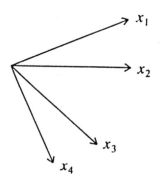

FIGURE 12.8. Geometric representation of the correlations between four variables.

Let's look at this by means of a simple example (Figure 12.8). Here we have a diagram representing the relations between four variables whose correlations are represented by the angles between them. Obviously, the average variable summarising these four will be somewhere between x_2 and x_3. How good such averages are at representing the original variables is a relevant question which may strike you. We'll see how this may be assessed later but for the moment the immediate question is how do we find out precisely where the average is?

TABLE 12.1.　Angles between variables shown in Figure 12.8.

	x_1	x_2	x_3	x_4
x_1	0	22	61	84
x_2	22	0	40	62
x_3	61	40	0	24
x_4	84	62	24	0

The first thing to do is note the exact values of all the angles and then the corresponding correlations/cosines (Tables 12.1–12.2). Having done this we can obtain the total sum of correlations for each variable (Table 12.2), remembering that the largest sum of correlations corresponds to the smallest sum of angles. We can see that, as expected, x_2 and x_3 have the largest sum of correlations and are therefore closest to the average, but we still haven't obtained the exact position of the average variable itself. This requires several more steps.

TABLE 12.2.　Correlations between variables shown in Figure 12.8.

	x_1	x_2	x_3	x_4
x_1	1.000	0.927	0.485	0.105
x_2	0.927	1.000	0.766	0.469
x_3	0.485	0.766	1.000	0.914
x_4	0.105	0.469	0.914	1.000
Sum	2.517	3.162	3.165	2.488

The total number of entries in the body of this matrix is 16, the square of the number of variables. If each correlation value were 1.0 then the total sum of correlations in the table would be 16.0. In the present case, of course, it isn't: the total sum of correlations is found by adding the separate sums for each variable: $2.517 + 3.162 + 3.165 + 2.488 = 11.332$.

Going back to our hypothetical example for a moment, if the total sum of correlations in the table was 16.0 then the maximum possible for any single variable would be 4.0, the square root of 16.0. Similarly here, the total sum of correlations is 11.332; thus the total sum possible for any single variable is $\sqrt{11.332}$, which is 3.366. This defines the variable with the largest possible overall correlation with all the other variables, or the one which is overall closest to the other variables in terms of angular distance. In other words, it is the average variable we are looking for, otherwise known as the first *principal component*. What we still do not know though is where this component lies in relation to the other variables.

Let us suppose that one of the original variables in this case coincided with the average variable or first principal component, i.e. the angle between them was 0 degrees. It too would have a sum of correlations of 3.366 and its correlation/cosine with the component would be 1.0; that is to say, it would correspond to the ratio of the sum of correlations for the original variable to the sum of correlations for the new principal component; here 3.366/3.366 = 1.0, corresponding to 0 degrees.

The same rationale applies, of course, whether or not any of the original variables coincides with the component: if we divide the sum of correlations for a variable by the sum of correlations for the component, the result is the correlation between the two, which can then be turned into an angle via the cosine. Let us carry out this operation for our example (Table 12.3), and put the component on our original diagram of the relations between the variables (Figure 12.9). By finding this component we have obtained a single variable averaging the four original ones, whether or not for the moment we think it's a good summary or average and would be prepared to use it in some analysis instead of the original variables.

TABLE 12.3. Correlations and angles between the four original variables and the first principal component. Total sum of correlations (TS) = 11.332, $\sqrt{TS}$ = 3.366.

	x_1	x_2	x_3	x_4
Sum	2.517	3.162	3.165	2.488
Sum/$\sqrt{TS}$	0.748	0.939	0.940	0.739
Angle	42°	20°	20°	42°

The method works in exactly the same way in the case where there are strong negative correlations, as we may briefly illustrate with the following example, in which x_1 and x_2 are highly correlated with each other and both strongly negatively correlated with x_3 (Figure 12.10).

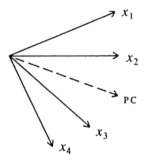

FIGURE 12.9. Geometric representation of the correlations between four variables, with the first principal component added.

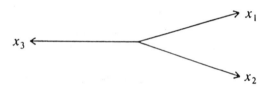

FIGURE 12.10. Geometric representation of the correlations between three variables.

The actual angles are shown in Table 12.4, and the correlations/cosines in Table 12.5. Putting in the component results in Figure 12.11. In this instance then x_1 and x_2 have strong positive correlations with the new component and x_3 a strong negative one.

TABLE 12.4. Angles between variables shown in Figure 12.10.

	x_1	x_2	x_3
x_1	0	34	164
x_2	34	0	162
x_3	164	162	0

TABLE 12.5. Correlations between variables shown in Figure 12.10.
TS = 0.884, $\sqrt{TS}$ = 0.913.

	x_1	x_2	x_3
x_1	1.000	0.829	−0.961
x_2	0.829	1.000	−0.951
x_3	−0.961	−0.951	1.000
Sum	0.868	0.878	−0.912
Sum/$\sqrt{TS}$	0.950	0.962	−0.999
Angle	18°	16°	177°

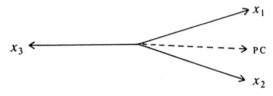

FIGURE 12.11. Geometric representation of the correlations between three variables, with the first principal component added.

These examples should have given you a feel for what a principal component is since they show one way in which they may be derived. It may be worth adding that this is not how they are actually calculated by the computer programs which carry out principal components analyses; these arrive at the same end by a different means.

At this point we can look again at the results of the first example to see what more may be said now that the first component has been located. As we saw, the angle between the component and the original variables was obtained by dividing the sum of correlations for a given variable by the square root of the total sum of correlations, to give a value for the correlation of the variable with the component, corresponding to the cosine of the angle between them.

It is these correlations with the variables which actually define the component: they are known as *component loadings* and they have exactly the same interpretation as ordinary correlation coefficients. In particular, we can use them now to get an answer to the question of how representative our new average variable is of the original variables, for the squared values of the correlations between the variables and the component (of the component loadings in other words) correspond precisely to the r^2 coefficient of determination values which we have seen in our discussion of regression. That is to say, by squaring the component loading of a variable we can find out the percentage of the variation in that variable that is accounted for by the new component (but see the comment on eigenvalues below). The figures for our example are presented in Table 12.6. In this case it appears that the new component accounts for 56 per cent of the variation in variable x_1, 88.2 per cent of the variation in x_2 and so on. If we sum all these values we have the sum total of all the variation accounted for by the component. For reasons arising from the matrix algebra derivation of the quantity, this sum total is usually known as the *eigenvalue* or *latent root* of the matrix, the matrix in question being the original matrix of correlations/cosines describing the relations between our four variables.

However, it is important to note that many computer programs normalise the component loadings so that their squared values sum to 1.0 rather than to the eigenvalue; in these circumstances the squared loadings do not correspond to r^2 values nor the loadings themselves to correlation coefficients. To produce this correspondence the normalised loadings must be squared and then multiplied by the eigenvalue for the component. This gives the corrected squared loading corresponding to an r^2 value; the square root of this in turn gives a loading corresponding to a correlation coefficient.

Assuming that the squared loadings are normalised to sum to the eigenvalue its formula is

$$\lambda_i = \sum_{j=1}^{p} L_{ij}^2$$

Where λ_i is the eigenvalue for component i, L_{ij} is the loading of variable j on component i, and the summation is over all variables, from 1 to p. In this case we have

$$\lambda_1 = 0.56 + 0.882 + 0.884 + 0.546 = 2.872$$

TABLE 12.6. Correlations and squared correlations of four variables with the first principal component, from the data in Table 12.3 and Figure 12.9.

Variable	Component loading	Squared loading (r^2)
x_1	0.748	0.560
x_2	0.939	0.882
x_3	0.940	0.884
x_4	0.739	0.546

As it stands it is difficult to attribute much meaning to this quantity. It is more helpful from the point of view of interpretation of a component to relate its eigenvalue to the total variation in the variables. Because we are dealing with a matrix of correlation coefficients, in which the variance in each variable has been standardised to 1.0, the sum total of the variation in the data is given by the number of variables in the analysis. To find the percentage of the variation in all the variables taken together accounted for by the component, we divide the eigenvalue for the component by the number of variables and multiply by 100:

$$\text{percentage accounted for} = \frac{\lambda_1}{n} \times 100$$

Here

$$\text{percentage accounted for} = \frac{2.872}{4} \times 100 = 71.8 \text{ per cent}$$

We can see that our new variable or principal component accounts for 71.8 per cent of the variation in the original four variables. To reiterate the point, the idea here is exactly analogous to that we have already seen in regression analysis. In multiple regression we were using a number of independent variables to account for variation in a dependent; here we are using a new variable we have defined to account for variation in the set of variables with which we started. In terms of our aim of trying to reduce the complexity in our data by reducing the number of variables with which we have to deal, we are already doing quite well in this case; we have replaced just over 70 per cent of the variation in four variables by a single new one. In the case of two of our original variables the component accounts for 88 per cent of the variation; for the other two, x_1 and x_4, it is not so high, at around 55 per cent.

The next question is whether we cannot account for at least some of the balance, both in the individual variables and over-all, by obtaining a second component. To relate what is involved to regression again, we can say that the variation unaccounted for by the first component is the residual variation from it – the variation which has zero correlation with it. Accordingly, the best way of accounting for this variation will be in terms of a component which is uncorrelated with the first, that is to say, at right angles or orthogonal to it.

TABLE 12.7. Correlations and angles between the four variables rep-resented in Figure 12.8 and Tables 12.1–2, with the second principal component derived from them.

Variable	Loading on second component	Angle between variables and second component
x_1	−0.661	131°
x_2	−0.336	110°
x_3	0.335	70°
x_4	0.676	47°

The loadings of the four variables on the second component, together with their conversion into angles, are shown in Table 12.7. If we now draw in the second component on our original diagram of the relations between our four variables and between them and the first component, we can see that the second one is indeed at right angles to the first (Figure 12.12).

We can also go on, as with the first component, to calculate the amount of variation in each of the individual variables, and the sum overall, accounted for by the second component, by simply squaring the component loadings. Likewise, these squared loadings can be summed to give the eigenvalue for the second component. The results of this operation are presented in Table 12.8, together with the results for component 1 already given, for reasons which will become clear in a moment.

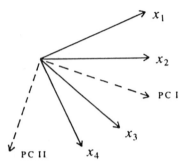

FIGURE 12.12. Geometric representation of the correlations between four variables, with the first principal component added.

TABLE 12.8. Squared correlations of four variables with principal components 1 and 2, from Figure 12.12.

Variable	Squared loading on component 2	Squared loading on component 1
x_1	0.437	0.560
x_2	0.113	0.882
x_3	0.112	0.884
x_4	0.457	0.546
Sum	1.118	2.872

From this we can see that component 2 accounts for 43.7 per cent of the variation in variable x_1, 11.3 per cent in x_2, and so on. Overall, the eigenvalue of the component is 1.118; to find the percentage of the variation in all the variables taken together accounted for by the second component we carry out the same calculations as for the first:

$$\text{percentage accounted for} = \frac{\lambda_2}{n} \times 100$$

Here

$$\text{percentage accounted for} = \frac{1.118}{4} \times 100 = 28.0 \text{ per cent}$$

At this point we can start looking at the results for the two components together. The first component accounted for 71.8 per cent of the variation; the two together account for 99.8 per cent, or 100 per cent within the limits of rounding error. Similarly, if we look directly at the eigenvalues we see that they sum to 3.99, while the sum total of variation in the correlation matrix from which the components were derived was 4.0, the number of variables. Likewise, if we look at the results for the individual variables and sum the squared loadings for each, they all come to more or less 1.0, or 100 per cent, again within the limits of rounding error.

In other words, our two new components have accounted for 100 per cent of the variation in the original four variables. This tells us that we can describe the variation in four variables in terms of two new ones without losing any of the information originally present. This is satisfactory in itself since it means that our data are immediately simplified and we are therefore more likely to be successful in detecting and understanding patterning within them. In visual terms, instead of looking at a series of scattergrams of the relationships between our four variables two at a time, we can simply look at one scattergram in two dimensions. In fact, we can note that if we had not been able to account for all the variation with two components, then it would have been impossible to represent the relationships between the original four variables correctly on a flat piece of paper. Conversely, if we could draw a diagram of the correct relations between 100 variables on a sheet of paper, we would know in advance that they could be reduced to two components.

So far we have only looked at components in connection with a series of abstract variables arbitrarily defined to have certain relationships. When dealing with real data we start off with cases which have values on a set of variables and it is in terms of these values and their relationships that we arrive at the correlations between the variables. Presumably then, if we can replace a set of correlated variables with new uncorrelated ones then we can replace the values of our cases on the original variables with their values on the new ones and it is these new values which we use to construct our now simplified scattergrams; these new values are known as *component scores*. As usual, how they are obtained is best illustrated with a two-variable example.

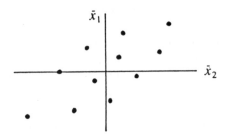

FIGURE 12.13. Scattergram of data points with values on two variables, x_1 and x_2.

When the observations on two variables are correlated, the scattergram will appear as in Figure 12.13, with the centre of gravity of the distribution at the intersection of the two means. We can imagine enclosing this distribution within an ellipse. If we do this, the angle between the axes defining the ellipse is given by the correlation between the two variables concerned, in the way we've already seen above; the origin is at the intersection of the two means. What is involved is shown in Figure 12.14.

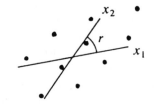

FIGURE 12.14. Axes of the ellipse defining the scatter of data points in Figure 12.13. The angle between the axes corresponds to the correlation between the variables.

When we find the principal components we are defining different axes for this scatter. The first principal component corresponds to the long axis of the ellipse and the second to the short axis, at right angles to the first. The lengths of the new axes or components correspond to their eigenvalues. The result is shown in Figure 12.15. In fact, the process of producing these components may be seen as a kind of regression. We have a scatter of points in a number of dimensions, two in the illustration, and we fit a line which goes through the longest axis of the scatter. With principal components analysis, however, the line of best fit is determined not by the *vertical* distances of the points to the line, as in regression, but by the distances *perpendicular to the line* itself. The residuals from this line will then be accounted for in the two-dimensional case by the second component, at right angles to the first. Where there are many dimensions we can continue to define new components at right angles to all the existing ones although it's impossible to visualise them.

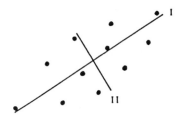

FIGURE 12.15. The principal components of the scatter of data points in Figure 12.13.

When we are simply moving from one pair of dimensions to another pair, as in this example, we are not perhaps doing a great deal, but even here it's not without significance. To the extent that the variables are correlated the first component will account for a greater part of the variation in the two variables and the deviations from it will be slight. On the other hand, if they are uncorrelated, the scatter of points will be circular so fitting components will not produce a better summary of the variation. However, it is, of course, the possibilities of space reduction which make principal components analysis particularly attractive.

You may wonder what all this has to do with the topic of component scores, for we seem to have done little more than repeat our derivation of principal components from a slightly different point of view. The component scores come in when we focus on what happens to a particular point when the axes are transformed in the way we have seen: how do we get from its values on the two original variables to its values on the new components? Again the matter is best illustrated by a diagram (Figure 12.16).

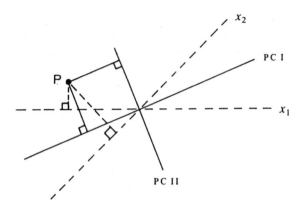

FIGURE 12.16. The relationship between the value of a data point on the original variables x_1 and x_2, and its score on the components PC I and PC II.

The position of point P is initially defined by its values on variables x_1 and x_2; the dashed lines projected down from the point to meet these two axes at right angles show the values of point P on these two variables. When we find the principal components we don't actually do anything to point P but we now have a new coordinate system in terms of which to describe its position. Its position in terms of the new axes is given by the solid lines projected from point P to meet the component axes at right angles. The point's position on each of these new axes is known as its component score for that axis, and just as we plotted scattergrams of our data so we can plot scattergrams of our data points in terms of their component scores; we will see below ways in which this can be helpful to us.

Component scores are obtained from the formula

$$S_{ik} = \sum_{j=1}^{p} x_{ij} L_{jk}$$

where S_{ik} is the score of observation i on component k, x_{ij} is the standardised value for observation i on variable j, L_{jk} is the loading of variable j on component k, and p is the number of variables. In words, we start by taking the standard score for observation i on variable j; we noted at the beginning of our account of principal components that we would be describing it in terms of a matrix of correlation coefficients, which therefore implied that we were dealing with standardised values for our variables. We then multiply this standardised value by the loading of that variable on the component of interest, i.e. by the correlation of that variable with the component, which in turn gives us the angle between the variable and the component. It is obviously necessary to know this angle if we are to change from one set of coordinates to another. In fact, of course, we need to know the relationship between every variable used in the analysis and the component currently of interest to make the transformation of coordinates successfully. We have to note each loading and the value of our data point on each variable, multiply them together and then sum all the results, for as many variables as we have.

At the end of the process of calculating component scores – which, of course, is done by computer – we have a table of the scores of our individual cases on each of the components, in the same way as initially we had a table of their scores on the variables we'd measured. As we will see, these scores, which in effect provide a summary of the main features of each of the data points, can be invaluable in interpretation. Furthermore, the fact that the components are by definition uncorrelated with one another means that a cluster analysis of the observations based on their component scores can often be more useful and informative than one based on the original variable values.

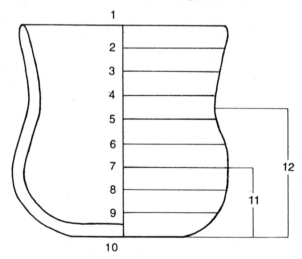

FIGURE 12.17. The measurements used to describe the shape of a number of late neolithic ceramic vessels from Central Europe.

AN ARCHAEOLOGICAL EXAMPLE

At this point we are badly in need of an archaeological example to bring together all the strands of our methodological account in a concrete substantively comprehensible fashion. The analysis to be described is concerned with the problem of understanding variation in the shape of sixty-five Bell Beaker ceramic vessels, from burials dating to the end of the neolithic period in Central Europe. Two sets of analyses were carried out, one using all sixty-five vessels and one using a randomly selected subset of twenty-two vessels. As the latter produced identical results it is the one presented here, for ease of illustration. The shapes of the vessels are described in terms of twelve measurements, shown in Figure 12.17.[1] Ten measurements were taken at intervals from the top to the bottom of the vessel (cf. Shennan and Wilcock, 1975); the measurements were taken from, and at right angles to, the centre line of the vessel drawing to the nearest point on the exterior of the vessel. Two further measurements were also taken: the height of the belly of the pot and the height of the bottom of the neck. In order that vessel size, as measured by overall vessel height, should not be a major aspect of the variation, all the measurements were standardised by division by overall vessel height. The correlations between the resulting ratios were then obtained (see Table 12.9) and a principal components analysis carried out on the matrix of correlation coefficients of each variable with every other variable. The eigenvalues and the variance accounted for by the components are shown in Table 12.10.

As you can see, we started with twelve variables and there are twelve components, but the majority of them only account for minute proportions of the variance. The question obviously arises here, as in many other cases, of how many of the components should be taken seriously. There is no fixed rule for this and it is a problem we will look at again below, but the guideline most often adopted is to take seriously only those components

---

1. More sophisticated methods of vessel shape description are now available; see, for example, the use of contour codes by Kampffmeyer and Teegen (1986) or Durham et al.'s (1995) use of the Generalised Hough Transform, a technique from image analysis. Note too Read's (1994) discussion of the problems raised by too much redundancy in artefact descriptions.

TABLE 12.9. Matrix of correlations between the twelve measurements defining vessel shape shown in Figure 12.17.

	1	2	3	4	5	6	7	8	9	10	11	12
1	1.000	0.978	0.901	0.509	0.280	0.283	0.328	0.369	0.359	0.477	-.048	-.353
2	0.978	1.000	0.956	0.553	0.357	0.378	0.419	0.455	0.437	0.478	-.023	-.349
3	0.901	0.956	1.000	0.704	0.565	0.588	0.606	0.606	0.568	0.512	0.107	-.187
4	0.509	0.553	0.704	1.000	0.924	0.859	0.758	0.665	0.540	0.342	0.627	0.350
5	0.280	0.357	0.565	0.924	1.000	0.973	0.895	0.807	0.694	0.340	0.553	0.469
6	0.283	0.378	0.588	0.859	0.973	1.000	0.964	0.890	0.781	0.376	0.429	0.394
7	0.328	0.419	0.606	0.758	0.895	0.964	1.000	0.968	0.890	0.457	0.208	0.292
8	0.369	0.455	0.606	0.665	0.807	0.890	0.968	1.000	0.960	0.517	0.032	0.203
9	0.359	0.437	0.568	0.540	0.694	0.781	0.890	0.960	1.000	0.630	-.082	0.133
10	0.477	0.478	0.512	0.342	0.340	0.376	0.457	0.517	0.630	1.000	-.035	-.266
11	-.048	-.023	0.107	0.627	0.553	0.429	0.208	0.032	-.082	-.035	1.000	0.460
12	-.353	-.349	-.187	0.350	0.469	0.394	0.292	0.203	0.133	-.266	0.460	1.000

TABLE 12.10. Eigenvalues and percentages of variance accounted for by the twelve principal components of the shape measurement data.

	1	2	3	4	5	6	7	8	9	10	11	12
Eigenvalues	6.77	2.67	1.41	0.63	0.34	0.07	0.05	0.03	0.01	0.01	0.00	0.00
%	56.41	22.23	11.75	5.24	2.81	0.61	0.46	0.28	0.11	0.05	0.02	0.02
Cum %	56.41	78.64	90.39	95.63	98.45	99.06	99.52	99.80	99.91	99.96	99.98	100.0

with an eigenvalue of 1.0 or more. The reasoning behind this is that 1.0 represents the variance of a single variable in the correlation matrix, so that if a component has an eigenvalue of less than this it actually accounts for less of the variation in the data than any one of the original variables (see for example Johnston, 1978, p. 146). An alternative is to plot the eigenvalues as the vertical axis against the components as the horizontal axis and to look for a kink in the curve of declining eigenvalues; Baxter (1994, pp. 59–62) discusses both options.

If we adopt the first approach in this case we see that we only have to deal with three components, all together accounting for 90 per cent of the variation in the data. Thus, in terms of one of the main aims of principal components analysis, data reduction and simplification, we have achieved a reduction from twelve variables to three new ones while still retaining the vast majority of the original information. Of these three, the first is by far the most important, as Table 12.10 shows.

It appears then that there are some major trends behind the initially confusing variation in the raw data, and the next step is to see which variables are involved in those trends. To do this we need to look at the loadings of the variables on the components, and also at their squared values, to see the percentage of the variation in the variables accounted for by the components. These are shown in Table 12.11.

TABLE 12.11. Loadings and squared loadings of the shape measurement variables on the first three principal components.

	Comp. 1		Comp. 2		Comp. 3	
Var.	Loading	Squared	Loading	Squared	Loading	Squared
1	0.61	0.37	−0.68	0.46	0.34	0.12
2	0.68	0.46	−0.65	0.42	0.30	0.09
3	0.82	0.67	−0.46	0.21	0.26	0.07
4	0.88	0.77	0.22	0.05	0.38	0.14
5	0.90	0.81	0.41	0.17	0.08	0.01
6	0.92	0.85	0.34	0.12	−0.06	0.00
7	0.93	0.87	0.21	0.04	−0.26	0.07
8	0.90	0.81	0.08	0.01	−0.39	0.15
9	0.84	0.71	−0.02	0.00	−0.51	0.26
10	0.58	0.37	−0.39	0.15	−0.26	0.07
11	0.30	0.09	0.58	0.37	0.66	0.44
12	0.18	0.03	0.84	0.71	0.05	0.00

If we look first at component I, we can see that the vast majority of the variables have high positive correlations with it; it accounts for more than 50 per cent of the variance for variables 1 to 9. Component I defines a pattern of variation common to all these. On the basis of the series of high correlations we can say that when a case has high values on one of these it will have high values on the others, and when it has low values on one it will have low values on the others. This pattern is condensed to a single trend defined by component I and, as we have seen, accounting for 56 per cent of the variance in the data. Precisely what that trend is will become clearer when we examine the scores of our individual cases on component I, because that is where the abstractions of the analysis can be directly related to the raw archaeological data. For the moment, however, we will continue with our examination of the component loadings.

A glance at those for component II, in combination with the fact that it accounts for only 22 per cent of the overall variance, shows immediately that in general this is much less important than the first – it accounts for only small proportions of the variation in most of the variables. The main exceptions are variables 1 and 2 on the one hand, which have quite high negative loadings, and variables 11 and 12 on the other, which have quite high positive ones. It appears that when rim diameter is large so is the diameter below the rim, and when one is small the other is small; similarly, when height of belly is high so is height of neck; when one is low the other is low. However, the two pairs of variables are negatively correlated with one another – high values for height of neck and belly tend to go with low rim diameter values and vice versa.

Component III, of course, is even less significant, as its overall percentage variance of 11.75 indicates; in only one case does it account for more than 30 per cent of the variance in a single variable. Variable 11, belly height, has a reasonably strong positive loading and variable 9, the next-to-base diameter, is fairly strongly negatively correlated with it. This seems to make sense in that when the belly is low the next-to-base measurement is likely to be larger, and vice versa. However, in order to see what the components mean in more detail we can look at the scores of the individual objects, the vessels.

TABLE 12.12. Scores of the vessels on the first three principal components, on the basis of their shape measurements.

Vessel	Comp 1	Comp 2	Comp 3
1	0.56	-0.42	0.21
2	-0.42	0.04	0.13
3	0.04	0.04	-0.26
4	0.32	0.03	-0.52
5	0.77	-0.14	-0.15
6	-0.22	-0.11	0.14
7	-0.80	-0.06	-0.03
8	-0.49	0.05	0.01
9	-0.69	-0.47	0.41
10	-0.69	-0.14	-0.19
11	-0.18	0.77	0.37
12	-0.25	0.58	0.21
13	1.04	0.47	0.40
14	-0.42	0.14	0.20
15	-0.21	0.13	-0.31
16	0.45	0.45	-0.36
17	0.28	0.04	-0.15
18	-0.28	-0.53	-0.10
19	-0.02	-0.23	-0.05
20	-0.57	0.01	-0.17
21	0.88	0.03	-0.09
22	0.91	-0.70	0.29

In Table 12.12 the scores of the twenty-two cases on the first three principal components are listed. These scores provide us with a means of obtaining a direct insight into the archaeological meaning of the components. If we note which cases have the highest negative values on the component and which have the highest positive values we can refer to our measurements or drawings of the individual vessels and see what it is that the vessels at each end have in common and what differentiates those at one end from those at the other. The component will then represent a trend from one to the other of these extreme types.

If we look at component I we see that cases 7, 9, 10 and 20 have large negative values and 5, 13, 21 and 22 have large positive values. For component II cases 1, 9, 18 and 22 have large negative values, 11, 12 and 13 have high positive ones.

Finally, for component III cases 4, 15 and 16 are at the negative end and cases 9, 11 and 13 are at the opposite end.

The raw data values for the cases – measurements expressed as percentages of vessel height – are presented in Table 12.13. If we look at the cases which have high negative values on component I, we see that they all have generally low values on the first nine variables, while those cases at the opposite end have high values for these variables. Remembering that all these values are width measurements in relation to height, we can see that all those with low values are slim vessels, all those with high values fat or squat ones. In other words, component I represents a trend from slim to squat in vessel shape, a trend summarising the majority of the covariation between these width measurements; obviously, in general, if one of them tends to be large or small then the others will tend to follow suit, hence the values of the loadings which we have already seen. Referring back to the loadings, the only width measurement which does not fit this pattern so strongly is the base.

We can now turn to component II. As we'd expect from the loadings, the distinctions here concern the height of the belly and neck (variables 11 and 12), on the one hand, and the rim diameter (variables 1 and 2) on the other. Vessels at the negative end have relatively large rim diameters and relatively low neck and belly heights, and those at the positive end have relatively small rim diameters and relatively high neck and belly height values. Component II represents a trend from one to the other. By definition this trend in variation is independent of that defined by the first component.

For component III it appears that the vessels at the negative end have a large next-to-base diameter in association with a low belly height while at the positive end the situation is reversed – high belly heights going with relatively small next-to-base diameters.

Examination of the component scores, then, is important for understanding precisely what the PCA is telling us about our data. It is, as we have seen, where the abstract analysis and the archaeological data confront each directly. But the identification of the individual cases in relation to the components is important in another respect. In this example we have simply defined the archaeological meaning of the components in terms of variation

TABLE 12.13. Values of the shape measurement variables for the twenty-two vessels.

	1	2	3	4	5	6	7	8	9	10	11	12
1	60.36	55.86	51.35	48.65	50.45	53.15	54.05	50.45	42.34	27.93	37.84	65.77
2	41.28	37.61	35.78	36.70	39.45	43.12	42.20	38.53	33.03	25.69	38.53	77.06
3	40.96	38.55	37.35	37.35	48.19	53.01	54.22	50.60	43.37	21.69	33.73	68.67
4	34.88	34.88	38.37	40.75	50.00	56.98	59.30	55.81	47.67	33.72	34.88	62.79
5	54.84	50.54	47.31	48.39	53.76	59.14	62.37	58.06	46.24	31.18	34.41	75.27
6	47.62	41.90	39.05	41.90	44.76	45.71	45.71	42.86	36.19	20.00	36.19	70.48
7	38.40	34.40	32.00	40.00	33.60	36.80	39.20	38.40	32.00	16.80	30.40	71.20
8	40.00	36.47	34.12	35.29	36.47	41.18	44.71	42.35	32.00	17.65	36.47	72.94
9	48.24	44.71	38.82	31.25	35.29	44.71	40.00	38.40	36.47	16.80	37.65	51.76
10	37.50	31.94	30.56	35.29	31.76	38.82	35.29	25.88	25.88	15.29	31.25	64.58
11	32.18	27.59	28.74	31.25	34.72	38.89	42.36	40.28	34.03	24.31	55.17	81.61
12	32.86	34.29	37.14	42.86	52.87	50.57	47.13	41.38	33.33	22.99	41.43	84.29
13	50.75	47.76	47.76	64.18	70.15	51.43	50.00	56.72	34.29	8.57	49.25	79.10
14	35.71	34.52	35.71	39.29	44.05	46.43	45.24	39.29	41.79	20.90	41.67	66.67
15	35.29	34.31	33.33	44.12	49.12	49.02	50.98	49.02	30.95	20.24	32.35	70.59
16	37.33	36.00	36.00	45.33	54.67	61.33	62.67	60.00	41.18	20.59	37.33	78.67
17	44.00	42.67	41.33	41.33	50.67	56.00	57.33	54.67	48.00	21.33	36.00	69.33
18	51.39	45.83	38.89	37.50	37.50	40.28	44.44	45.83	37.50	22.22	26.39	59.72
19	46.74	43.48	40.22	41.30	48.91	48.91	52.17	46.74	38.04	22.83	32.61	63.04
20	32.17	32.17	31.30	33.04	39.13	43.48	44.35	42.61	35.65	21.74	34.78	62.61
21	50.53	48.42	48.42	54.74	52.31	62.11	62.11	58.95	48.42	27.37	36.84	73.68
22	66.15	64.42	56.92	52.31	52.31	55.38	55.38	53.85	46.15	33.85	41.54	56.92

in vessel shape. It might easily be, however, that these trends in shape relate, for example, to change through time, so that the vessels at one end of a component are early and those at the other end are late. By being able to consider the individual vessels, or whatever our cases might be, we have access to information which may exist about other aspects of their archaeological context: are they associated, for example, with other items for whose dating we have independent evidence?

So far, however, we have only looked at the scores of the cases on each individual component taken separately. This is obviously important if we're trying to define what the components mean in archaeological terms. Nevertheless, the possibility clearly exists of producing scattergrams of the scores of the cases on two components together. In the example of our vessels, a scattergram just using the first two components includes 78 per cent of the variation in the data, while if we use different symbols for the cases according to their scores on component III a further 12 per cent is added, bringing the total to 90 per cent. The possibilities of visual assessment of patterns in these circumstances, as compared with dealing with the original twelve variables, are certainly far greater. Furthermore, if the program being used operates the appropriate scaling procedure, it is also possible to include the variables on the same scattergram, with their positions defined by their loadings on the relevant components.

Such scattergrams are useful in a variety of ways. First, it may be that such patterns as chronological trends in the variation in our data will not be apparent in terms of a single dimension but will become clear when we are dealing with two. Second, as was noted already in the previous chapter, such scattergrams can provide a supplement to cluster analysis. Because the small number of important dimensions often resulting from the ordination contain a large amount of information, we can get a good idea whether genuine clusters of data items exist, or whether clusters would represent a relatively arbitrary division of a continuum; and whether certain points are outliers which do not really belong with any of the others. In addition, we can see, for example, whether all the cases in particular parts of the scattergram come from a particular site. Finally, if the loadings of the variables are shown on the scattergram as well, we can see which variables are most important in defining the position of particular data points.

Figure 12.18b shows the scattergram of the vessels plotted in terms of their values on the first two principal components, together, as we have seen, accounting for over 78 per cent of the variation in the data. Also shown (in Figure 12.18a, below) are the variables, defined by the loadings of the variables on these components, so that we can see how the variables and cases relate to one another. So, for example, all those vessels which are broad and squat are at the right hand of component I together with the main set of variables positively correlated with squatness, i.e. large diameter values; slim vessels are at the opposite end of the scattergram from these. However, the squat vessels are quite spread out vertically at the right-hand end of component I because they have varying characteristics significant in relation to component II.

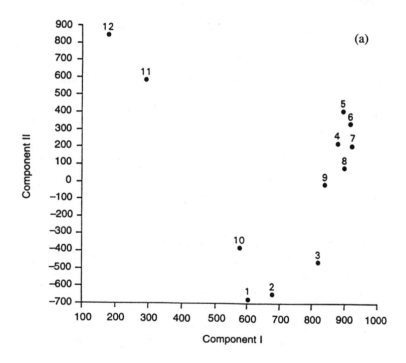

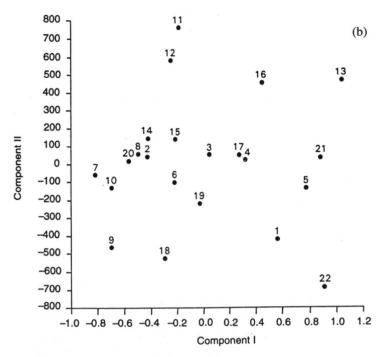

FIGURE 12.18. (a) Scattergram of vessel measurement variables against the first two principal components. (b) Scattergram of individual vessel scores on the first two principal components.

SUMMARY OF PRINCIPAL COMPONENTS ANALYSIS

PCA carries out a number of extremely useful tasks as far as trying to make sense of complex data tables is concerned, as Doran and Hodson (1975, p. 196) and many others since them have pointed out.

1. It gives a helpful indication of the relationships between variables.
2. It also provides information about the relationships between units.
3. It suggests whether there are any major summary trends within the data, and which variables are mainly involved in the trends.

4. It provides a transformation of the data in which, in general, a very large percentage of the variation in a large number of variables is compressed into a smaller number of variables.
5. The transformation is carried out in such a way that the new variables are uncorrelated with one another.

These characteristics make PCA in general more informative than cluster analysis, because variables and cases are dealt with together but also because the variation in the data is in a sense disentangled, separated out into different independent dimensions and therefore easier to grasp.

But what are the assumptions of PCA and what problems are there with using it? First, PCA is most appropriate for numeric data, like measurements, or elemental compositions obtained from characterisation processes of various kinds. Although it can be used where the data are counts, for example counts of the number of animal bones of different species in an assemblage, particularly if they are appropriately transformed (see for example Baxter, 1994, Chapter 4), in general it is preferable to use the related method of correspondence analysis (see next chapter) for counted data. PCA is usually based on the matrix of covariances between the variables concerned, which may or may not have been transformed into a matrix of correlations (see below). Clearly, this presupposes that the assumptions discussed above in the regression chapters are met; in particular, the relations between the variables must be linear or the covariance/correlation will not adequately represent the relations between the variables. This point may be investigated by examining the bivariate scattergrams of relations between pairs of variables. Alternatively, if the individual variable distributions are normal it is likely that the use of correlations/covariances will be satisfactory. If problems appear, it may be possible to resolve them by means of transformations of the kind discussed above in Chapter 6, but an alternative is to carry out the analysis on a matrix of rank correlation coefficients (Wright, 1989, p. 38), since their use does not presuppose any distributional assumptions.

However, even if the data are numeric, care must be taken if they are in the form of proportions, particularly if they involve only a small number of variables, because proportions have in-built inter-correlations. Thus, if three variables together sum to 100 per cent and one goes up by 10 per cent, it means that the other two between them must go down by 10 per cent; they are automatically negatively correlated with one another. The issues raised by this and the various possible solutions to the problem are discussed by Baxter (1994) and Wright (1989).

An important issue with regard to PCA, already noted several times in passing, is the question of standardisation of the variables to Z scores, so that they have a mean of 0 and a standard deviation of 1.0. The results of a PCA of standardised variables may well be very different from those of an unstandardised one. If the data are numeric then the usual option is to standardise so that variables which vary over narrow ranges will have as much weight as those which vary over much greater ranges; thus, for example, blade thicknesses will have as much influence in an analysis as blade length. This is probably desirable more often than not but it shouldn't be done without thinking. On the other hand, if the data are counts then small numbers mean few observations, which may easily be unreliable, so we may not want to give much influence to these. The issues are discussed by Baxter (1994, Chapter 4) and Wright (1989).

A further point to be borne in mind is that since PCA is designed to extract axes from matrices it will do this regardless of any substantive meaning or importance they may have. In any matrix of correlations between even a moderate number of variables there will be a large number of values. Some of these will be quite large and statistically significant purely by chance, even if the matrix is derived from a set of random numbers. On the basis of these chance large values apparently significant components may result from a PCA, which may even be apparently interpretable in substantive terms to the archaeologist eagerly searching for patterns. This problem is discussed in an archaeological context by Vierra and Carlson (1981) and also by Wright (1989) and Baxter (1994), who point out that it is possible to test the correlation matrix prior to PCA to see if there is a significantly large number of significant correlations. By this means illusory results may be avoided.

It is also important to point out that the process of interpreting components is not mathematically rigorous. For example, various suggestions were described above for deciding on the number of components worth taking seriously and trying to interpret, but they are just that – suggestions which have been found useful – and they won't necessarily produce the same answer. We have the same problem in trying to interpret individual components. In trying to decide which variables are important in defining a component, how high do the variable loadings have to be before we start regarding them as substantively significant and use them in our interpretation? The answers vary (cf. Krzanowski, 1988, pp. 68–70).

Finally, we need to consider a more general issue which is similar to those issues raised in the previous chapter's discussion of cluster analysis. If there is correlational structure among the variables in a data set, are we bound to find it and define it correctly using PCA? The answer is, not necessarily. The point was demonstrated by Whallon (1982) in a study of pottery shapes defined by measurements. His argument may be illustrated by a simplified example. Suppose there are two pottery types – one tall and slim, the other an open, flat dish form – defined by two measurements – rim diameter and height. In each case, let us suppose, there is a strong correlation between height and diameter. However, if we plot them on a scattergram, we will find that the slope of the line defining the relationship is different in the two cases: height and diameter covary differently in the two types. If we then put both types together into a single data set and carry out a PCA on the measurements, then the two different relationships will tend to cancel one another out; the strong correlation structure present will be diluted. In a simple and obvious case such as this the two groups would almost certainly be distinguished by the PCA anyway but Whallon showed that there were circumstances where they would not be. Correlational methods in effect presuppose a single overall correlational structure in the data, not two different ones. The point is similar to the situation when we have a single distribution which is multimodal – it's often best to divide it up according to the modes and examine each part separately. Here too, once we recognise distinct sub-groups we should analyse them separately, in the way illustrated at the end of the previous chapter. The point is also discussed and illustrated by Madsen (1988, pp. 15–16), and by Read and Russell (1996).

Rotation

So far an account has been presented of standard PCA, how it works and the issues it raises, but we cannot leave the topic without mentioning the controversial subject of *rotation*.

What is involved is best illustrated by looking again at the situation at the end of our simple initial illustration of the principles of PCA, shown in Figure 12.12. We had a first average component, summarising the majority of the variation in the four variables, and a second, independent of and at right angles to the first, which summarised the residual variation. But if we think about one of the aims of PCA as being to summarise the variables and thus make the variation easier to understand, we can see that if we could rotate the two components anti-clockwise, still keeping them at right angles to one another, then we could more or less line up PC I with variables 1 and 2 and PC II with variables 3 and 4; in this way we would have a more direct and quite possibly more interpretable summary of their variation. This is the operation of rotation and it can be seen that it has a plausible intuitive appeal.

The rules which have been devised and implemented for carrying out this procedure are many and varied. Some of them even drop the stipulation that the new axes should be at right angles to one another, but these are not considered here and the most commonly used ones keep this constraint; they are therefore known as orthogonal rotations. The idea is to rotate the axes to a position which is as close as possible to an ideal referred to as *simple structure*. This ideal is that each variable should be completely identified with one single rotated axis and no other. In numerical terms the aim is that each variable should have a loading of 1.0 on one axis and 0.0 on all the others. Obviously, it is impossible to achieve this ideal with any real data set in practice, but computer methods are available which approximate it as closely as possible for any given case. As far as our example in Figure 12.12 is concerned, we can simply do the rotation visually (Figure 12.19), but this will be impossible in real examples.

As you can see, once rotation has taken place we have not only reduced the variation in the data to a smaller number of dimensions, we have identified the new dimensions as far as possible with specific sets of variables. This can potentially be very helpful in clarifying the main aspects of variation in our data, although in the case of the vessels in the detailed example described above rotation made no difference to the results or their interpretation.

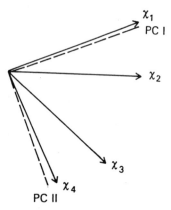

FIGURE 12.19. Rotation of the principal components shown in Figure 12.12.

But rotation brings its own set of problems, since the decision about the number of components to be rotated determines the way in which the dimensions are defined: rotating two will give two groups of variables and rotating three will give three. Furthermore, the introduction of the third will not simply add a dimension associated with a group of variables to the first two groups; it is likely to change the definition of the first two. This is intuitively obvious if you think about what is involved in rotating a fixed set of axes at right angles to one another through a cloud of data points: the best position for three axes in terms of the criterion specified above is unlikely to be the same as that for two. When the nature of the summary dimensions can be affected by relatively arbitrary choices about the number of axes to be rotated then caution is clearly required.

Another issue arises from the fact that the first principal component often represents a general 'size' dimension, which is relevant to some extent to most if not all of the variables, which are positively associated with it. In the case of our example it was general vessel width, or squatness. It can often be the case that this is lost when the axes are rotated. The 'size' dimension is distributed around other more specific dimensions, which may or may not be satisfactory.

The issues raised by rotation are extensively discussed by Baxter (1994, pp. 83–5) and Wright (1989, pp. 35–7). The former is very dubious whereas the latter is very much for it, arguing that rotation of PCA axes usually enhances interpretation. He also points out that if it is felt to be important to keep a general 'size' axis unaltered, it is possible to leave this out and simply rotate the others which are felt to be important; his MV-ARCH program provides the facility to do this.

FACTOR ANALYSIS

It remains briefly to consider the technique, or set of techniques, known as *factor analysis*. This is a term surrounded by confusion, as Baxter (1994, pp. 85–90) documents. On the one hand, it has often been used as a general term for techniques which work on a data matrix of objects and variables to reduce their dimensionality, including PCA. On the other hand, it has a more specific meaning, referring to a technique which is similar to but has different theoretical foundations from PCA, foundations which many, especially statisticians, regard as dubious.

The essential difference between factor analysis and PCA may seem fairly minor but it does have quite important consequences. Principal components analysis extracts components from all the variance in the data. Factor analysis works on a different principle. It assumes that the variance in a variable can be divided into two segments, one part which it has in common with other variables and reflects its relations with them, and another part which is unique to itself and does not relate to anything else; these two parts are referred to as the *common variance* and the *unique variance*. The argument is that as factor analysis is concerned with defining underlying patterns of variation common to several variables then it should only operate on the common variance and leave the unique variance out of account: to include all the variance in the analysis is to confuse the issue. The question which arises then is how to estimate the unique variance of the variables in the analysis so that it may be removed from consideration; the remaining common variance of a variable is often referred to as its *communality* in the jargon of factor analysis.

What is involved in technical terms in the factor analysis case is best illustrated by a comparison with PCA. We saw above that when components were extracted from a correlation matrix the entries down the principal diagonal of the matrix were all 1.0, the standardised variance of each variable. In factor analysis the values along the diagonal are not 1.0 but are the communality estimates for the different variables. These are usually the multiple R^2 values of the individual variables and will, of course, vary from one variable to another. You will remember from Chapter 10 on multiple regression that the multiple R^2 value gives the proportion of the variation in a dependent variable accounted for by the effect of all the independents acting together and separately. Thus, to obtain the communalities, each variable in turn is treated as dependent on all the others. The argument is that the amount of variance accounted for by the other variables is a measure of what a given variable has in common with them; whatever the source of the rest of the variance, it is not relevant to the point at issue. The sum of the communalities is the total amount of variation in the analysis. If a given variable has only a small communality – in other words, the way in which it varies has little in common with the others – then it will play only a small role in the analysis.

In terms of our graphical illustration of the extraction of principal components, there the lines or vectors representing the individual variables were of equal length and each variable played an equal role in defining the position of the first component; in factor analysis the vectors corresponding to the variables would be of different lengths, the lengths corresponding to the communality value, and the position of the first average variable, or factor in this case, would be more strongly affected by those with the larger communalities; a variable with twice the communality of another would have twice the influence on the position of the factor.

As with PCA, but using this different matrix, we obtain the loadings of each of the variables on the factor. Correspondingly, the squared factor loadings give us the proportion of the variance in the variables accounted for by the factor. It is then normal in the case of factor analysis to go on to the rotation procedure described above.

More extensive discussions of factor analysis may be found in Krzanowski (1988, Chapter 16) and Baxter (1994, pp. 85–90), both of whom express considerable doubts about it. Wright (1989, pp. 36, 85–7) typically takes a robust pragmatic view suggesting that using PCA or true factor analysis usually makes very little difference in practice. This would point to the general use of PCA as the less controversial method.

EXERCISES

12.1 Carry out a principal components analysis of the data on Uruk bevel rim bowls provided for Exercise 11.1. Comment on all aspects of the results which you consider to be relevant, giving special attention to the archaeological interpretation of the components and their significance. Try rotating the principal components and compare the results with the unrotated versions.

12.2 A study is being carried out of the size of lithic waste in a series of soil samples in order to try to distinguish deposits which represent primary refuse from lithic production from those which represent secondary dumps of such material (Healan, 1995). It is assumed that a greater proportion of very small fragments is likely to indicate primary refuse while a greater proportion of larger ones is more likely to be indicative of dumping.

For each sample the lithic debitage was recorded in terms of five size categories and the total weight of lithics in each category was recorded. These weights were divided by the sample volume to give a standardised measure of density. There were fifty-nine samples in all.

The tables below show the correlations between the size classes and the results of a principal components analysis of these data, including both rotated and unrotated component loadings; the size classes are given in millimetres. The figure shows the plot of the sample scores on the two rotated components; the different samples are coded in terms of whether they come from interior or exterior surfaces, from what are believed on other grounds to be refuse deposits, or from general layers.

Discuss the results from a statistical and an archaeological point of view, with particular reference to whether there is evidence for a differential distribution of large and small debitage.

Matrix of correlations between size classes

	7.9–15.0	5.7–7.9	4.0–5.7	2.8–4.0	2.0–2.8
7.9–15.0	1.000				
5.7–7.9	0.714	1.000			
4.0–5.7	0.792	0.686	1.000		
2.8–4.0	0.555	0.566	0.817	1.000	
2.0–2.8	0.292	0.333	0.608	0.908	1.000

Unrotated component loadings and eigenvalues

Size class	Factor				
	1	2	3	4	5
7.9–15.0	0.800	−0.491	−0.490	−0.577	−0.040
5.7–7.9	0.782	−0.433	−0.793	0.015	−0.081
4.0–5.7	0.937	−0.090	0.348	0.757	−0.224
2.8–4.0	0.920	0.363	−0.027	−0.032	0.790
2.0–2.8	0.749	0.643	−0.097	−0.307	−0.563
Eigenvalue	3.536	0.982	0.318	0.129	0.036
% variance	70.717	19.631	6.368	2.573	0.711

Varimax rotated component loadings

Size class	1	2
7.9–15.0	0.922	0.176
5.7–7.9	0.870	0.206
4.0–5.7	0.753	0.565
2.8–4.0	0.435	0.888
2.0–2.8	0.1208	0.980

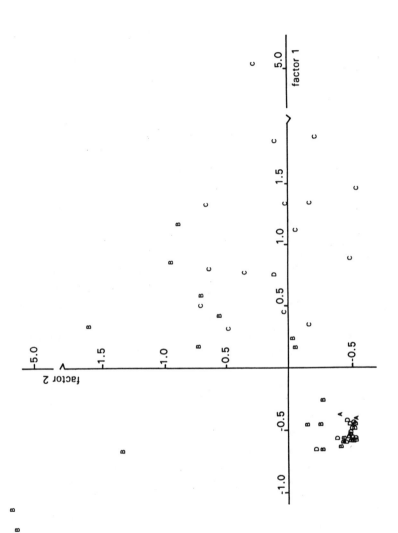

KEY: A interior surface; B exterior surface; C refuse deposit; D other general strata (after Healan, 1995, fig. 4).

Thirteen

CORRESPONDENCE ANALYSIS AND OTHER MULTIVARIATE TECHNIQUES

The previous chapter described PCA, the key technique for reducing the dimensionality of real numeric data, such as physical measurements. However, although PCA is in a sense the foundational technique, it is not especially suited to the analysis of data consisting of counts or presence/absence of nominal categories. But such data are arguably much more widely found in archaeology than numeric measurements – whether we are talking about counts of types in ceramic assemblages, presence/absence of particular types of grave goods, or numbers of different lithic types in a stone artefact assemblage; indeed, any case where we are looking for patterning in terms of counts (abundance data) or presence/absence (incidence data) of some feature.

In these situations the technique to use is correspondence analysis, which may be regarded as the PCA for this kind of data. The technique is a more recent development than the others described. It was developed particularly in France and although its potential was quickly appreciated by French archaeologists (cf. Djindjian, 1980) and thereafter in Scandinavia (e.g. Madsen, 1988), it took a long time to percolate into Anglo–American circles, at least partly because of the delay before it was incorporated into widely used statistics packages. Instead, normal PCA was used or the data were converted into similarities/distances and investigated by means of cluster analysis (Chapter 11) or principal coordinates analysis (see below). The virtue of correspondence analysis is that it carries out a PCA-type analysis directly on the original data matrix of values of objects on variables, without the intervening information-losing step of creating similarities/distances.

As usual, what is involved is best illustrated by examples. The principles will be illustrated by means of a very simple data set and then an analysis of a more realistic set of archaeological data will be carried out. The description of the principles is derived from Greenacre (1993), who offers a very full account of the method at the sort of level which is appropriate here.

Table 13.1 contains a small subset of the information from Baxter, 1994 (Table A3) describing a set of mesolithic assemblages in terms of counts of a number of types.

TABLE 13.1. Composition of five mesolithic assemblages in terms of the counts of three different lithic types.

| Assemblages | Types | | | |
	Microliths	Scrapers	Burins	Total
1	68	37	8	113
2	136	95	3	234
3	41	0	3	44
4	690	181	26	897
5	78	165	19	262
Total	1013	478	59	1550

Clearly, if we want to make a comparison of these assemblages in terms of the representation of the different types we need to take some measures to make them comparable with one another, by removing the effect of the differential assemblage sizes. We do this by converting the figures into percentages or proportions so that what we end up with is a comparable *profile* for each row. Such profiles are the starting point for correspondence analysis (hereafter CA). Those for the data in Table 13.1 are shown in Table 13.2.

Thus, we can see, for example, that microliths tend to dominate in the majority of the assemblages and are overwhelmingly predominant in assemblage 3, while assemblage 5 is unusual in that scrapers are the most important type. At the bottom of the table we have the *average profile*, obtained by taking the total number of lithics overall, as given in Table 13.1 (1550), and then dividing each of the individual type totals by this grand total. Overall, in other words, microliths make up approximately 65 per cent, scrapers 31 per cent and burins 4 per cent of the lithics.

TABLE 13.2. Composition of five mesolithic assemblages in terms of the proportions of three different lithic types.

	Types		
Assemblages	Microliths	Scrapers	Burins
1	0.60	0.33	0.08
2	0.58	0.41	0.01
3	0.93	0.0	0.07
4	0.77	0.20	0.03
5	0.30	0.63	0.07
Average	0.654	0.308	0.038

But as well as looking at the rows – the individual assemblages – of Table 13.1 and comparing them with one another, we can also look at the columns, which tell us how the types are distributed between the assemblages. Here too, if we want to compare the distribution of the types over the assemblages we have to remove the effect of the different totals – 893 microliths compared with 59 burins, for example – by again turning the figures into proportions or percentages. If we do this, we end up with *column profiles*. Those for Table 13.1 are shown in Table 13.3.

TABLE 13.3. Proportions of three different lithic types in five mesolithic assemblages.

	Types			
Assemblages	Microliths	Scrapers	Burins	Average
1	0.07	0.08	0.14	0.07
2	0.13	0.20	0.05	0.15
3	0.04	0.00	0.05	0.03
4	0.68	0.38	0.44	0.58
5	0.08	0.35	0.32	0.17

From this we can see, for example, that the majority of the microliths are found in assemblage 4, while scrapers and burins are not nearly so concentrated in a single assemblage, with quite large proportions in assemblages 4 and 5. If we look at the average column, obtained by dividing the total for each assemblage by the sum total for all the assemblages together, we see clearly that 58 per cent of all the lithics belong to assemblage 4, with the remainder divided not too unequally between the other four assemblages.

Because we only have three variables here – microliths, scrapers and burins – and for each assemblage the three together sum to 100 per cent, we can represent the assemblages on a so-called *ternary diagram* or *tripolar graph*. This is because percentages and proportions are closed scales; once we know two of the values the third one is fixed. Thus, in the case of assemblage 2, once we know that 0.58 of the assemblage is made up of microliths and 0.41 of scrapers, then the value for burins must be 0.01.

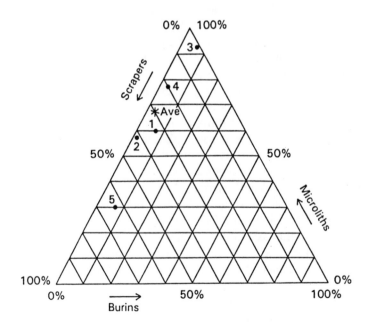

FIGURE 13.1. Tripolar graph of the composition of five mesolithic assemblages in terms of the percentages of microliths, scrapers and burins. The overall average composition is also shown.

Figure 13.1 shows the tripolar graph for the lithic assemblages. Each side of the triangle represents a percentage scale, in this case one for microliths, one for scrapers and one for burins. Obviously, if we had four or five lithic types with the frequencies turned into proportions we would still have a closed scale but it would no longer be possible to represent it in two dimensions. Four variables would need a three-dimensional representation (a tetrahedron) and so on. In the present case, though, two dimensions are sufficient.

How do we read it? At the extreme, an assemblage in the corner at the bottom right would have 100 per cent burins and nothing else, an assemblage in the corner at the bottom left would be 100 per cent scrapers, and one at the very top would be 100 per cent microliths. But let us also look specifically at assemblage 1. This lies at the 0.6 or 60 per cent point on the microlith scale, at the 33 per cent point on the scraper scale and the 8 per cent point on the burin scale. The row average is also marked on the diagram and we can see that some assemblages are closer to the average than others. Another way of looking at it is to see the individual assemblages as representing different combinations of the three extremes noted above.

We obtained the row average shown on the diagram and given in Table 13.2 by simply totalling the numbers of microliths, scrapers and burins and dividing by the total number of lithics. But we can also think of it another way, as a weighted average of the individual rows. To see what this means let us focus on the microliths. If we sum the proportions of the microliths in the five assemblages a glance will show that the answer will not be 0.65. What's wrong? The answer is that each row or assemblage must be weighted by how big it is in proportion to the total. Thus, if we look at the right-hand column in Table 13.3, we see that assemblage 1 makes up only 0.07 (7 per cent) of the total number of lithics, whereas assemblage 4 makes up 0.58 (58 per cent). It makes sense for assemblage 4 to have a bigger effect on the average than assemblage 1 does, and this is what happens. Accordingly, to keep with the microliths, if we take the 0.6 of assemblage 1 that is made up of microliths and multiply this by the 0.07 that assemblage 1 makes up of the total we will give it the correct weight. If we do this operation for each assemblage and sum the results, we obtain 0.65, the correct overall proportion of microliths. Of course, we can do the same for the scrapers and burins.

In other words, although we are dealing all the time with proportions rather than frequencies, we still take into account the size of the assemblages. Bigger assemblages have more weight, which seems intuitively correct. Here the profile of assemblage 4 has most weight and that of assemblage 3 the least. In correspondence analysis the weight of a profile is known as its *mass*. The greater the mass of a row (or column, the point applies equally to these), the more influence it has on the CA result.

At this point we can ask: to what extent are the individual assemblages different from the average? Answering this question takes us back to the contingency table chi-squared test described in Chapter 7. We have found that the average assemblage consists of 1013/1550 = 65.4 per cent microliths, 478/1550 = 30.8 per cent scrapers and 59/1550 = 3.8 per cent burins (see Table 13.1). If the individual assemblages were like this average we would expect them to be split up in these same proportions.

TABLE 13.4. Composition of five mesolithic assemblages in terms of the counts of three different lithic types, with the expected values for each category based on the assumption of no difference between the assemblages shown in parentheses beneath.

| Assemblages | Types | | | |
	Microliths	*Scrapers*	*Burins*	*Total*
1	68	37	8	113
	(73.8)	(34.9)	(4.3)	
2	136	95	3	234
	(152.9)	(72.2)	(8.9)	
3	41	0	3	44
	(28.8)	(13.6)	(1.6)	
4	690	181	26	897
	(586.2)	(276.6)	(34.1)	
5	78	165	19	262
	(171.2)	(80.8)	(10.0)	
Total	1013	478	59	1550

Thus, referring to assemblage 1, which has 113 lithics, if it was like the average it would have 0.654 × 113 = 73.8 microliths,

0.308 × 113 = 34.9 scrapers and 0.038 × 113 = 4.3 burins. In actual fact, the figures are 68, 37 and 8 respectively. Of course, we can obtain the expected values for all the cells in the table (see Table 13.4) and calculate the total chi-squared value which, at 235.1 with 8 d.f., is highly significant. In other words, the table is not homogeneous. The distribution of microliths, scrapers and burins does not correspond to what we would expect if the rows of the table were all essentially the same as one another, i.e. if they all corresponded to the average.

This is all very well, but our interest is really in comparing the row *profiles* of the table, not the absolute frequencies. In fact, it is quite straightforward to do this. Let us take the chi-squared calculations for assemblage 1.

$$\frac{(68-73.8)^2}{73.8} + \frac{(37-34.9)^2}{34.9} + \frac{(8-4.3)^2}{4.3}$$

We can re-express this in terms of the row profile elements from Table 13.2 and the row total, which in this case is 113, the total number of lithics in assemblage 1:

$$113\,\frac{(0.60-0.654)^2}{0.654} + 113\,\frac{(0.33-0.308)^2}{0.308}$$

$$+113\,\frac{(0.08-0.038)^2}{0.038}$$

Thus, the general formula is

> (*row total* × (*row profile element – expected row profile element*)^2/*expected row profile element*)
> (Greenacre, 1993, eq. 4.3)

And we can do this for all the rows in the table, adding all the elements to obtain our chi-squared result.

But there is one more step to be taken. We saw in Chapter 7 that if we divide the chi-squared value by the sample size we end up with a measure of the strength of the association between the two variables concerned, or the *extent* of the departure of observed from expected values. We can apply that idea here, where $n = 1550$

$$\frac{\chi^2}{1550} = \frac{113}{1550} \left[\frac{(0.60-0.654)^2}{0.654} + \frac{(0.33-0.308)^2}{0.308} \right.$$

$$\left. + \frac{(0.08-0.038)^2}{0.038} \right] + \textit{the corresponding terms}$$

for the other assemblages

For each row (each assemblage here) this formula gives us a measure of its distance from the notional average row or assemblage. In fact, it is a distance measure analogous to the Euclidean distance measure we saw in Chapter 11, except that the squared distances are weighted by their corresponding expected values. Because of this it is known as the *chi-squared distance*: a measure of the distance of each row from the overall row average.

But there is one more element of the equation that needs mentioning, the 113/1550 element at the beginning. This 113/1550 is 0.07 which, as we have already seen, is the mass of row 1, the proportion that row 1 makes up of the total number of observations. In other words, the contribution that each row makes to the total departure from expectation is weighted by its mass; rows containing more of the observations have more influence on the result.

To summarise this rather elaborate procedure, if we take each row, sum the (observed – expected) terms to obtain its distance from the average and weight that distance by the mass of the row, repeat that operation for all the rows and add up the result, we have the *chi-squared/n* term. The sum of weighted distances which this represents is known as the *total inertia* in the table, the total amount of departure from the average. Those rows which contribute the most to this will be those which have the largest departures from the average and the largest mass.

In a table where the expected and observed values do not depart too much from one another χ^2/n, the total inertia, will be relatively slight. Where the departure is large, it will obviously be much greater.

This has all been described in terms of differences between the rows, the assemblages in this case; we are investigating whether the assemblages are different in terms of the proportional distribution of types across them. But we can do exactly the same analysis for the columns, asking whether the different lithic types are differentially distributed across the assemblages. Clearly, the total inertia in the table is still exactly the same and so are the individual cell values, the $(O - E)^2/E$ terms, but now we sum them for each column and weight them by their column mass, to give the overall departure or distance of each *column* from the average, and the total for all the columns sums to the total inertia.

These chi-squared distances are satisfactory as they stand in the context of the triangular space in which they have been set up. But we are more used to straight-line Euclidean distances of the type we saw in Chapter 11, which presupposes spaces defined by axes at right angles to one another. We need to transform our chi-squared distances so that they correspond to straight-line distances in Euclidean space (Greenacre, 1993, p. 33). This involves dividing the individual row profile elements, which specify the position of the rows in the equilateral triangular space, by the square root of the corresponding column average. This operation, in effect, stretches the three sides of the triangle differentially so that it is no longer an equilateral one. Thus, the absolute distance to go from 0 per cent to 100 per cent on one axis will be longer than that on another. Once this is done the chi-squared distances can indeed be read as Euclidean ones.

The transformed values for assemblages 1 and 2 are as follows:

$$\frac{0.6}{\sqrt{0.654}} \qquad \frac{0.33}{\sqrt{0.308}} \qquad \frac{0.08}{\sqrt{0.038}}$$

$$\frac{0.58}{\sqrt{0.654}} \qquad \frac{0.41}{\sqrt{0.308}} \qquad \frac{0.01}{\sqrt{0.038}}$$

Thus, for assemblage 1 we have [0.74 0.59 0.41] and for assemblage 2 [0.72 0.74 0.05].

For each assemblage these three values represent its location in a three-dimensional Euclidean space represented by the three variables, microliths, scrapers and burins. The position of the average is at [0.81 0.55 0.19]. We can obtain the straight-line distances between these points, and in particular between the individual rows or assemblages and the overall average. The sum total of these distances, weighted by the mass of the corresponding row, gives us the total inertia in the data, as we have seen. The transformed coordinates for all the assemblages are shown in Table 13.5 and they are represented in Figure 13.2.

TABLE 13.5. Transformed coordinates of five mesolithic assemblages in the three-dimensional Euclidean space shown in Figure 13.2.

	Types		
Assemblages	*Microliths*	*Scrapers*	*Burins*
1	0.74	0.59	0.41
2	0.72	0.74	0.05
3	1.15	0.00	0.36
4	0.95	0.36	0.15
5	0.37	1.14	0.19
Average	0.81	0.55	0.19

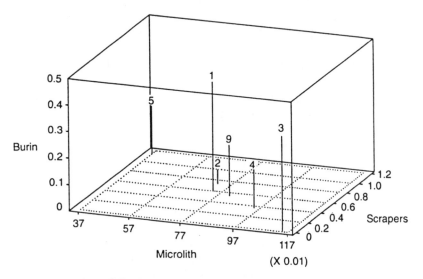

FIGURE 13.2. 3-D plot of the composition of five mesolithic assemblages in terms of the percentages of microliths, scrapers and burins, with the values scaled so that the straight-line distances between the points are Euclidean. The position of the overall average is given by the point labelled 9.

We have now got to the point where we can represent our assemblages in a Euclidean coordinate system, where the distances between them relate to their departure from the average of the data as a whole, within a framework based on the analysis of contingency tables, in which we have values for both rows and columns (objects and variables). When the distances are weighted by the mass of the rows (or columns) concerned, we get a measure of the contribution to inertia of those rows (or columns) and the sum total for all the rows (or columns) is the total inertia in the data.

In the case of three variables there is no problem about representing the result but clearly, once the number of variables increases, such a representation becomes impossible and we are back with the issue raised by PCA. Is there some way in which we can reduce the dimensionality of the data and still retain most of the information? With CA as opposed to PCA, however, instead of dealing with a scatter of points whose position is defined by their values on a series of more or less correlated variables, the position of the points is now defined in terms of their chi-squared distance from the overall average.

If the cloud of points is equally scattered in all directions, there is not a lot we can do about it. However, as with PCA, if the scatter is elongated in some specific direction then we can fit a line through the points in that direction and project the points onto that line. In PCA, if such a line or axis is a good one, it accounts for a large proportion of the variance in the data, as we saw in the previous chapter. Hopefully, a small number of PC axes accounts for most of the variance. In CA the principle is exactly the same but instead of variance we are dealing with inertia. If there is one particular direction in which the weighted distances of the points from the average – their inertia – are particularly great then an axis or line placed along that direction will account for most of the inertia in the data. As usual, we can measure the deviations of the points from the line in terms of the sum of squared deviations – the best-fit line is that which minimises the sum of squared chi-squared deviations, taking into account the mass of the data points. Ideally, we will be able to represent the data in a space of two or three dimensions defined by these new axes, which accounts for a high percentage of the inertia in the data. CA involves finding the successive axes, in exactly the same way as PCA.

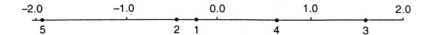

FIGURE 13.3. The five mesolithic assemblages plotted onto the first CA axis of a space defined by the variables.

The one-dimensional display for the five mesolithic assemblages is shown in Figure 13.3 (cf. Greenacre, 1993, exhibit 6.3). Since there are three variables in this case the number of dimensions required to represent accurately the chi-squared distances between the row profiles is two, so the distances between them along this single dimension are only approximate – a certain amount of distortion is going on. However, in this analysis the first axis accounts for 94.5 per cent of the inertia in the data so the loss or distortion is not very great.

The space in which the assemblages lie is defined by their proportions of scrapers, burins and microliths and, as we have seen, can be represented by the stretched sides of a tripolar graph: an assemblage with all microliths would be at one corner, one with all scrapers would be at another and one with all burins would be at the third. But although it is bound to involve a fair amount of distortion of the position of at least one of the variables, we can also project the locations of our *variables* onto our single dimension (see Fig. 13.4) and this is likely to help our interpretation. In this case the important scraper and microlith variables are represented pretty accurately; it is only the relatively insignificant burin variable whose position is drastically distorted. We can see from the diagram that assemblage 5 is strongly towards the scraper end of the axis while assemblage 3 is at the microlith end. In the simple case that we're illustrating here this was, of course, obvious from the start, but when there are more realistic numbers of variables and units this is not the case.

So far we have described the analysis of the assemblages, the row profiles of our data matrix, but in fact there is also an analysis of the variables, the lithic-type column profiles, which has been mentioned only in passing. If you feel more at ease with the idea that it is the rows of a data matrix that we analyse, imagine turning the data matrix on its side so that now the three columns (the types) become three rows and the five assemblages make up the columns. We can now ask how the types lie in terms of their distribution across the assemblages. This is the columns analysis that CA carries out at the same time as it carries out its row analysis. The result is the same, in that the first axis again accounts for 94.5 per cent of the inertia, but this time it is the inertia in the lithic type profiles, not the assemblage

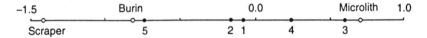

FIGURE 13.4. The five mesolithic assemblages and the variables plotted onto the first CA axis of a space defined by the variables.

profiles. The analysis has defined a space in which the types are located in terms of the assemblages. Figure 13.5 shows the one-dimensional result for the types, with the assemblages also projected onto the axis. Note that because it is now the assemblages which define the space it is their locations which are markedly distorted. Note too that whereas in the first analysis the assemblages were 'inside' the types, it is now the types which are 'inside' the assemblages, and the configuration of the types represents a contracted version of that seen in the row analysis (Fig. 13.4); the distances are much smaller but the relationships are the same. Conversely, the configuration of the rows – the assemblages – represents an exactly corresponding expansion of that seen in the row analysis.

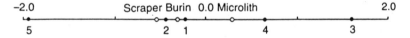

FIGURE 13.5. The three variables (microliths, scrapers and burins) and the five assemblages plotted onto the first CA axis of a space defined by the assemblages.

However, just as with PCA, rather than looking at the objects and variables merely in relation to a single dimension, we can also produce a two-dimensional scattergram, in which the horizontal and vertical axes can represent any pair of the CA principal axes that we want, although usually it is the first two that are of interest. Figure 13.6 shows the two-dimensional scattergram of the analysis of the assemblage profiles. As we have seen, the first axis represents 94.5 per cent of the inertia. Axis 2 represents the remaining 5.5 per cent, so between them we have an accurate picture of the locations of the assemblages in the space defined by the variables. The crossing point of the two axes represents the average profile, so locations away from this represent departures from the average. In this case we can see that the main trend of variation runs from high scraper proportions on the left to high microlith proportions on the right, the two being strongly inversely correlated with one another. Variation along this dimension is relatively continuous although there is a suggestion that assemblage 5, with its high scraper values, is distinct from the others. The burin dimension makes very little difference: there is only a tiny amount of variation in the vertical direction.

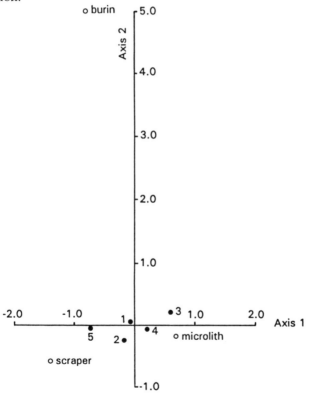

FIGURE 13.6. The five mesolithic assemblages plotted into a two-dimensional CA space defined by the variables, which are also shown.

In Figure 13.6 the positions of the assemblages, the row profiles, are defined in relation to the variables, the types, in the
principal axis space. Such a CA scattergram is said to be *asym-
metrically scaled* (Greenacre, 1993, p. 67). But, just as we saw
with the one-dimensional case, we can also have a two-dimensional display of the lithic types, the column profiles, in relation
to their distribution across the assemblages, in the principal
axis space. The result is shown in Figure 13.7. This too is an
asymmetric display and as we saw above, the two displays are
connected to one another by relations of expansion and contrac-
tion, which are especially easy to see in relation to the location
of the lithic types in the two scattergrams.

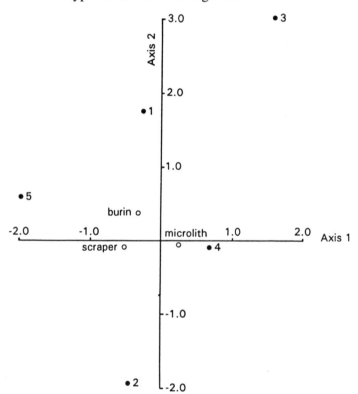

FIGURE 13.7. The three variables plotted into a two-dimensional CA
space defined by the assemblages, which are also shown.

However, it is also possible to produce a *symmetric* scattergram and, as Greenacre notes (1993, p. 69), this is by far the most popular option even though some care needs to be taken in the interpretation of such symmetric displays. In a symmetric display both the row profiles and the column profiles, the assemblages and the types, are plotted, but not one in terms of the other as in the asymmetric displays. In effect, the locations of the assemblages from 13.6 (assemblages in relation to types) and of the types from Figure 13.7 (types in relation to assemblages) are overlaid on one another even though, strictly speaking, they come from different spaces, the first a space defined by the types, the second one defined by the assemblages. The result is shown in Figure 13.8.

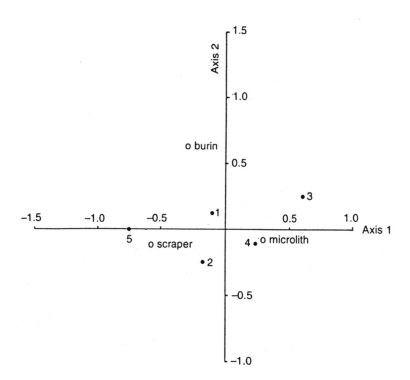

FIGURE 13.8. The assemblages and variables plotted into a two-dimensional symmetric CA space.

In such a space the distances between the assemblages (rows) correspond to their chi-squared distances (assuming that the display contains a high proportion of the inertia, as here) and the same is true of the distances between the lithic types (the columns). However, this is *not* true of the distances between the rows and the columns (the assemblages and the types); because they come from different spaces these distances *cannot be taken literally*. We can only talk in relative terms and point out, for example, that assemblage 5 is more associated with scrapers, while assemblage 3 at the other end of the axis is more associated with microliths. The dangers are indicated by the fact that assemblages 1 and 2 are reasonably close to burins but reference to Table 13.2 shows that in both cases the burin proportion is minute. Figure 13.6 is much more realistic in this respect since the distance interpretation of assemblage-type relations is more justified.

Finally, Greenacre (1993, pp. 71–2) makes the very important point that if we are interpreting distances on such scattergrams it is essential that the vertical and horizontal distances are scaled in the same way; in other words, the distance of one unit in the horizontal x direction must be the same as the distance of one unit in the vertical y direction. This needs checking carefully because even if the original is correctly scaled, importing it, for example, into a word-processing program for inclusion in a document may lead to the scales being altered automatically to fit the page.

However, in interpreting the results of a CA we are not just restricted to looking at the scattergrams and noting the percentage of the inertia accounted for by the axes. Other information is also available and of interest. To start with, we can go back to our original data table and calculate the contribution to inertia made by each individual cell of the table. Thus, the total chi-squared value for our table was 235.1, of which row 4, column 1 (assemblage 4 microliths) contributed 18.4, or 18.4/235.1 = 7.8 per cent. The table of contributions to inertia is shown in Table 13.6.

We can easily see from this that assemblage 5's scraper proportion contributes over 37 per cent of the total inertia and its microlith proportion contributes another 22 per cent or so. Similarly, we can sum these values for the rows and columns to establish the contribution that each of the assemblages and each of the types makes to the total inertia; these figures are also shown in Table 13.6. Thus, of the types, scrapers contribute by far the most inertia, at over 60 per cent with microliths second and burins contributing very little. Assemblage 5 contributes practically three times more of the inertia than any of the others, a massive 62.3 per cent.

TABLE 13.6. Cell contributions to inertia for the five mesolithic assemblages.

	Types			
Assemblages	*Microliths*	*Scrapers*	*Burins*	*Row contribution*
1	0.2	0.04	0.7	0.94
2	0.8	3.1	1.7	5.6
3	2.2	5.8	0.5	8.5
4	7.8	14.0	0.8	22.6
5	21.6	37.3	3.4	62.3
Column contribution	32.6	60.2	7.1	100

These row and column contributions are given again in Table 13.7, a table of CA diagnostics produced by the WINBASP program (Scollar, 1994), in the column headed *Inr*, except that they have been multiplied by 1000, as is usual CA practice, rather than 100; there are also small differences arising from rounding error. Thus, in Table 13.6 we have given the contribution of assemblage 5 as 62.3 per cent while here it is 620.

The column headed *Mass* gives the mass of the rows and columns as described above, but now expressed as a number out of 1000. The columns headed *Comp 1* and *Comp 2* give the co-ordinates of the assemblages and the types on the two principal axes. In this case the table refers to the symmetric display of assemblages and variables.

But the table also contains other information of interest. The first column, *Qlt* (quality) gives a measure of how well the two-axis CA space describes the position of the rows and columns. In this case, because the two axes between them account for 100 per cent of the inertia, the quality of the representation is 1000, or 100 per cent, in all cases. A low value for a particular row or column would be an indication that it is not very well characterised by these two dimensions.

TABLE 13.7. Correspondence analysis diagnostics for the five mesolithic assemblages

Units	Qlt	Mass	Inr	Comp 1	Cor	Ctr	Comp 2	Cor	Ctr
1	1000	73	16	−93	256	4	−158	744	217
2	1000	151	55	−170	522	30	163	478	481
3	1000	28	84	617	844	75	−266	156	239
4	1000	579	225	244	999	238	6	1	3
5	1000	169	620	−746	995	652	−55	5	60

Types	Qlt	Mass	Inr	Comp 1	Cor	Ctr	Comp 2	Cor	Ctr
micro	1000	654	324	275	999	343	−7	1	4
scraper	1000	308	599	−543	994	630	−41	6	62
burin	1000	38	77	−323	337	28	453	663	934

Further to the right are two columns labelled *Ctr*, the first referring to axis 1 and the second to axis 2. This tells us what proportion of the inertia accounted for by each axis is contributed by each of the assemblages and types (rows and columns). Thus, we can see that assemblage 5 contributes 652 (or 65.2 per cent) of the inertia accounted for by axis 1, assemblage 4 contributes 238 (23.8 per cent), and so on. Similarly for the variables; scrapers contribute 630 (63 per cent) of the inertia accounted for by axis 1, microliths 34.3 per cent and burins only 2.8 per cent. For axis 2 the biggest contribution is from assemblage 2, which contributes 48.1 per cent of the inertia it accounts for; of the types, burins contribute 93.4 per cent. These figures are referred to as *absolute contributions to inertia*.

But we can also ask a slightly different question: how much of the inertia in the individual row and column profiles does a particular axis account for? The sum total accounted for by all the axes produced (here two) put together is given by the quality figure we've already looked at. As we have seen, it is 100 per cent in all cases: the two axes account for all the inertia in the data. The contributions of the specific axes to accounting for inertia in a specific row or column are given by the two *Cor* columns, one for each axis. Thus, 99.5 per cent (995) of the inertia associated with assemblage 5 is accounted for by axis 1 and only 0.5 per cent by axis 2; in the case of assemblage 1 25.6 per cent is associated with axis 1 and 74.4 per cent with axis 2.

For the types we see that 99.9 per cent of the inertia associated with microliths and 99.4 per cent of that associated with scrapers is accounted for by axis 1, leaving only 0.1 per cent and 0.6 per cent respectively to be accounted for by axis 2. In the case of burins it is 33.7 per cent and 66.3 per cent respectively. Theses quantities, for both assemblages and types (rows and columns) are known as *relative contributions to inertia.*

There are various other aspects of CA which Greenacre (1993) describes, and readers are referred to this if they want more information. The account given here has been quite a detailed one which describes the key aspects of the method and its output. However, the simplified example doesn't give any indication of the dimensionality reduction capacities of the technique, so this treatment will be completed by the presentation of a more realistic archaeological example.

AN ARCHAEOLOGICAL CASE-STUDY: DANISH BRONZE AGE HOARDS

The case-study involves a set of Bronze Age hoards from present-day Denmark published by Levy (1982); the data have been slightly modified. Each hoard is described in terms of the frequency of occurrence (abundance) of a series of types. Only hoards containing more than a single type and types occurring more than once have been included in the analysis; the result is a dataset consisting of counts of twenty types in forty-four hoards; it is listed in Table 13.8. Most of the type names are self-explanatory but some deserve a brief comment: palstaves are bronze flanged axes; celts are stone axe/adzes; tutuli are small decorative sheet bronze cones; tubes are bronze tubes most probably used for decorating skirts; axes are bronze shaft-hole axes.

The hoards and their social significance have been extensively discussed by Scandinavian Bronze Age scholars, particularly in terms of gender symbolism and the extent to which the hoards can be considered as of male or female character (see for example Sorensen, 1992, and references therein).

TABLE 13.8. The contents of a series of Danish hoards.

Hoard	Types				
1	2 belt plates	2 neck collars	4 spiral finger rings	Tubes	33 tutuli
2	2 arm rings	1 belt hook	2 neck collars	3 spiral arm rings	13 tutuli
3	1 spear	1 weapon palstave			
4	3 arm rings	2 belt plates	2 neck collars	1 sickle	
5	1 belt plate	1 knife	2 plain palstaves		
6	2 arm rings	1 fibula	1 neck collar	1 spiral arm ring	
7	1 plain palstave	1 sickle	3 spears		
8	4 arm rings	3 belt plates	1 neck collar	31 tutuli	
10	2 neck collars	1 spiral arm ring			
11	1 chisel	3 spears	1 sword		
13	1 celt	2 plain palstaves			
14	1 arm ring	1 belt hook	6 plain palstaves	1 sword	

No.								
17	1 arm ring	3 awls		2 neck collars	1 plain palstave	2 sickles	1 spiral arm ring	1 tutulus
18	1 belt plate	1 knife	1 belt plate 2 spiral arm rings					
21	1 belt plate	1 spear						
22	3 belt plates	3 neck collars	1 saw	1 sickle	4 spiral arm rings	8 spiral finger rings	21 tutuli	
24	6 sickles	4 spears						
25	2 belt plates	1 fish hook						
26	1 arm ring	2 plain palstaves	1 spear	1 sword				
29	2 belt plates	1 knife	1 neck collar	2 sickles	2 tutuli			
30	1 celt	1 weapon palstave						
33	2 knives	2 plain palstaves	15 sickles	16 spears	2 swords			
34	1 chisel	1 knife	8 sickles	5 spears	1 weapon palstave			
36	1 arm ring	3 belt plates	1 chisel	2 plain palstaves	4 sickles	1 spear		
37	3 belt plates	1 neck collar	7 tutuli					
40	2 sickles	3 spears						
42	1 plain palstave	2 sickles						
43	4 arm rings	1 neck collar						

Hoard	Types									
44	1 belt plate	1 celt	2 daggers							
45	Amber	1 awl	17 tutuli tubes							
48	1 belt plate	1 neck collar	6 tutuli							
49	1 belt plate	4 tutuli								
51	1 axe	1 sword								
52	1 celt	7 sickles	1 sword							
53	Amber	2 neck collars	1 sword							
55	7 plain palstaves	1 weapon palstave								
56	5 arm rings	1 awl	1 neck collar	5 tutuli						
57	1 celt	1 chisel	2 plain palstaves	1 sword						
58	1 celt	1 weapon palstave								
59	2 belt plates	1 celt	1 chisel	1 dagger	2 neck collars	4 plain palstaves	2 sickles	3 spears	2 spiral arm rings	18 tutuli
60	19 plain palstaves	3 spears								
61	1 belt plate	2 spears								
62	1 axe	1 celt	1 plain palstave	6 spears	1 sword					
63	4 plain palstaves	2 sickles								

Tables 13.9 and 13.10 show the results of the CA of these data. The number of axes selected is four and Table 13.9 shows that together these account for roughly 50 per cent of the inertia in the data, the most important, axis 1, accounting for 18 per cent of this. We can now take an initial look at the diagnostics from the analysis (Table 13.10), starting with the *mass* column which, as we have seen above, gives a measure of the weight of the individual units and variables (rows and columns). With regard to the variables, we can see that the tutuli have by far the greatest mass because of their large number of occurrences; spears, sickles and plain palstaves also have masses of more than 100, an indication of a fairly high number of occurrences, whereas axes, amber, tubes and belt-hooks, which occur only twice, have a mass of 4. There is not much variation in the mass of the individual hoards; the biggest is hoard 1, with a mass of 84 and hoard 22, with a mass of 80.

TABLE 13.9. Danish hoard correspondence analysis: summary statistics.

Component	Eigenvalue	% Inertia	Cumulative % inertia
1	0.805569	18.3	18.3
2	0.538717	12.3	30.6
3	0.450089	10.2	40.8
4	0.380434	8.7	49.5

We can now turn to the inertia (*Inr*) column. As we have seen, the inertia of a row or column (hoard or type) is a measure of the distance of that row or column from the average, weighted by its mass. Hoards (rows) and types (columns) which have a high inertia will have a major impact on the CA result. A look at the inertia values of the columns (types) shows that the differences between them are not great: plain palstaves make the greatest contribution to inertia with a value of 116 (i.e. they make up 11.6 per cent of the inertia in the variables; behind them is a group of variables contributing around 7 per cent: tutuli, arm-rings, weapon palstaves, spears, sickles, daggers and axes; whereas tubes contribute only 1.4 per cent. If we now look at the hoards, we see that most of the inertia values are very low, between 1 per cent and 4 per cent, but hoard 44, which contains a belt-plate, a celt and a dagger contributes 8.2 per cent; and

TABLE 13.10. Correspondence analysis diagnostics for the Danish hoards.

Name	Qlt	Mass	Inr	Comp 1	Cor	Ctr	Comp 2	Cor	Ctr	Comp 3	Cor	Ctr	Comp 4	Cor	Ctr
beltpla	98	62	27	379	76	11	-110	6	1	-169	15	4	-14	0	0
neckcol	491	48	37	740	165	33	79	2	1	312	29	10	992	296	125
tutuli	891	351	75	825	723	297	1	0	0	-80	7	5	-389	161	140
awl	141	10	38	541	18	4	125	1	0	527	17	6	1329	106	47
tubes	100	4	14	994	63	5	-7	0	0	-134	1	0	-761	37	6
chisel	84	10	24	-868	72	9	-320	10	2	-137	2	0	24	0	0
arm ring	767	48	70	551	48	18	340	18	10	674	72	49	1997	629	505
spirarm	127	28	36	683	83	16	49	0	0	180	6	2	464	38	16
belthook	109	4	17	-91	0	0	1278	87	12	574	18	3	274	4	1
weapals	507	10	75	-1418	62	25	593	11	7	-3686	417	303	772	18	16
celt	709	18	48	-828	59	15	362	11	4	-2669	610	286	575	28	16
spear	716	104	74	-1180	447	181	-891	254	154	187	11	8	-105	4	3
sickle	624	120	69	-829	272	103	-921	335	190	194	15	10	-762	2	1
plainpal	989	112	116	-1167	301	190	1689	632	596	384	33	37	-323	23	31
knife	94	12	27	-682	47	7	-626	39	9	275	8	2	-63	0	0
sword	250	18	35	-1320	207	39	-337	14	4	223	6	2	438	23	9
spirfin	244	24	32	965	159	28	-36	0	0	-90	1	0	-696	83	31
dagger	389	6	77	-24	0	0	324	2	1	-4497	362	271	1179	25	22
axe	82	4	67	-1681	38	14	-1114	17	9	60	0	0	1400	27	21
amber	47	4	43	1028	22	5	87	0	0	319	2	1	1022	22	11

Average
Type QLT 373

Units Name	Qlt	Mass	Inr	Comp 1	Cor	Ctr	Comp 2	Cor	Ctr	Comp 3	Cor	Ctr	Comp 4	Cor	Ctr
1	846	84	26	910	610	87	-6	0	0	-101	8	2	-557	229	69
2	420	42	17	810	373	34	148	12	2	145	12	2	200	23	4
3	351	4	24	-1448	80	10	-203	2	0	-2607	259	61	541	11	3
4	677	16	16	427	42	4	6	0	0	466	50	8	1595	585	107
5	208	8	14	-734	73	5	900	109	12	326	14	2	-293	12	2
6	768	8	14	703	64	5	275	10	1	686	61	8	2209	633	103
7	625	10	7	-1234	485	19	-519	86	5	340	37	3	-232	17	1
8	654	78	20	847	637	70	40	1	0	0	0	0	-130	15	3
10	211	6	17	804	53	5	94	1	0	399	13	2	1324	144	28
11	288	10	20	-1277	189	20	-907	95	15	193	4	1	48	0	0
13	567	6	12	-1174	151	10	1699	317	32	-944	98	12	-39	0	0
14	624	18	29	-973	136	21	1728	429	100	625	56	16	139	3	1
17	198	24	36	252	10	2	75	1	0	445	30	11	1020	157	66
18	20	8	26	296	6	1	-217	3	1	173	2	1	346	8	3
21	125	4	5	-447	37	1	-682	86	3	14	0	0	-96	2	0
22	422	80	37	844	354	71	-37	1	0	-40	1	0	-366	66	28
24	769	20	16	-1080	331	29	-1238	436	57	285	23	4	-142	6	1
26	513	10	9	-954	237	11	679	120	9	553	79	7	546	77	8
29	94	16	8	112	5	0	-444	85	6	89	3	0	-6	0	0
30	679	4	34	-1251	42	8	650	11	3	-4736	594	200	1092	32	13
31	551	52	10	436	232	12	-239	70	6	-205	51	5	-403	198	22
33	911	74	44	-1134	497	119	-980	372	132	309	37	16	-119	5	3

Units Name	Qlt	Mass	Inr	Comp 1	Cor	Ctr	Comp 2	Cor	Ctr	Comp 3	Cor	Ctr	Comp 4	Cor	Ctr
34	723	32	23	-1079	374	46	-1037	345	64	-99	3	1	-41	1	0
36	195	24	11	-558	150	9	-171	14	1	219	23	3	125	8	1
37	448	22	8	775	395	16	-30	1	0	-103	7	1	-261	45	4
40	784	10	9	-1159	355	17	-1230	401	28	283	21	2	-152	6	1
42	359	6	5	-1049	299	8	-70	1	0	383	40	2	-257	18	1
43	753	10	30	656	33	5	392	12	3	897	61	18	2912	647	224
44	466	8	82	-139	0	0	306	2	1	-4409	432	347	1183	31	30
45	432	38	19	914	372	40	17	0	0	41	0	0	-364	59	13
48	241	18	16	874	201	17	-5	0	0	-78	2	0	-381	38	7
49	651	10	3	819	459	8	-29	1	0	-146	15	0	-509	177	7
51	80	4	69	-1672	37	14	-988	13	7	212	1	0	1490	30	23
52	363	18	22	-984	180	22	-973	176	32	-180	6	1	87	1	0
53	104	6	49	932	24	6	111	0	0	468	6	3	1625	74	42
55	866	16	27	-1335	242	36	2115	607	133	-186	5	1	-302	12	4
56	713	24	22	758	146	17	217	12	2	473	57	12	1400	498	124
57	276	10	20	-1192	161	18	840	80	13	-514	33	7	127	2	0
58	679	4	34	-1251	42	8	650	11	3	-4736	594	200	1092	32	13
59	373	72	6	212	117	4	101	26	1	-233	141	9	-185	89	6
60	951	44	58	-1302	292	93	1822	571	272	533	49	28	-476	39	26
61	259	6	7	-736	107	4	-859	146	8	102	2	0	-121	3	0
62	375	20	28	-1346	295	45	-646	68	16	-131	3	1	236	9	3
63	776	12	11	-1174	356	21	1116	321	28	478	59	6	-391	39	5

Average
Unit QLT 487

hoard 51, containing an axe and a sword contributes 6.9 per cent.

It is now time to turn to the results of the CA itself and specifically to the locations of the hoards and the types in the CA space. These are given by the *Comp 1* to *Comp 4* columns in Table 13.10; more informatively, they are also shown in Figures 13.9–13.11. These are *symmetric* displays of the types and hoards against pairs of CA axes: 1 and 2; 1 and 3; and 1 and 4. Because they are symmetric displays we have to take care how we interpret the relations in the scattergram between the type configuration and the hoard configuration, but in both cases the crossing point of the two axes represents the average position.

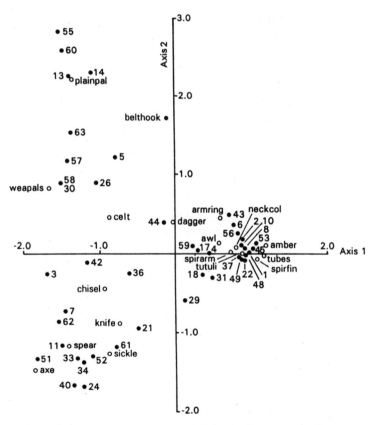

FIGURE 13.9. The Danish hoards and the artefact types they contain plotted into a symmetric space defined by CA axes 1 and 2.

We will first look at Figure 13.9, the scattergram for axes 1 and 2, and specifically at the distribution of types. Axis 1 is the most important, accounting for 18 per cent of the inertia, and it is apparent that it opposes two sets of types: amber, tubes, spiral finger-rings, awls, tutuli and belt-plates at the right-hand end; and a group at the other end made up of axes, spears, sickles, knives, chisels, swords and celts, which are, however, differentiated among themselves with respect to the second axis. In other words, we have personal ornaments at one end of the axis and tools and weapons at the other, and one possible inference is obviously that some sort of gender distinction is being symbolised here, so that there are 'male' hoards and 'female' hoards, although equally obviously such a system would need substantiation, perhaps by looking at the types of grave goods occurring with skeletons of known sex.

The basis of the differences among the putatively 'male' hoards at the left-hand end of axis 1 is not so clear. It is certainly not one between tools and weapons because these are inter-mixed with one another. It may be significant that all three of the upper types are non-shaft-hole axes of various types, both bronze and stone, but it is difficult to say any more, even though this axis does account for 12 per cent of the inertia.

The pattern in the types is clearly mirrored by the hoards and a glance at the contents of some of the individual hoards in Table 13.8 makes it perfectly clear why they are located where they are. What is more apparent with the hoards is that there is a suggestion of a roughly V-shaped trend in their distribution in the principal axis space, starting in the top left with hoard 55, going more or less vertically down and then going slightly up and across to the right, to the group of hoards associated with the ornament categories. This sort of pattern is very characteristic of correspondence analysis (see for example Madsen, 1988).

We can carry out exactly the same examination of the scatter-gram of hoards and types on axes 1 and 3 (Fig. 13.10). This time the contrast between the ornament group of types (and hoards) and the weapon/tool group is even more apparent, because the latter group is now more or less as concentrated as the former. Axis 3 seems to pick out solely a few outliers, daggers, celts and weapon palstaves as types, and the small group of four hoards particularly associated with them.

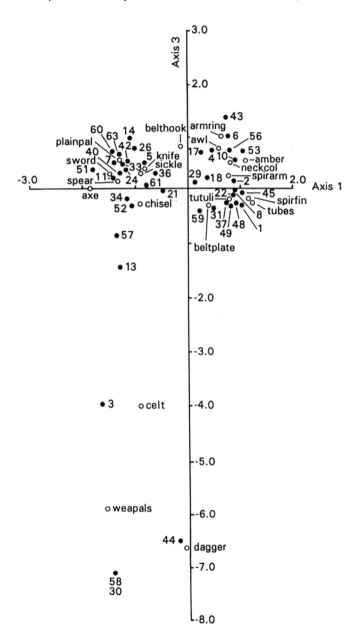

FIGURE 13.10. The Danish hoards and the types they contain plotted into a symmetric space defined by CA axes 1 and 3.

Finally, if we look at Figure 13.11 we can see the scattergram of axes 1 and 4. In some ways this is the converse of Figure 13.9. Now the weapon/tool complex is closely bunched together but the ornament group is spread out vertically, indicating some differences among ornament-dominated hoards along axis 4, accounting for about 8 per cent of the inertia. Here too there is a suggestion of a roughly V-shaped scatter of hoards and types.

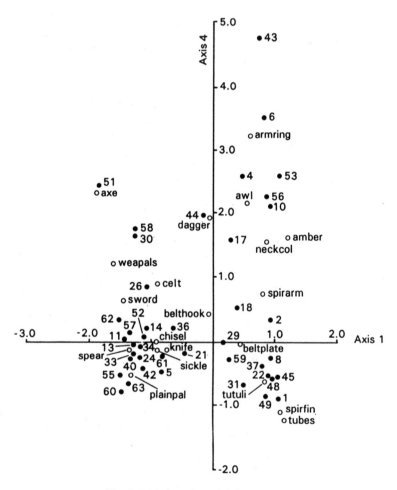

FIGURE 13.11. The Danish hoards and the types they contain plotted into a symmetric space defined by CA axes 1 and 4.

As we saw with our simple example, the diagnostics, which we have already begun looking at, can throw further light on these results. The *Qlt* (quality) column gives us a measure of how well our four-axis CA space describes the position of the types and hoards. If the four axes between them accounted for 100 per cent of the inertia, the quality would be 1000 (100 per cent) in all cases. In the present case the four axes only account for 50 per cent and the quality of the four-dimensional representation will vary from hoard to hoard and type to type. Those with high quality values will be well represented and those with low values poorly characterised by these four dimensions.

If we look first at the types, we can see that the average type quality of fit on the four axes used is 373; at the extremes, the quality of fit of plain palstaves is virtually perfect, while at the other extreme the quality of fit of amber to these four dimensions is virtually 0. Those with above-average values are neck-collars, tutuli, arm-rings, weapon palstaves, celts, spears, sickles, plain palstaves and daggers. The average quality of fit of the individual hoards is higher, at 487, and in some cases, such as hoard 60 with a value of 951, it is very high indeed; hoard 18, on the other hand, has a value of only 20.

The *Ctr* column for each axis, as we saw above, tells us what proportion of the inertia accounted for by each axis is contributed by each of the hoards and types (rows and columns); these are the *absolute contributions to inertia* described earlier. In the case of the types and axis 1 we see that tutuli contribute 297 (29.7 per cent) of the inertia accounted for by this axis, spears contribute 181 (18.1 per cent), sickles 103 and plain palstaves 190; all the other type contributions to this axis are relatively small. The differences between the hoards are relatively slight, the largest value being associated with hoard 33, which contributes 11.9 per cent of the inertia associated with axis 1 and contains among other things spears, sickles and plain palstaves. These three are also the main types associated with axis 2, contributing respectively 15.4 per cent, 19.0 per cent and 59.6 per cent of the inertia associated with this axis.

In the case of axis 3 it is weapon palstaves (303), celts (286) and daggers (271) which make the main contributions, as one might expect from the scattergram; hoard 44 contributes 347 and hoards 30 and 58 contribute 200 each, leaving the remaining

25 per cent of the inertia associated with this axis to be contributed in small quantities by the other 41 hoards.

Finally, arm-rings contribute over 50 per cent (505) of the
inertia associated with axis 4 and all the other values are small
in comparison; hoards 4, 6, 43 and 56 all make significant contributions to this axis.

It remains to look at the *Cor* columns for the individual axes.
As we saw above, in contrast to the *Ctr* columns, which give the
contribution that each hoard and type makes to each axis (the
absolute contribution to inertia), these columns tell us how
much of the inertia in each type and hoard is associated with
each axis (the relative contribution to inertia); together they sum
to the quality value.

We can illustrate how it works with the first item on the type
list, belt-plate. Overall, the four axes account for 9.8 per cent of
the inertia in this type; this is made up of 7.6 per cent from
axis 1, 0.6 per cent from axis 2, 1.5 per cent from axis 3 and
nothing from axis 4. We can use this information to see, for
example, which hoards and types are best represented on the
scattergram of axes 1 and 2. These will be items which have a
fairly high overall quality value, most of which is associated
with axes 1 and 2. The position of other items on this scattergram (or any of the others) is to a greater or lesser degree distorted. Examples of types well represented on the axis 1 and 2
scattergram are tutuli (*Qlt* 891; associated with axis 1, 723);
spear (*Qlt* 716, associated with axis 1, 447, with axis 2, 254);
sickle (*Qlt* 624, axis 1, 272, axis 2, 335); and plain palstave (*Qlt*
989, axis 1, 301, axis 2, 632). Neck-collars, on the other hand,
are best represented by the axis 1 and 4 scattergram (accounting
for c. 46 per cent of their inertia), weapon palstaves by axes 1
and 3 (48 per cent); and so on. The procedure can, of course, be
repeated for the individual hoards.

It will be apparent from this that there is a great deal of information available from a CA which can be used to build-up,
strengthen and cross-check our initial interpretation, although
the scattergrams remain the most important element. In the case
of the hoards, the main points to emerge concern the distinction
between ornament hoards and tool/weapon hoards, which may
have a significance in terms of gender symbolism; however, we
also found that there are distinctions within both of these categories. If we were following this up as a substantive study of the

Danish Bronze Age we would want to cross-check and develop our interpretation not just in relation to independent evidence regarding sex and gender, as noted above, but also in relation to such aspects as geographical patterns in the distribution of different types of hoards and deposition circumstances; for example, whether or not the hoards appear to have been deliberately deposited in a river or a bog.

This completes our treatment of correspondence analysis but it is now necessary to turn, albeit briefly, to a substantive archaeological topic which has close methodological links with this technique – seriation.

SERIATION

Seriation refers to the process of putting items in a series or order on the basis of their intrinsic properties; the order of interest has usually been chronological. The procedure was in effect invented in a famous study by the Egyptologist Sir Flinders Petrie (1899), in an examination of burials of the predynastic period in Egypt. Petrie had information on the grave goods found in a large number of graves and he was interested in finding out the chronological order in which the burials were deposited, given the assumption that one of the most important factors affecting the goods deposited in a particular grave would have been variation in the types which were in fashion at any one time. As Kemp (1982) describes, Petrie's conclusion was that the ordering of the graves which would best approximate their chronological sequence would be one in which the lifespans of the individual types would be the shortest possible; the idea being that a type comes into fashion, has a period of increasing popularity, is widely used for a time, then declines in popularity and disappears from use. Petrie's practical solution to the problem involved writing out the contents of each grave on a strip of cardboard, laying all the strips in a line and then shuffling them around to try and get all the occurrences of a given type bunched together. This is by no means a straightforward procedure since the lifespans of different types overlap, so that grouping together the occurrences of one type may have the effect of dispersing those of another, but eventually Petrie achieved an ordering with which he was satisfied.

At the beginning of the 1950s Brainerd and Robinson

(Brainerd, 1951, Robinson, 1951) wished to order pottery assemblages. They made the same assumption as Petrie about the way in which types come into fashion and go out again, but rather than working with strips of cardboard they took their assemblages and, on the basis of a comparison of the relative proportions of the different pottery types in each pair of assemblages, they calculated a measure of similarity between each assemblage and every other, in the way described above in Chapter 11. They then shuffled the order of the assemblages in the similarity matrix with the aim of grouping all the highest similarities along the principal diagonal and thus producing a sequence.

The modern way of achieving this aim of seriation is to use CA. However, the process deserves some discussion. Correspondence analysis is the obvious technique because usually we are seriating items in terms of counts of the types they contain, whether they be graves containing grave goods, hoards containing different metal types or settlements containing pottery assemblages. In fact, the last of these examples is already somewhat problematic, because although it is easy to see that the deposition of a hoard or a grave normally involves a single event and those events can in principle be put in a strict sequence, this is not necessarily true of settlement occupation phases; moreover, if, as is likely, the settlements are some distance apart from one another, there may be time-lags in the fashion changes between one settlement and the next.

Setting these problems aside, however, the normal procedure in such circumstances is to take the first axis of a correspondence analysis as the best seriation order. It may seem very trite and obvious to point it out but such an ordering will only be a chronological seriation if the types in terms of which the units are being described are chronologically sensitive; there must be reasons to believe this in the first place, such as independent stratigraphic or radiocarbon evidence. As an example where this is *not* the case we can use the first axis of the CA of Danish hoards described above to produce a seriation. Figures 13.12–13.13, produced by the WINBASP program, show the result, in the first case with the hoards forming the vertical dimension and in the second case the types; the hoards have been ordered and the types have been concentrated, but there is no basis for suggesting that the ordering is chronological. If anything, the trend may be suggested as going from extremely male types and hoards to extremely female ones, although, as we have noted already, that suggestion would need to be substantiated.

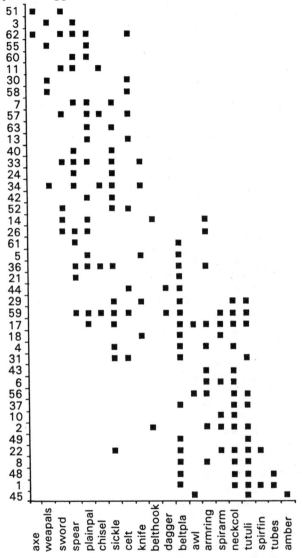

FIGURE 13.12. A seriation of the Danish hoards and artefact types based on their positions on the first CA axis. Vertical axis shows the different hoards, horizontal axis the different types.

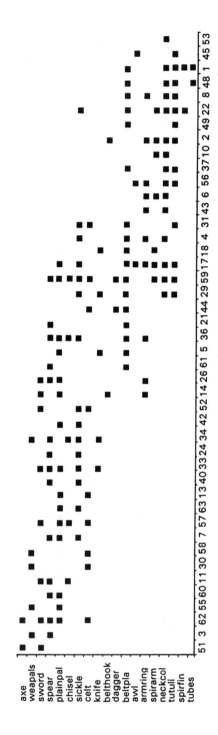

FIGURE 13.13. A seriation of the Danish hoards and artefact types based on their positions on the first CA axis. Vertical axis shows the types, horizontal axis the hoards.

Furthermore, not only must the types defined be chronologically sensitive but the pattern of their occurrence through time is also very important. If this does not follow the standard pattern of first appearance, rise in popularity, peak, decline and disappearance which was assumed by Petrie then correspondence analysis will not produce a correct sequence even when the types are chronologically diagnostic; the issue is discussed by Baxter (1994, pp.118–23). It is not necessarily easy to confirm this assumption in any given case; indeed, if we could it would probably mean that we had sufficient independent chronological information not to need a seriation anyway.

Finally, we can point out that although the ordering of units on the basis of types they contain has been the normal way of obtaining an ordering of archaeological material using its intrinsic properties, it is not the only way, or even necessarily the best; other methods may be available. Thus, Braund (1985) shows that in the first millennium AD in the eastern United States ceramic vessel thickness changed directionally through time, so that it could be used to put assemblages of unknown date in order. Similarly, it has been shown that the diameter of the bore in clay pipe stems also changes directionally with time in a way which can be consistently calibrated with date, so that they can be independently dated themselves and also be used to assist in the dating of the contexts in which they are found. In such cases as these seriation is a straightforward process simply involving a single variable.

OTHER TECHNIQUES

Although principal components analysis and correspondence analysis are nowadays by far the most important multivariate techniques used in archaeology, others exist which may also be useful in particular circumstances and it is worth giving brief accounts of them here which can be followed up by more detailed reading (e.g. Baxter, 1994) if necessary.

Principal Coordinates Analysis

This technique is very similar to PCA and CA in its principles but operates on a matrix of distances or similarities instead of a raw data matrix and thus becomes appropriate when the calculation of a similarity or distance measure is felt to be a required initial step in an analysis.

Thus, suppose we are analysing the graves in a cemetery and have decided that we must calculate a similarity measure between them rather than working directly on the raw matrix of frequency counts or presence/absence. We now want to find out if there is any patterning in this matrix. One way of doing this is by means of cluster analysis as we saw in Chapter 11, but this has its problems, as we also saw. An ordination approach would be as follows.

We can imagine trying to represent the graves under study as points in a space, such that the similarities between the graves are represented by the distances between the points. In order to represent the relationships accurately we would need a space of many dimensions. We can further imagine that within this space the points will not necessarily be scattered equally in all directions; they may be distributed over a relatively short distance in some directions and a considerably longer one in others. It is possible to define the orientation of these different directions or axes and also the lengths over which the points are distributed along them. Once we have defined the orientation of the longest axis and its length, we can then define the axis which goes through the next longest part of the point scatter, subject to the proviso that it must be at right angles to the first, and we can obtain its length too. It is possible to go on doing this for as many independent dimensions of our space as exist. As with PCA and CA, these axes often have a substantive interpretation in terms of the data from which they are derived and we can establish a set of coordinates of our points (graves) in relation to these axes and use these new coordinates to produce scattergrams. This is the process of *principal coordinates analysis*.

In other words, in order to create a low-dimensional space for the purpose of understanding patterning in data we do not need to define the space in terms of *variables*; we can do so in terms of the space defined *by the similarities between the units*. In the same way as we could define PCA and CA axes and their associated eigenvalues for the space created by the variables, we can define principal axes and eigenvalues for the space created by the similarities, that is to say, for the similarity matrix. The size of the eigenvalue gives the importance of a given dimension in accounting for variation in inter-point distances and can be converted as before into a figure for the percentage of the inter-point distance in the data accounted for by that dimension. Again the first few dimensions may well account for the major part of it, although not as markedly as is often the case with PCA and CA. After all, if the starting point of the analysis is a matrix of similarities between 150 items then at the start we are dealing with 149 dimensions, far more than is likely to be the case with most principal component and correspondence analyses. The principal axes of the space enable us to obtain the equivalent of a component score for each of our cases on each of the orthogonal axes of the space. Thus, we move from a relative representation of the cases or data points in relation to one another, to their representation in terms of their positions on the new axes. As noted already, we can use these axes to produce scattergrams of our data points which we can examine for trends and clusters as with PCA and CA scattergrams.

However, the consequence of the fact that principal coordinates analysis works only on similarities between cases, as opposed to correlations between variables or chi-squared distances between variable profiles, is that there are no loadings of variables on components, or contributions of variables to axes accounting for inertia, to be considered and to be used as a basis for the interpretation of results. It is *only* the equivalent of component scores or item (row) contributions to axes which principal coordinates analysis produces and it is these which must be interpreted to arrive at the substantive meaning of the new axes. Nevertheless, as we have seen above, this is not a problem. One has to note which cases are at one end of a given axis, which at the other, and then go back to the raw data on which the coordinates were based to see what differentiates these from one another. Thus, if we were dealing with the results of a principal coordinates analysis of a matrix of similarities between graves then we could refer back to our initial listing of the values of the variables which were used to characterise the graves, different graves goods types for example. By this means we would obtain a substantive archaeological knowledge of the main factors behind the variation in the burials.

Non-metric Multidimensional Scaling

This technique approaches essentially the same problem as principal coordinates analysis from a rather different angle; for a given set of data it should produce very similar results, in terms of the relationships between points in the low-dimensional space which the method tries to achieve.

The conceptual basis of the technique is straightforward. The starting point is the same as for principal coordinates analysis: a measure of similarity or dissimilarity between our *n* cases, and a representation of the relationships between the cases in a multidimensional space, the number of dimensions being one less than the number of cases. From this starting point the method successively reduces the number of dimensions in which the points are represented, at the same time trying to keep to a minimum the distortion in the relations between the points, which begins to arise as the number of dimensions is reduced. The specific feature of the method is that, in contrast to principal coordinates analysis, it is *non-metric*: it works not on the actual numerical values of the similarities/distances between the cases but on their rank-ordering. That is to say, it is the rank-ordering of the distances/similarities between the points which the method tries to preserve as the dimensions are reduced. Thus if the distance between point (item) x_i and point (item) x_j is the tenth smallest distance in the original distance matrix, it should remain the tenth smallest as the number of dimensions of the multidimensional representation is reduced. This property means that the similarity/distance measure used to create the matrix does not have to be fully quantitative, so long as we have a basis for saying 'this is nearer to this than to that'.

Of course, the method has to maintain the rank-order distances not just for one pair of cases but for all of them at the same time: the rank-ordering of all the distances in the reduced space should correspond to the original ordering of all of them. It goes without saying that the relevant juggling is difficult and that it is almost impossible for the original arrangement of the points in terms of the rank-order of their distances to be perfectly preserved in a space of few dimensions. A key part of the method is that it provides a measure of the success with which the ordering is maintained as the number of dimensions is reduced; the measure is known as *stress*.

In the same way as the eigenvalues associated with axes in the methods we have previously seen indicate the importance of those axes in accounting for variation in the data, so stress gives a measure of the number of dimensions important in representing the data in non-metric multidimensional scaling. The measure is calculated for each successively decreasing number of dimensions and the idea is to look for the number of dimensions at which a large increase in the measure suddenly occurs: this indicates a sudden increase in the amount of distortion in the data, which would arise when a dimension important in accounting for variation in the data is removed.

The idea, as with the other methods we have seen, is that if the variation in a set of data is reducible to a small number of major trends then the stress at the appropriate small number of dimensions will be lower than for comparable data where the variation is not reducible in this way. A low stress value at a particular number of dimensions would correspond to the case in principal coordinates analysis where that number of dimensions accounts for a high percentage of the variation in inter-point distances. Furthermore, the substantive archaeological meaning of the dimensions can be established in the same way, by looking at which cases lie where on the various axes or dimensions. In general, the results of the two techniques on a given data set should be pretty similar.

In recent years non-metric multidimensional scaling has not been all that widely used in archaeology, not least because of the rise of correspondence analysis. Kemp (1982) used it in his re-analysis of Petrie's Egyptian Predynastic cemeteries, while Cherry and others have used it to construct maps of Aegean Bronze Age states on the basis of co-occurrences of names of places on clay tablets (Cherry, 1977, Kendall, 1977). This last example is particularly appropriate for the technique since there is no real justification for treating the co-occurrences of names as representing a strictly quantitative measure of distance. Much fuller accounts of the technique are given elsewhere (Doran and Hodson, 1975, pp. 214–17; Kruskal and Wish, 1978; Gordon, 1981, pp. 91–101).

Discriminant Analysis

Before finally leaving multivariate analysis there is one more technique that must be mentioned, albeit only briefly, even though it is rather different in nature from any we have looked at so far. All these have been concerned with looking for patterning in a set of data, with very little in the way of prior assumptions as to what the patterning is like. The technique of *discriminant analysis* presupposes that we can divide our observations into groups on the basis of some criterion and then attempt to find ways of distinguishing those same groups on the basis of some independent criterion derived from the data.

In fact, the procedure has already been referred to early in Chapter 11, where we distinguished *classification* from *discrimination* and gave an example of the latter. We have a number of undecorated ceramic vessels of a particular type, found at different sites. Do the vessel shapes, described in terms of a series of ratio measurements, differ from site to site? In discriminant analysis we tell the program how many vessels come from each site and the analysis then attempts to reproduce correctly the assignment of vessels to the site groups, but based solely on the measurements describing the vessel shape. If it is successful at doing this it means that the vessels from the different sites do differ from one another; if it isn't, it means they do not. This can be a very useful thing to do. One area in which it has found considerable archaeological use is artefact characterisation studies, where quantities of trace elements in lithic artefacts or pottery are used to try to discriminate material from different sources.

Whereas principal components and related techniques construct new variables according to a criterion of maximising the variance or inertia accounted for, discriminant analysis involves constructing new variables from the original ones with the criterion that these variables must maximise the differences between the groups previously defined, the different sites in the example outlined above. What is involved is, as usual, best indicated by a simple example and a diagram (Fig. 13.14). Suppose we have assemblages of flint flakes from two distinct phases at the same site and have described the size and shape of the flakes in terms of measurements of length and breadth. Do the sizes or shapes of the flakes in the two phases differ?

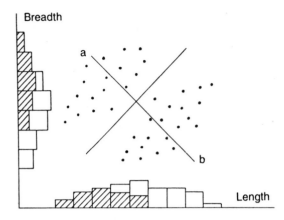

FIGURE 13.14. Discriminating between two groups of lithic debitage on the basis of the length and breadth of the individual pieces.

If we look at our two original variables, length and breadth, we can see from the histograms illustrated on Figure 13.14 that neither of the variables discriminates between the flakes from the two phases: there is a considerable overlap in both length and breadth between the two. However, if we look at the scattergram of the two variables together, we can see that there are indeed two distinct groups corresponding to the phases. However, we do not actually need two dimensions to show this. A single axis does exist along which the two groups are distinguished perfectly – the line $a - b$ in the diagram, which is a composite of both length and breadth. This is the *discriminant function* in this case; a line cutting it at right angles between the two groups divides them with complete success.

Of course, in a real case with several variables we cannot see this immediately by eye as we could in our example. Discriminant analysis programs carry out the operation of finding the best discriminating axes in the multivariate case and in the same way as for PCA and related techniques we are told the eigenvalue of each function and the contribution of each of the original variables to it.

The above account is intended to do no more than give you an idea of what is involved in the technique, which is too important to omit altogether. It is described in detail by Baxter (1994,

Chapters 9 and 10) and is widely available in the standard statistics packages. It is not really an exploratory technique like the other multivariate methods described but can be very useful when it comes to testing archaeological hypotheses.

If you have managed to get this far with the multivariate analysis chapters in this book you will have a very good basis for understanding the issues raised by Baxter (1994) in his more detailed account, and also for appreciating the value of the advice given by Wright (1989) when you embark on your own analysis.

EXERCISES

13.1 Excavation of a settlement midden in northern Norway produced large numbers of animal bones from the fourteen layers (layer 1 being the most recent and layer 14 the oldest). The bone frequencies are presented in the table below. In order to investigate patterning in the composition of the bone assemblage through time a correspondence analysis was carried out. The scattergram of the layers and species against the first two axes is shown below in a symmetric display. The first axis accounts for 68 per cent of the inertia, the second for 29.5 per cent. Discuss the results for the layers and for the species and the relation between them (data from Mathiesen et al., 1981).

TABLE Exercise 13.1 Osteological material from layers 1–14 of trench 1 of the farm mound of the island of Helgøy (see key to Figure over page for details of assemblage) (after Mathiesen et al., 1981).

	A	B	C	D	E	F	G	H	I	J	K	L	M	N	P	Q	Sum
1	27	42	33	1	3	0	272	5	40	31	3	0	0	0	17	0	474
2	54	122	35	0	4	0	1080	36	15	73	11	1	0	0	47	0	1578
3	44	83	54	3	4	0	842	24	71	81	35	12	0	0	32	0	1284
4	101	151	90	2	6	0	3247	14	128	81	20	23	3	0	34	1	3901
5	101	202	58	4	0	4	3204	95	99	216	24	92	33	0	22	4	4158
6	43	61	33	6	13	1	1082	37	170	138	17	1	5	0	4	4	1615
7	24	40	17	0	23	4	545	23	3	88	3	0	1	3	2	1	777
8	17	24	14	1	30	3	597	22	4	46	4	1	0	0	2	0	765
9	27	42	10	2	14	2	294	8	7	33	2	11	0	0	9	0	461
10	24	53	20	0	6	0	100	6	3	22	0	28	0	0	14	1	277
11	45	78	35	0	30	1	128	4	9	20	0	17	1	0	2	9	379
12	109	367	167	1	142	8	348	1	13	38	1	80	1	0	13	6	1294
13	15	18	17	0	7	8	25	0	0	4	0	14	0	0	0	1	109
14	42	41	34	0	15	3	93	0	0	0	0	14	0	0	6	0	248
Sum	673	1324	617	20	297	34	11857	275	662	871	118	294	44	3	204	27	17320

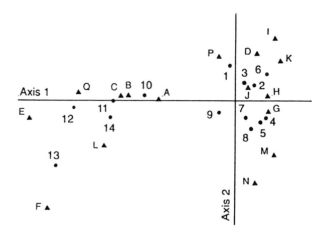

Layers 1–14

A	Cattle	*Bos taurus*
B	Sheep/goat	*Ovis aries/Carpa hircus*
C	Pig	*Sus scrofa dom.*
D	Reindeer	*Rangifer tarandus*
E	Seal	Phocidae
F	Grouse	*Lagopus*
G	Cod	*Gadus morrhua*
H	Haddock	*Melanogrammus aeglefinus*
I	Coalfish	*Pollachius virens*
J	Ling	*Molva molva*
K		*Brosme brosme*
L	Halibut	*Hippoglossus hippoglossus*
M		*Sebastes marinus*
N		*Anarchichas lupus*
P	Auk	Alcidae
Q	Hen	*Gallus gallus f. dom.*

FIGURE Exercise 13.1 Correspondence analysis of the data from the table on previous page (after Mathiesen et al., 1981).

13.2 Information is available from the palaeolithic cave site of Ksar Akil concerning the numbers of different types of lithic waste from ten successive levels (see table below); layer 1 is at the top and layer 10 is at the bottom. The question of interest is whether there are any clear patterns of assemblage variation between the layers, whether any such variations show chronological trends, and which of the different lithic types are the most significant in any patterns which emerge. In order to answer these questions a correspondence analysis of the data has been carried out. The results are shown in the tables below and in the symmetrically scaled scattergram of the types and the layers against the first two axes.

Frequencies of lithic debitage classes from Ksar Akil

Level	Partially cortical	Non-cortical	Flake-blades	Blades	Bladelets
1	2	12	6	12	4
2	16	44	14	6	4
3	72	105	54	55	69
4	111	87	114	148	115
5	35	40	48	47	55
6	60	74	76	53	56
7	62	51	206	127	66
8	24	50	80	67	30
9	52	177	344	205	75
10	21	81	138	31	22

Partially cortical = flakes with patches of the outer skin of the flint nodule (known as the cortex)

Non-cortical = flakes with no trace of cortex

Diagnostics for: Ksar Akil lithic correspondence analysis

Component	Eigenvalue	% Inertia	Cumulative
1	0.076087	59.4	59.4
2	0.040947	32.0	91.4

Types

Name	Qlt	Mass	Inr	Comp 1	Cor	Ctr	Comp 2	Cor	Ctr
Partcort	908	130	194	416	905	295	23	3	2
noncort	974	206	231	67	31	12	−368	943	681
flakblad	955	308	301	−345	953	483	18	3	2
blade	685	214	110	−39	24	4	209	661	228
bladelet	913	142	164	332	743	205	159	171	88

Average
Type QLT: 887

Units

Name	Qlt	Mass	Inr	Comp 1	Cor	Ctr	Comp 2	Cor	Ctr
Level 1	99	10	21	42	7	0	−154	92	6
Level 2	959	24	139	253	86	20	−805	873	379
Level 3	998	101	155	399	816	212	−189	182	88
Level 4	986	164	150	284	688	174	187	298	140
Level 5	800	64	57	275	671	64	121	129	23
Level 6	896	91	46	230	820	63	−70	76	11
Level 7	905	146	103	−177	346	60	225	560	181
Level 8	470	72	15	−100	389	9	46	81	4
Level 9	950	244	170	−291	946	270	−18	4	2
Level 10	881	84	145	−339	516	126	−285	365	166

Average
Unit QLT: 794

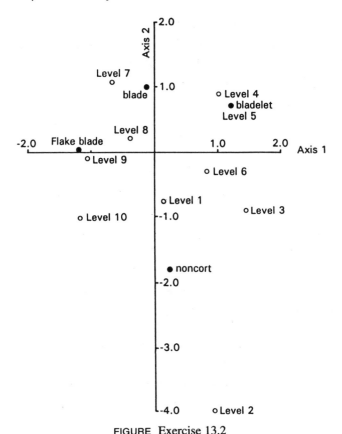

FIGURE Exercise 13.2

13.3 Data have been gathered on the content of a series of material culture assemblages collected by ethnographic field-workers at different locations in New Guinea in the early part of this century (see Moore and Romney, 1994; Welsch et al., 1992). In order to see if there is any patterning in these data a correspondence analysis has been carried out. In addition to the data on material culture assemblages which were subject to correspondence analysis, information was also collected on the family of the language spoken where the artefacts were collected, and on the site's geographic location. The first table below shows the raw data and the second the correspondence analysis diagnostics. The first figure shows the scattergram of sites and artefacts against CA axes 1 and 2 in a symmetric display; the second shows the locations of the collecting sites.

On the basis of the CA, discuss the relations among the variables, among the sites and between the two and consider also how these relate to the language spoken and the location of the collecting site.

Location	Language	Pottery	Wooden dish	String bag	Basket	Mask	Carving	Bows/ arrows	Spears	Shields	Clubs	Lime container
1	AN	14	2	3	1	0	4	121	2	0	0	47
2	Sko	2	0	0	0	0	10	55	0	0	0	11
3	Sko	0	0	0	0	0	0	47	0	3	0	0
4	Sko	2	2	11	1	0	12	270	7	5	0	11
5	Sko	0	0	0	0	0	0	171	0	1	0	0
6	AN	10	17	2	16	0	0	43	0	25	13	13
7	Sko	0	37	0	0	3	2	127	0	25	1	0
8	AN	0	0	8	0	0	0	16	0	4	1	7
9	AN	93	11	7	7	0	0	258	2	2	9	6
10	AN	0	14	25	10	3	5	2	2	0	11	14
11	AN	1	5	11	6	3	4	132	1	1	8	23
12	AN	2	17	7	6	0	3	89	5	0	10	2
13	Torr	2	6	0	0	1	4	5	2	0	0	1
14	AN/Ndu	1	8	52	1	17	27	23	34	5	10	1
15	Ndu	0	51	20	4	13	12	29	0	0	0	0
16	Ndu	1	17	5	0	2	17	0	0	0	0	0
17	AN/Ndu	0	0	2	0	13	21	6	0	1	0	2
18	Sepik	6	2	1	0	51	32	0	1	0	0	0
19	Sepik	13	5	14	8	16	22	0	0	4	3	6
20	Sepik	19	4	3	0	34	8	0	7	0	0	3

Diagnostics for: New Guinea material culture

Component	Eigenvalue	% Inertia	Cumulative
1	0.541707	39.0	39.0
2	0.250016	18.0	56.9

Types

Name	Qlt	Mass	Inr	Comp 1	Cor	Ctr	Comp 2	Cor	Ctr
pottery	192	62	89	−35	2	0	617	191	94
wooddish	410	74	104	−374	71	19	−815	339	195
strngbag	696	64	88	−690	249	56	−925	448	218
basket	313	22	37	−151	10	1	−832	303	62
mask	931	58	201	−1896	750	386	930	181	202
carving	733	68	117	−1302	713	214	215	19	13
bowarrow	917	520	134	545	832	285	175	86	64
spear	241	24	71	−846	171	31	−545	71	28
shield	136	28	63	190	12	2	−617	124	43
club	434	25	32	−128	9	1	−875	425	75
limecont	42	55	66	215	28	5	−158	15	5

Average
Type QLT: 459

Units

Name	Qlt	Mass	Inr	Comp 1	Cor	Ctr	Comp 2	Cor	Ctr
1	262	72	48	458	228	28	174	33	9
2	343	29	12	335	197	6	289	147	10
3	692	19	11	711	613	17	255	79	5
4	652	120	39	509	576	57	185	76	16
5	733	64	42	737	604	64	341	129	30
6	254	52	64	182	19	3	−635	235	84
7	198	73	47	360	146	17	−216	52	14
8	224	13	13	202	31	1	−503	193	14
9	400	147	82	427	237	50	355	163	74
10	690	32	58	−556	122	18	−1199	568	185
11	450	73	17	375	446	19	−38	4	0
12	415	53	13	263	196	7	−279	220	16
13	241	8	8	−531	207	4	−213	33	1
14	513	67	123	−932	339	107	−667	174	119
15	427	48	67	−610	192	33	−677	236	88
16	438	15	43	−1174	356	39	−563	82	19
17	714	17	45	−1494	597	69	661	117	29
18	943	35	149	−2059	710	272	1181	233	194
19	672	34	41	−1057	671	70	−46	1	0
20	782	29	80	−1477	573	117	891	209	92

Average
Unit QLT: 502

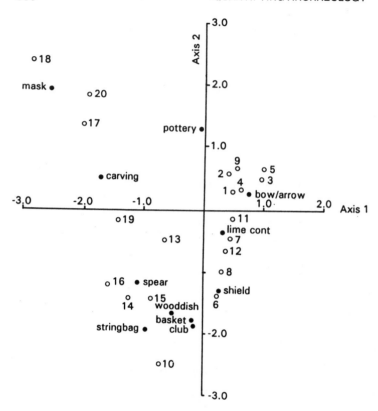

FIGURE Exercise 13.3

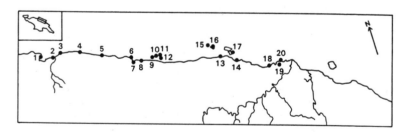

FIGURE Exercise 13.3

Fourteen

PROBABILISTIC SAMPLING IN ARCHAEOLOGY

In its most general sense 'sampling' embodies the idea of using information from a part of something to make inferences about the whole. Since archaeologists have always been acutely aware of the partial nature of the evidence they recover – they only ever recover a 'sample' – the idea of a methodology which could help to solve the problems posed by this situation has an almost mystical attraction. The belief that forms of probability sampling could provide such solutions was one of the reasons for the popularity of this subject in the 1960s and 1970s, and the disillusion when it was realised that such techniques did not provide any sort of panacea is one of the reasons why it has subsequently faded from attention. Nevertheless, the problems posed by the fact that we never have enough time or money for archaeological projects have not gone away. They have, if anything, become more pressing as the need for obtaining the maximum amount of archaeological information for the minimum cost in advance of planning and engineering decisions about development projects has increased. This is not to say that they can all be solved by statistically-based sampling methods but these do have a role to play and it is worth being aware of the possibilities they offer. In this chapter it will not be possible to do any more than sketch out the basic principles and indicate some sources of further reading, so that you are aware of some of the possibilities and can follow them up if need be.

It is important to be clear from the start that 'sampling' is concerned only with making inferences about some defined piece of the extant archaeological record on the basis of a study of some part of it. It is not directly concerned with making inferences from the extant record to the material results of human behaviour in the past, still less to the nature of the behaviour which produced them, although this is not to say that methods for doing this won't involve probability considerations (e.g. Orton, 1982; Fieller and Turner, 1982).

Of course, archaeologists have always practised sampling in the sense that they have selected sites to excavate in regions, and places to put trenches within sites, and they have not restricted their conclusions to those specific sites or trenches. The change which occurred in the 1960s was the introduction and advocacy of *probabilistic sampling*: the selection of the part of the archaeological record to be investigated in such a way that probability theory can be used to evaluate the inferences made from that part to the whole from which it was selected, in terms of the probability that the inferences are correct. The idea then is to ensure that the sample selected is representative of the whole. Probability theory provides the rules for both making the selection and making the inferences from it.

But what inferences can we make in this way? Statistical sampling theory becomes relevant when the aim of the study is to use the sample selected to make estimates of characteristics of the population from which it is drawn. The aim in these circumstances is to draw a sample which is an 'honest representation' of the population and which leads to estimates of population characteristics with as great a precision as we can reasonably expect for the cost or effort expended (cf. Barnett, 1974). Probably the best-known field where these issues impinge on modern life is in the context of political opinion polls, where the object is to question a small number of people about their voting intentions with the aim of projecting the resulting percentages onto a national level. Archaeologists, of course, have a more difficult life than this since the populations of interest to us are very often invisible, but we are not the only ones with such problems: imagine what it's like to be a marine ecologist trying to estimate the world population of blue whales!

If we use a probabilistic sampling scheme, the result will be an estimate whose reliability and precision may be quantified; in other words, one for which we can supply a *confidence interval*. As we saw in Chapter 6, in specifying a confidence interval we are saying that in a given percentage of the samples generated by this means, the population characteristic (or parameter) concerned will fall within some specified interval estimated from the sample. We have already seen (in Chapter 6) that we can use our theoretical knowledge after the event, when our data have been collected, to obtain such confidence intervals for estimates in which we are interested. However, as we will see below, we can also use it before collecting the data, to obtain an estimate of the sample size required to obtain a confidence interval of a desired width. It is obviously better, if it is at all possible, to follow the latter procedure rather than finding out late in the day that time and effort have been spent on unnecessary data gathering or, worse, that from the data collected we can only specify an interval which is uninformatively wide.

But probability sampling isn't the only approach available. Judgemental or purposive sampling involves investigators making their choice about, for example, which part of a site to excavate or which part of a region to survey on the basis of their academic judgement without regard to any statistical criteria. The aim may or may not be to obtain a representative sample. If it is, and the investigator possesses a great deal of relevant knowledge, then the sample may indeed be an excellent representation of the population. The main problem with this approach to sampling, if the aim is to achieve representativeness, is not that the estimates resulting from it may be distorted but that we have no means of evaluating the representativeness of the sample selected other than through an evaluation of the selector and our own knowledge of the substantive situation. On the other hand, there are many archaeological questions to which the techniques of probability sampling are not relevant.

CALCULATING CONFIDENCE INTERVALS AND SAMPLE SIZES

You may or may not remember from earlier chapters that a distinction has to be made between the characteristics of samples (statistics) and those of populations (parameters). For a given population any parameter value will be fixed but unknown. In probability sampling the aim is to use statistics calculated from a sample to estimate the population parameters. Since we do not know the population parameters, and would not need to take a sample if we did, we can never know how close our estimates are to the parameter value. Our rationale for having some confidence in the estimates therefore has to be based on a method of sample selection which has secure theoretical foundations to justify the claims we make.

In Chapter 6 we saw how to obtain a confidence interval for the population mean on the basis of a simple random sample. This depended on using the standard deviation of the sample and the sample size to estimate the standard error of the mean:

$$s_{\bar{y}} = \sqrt{\frac{s^2}{n}}$$

If we stop before the square root stage we have $s_{\bar{y}}^2$, the variance of the mean, and in what follows we will use both this and the standard error.[1]

But there is another aspect of sample size which also makes a difference to our estimates of the standard error of the mean; it was not considered in Chapter 6 but is relevant now, in the context of actually taking a sample from a finite population. If our sample was so large that it included the entire population of interest we would know the population mean exactly and our estimate would have no error at all. By extension of this, as our sample becomes an increasingly large fraction of our population, our estimate of the standard error can be narrowed down. This is done by adding to the basic formula something called the *finite population correction factor*. Now we have:

$$s_{\bar{y}} = \sqrt{\frac{s^2}{n} \left(\frac{N-n}{N}\right)}$$

where n is the sample size and N is the population size.

Thus, the formula for constructing a confidence interval that we saw in Chapter 6 becomes

$$\bar{y} \pm Z_\alpha \sqrt{\frac{s^2}{n} \left(\frac{N-n}{N}\right)}$$

---

1. The notation in this chapter is slightly different from Chapter 6, in that instead of referring to our variable of interest as x, we will now refer to it as y. The reason for this is that later in this chapter we will be considering our estimated quantities as *dependent* on the values of other variables.

where Z_α is the number of standard errors associated with a particular probability level, s^2 is the sample variance, n is the sample size and N is the population size.

As before, we substitute $t_{\alpha,df}$ for Z_α where the sample size is smaller than about forty or so, with $n-1$ degrees of freedom.

To construct a confidence interval, of course, we must already have the relevant information to hand. This is all very well, but in the situation in which we find ourselves at the beginning of an archaeological investigation for which we only have limited resources, one of the key questions is precisely how large a sample we should select. If it is too small, the confidence intervals for our estimates of the quantities in which we're interested will be too wide to be of any use; if it is larger than we need, then resources are being wasted which could be used for something else. How can we calculate a required sample size?

Let us look again at the formula for constructing a confidence interval, assuming that we are dealing with the normal distribution and ignoring for the moment the finite population correction. The formula for the interval around the mean is

$$Z_\alpha \sqrt{\frac{s^2}{n}}$$

Let us designate this tolerance (or $\pm$) factor as d. We then have

$$d = Z_\alpha \sqrt{\frac{s^2}{n}}$$

This can be rearranged to give

$$\sqrt{n} = \frac{Z_\alpha s}{d}$$

or

$$n = \left(\frac{Z_\alpha s}{d}\right)^2$$

We have then a formula for estimating what the sample size should be in a given case, provided that we can specify the three quantities on the right-hand side of the equation.

Fixing a value for Z_α is straightforward enough: it is simply a matter of deciding on the probability we wish to have that our interval will include the parameter in which we are interested. Specifying the tolerance, the ± factor which we are prepared to accept is also straightforward enough in principle, although less so in practice. Why should we decide on a particular tolerance level? Ideally, it should stem from the specific question which we are investigating, but in practice the decision may be rather arbitrary. The point is that if we are prepared to settle for an estimate with an error factor rather than insisting on obtaining the exact value of the population parameter, we can save a great deal of effort in terms of the number of units or items we have to examine.

The third quantity, s, has been written in lower case here and throughout because although it is the population standard deviation, S, which interests us, we have been using s, the sample-based estimate of S, since the latter is, of course, unknown. When we wish to calculate a sample size, however, even obtaining s is problematical. In the case of constructing a confidence interval we could obtain it from our sample. Before taking the sample, trying to decide on the sample size, we are not in this position! What can we do?

In general terms there are two possible answers, neither of which is ideal. One is to carry out some sort of pilot study on the population of interest, before the main investigation, and thus obtain a preliminary sample-based estimate of the population standard deviation with which to work. Another is to use the results of previous work on similar populations which has already produced variability estimates. In both cases we might want to increase the resulting estimate of the population standard deviation slightly in case it turns out to be an underestimate and our confidence intervals end up being wider than we would wish.

Having used the formula presented above to obtain an initial estimate of the required sample size we should then consider whether or not this represents a sufficiently large fraction of the total population for the finite population correction to be required. To obtain the required size taking the sampling fraction into account we have

$$n = \cfrac{1}{\cfrac{1}{n} + \cfrac{1}{N}}$$

where N is the population size and n is the sample size as initially calculated.

At this point it is worth going through a numerical example of calculating the correct sample size to estimate a mean, to see how the procedure is carried out (cf. van der Veen and Fieller, 1982). Let us look again at the 2,000 hypothetical arrowheads for whose mean length we calculated a confidence interval in Chapter 6 and imagine that we are now at the stage before that, where we need to ask how many we should measure in order to estimate their mean length with a given degree of precision, on the assumption of selection by means of simple random sampling. Prior knowledge tells us that such a distribution of lengths will probably have a tendency to be positively skewed, but this skewness is unlikely to be so great as to have a major effect on the normality of the notional distribution of sample means, which is what matters. Applying the formula

$$n = \left(\frac{Z_\alpha s}{d} \right)^2$$

we need to fill in some numbers:

Z_α: we will assume that we are interested in the 95 per cent probability level so this may be set at 1.96.

s: we will assume that we have selected a small number of arrowheads for measurement as a pilot sample and that this has given us a value of 4.00 mm as an estimate of the population standard deviation. To be on the safe side we have decided to increase this by 1.0 mm and to use an estimate of 5.0 mm for the population standard deviation.

d: we will assume that we want to estimate the mean within a tolerance of ± 1.0 mm, an effectively arbitrary decision.

$$n = \left(\frac{1.96 \times 5.0}{1.0} \right)^2 = 96$$

Applying the finite population correction,

$$n' = \cfrac{1}{\cfrac{1}{n} + \cfrac{1}{N}}$$

$$n' = \cfrac{1}{\cfrac{1}{96} + \cfrac{1}{2000}} = 91.6$$

In this case, because n is such a small fraction of N, applying the correction does not make a great deal of difference.

To show the difference that varying the tolerance makes, let us recalculate the sample size figure, supposing that we will be satisfied with a tolerance of ± 2.0 mm instead of 1.0 mm.

$$n = \left(\frac{1.96 \times 5.0}{2.0}\right)^2 = 24$$

Alternatively, if we wanted it to within ± 0.5 mm:

$$n = \left(\frac{1.96 \times 5.0}{0.5}\right)^2 = 384$$

It is obviously worth giving the matter of the tolerance level some thought, as it has an enormous effect on the required sample size.

It may be, of course, that our sample size is going to be determined simply by the amount of time and money available. On the basis of knowledge of the cost of collecting information on one item, or of experiments or prior knowledge of the time taken to collect it, we may know our maximum possible sample size in advance. If, given an estimate of the likely population standard deviation, it turns out that a sample of this size will only produce a confidence interval which is too wide to be at all informative about the parameter in question, then we really need to rethink our whole project.

Estimating Totals

Now that we have seen the procedure for estimating the confidence interval for a population mean with a given probability level, and how to rearrange the information to estimate required sample sizes, we can look at the question of estimating population totals; this can be done much more briefly since it is only a minor variation on what we have just seen, and saw earlier, in Chapter 6.

You may be puzzled by the whole idea of estimating a total. After all, do we not in effect need to have a total list of our population in order to select a sample? The answer is that the list of items which we are sampling may not be the same as the list of items in which we are interested. An archaeological example arises in regional survey. A normal procedure would be to divide the region up into a number of squares and to sample the squares: the squares then form the list of items we are sampling, a list that we can completely enumerate if required. We are certainly not interested in the total number of squares but we may well be interested in the total number of sites within the area, perhaps of a particular type or period. To find this we will need to have a sample-based estimate of the mean number of sites per square which can then be multiplied up by the total number of squares. We can write this as

$$y_T = N\bar{y}$$

where y_T is the total number of items of interest, $\bar{y}$ is the mean number of items of interest per sample unit, and N is the total number of sample units in the population.

This is straightforward enough, but, as with estimating the mean, we are generally not just interested in a point estimate but in being able to specify a confidence interval. Fortunately, this too is very easy. As you might expect, it is simply a matter of including N in the formulae for obtaining confidence intervals and sample sizes which we have already seen for the mean. Thus, for the confidence interval we have

$$y_T \pm Z_\alpha \sqrt{\frac{s^2}{n}(N-n)N}$$

with $t_{\alpha,df}$ substituted for Z_α with small sample sizes. And for the sample size calculation we have

$$n = \left(\frac{Z_\alpha sN}{d}\right)^2$$

and, as before

$$n' = \frac{1}{\dfrac{1}{n} + \dfrac{1}{N}}$$

Estimating a Population Proportion

This looks at first sight rather different from the two cases we have examined so far but in fact it is closely related. The situation is one which arises frequently in archaeology. We may, for example, want to estimate the proportion of sherds in an assemblage which have some specified characteristic or belong to a particular type. The difference between this and the previous examples lies not in what we are trying to do but in the simple structure of the values in the population and the sample, which can only take one of two states: a particular sherd, for example, either has the characteristic in question or it does not.

As with the mean, the best estimate of a population proportion will be the corresponding sample proportion, but again we want a confidence interval, and for this we need to know the standard error of the proportion.

The standard deviation of a population of ones and zeroes is $\sqrt{P(1-P)}$, where P is the proportion of interest. This can be estimated using p, the sample proportion. To obtain the standard error of the proportion we must divide this by $\sqrt{n}$, the square root of the sample size, as with the mean. Thus, the standard error of the proportion is $\sqrt{\dfrac{p(1-p)}{n}}$.

Obviously the shape of such a distribution is not going to be normal. Nevertheless, the shape of the notional distribution of sample means will be, so long as the sample is reasonably large, say greater than fifty. In these circumstances we can once again construct the confidence interval by multiplying the standard error of the proportion by Z_α, the number of standard errors corresponding to the probability level in which we are interested, since the distribution is a normal one. Finally, the finite population correction has the same role as before. Thus a confidence interval for P, the population proportion, will be given by

$$p \pm Z_\alpha \sqrt{\frac{p(1-p)}{n-1} \left(\frac{N-n}{N} \right)}$$

where p is the sample proportion.

This is straightforward enough when we have the information from a sample and want to construct a confidence interval for P on the basis of it, but how do we estimate sample size? We saw above that we could re-arrange the formula for the confidence interval for a mean or a total to obtain the sample size required for a given precision and probability. If we now do this for the case of proportions we have

$$n = \frac{Z_\alpha^2 p(1-p)}{d^2}$$

This tells us that in order to calculate an appropriate sample size to obtain an estimate of a proportion with a certain level of probability, we first need to make an estimate of what the proportion is. This seems rather paradoxical even by the standards of statistics. Fortunately it is not quite as bad as it looks.

For a given tolerance and a given probability level, the maximum sample size n we will need will be when $p(1-p)$ takes the maximum value it can possibly take. Quite simply, this will be when $p = (1-p) = 1/2$. The product of the two in this case will be $1/4$ and the product of no other pair of values will be so great. In other words, in the case of proportions, unlike other means and totals, we can always find the maximum size of the sample we will need to attain a certain tolerance with a certain probability, simply by assuming that the population proportions P and $(1-P)$ are $1/2$ – we don't need to bother estimating them with sample proportions at all.

For actual values of P between 0.3 and 0.7 this maximum will not be too extravagant an estimate of the required sample size for a given confidence interval. On the other hand, as P gets larger or smaller than this, the required n begins to decrease fairly considerably so assuming $P = 1/2$ will create a fairly large amount of unnecessary work. In many cases, however, it will be possible to have a reasoned guess as to whether the proportional occurrence we are investigating is very rare or very common (one is obviously the converse of the other), or only reasonably frequent.

As with the other sample size estimates we have seen, we can correct for the sampling fraction as above.

It remains to consider an example of estimating the required sample size for a proportion. Suppose we have a large collection of sherds and we know that the fabric of some of them contains a particular mineral which is diagnostic of a specific origin. How many sherds do we have to select by simple random sampling to examine in detail in order to find the proportion or percentage of sherds containing the mineral and therefore originating from this particular source?

Let us assume that we wish our estimate to have a tolerance of ± 0.05 (5 per cent) and a probability of 95 per cent. We think it likely that the type is fairly frequent and we want to be on the safe side, so we assume that $P = 1/2$, giving the largest possible sample size:

$$n = \frac{Z_\alpha^2 p(1-p)}{d^2}$$

In this case

$$= \frac{Z_\alpha^2 \frac{1}{4}}{d^2} = \frac{Z_\alpha^2}{4d^2}$$

Substituting numbers:

$$n = \frac{1.96^2}{4 \times 0.05^2} = 384.16$$

If this represents a reasonably large fraction of the population of sherds then we can modify the initial estimate by using the finite population correction.

A more complex situation would be where we want to estimate the proportions of a whole series of different fabrics in a ceramic assemblage and before we start we don't even know how many fabric types there are. The worst case figures for this situation have been calculated by Thompson (1987, 1992), who provides a table of the relevant sample sizes for a tolerance of 0.05 and varying probability levels (1992, p. 39); in the case of a 95 per cent confidence interval the initial sample size required would be 510, to be modified if necessary by the finite population correction.

SELECTING A SAMPLE

At this point we have seen a great deal about constructing confidence intervals and estimating required sample sizes on the basis of simple random samples but we have not yet specified how to go about selecting one.

To select any sample at all it is obvious that we need a set of *sampling units*: discrete, definable entities amongst which samples may be chosen. The list of sampling units from which samples may be drawn is known as the *sampling frame*. Without a sampling frame containing the list of all the items in the population which we wish to sample we cannot go any further.

It is important to emphasise again here that the sample units making up the list do not have to be the real items of interest: they may merely contain them. Thus, in an archaeological context, the fact that before we excavate a site we do not usually know how many features there will be, and that if we did know this, for some purposes at least we would not need to bother taking a sample, is completely irrelevant to the process of taking a sample. In all such cases we can sample from known populations which contain the one in which we're interested. At the regional level we can sample units of land and at the site level grid squares. It is then possible to discuss the attributes of these arbitrary units and talk about, for example, the number of sites per sq.km., or the number of sherds per grid square. Or we can talk about aspects of the sites or artefacts themselves, in which case any statistical inference procedures must take into account the fact that they are dealing with cluster samples (see below).

As we have already seen (Chapter 6), *a simple random sample* is a sample which has the characteristic that any individual, and any combination of individuals, has an equal chance of occurring in the sample. Such a sample can be obtained by drawing members from the population one at a time *without replacement*; this means that once an item has been selected it is withdrawn from the selection pool and does not have a second chance of being chosen.

The method may be illustrated by means of a *random numbers table*. The sampling units in the population are numbered in sequence. As many random numbers are selected from the table as are required to give a sample of the size decided, subject to the stipulation that if a number comes up which has already occurred it is ignored. How is the table to be read?

Suppose the case above, where we wanted to select a sample of arrowheads from an assemblage of 2000, and each arrowhead has been given a number from 1 to 2000. Because 2000 is a four-digit number we need four-digit random numbers; these are obtained by reading four adjacent digits together from the random numbers table; a small extract from one is presented here to illustrate the procedure:

10	09	73	25
37	54	20	48
08	42	26	84
99	01	90	25

We don't need to start at the top of the table and we can make our blocks of four digits by amalgamating any adjacent four. We might, for example, begin with the second row and the fourth digit across. Reading across and then down we would have 4204, 2268, 1902. Since only one of these falls within the range 1–2000 only this one is selected, the other two are ignored. You continue reading the table until the required number of numbers has been selected, without duplication. If the population contained only 100 elements then only two-digit numbers would be required, with 00 counting as 100.

If the sampling units are spatial ones defined in terms of a grid over an area, individual units may be selected by means of two random numbers specifying the coordinates of a corner of the unit. A spatial random sample is shown in Figure 14.1.

Normally the random numbers required are obtained directly from a computer random number generator, for which the range required can be specified in advance. Of course, for a random sample the numbers are obtained from a uniform distribution, where every number within the specified range has an equal probability of being selected. It is worth noting that many of these generators produce a fixed set of numbers that you will obtain every time unless you take explicit action to randomise the starting point.

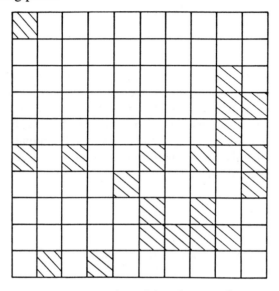

FIGURE 14.1. A spatial random sample.

ALTERNATIVE AIMS AND ALTERNATIVE METHODS

We are not always, or even often, simply interested in obtaining an overall estimate of some quantity from a sample. This is likely to be especially true if we are carrying out fieldwork, where we will be interested in spatial variation in our items of interest at least as much as in overall figures. One way of viewing this in a sampling context is that we are often interested in estimates for particular subsections of the population of interest; for example, the number of sites located on a particular soil or in a specific part of the region, or the proportion of a given lithic type that has a particular pattern of use-wear.

Of course, we can obtain such estimates for particular sub-populations from a simple random sample if after the event we decide that we want to do so for some reason. A confidence interval for the mean of some sub-population k can be obtained by using the following formula from Thompson (1992, pp. 42–3), first finding the variance of the sub-population sample and then dividing this by the sample size:

$$\bar{y}_k = t \sqrt{\frac{\sum\limits_{i=1}^{n_k} (y_{k_i} - \bar{y}_k)^2}{n_k - 1}} \left(\frac{1}{n_k}\right)$$

where t is the t value corresponding to the confidence level of interest and the number of degrees of freedom is given by $n_k - 1$, where n_k is the number of sample units taken from the kth sub-population; and where y_{k_i} is the value of the ith observation in sub-population k and $\bar{y}_k$ is the mean of sub-population k.

As usual, this can be modified by taking into account the finite population correction:

$$\frac{N_k - n_k}{N_k}$$

where n_k is again as above and N_k is the total size of the relevant sub-population.

Stratified Sampling

The problem with this approach is that we can't guarantee that our simple random sample will include any items from a particular sub-population which may turn out to be of interest. It makes more sense to divide our population into sub-populations of interest first if we can do it and then randomly sample each of the sub-populations; this will guarantee getting the information we want. This is the method known as *stratified random sampling*, because the technical name for the sub-divisions is *strata* (nothing to do with archaeological layers as such, although we might want to use these as sampling strata for some purpose).

It is easy to think of examples where this possibility is relevant. For example, if an archaeological survey of a region is being carried out, it may be decided to divide the region into environmental zones on the basis of some criterion and to sample each; or if a site is being excavated and it appears from preliminary work that it is functionally differentiated, then each of the functionally different sections may be sampled; or again, if we are selecting a sample of sherds from a multi-period site for scientific analysis we will probably want to take measures to ensure that all periods, or certain specific ones of particular interest, are represented. As far as fieldwork is concerned, we may simply divide an area of interest into arbitrary sub-areas, say squares, and randomly sample within these squares, just to make sure we have reasonably even coverage.

In effect, what we are saying in such cases is that we don't just want to predict, say, overall site density for a region, but the varying densities at different places within it. However, stratified samples can have a further benefit. If our sub-populations are homogeneous with respect to the phenomenon of interest but differ among themselves, we will get a better estimate (i.e. one with a narrower confidence interval) of our overall parameter of interest with a stratified sample than with a simple random one, for a given size of sample. Thus, if we stratify a region by soil type and sample-quadrats within a given soil type have very similar numbers of sites, while the numbers of sites in quadrats on different soil types are very different, then it is the stratified sample which will give the better estimate. An example of a stratified sample is shown in Figure 14.2.

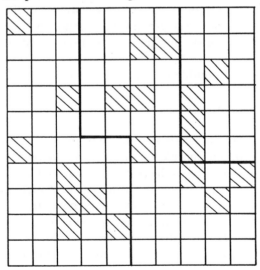

FIGURE 14.2. A stratified spatial random sample.

To obtain a confidence interval for the mean of any particular stratum is straightforward enough. It is the simple random sample formula we have already seen, applied separately to each stratum. To find an interval for the overall mean of a population sampled by stratified random sampling we need the following formulae (Thompson, 1992, pp. 104–5); first a point estimate for the mean:

$$\bar{y}_{st} = \frac{1}{N} \sum_{h=1}^{L} N_h \, \bar{y}_h$$

where $\bar{y}_{st}$ is the overall mean from stratified sampling; N is the overall population size; N_h is the size of the population in stratum h; $\bar{y}_h$ is the mean value for stratum h; and L is the number of strata.

The standard error of this overall mean (taking into account the finite population correction) is given by the square root of the following:

$$\text{var}\,(\bar{y}_{st}) = \sum_{h=1}^{L} \left(\frac{N_h}{N}\right)^2 \left(\frac{N_h - n_h}{N_h}\right) \frac{s_h^{\,2}}{n_h}$$

where quantities are as above and, in addition, n_h is the size of the sample in stratum h; and s_h^2 is the variance of the values in stratum h, obtained by squaring the differences between the stratum mean and the stratum individual observations in the usual way.

To obtain the confidence interval we have

$$y_{st} \pm t\sqrt{\text{var}\,(\bar{y}_{st})}$$

where the t value depends as usual on the probability we wish to associate with our confidence interval and the relevant number of degrees of freedom. If the population size and the sample size for each stratum are the same, the number of degrees of freedom is $n - L$ (the sample size minus the number of strata), but if this isn't the case a more complex approximation must be used (Thompson, 1992, p. 106); however, if all the stratum sample sizes are greater than thirty then the Z_α value may be used instead of t.

After these slightly numbing formulae an example may help.

A regional survey has been carried out on a non-site basis, recording lithic artefact densities, and the area has been divided into four strata based on a combination of topography and soil type; the elements of the population are one-hectare quadrats; the results are shown in Table 14.1.

TABLE 14.1.

Stratum	Stratum pop. size (N_h)	Stratum sample size (n_h)	Stratum mean lithic density $(\bar{y}_h)$	Stratum lithic density variance (s_h^2)
1	400	40	15.2	20.3
2	310	31	21.1	62.4
3	360	36	12.6	7.4
4	430	43	19.2	50.9

Using the formulae given above we first need to calculate the overall mean:

$$\bar{y}_{st} = \frac{1}{1500} [(400 \times 15.2) + (310 \times 21.1) + (360 \times 12.6) + (430 \times 19.2)]$$

$$= \frac{25413}{1500} = 16.942$$

So the overall mean density of lithics per hectare is estimated to be 16.94. The next step is to calculate the standard error of the mean, taking into account the finite population correction.

$$\text{var}(\bar{y}_{st}) = \frac{1}{1500^2} [400(400-40) \frac{20.3}{40} + 310(310-31) \frac{62.4}{31}$$

$$+ 360(360-36) \frac{7.4}{36} + 430(430-43) \frac{50.9}{43}]$$

$$= \frac{1}{1500^2} (730800 + 174096 + 239760 + 84702960)$$

$$= \frac{85847346}{1500^2} = 38.15$$

So for a 95 per cent confidence interval we have

$$\bar{y}_{st} \pm 1.96 \sqrt{38.15}$$

Here 16.94 ± 12.11

or $4.83 - 29.05$

In other words, there is a 95 per cent probability that the lithic density/ha lies in the range 4.83–29.05.

This kind of stratified sampling approach can go a long way towards satisfying our usual requirement that a sample should tell us not only about overall quantities of interest but also sub-population variation, where the latter will often have a spatial dimension in an archaeological context. Moreover, the method has the virtue of building into the estimation procedure specific information relevant to the case.

Systematic Sampling

An alternative way of ensuring an even spread of coverage so that we have information about internal variation within a population as well as overall coverage is *systematic sampling*. With this technique (which is in fact a special case of cluster sampling – see below) the interval between the sample points is fixed by the relation between the size of the proposed sample and the size of the population. Thus, if we wanted to select a sample of 30 from a population of 300 we would select every 300/30th item – every 10th in other words. Whether the 1st, 11th, 21st, etc. are chosen, or the 5th, 15th, 25th etc., or whatever, is determined by selecting a random number between 0 and 9 for the starting point. Figure 14.3 shows an example of spatial systematic sampling.

One of the reasons for selecting a systematic sample is that it is often easy and convenient to put the procedure into operation, and the other is the aim of ensuring even coverage already noted. However, systematic samples do present problems, even for ensuring even coverage, unless they are carefully thought out (see below). The difficulty in this respect arises from the fact that there may be periodicities in the values of the population elements being sampled. This is particularly likely to be the case

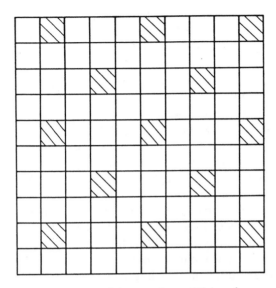

FIGURE 14.3. A systematic spatial sample.

in the sampling of spatial distributions. On a settlement excavation, for example, a regular grid of sampling units at a given
level might find all the houses or miss them, if, as is likely,
they are systematically distributed in some way. Furthermore,
whichever turned out to be the case, any estimate of the total
number of houses based on the number in the sample would
prove erroneous (cf. Winter, 1976). As far as the aim of obtaining such overall estimates is concerned, the problem with systematic sampling is that any single systematic sample has a
sample size of only one. This is because only the first item in the
sample is selected at random; once that choice has been made
all the other items in the sample are given. In Thompson's ter-
minology (1992, p. 113) there is a single *primary* sampling unit,
made up of systematically spaced *secondary* units. Because there
is only a single item in the sample it is impossible to calculate a
standard error and thus obtain a confidence interval.

One way round this is to treat the secondary units as if they
were a simple random sample, but this is obviously only satisfactory if it is reasonable to assume that the order of items in the

sampling frame is random. This option should be used with caution since periodicities and trends within the population may not be at all obvious. Furthermore, as Thompson points out (1992, p. 119), if we are sampling spatial populations it is more often than not the case that values of some phenomenon are similar for points which are close together and less similar when they are further apart. Since a systematic sample places the units maximally far apart, the estimate of the standard error of the mean or total which results is likely to be exaggerated.

A variety of other ways have been suggested for estimating the standard error from a single systematic sample. Most of them require some sort of prior knowledge of the structure of the population being sampled in order to use an appropriate method, but such knowledge may well not be available. Bellhouse (1980; Bellhouse and Finlayson, 1979) extended the idea of using prior knowledge by developing a computer program for calculating the outcome of different sampling schemes, including systematic sampling, in terms of the standard error of the estimate. The problem is that in order to provide an appropriate sampling scheme for a particular case, whether region or site, the method presupposes that complete information is available for a similar region or site, to provide the information on which the performance of the sampling scheme may be assessed; nevertheless, for well-known site types such information is likely to be available.

Cluster Sampling

It was noted above that systematic sampling is in fact a special case of cluster sampling. As Thompson explains (1992, p. 113), the key idea of cluster sampling is that the population is divided up into *primary units*, each of which is made of *secondary units*. Even though it may be the secondary units that we want to study it is the primary units that we select. If one member of a cluster is selected then so are the others.

An archaeological example of the difference between cluster sampling and the other forms of sampling we have seen so far may make clearer what is involved. Let us suppose that a large number of pits has been excavated at a site. We are interested in studying the pottery from them but we do not have the resources to study all of it, so a sample must be taken.

If we were taking a simple random sample we would treat all the pottery from all the pits as the population and select randomly from that population without regard to the pits from which the pottery comes. It is likely that such a procedure would be extremely difficult (and expensive) to put into practice because of the way material is stored and organised after an excavation, and also that some pits would not be represented in the sample while others would only have very few sherds selected.

If we were using stratified random sampling we could take the individual pits as our strata and select a random sample of pottery from within each pit. Although this would be very good from the point of view of ensuring that all pits were represented and of estimating various properties of the population, it would almost certainly be very laborious to put into operation because we would have to organise the procedure of selecting a random sample from each pit; moreover, rare items within a pit, which might be of particular interest, would probably never be included in a sample.

The cluster sampling approach would be to take a random sample of pits and study the pottery from the pits selected. This would have the disadvantage that not all the pits would be examined, and that cluster samples almost always give greater sampling errors than simple random samples of the same size (see below). On the other hand, it would almost certainly be the easiest procedure to put into practice, probably by a considerable margin, which would mean that we could actually look at more pottery for the same amount of time and effort. In cluster sampling, then, we do not sample among individual units independently but among clusters or groups of sample units. The example just described is very characteristic of the kind of situation which occurs in archaeology; often there is not much choice about dealing with cluster samples. A spatial cluster sample is shown in Figure 14.4.

The formulae for obtaining confidence intervals of estimates of means and totals are the same as for simple random sampling but the results in this case refer to the primary units only, not the secondary units. So, for example, by this means, if we were

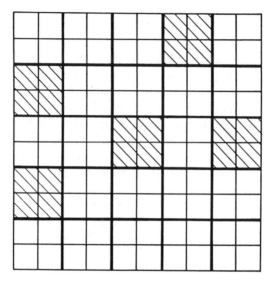

FIGURE 14.4. A spatial cluster sample.

carrying out a study of site formation processes we could produce a confidence interval for the overall mean sherd size per pit
of a particular fabric type.

The main problem with clusters, for example the contents of
the pits in the hypothetical example described above, is that they
tend to be relatively homogeneous and any single cluster is likely
to represent only a fraction of the full range of variation in the
population as a whole. This means that in selecting only certain
clusters we may be failing to consider some of the variation in
the population. The relative efficiency of a cluster sample to a
simple random sample of equivalent size (i.e. where the size of
the random sample is the same as the total number of *secondary*
units in the cluster sample) is determined by the ratio of the variance of the simple random sample to that of the primary units of
the cluster sample, so that if there is little variation they will be
more efficient. As noted above, more often than not this will not
be the case and there will be fairly considerable variation
between sampling units; in spatial sampling this arises because
nearby things tend to be similar to one another and more distant
things less so.

Spatial Prediction

However, this fact about spatial variation is not simply a problem. It is also something that can be turned to our advantage. We said earlier that it was unlikely that we would just be interested in an overall estimate of some attribute of our site or region; more often than not we are interested in the internal variation. In fact, if we can characterise the internal variation well we are also likely to get a better estimate of the overall figure. We saw that one way of doing this is to stratify our sample, perhaps in terms of environmental characteristics; but this is not the only possibility. More generally, we can use techniques of spatial prediction which exploit the facts of spatial variation noted above, i.e. that values of a variable at one location are not independent of those at another, so that typically items which are very close together will be very similar but this similarity will decline with distance. If we have a set of sample values scattered across an area of interest we can use this phenomenon to make inferences about what is happening in between. In order to do this we need to know the rate at which similarity falls off with distance, and whether this is the same in all directions. However, this too can be estimated from our sample points. This kind of prediction is known as *kriging* and has been particularly developed in the field of geostatistics, where the aim has been to predict such phenomena as underground ore distributions. It has been little used in archaeology (see for example Zubrow and Harbaugh, 1978) but has considerable potential, especially in association with stratified sampling techniques. Thompson (1992, Chapter 20) discusses its role in sampling while a good introduction to the techniques is given by Isaaks and Srivastava (1989).

Adaptive Sampling

Like stratification, spatial prediction makes use of information from the data – in this case the spatial dependence structure – to improve predictions. However, one obvious way of using information has not so far been considered. As we start collecting our sample we will in that very process start acquiring new information. Normally we do not let that information affect how we go about sampling, but the use of adaptive designs as part of a multistage sampling procedure enables us to do this; that is to say, 'the procedure for selecting sites or units to be included in the sample may depend on values of the variable of interest observed during the survey' (Thompson, 1992, p. 263).

The purpose of using such an approach is to obtain better estimates of such population parameters as means and totals than are likely to be attainable by other methods but they can also provide more information than would otherwise be available about other aspects of the population which are of interest. They are particularly relevant to the kinds of situations which arise in archaeological surveys, whether these involve surface survey or test-pitting. More often than not archaeological material is clustered in space and these clusters may be relatively uncommon; furthermore, increased clustering or clumping of material

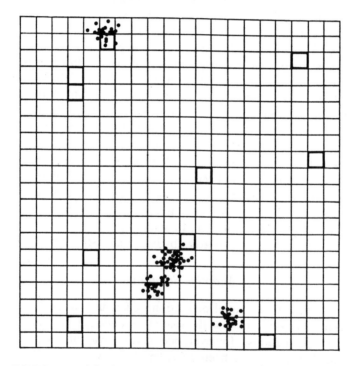

FIGURE 14.5. Adaptive cluster sampling to estimate the number of point objects in a study region of 400 units. An initial random sample of ten units is shown (after Thompson, 1990, 1992).

drastically increases the standard error of any estimates, so that problems are potentially posed for standard methods. We may end up with estimates of, for example, site mean density in a region, with intervals which are so wide as to be completely useless. In addition, if we find a cluster we are quite likely to want to know more about it than our initial sample units will tell us. Thus, the need for methods which can cope with this sort of situation and give estimates of high precision is clear enough and methods of *adaptive sampling* satisfy this need by greatly improving the precision of estimates in such circumstances. On the other hand, methods which increase the representation of selected areas on the basis of earlier stages of the survey may well give us biased estimates. What we need are estimates of means and variances which are unbiased in such circumstances, and in particular estimators whose unbiasedness does not depend on the characteristics of the population being sampled. Thompson (1992) provides an extensive description of such methods which it is impossible to summarise here, but it is worth showing what is involved by going through his example of adaptive cluster sampling.

Figure 14.5 shows a clustered spatial population in a region and the location of ten randomly located sample quadrats, two of which happen to intersect two of the clusters present. In this case the rule is that if a quadrat locates an observation of interest then the four nearest neighbour quadrats above, below, left and right are also surveyed. Similarly, if any of these produces an observation of interest the procedure is repeated until no more observations are found. The result is the scheme shown in Figure 14.6.

We now need to obtain an unbiased estimate of the mean density of items in our population of grid squares and its variance, so we can calculate a confidence interval. This first requires us to define what is known in the jargon as a *network*. A network is a sub-collection of sampling units where the selection of any one unit within the network containing an observation of interest leads to the selection of all the others with such observations by the procedure defined above of adding sampling units. Thus, in the case of the upper cluster of points in Figure 14.6 the network size is six units and for the lower cluster it is eleven units.

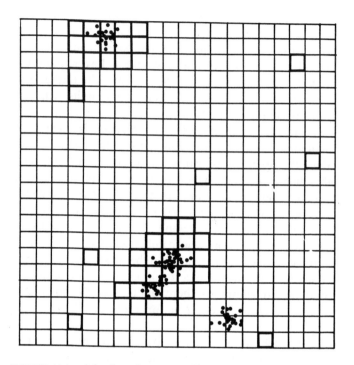

FIGURE 14.6. Adaptive cluster sampling to estimate the number of point objects in a study region of 400 units. Adjacent neighbouring units have been added to the initial ten unit sample whenever one or more of the objects in the population is observed in a selected unit (after Thompson, 1992).

Those units containing no observations count as networks of one unit. To work out the average value for a given network of units we divide the total number of observations in the network by the number of units (Thompson, 1992, p. 271):

$$w_i = \frac{1}{m_i} \Sigma y_j$$

where w_i is the mean value for network i; m_i is the number of units in network i; and y_j is the value of a given jth unit of network i.

In the case of the upper cluster in the figure the number of observations is 36 and the number of units is 6, so the mean is 6.

We now need to estimate the mean density of items for the region as a whole:

$$\bar{y} = \frac{1}{n} \sum_{i=1}^{n} w_i$$

where n_i is the number of initial independent sampling units and the w_is are as calculated above.

In this case

$$\bar{y} = \frac{1}{10} \left(\frac{36}{6} + \frac{107}{11} + \frac{0}{1} + \ldots + \frac{0}{1} \right)$$

$$= 0.1(6 + 9.727 + 0 + \ldots + 0) = 1.573$$

That is to say, the mean number of items per unit in this case is 1.573. If we want to obtain an estimate of the total number of items in the population of 400 sampling units we simply multiply by 400 to give 629.

We now need an estimate of the variance of this figure in order to produce our confidence interval. This is done in the usual way, taking into account the finite population correction and based on the squared differences between the value for each of our networks and the overall mean (Thompson, 1992, p. 271).

$$\text{var}\,(\bar{y}) = \frac{(N-n)}{Nn(n-1)} \sum_{i=1}^{n} (w_i - \bar{y})^2$$

In this case we have

$$\frac{(400-10)}{400(10)(10-1)} \left[(6-1.573)^2 + (9.727-1.573)^2 + (0-1.573)^2 + \ldots + (0-1.573)^2 \right]$$

$$\frac{390}{400(10)} (11.675) = 1.147$$

The variance of the total is

$$N^2(\text{var}\,(y))$$

$$= 400^2(1.147) = 183520$$

To obtain a 95 per cent confidence interval we need

$$\bar{y} \pm t_{\alpha,df} \sqrt{\operatorname{var}(\bar{y})}$$

where $t_{\alpha,df}$ = 2-tailed 0.05 and d.f. = $n-1$ = 9

Here we have

$$1.573 \pm 2.262(1.071)$$

$$= 1.573 \pm 2.423$$

So the mean density lies between −0.85 and 3.996 items per quadrat and, in fact, since its lower limit is negative, it is not significantly different from zero.

For the total the corresponding figures are

$$629 \pm 2.262 \,(428.39)$$

or −340 to 1598.

Needless to say, if we had treated the forty-five units eventually included in the sample as a simple random sample we would have ended up with a gross overestimate. However, in addition to a much better estimate this method also provides far more data for subsequent analysis as well as an excellent basis for estimating the variogram which is the essential basis of spatial prediction models (Isaaks and Srivastava, 1989).

Thompson (1992) also develops results for other forms of adaptive cluster sampling.

DETECTABILITY

A relevant aspect of much archaeological fieldwork is the question of detectability: when we walk across a site in the course of an archaeological survey, for example, we're not necessarily guaranteed to find it, and the same when digging test pits; similarly, if the fieldwalkers on a survey are fifteen metres apart, they'll only find sites ten metres across some of the time.

Nance (1983) was one of the first to discuss this question in archaeology and Kintigh (1988) has subsequently developed methods for calculating detection probabilities for different combinations of test-pit sizes and densities of finds and features; the use of these methods is illustrated below. However, archaeology is not the only subject to be faced with detectability problems when taking samples: ecological surveys in particular face similar difficulties, for example in estimating the numbers of birds or fish in a particular area. At least archaeological sites don't move, or anyway not very far! In all such cases it is necessary to take detectability factors into account when making estimates. This presupposes being able to estimate detectability. Kintigh (1988) has done this for the particular technique he has modelled but in general it is possible to do it by carrying out experiments in total survey coverage or by conducting retrospective sampling experiments on well-documented totally excavated sites.

Clearly, whether we are interested in estimating overall parameters for populations or characterising sub-populations by such techniques as stratification and spatial prediction, if we do not take into account detectability we are not going to come up with valid estimates. Not only that, but lower detectability values also lead to higher variances for our estimates, and this effect is still further enhanced when our detectability value is itself an estimate with a variance. Full details of what is involved are given by Thompson (1992, Chapter 16) but it may be useful to illustrate the issue with an example.

Suppose we have an area selected for development, but before development is allowed to go ahead it is decided that an archaeological evaluation based on test-pitting should be carried out, with the aim of estimating the total number of artefacts in the area to be affected. The area to be covered is 2 ha and it has been decided to take a simple random sample of 40 2×2 m test-pits. Earlier work suggests that the detectability of artefacts in this soil type by this team, assuming sieving of the soil from the test pits, is 0.8, with an estimated standard error of 0.025. The mean artefact density from the sample is 2.03 per quadrat, with a standard deviation of 1.97. The population size, N, is the number of quadrats in 2 ha, which is 5000. We will obtain a confidence interval for the total, first ignoring then taking into account the detectability level.

1. *Estimating the total without the detectability factor*

$$\bar{y}_T = 5000(2.03) = 10150$$

$$\text{var } (\bar{y}_T) = N^2 \left(\frac{N-n}{N}\right) \frac{s^2}{n}$$

$$= 5000^2 \left(\frac{5000-40}{5000}\right) \frac{1.97^2}{40}$$

$$= 25{,}000{,}000(0.992)(0.097)$$

$$= 2405600$$

$$s_{y_T} = \sqrt{2405600} = 1551$$

where $\bar{y}_T$ is the total number of artefacts.
  So the 95 per cent confidence interval is

$$10150 \pm (1.96)(1551)$$

i.e. there is a 95 per cent probability that the number of artefacts in the area is in the range 7110–13190.

2. Estimating the total using the estimated detectability factor of 0.8

$$\bar{y}_T = N \frac{\bar{y}}{p} = 5000 \left(\frac{2.03}{0.8}\right) = 12688$$

where $\bar{y}_T$ is the total number of artefacts, $\bar{y}$ is the mean number per quadrat and p is the detectability value.
  We now need to obtain an estimate of the variance of this quantity preparatory to calculating the confidence interval. This time the variance has two components, the normal sampling variance in the quantity being estimated and that in the detectability factor:

$$\text{var } (\bar{y}_T) = \frac{N^2}{p^2} [\left(\frac{N-n}{N}\right) \frac{s^2}{n} + \left(\frac{1-p}{N}\right) \bar{y} + \frac{\bar{y}^2}{p^2} \text{ var } (p)]$$

$$= \frac{5000^2}{0.8^2} [\left(\frac{5000-40}{5000}\right) \frac{1.97^2}{40} + \left(\frac{1-0.8}{5000}\right)(2.03) +$$

$$\left(\frac{2.03^2}{0.08^2}\right)(0.000625)]$$

$$= (39062500)(0.0962+0.0000812+0.4024)$$

$$= (39062500)(0.4987)$$

$$= 19480469$$

$$s_{y_T} = \sqrt{19480469} = 4414$$

95 per cent confidence $= 12688 \pm (1.96)(4414)$

i.e. there is a 95 per cent probability that the number of artefacts in the area is in the range 4036–21340.

Obviously, the mean has moved upwards considerably as a result of taking into account the detectability factor, but much more important is the effect on the standard error of the estimate, which is roughly three times as large as an estimate which doesn't take the detectability factor into account and thus gives a completely misleading impression of the precision of the estimate.

A Field Strategy Case-study

The use of test-pitting as a means of archaeological survey has grown increasingly important in the last twenty years, despite the problems associated with it. Indeed, as we noted above, Kintigh (1988) has proposed methods to deal with the problems; these bring us back to the topic of systematic sampling discussed above. It was stated then that a specific problem with this sampling method is that systematic samples are samples of one, because of the lack of independence of the sample units. However, there is another way of looking at systematic samples in situations where we can afford reasonably dense coverage and in these circumstances the sampling problem shades into a detectability problem.

As Kintigh (1988) explains, if we are carrying out a survey to locate *sites*, as opposed to estimating densities of artefacts, we have two problems – first, we must intersect the site with our survey method and then we must detect evidence of its presence. As far as test-pitting is concerned, he shows that the most efficient layout is a triangular/hexagonal pattern, because this minimises the size of the largest area that can go undetected. On

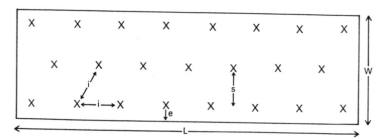

FIGURE 14.7. The design of test-pitting strategies based on a regular hexagonal layout. W = width of survey area, L = length of survey area, t = number of rows of test-pits, i = interval between test-pits in a row, s = interval between two rows of test-pits, d = maximum diameter of untested site, e = distance from transect to edge of survey area; $s = i \sqrt{3/2} = 0.866i$, $s = 3W/(t-1)$, $e = s/3$, $d = 2i/\sqrt{3} = 1\cdot155i$, $d = 4s/3$ (after Champion et al., 1996).

this basis, once a decision has been made on the smallest size of site one wishes to guarantee finding, spacing parameters for the test-pits can be selected to obtain the required results, using a set of formulae. What is involved is shown in Figure 14.7 (from Champion et al., 1996). The example used by Champion et al. involved the retrospective test-pitting of a 51-ha development area in which a site of 128 m diameter had been discovered. In this case:

L (length of development area) = 1429 m
W (width of development area) = 357 m

Using Kintigh's formula the resulting strategy would have been:

Number of rows of test-pits = 5
Spacing between rows = 76.5 m
Spacing between test-pits along rows = 88.3 m
Maximum diameter of an untested site = 102 m

So this strategy is guaranteed to intersect any site more than 102 m in diameter whose centre lies within the evaluation area; for smaller sites than this the probability of intersection obviously decreases as site size decreases.

However, intersection of the site does not guarantee detection: if the density of finds or features is low and/or highly clustered then a small test-pit is quite likely not to recover anything at all, so the site will not be found even if the trench is in the middle of it. Since it is likely that only one or two test-pits will intersect the site, it is essential that they are large enough to recognise it. How large that is cannot be specified absolutely — it depends on the density and distribution of finds and features. In addition to specifying test-pit layouts, the Kintigh simulations also provide information on the probability of site detection for particular test-pit sizes under specific assumptions about the density and distribution of finds/features. Information about likely distributions can be obtained from existing site reports and, as with site size, decisions can be made about the minimum density of finds/features which the investigator wishes to guarantee finding. As usual, such decisions will depend on aims: to discover mesolithic forager camps will be general need a denser layout and larger test-pits than a Roman rural settlement.

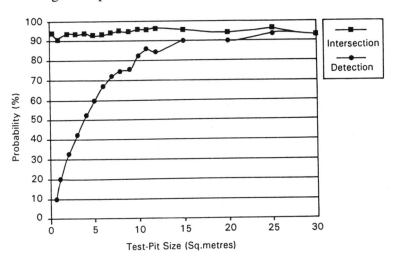

FIGURE 14.8. Site intersection and detection probabilities for a range of test-pit sizes, based on a retrospective analysis of the archaeology of a development area (after Champion et al., 1996).

Obviously, for a given density of finds/features the probability of detection increases as the test-pit size gets bigger. This is seen in Figure 14.8, based on a retrospective study of a totally excavated site. The test-pit size selected would normally be the value at which the curve of detection probability against test-pit size starts to level out, so that increasing the size doesn't greatly improve the probability of detection. In Figure 14.8 it can be seen that with the trench layout chosen a site of the size in question would be intersected with a probability greater than 90 per cent. However, if the test-pit was only 1 metre square it would only have a probability of 10 per cent of actually detecting it. A 10 sq.m trench, on the other hand, would have a probability of detection of 80 per cent. However, you would have to go up to 30 sq.m before the detection probability would correspond to the intersection probability; furthermore, we should note that these simulated probabilities depend on 100 per cent detection of finds/features present; real figures are likely to be worse than this.

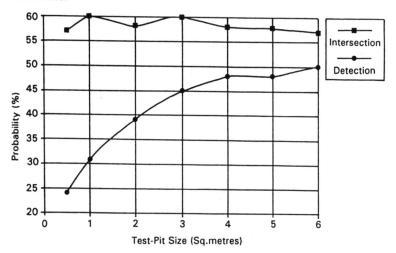

FIGURE 14.9. Site intersection and detection probabilities for a range of test-pit sizes, based on a retrospective analysis of the archaeology of a different development area (after Champion et al., 1996).

Another example from the study of Champion et al. is shown in Figure 14.9. The test-pit layout selected would intersect a site such as this of 48 m diameter approximately 60 per cent of the time and with a test-pit of 3 sq.m would detect the site with a probability of 45 per cent. This is obviously not particularly good. In this case the strategy was redefined with a denser layout to guarantee that at least *two* test-pits would intersect the site. In this case the detection rate with 3-sq.m test-pits rose to 74 per cent.

Finally, it is important to bear in mind that there may be more than one site in the area being test-pitted, and this too affects our strategies, because we need to establish the probability of a joint event: of finding site 1 *and* site 2 *and* site 3 etc., all of which individually have a probability of detection of less than 100 per cent. The results for another of the retrospective analyses carried out by Champion et al. are shown in Figure 14.10. From this we can see that with the intersection layout chosen, based on discovering sites larger than 25 m in diameter, while 1-sq.m test-pits would discover at least one of the sites with a 40 per cent probability, we would need test-pits of 15 sq.m to give a probability of detection for all five sites of greater than 50 per cent.

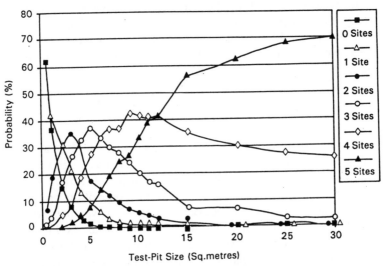

FIGURE 14.10. Probabilities of detecting different numbers of sites for a range of test-pit sizes, based on a retrospective analysis of the archaeology of a development area (after Champion et al., 1996).

But simply detecting the site or sites may not be enough. For example, a single test-pit is highly unlikely to provide an indication of what sort of site it is and may well not provide a date. In this situation it would be highly appropriate to use the sort of adaptive cluster sampling techniques described above. In Champion et al.'s retrospective study, following on the stage I test-pit design obtained from the simulation programs, a second stage of simulated work was carried out, in which trenches were allocated to the test-pits in the same proportion as they produced remains, so that a test-pit which produced 20 per cent of the stage I finds/features received 20 per cent of the simulated stage II trenching; the trenches were placed so that they extended north, south, east and west of the test-pits on which they were centred (Champion et al., 1996, p. 55).

In the case-study on the Charnham Lane development such a two-stage strategy detected all five sites, recovering nearly 50 per cent of the finds and nearly 40 per cent of the features in an area of 11745 sq.m, 8.7 per cent of the development area. The other case-study involved a mesolithic site without features. The total area 'excavated' by the two-stage adaptive procedure was 129 sq.m, 3.4 per cent of the development area. This led to the 'discovery' of 42 per cent of the finds, which would have made possible a detailed analysis of the assemblage, and enabled the definition of the site boundaries.

CONCLUSION

Probabilistic sampling procedures remain very useful in archaeology and the development of techniques such as adaptive cluster sampling, together with the increased use of sample-based spatial prediction methods, can get around some of the problems which sample-based methods once faced. However, they should not be assumed to be appropriate in all circumstances. Plenty of authors, for example, have argued that for certain archaeological purposes at the regional scale continuous survey coverage is essential, and this seems reasonable enough. But even continuous survey coverage cannot escape coming to terms with many of the issues discussed in this chapter because short of total excavation of the whole area, including sieving the topsoil, detectability issues always arise and have a probabilistic dimension which must be taken into account.

EXERCISES

14.1 An archaeological survey has been carried out of an area of 100 sq.km. The survey was based on a simple random sample of one-hectare quadrats, totalling 5 sq.km in all. Densities of material in each quadrat were recorded and for lithics the mean density was 16.95/ha, with a standard deviation of 7.03, and a distribution not far from normality, albeit positively skewed.

Calculate a confidence interval for the total number of lithic items in the survey area as a whole, with a probability of 99 per cent.

14.2 A hunter-gatherer occupation site was excavated on a grid of 2×2 metre squares. Below is a list of the number of lithic pieces found in each of the fifty squares excavated.

2	5	15	17	11	26	25	28	23	22
38	37	35	30	39	48	47	45	48	42
47	45	41	55	50	59	51	59	56	57
53	61	67	64	63	60	79	75	77	72
71	85	82	89	96	93	95	108	103	117

i) Work out the mean and standard deviation for the site as a whole.

ii) (a) Use random numbers to select ten simple random samples of ten squares; (b) obtain the mean and standard deviation for each sample, together with the mean of the means; (c) obtain the standard error of the mean for each sample, and 95 per cent and 99 per cent confidence intervals for the mean; (d) how do the confidence intervals relate to each other and to the overall population mean?

(iii) Repeat (ii) for samples of twenty squares.

NB The *t* distribution should be used for the confidence intervals.

14.3 A gridded surface survey using simple random sampling is being carried out on an archaeological site prior to excavation in order to get an idea of the overall total number of pottery sherds present. It is decided that the survey should make sure the total is estimated to a tolerance of $\pm$ 3000 sherds. The survey quadrats are 5 × 5 metres in size and it is assumed on the basis of previous work elsewhere that a reasonable estimate of the standard deviation of the number of sherds per quadrat is 6. The probability level required is set at 95 per cent.

i) How many quadrats will need to be surveyed to provide such an estimate, assuming that the site is 25 ha in extent? (Note that there are 10,000 sq.m in a hectare.)

ii) What difference would it make to the confidence interval if it was subsequently concluded that the detectability level of the survey method used was 90 per cent rather than 100 per cent?

14.4 The figure below shows the results of a sampling experiment on a totally surveyed area. Ten units have been initially selected by simple random sampling. Use adaptive cluster sampling methods to estimate the total number of sites in the area with a 95 per cent probability. Does the real total fall within the interval?

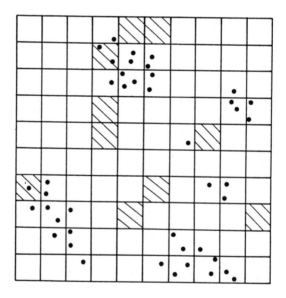

BIBLIOGRAPHY

Aldenderfer, M. 1982. Methods of cluster validation for archaeology. *World Archaeology* 14, pp. 61–72

Barnett, V. 1974. *Elements of Sampling Theory*. London: English University Press

Baxter, M. J. 1994. *Exploratory Multivariate Analysis in Archaeology*. Edinburgh: Edinburgh University Press

Baxter, M. J. and C. Beardah. 1995. Beyond the histogram – improved approaches to simple data display in archaeology using kernel density estimates. Paper presented at the IIIrd International Symposium on Computing and Archaeology, Rome 1995

Beazley, J. D. 1963. *Attic Red-Figure Vase-Painters*. Oxford: Clarendon Press

Bellhouse, D. 1980. Sampling studies in archaeology. *Archaeometry* 22, pp.123–32

Bellhouse, D. and W. D. Finlayson. 1979. An empirical study of probability sampling designs: preliminary results from the Draper site. *Canadian Journal of Archaeology* 3, pp. 105-23

Blalock, H. M. 1972. *Social Statistics*. New York: McGraw-Hill

Brainerd, G. W. 1951. The place of chronological ordering in archaeological analysis. *American Antiquity* 16, pp. 301–13

Braund, D. 1985. Absolute seriation: a time-series approach. In C. Carr (ed.), *For Concordance in Archaeological Data Analysis*, pp. 509–39. Prospect Heights, Illinois: Waveland Press

Brumfiel, E. 1976. Regional growth in the eastern valley of Mexico: a test of the 'population pressure' hypothesis. In K. V. Flannery (ed.), *The Early Mesoamerican Village*, pp. 234–49. New York: Academic Press

Buchvaldek, M. and D. Koutecky. 1970. *Vikletice: ein schnurkeramisches Gräberfeld*. Prague: Universita Karlová

Buck, C. E., W. Kavanagh and C. D. Litton. 1996. *Bayesian Approaches to Interpreting Archaeological Data*. New York: John Wiley & Sons

Buck, C. E., J. B. Kenworthy, C. D. Litton and A. F. M. Smith. 1991. Combining archaeological and radiocarbon information – a Bayesian approach to calibration. *Antiquity* 65, pp. 808–21

Buck, C. E., C. D. Litton and S. J. Shennan. 1994. A case study in combining radiocarbon and archaeological information: the early Bronze

Age settlement of St.Veit-Klinglberg, Land Salzburg, Austria. *Germania* 72 (2), pp. 427–47

Buck, C. E., C. D. Litton and A. F. M. Smith. 1992. Calibration of radio-carbon results pertaining to related archaeological events. *Journal of Archaeological Science* 19, pp. 497–512

Carr, C. 1985. Alternative models, alternative techniques: variable approaches to intra-site spatial analysis. In C. Carr (ed.), *For Concordance in Archaeological Data Analysis*, pp. 302–473. Prospect Heights, Illinois: Waveland Press

Champion, T., P. Cuming and S. J. Shennan. 1996. *Planning for the Past Vol. 3: Decision-making and field methods in archaeological evaluation*. London: English Heritage and University of Southampton

Chatterjee, S. and B. Price. 1977. *Regression Analysis by Example*. New York: John Wiley and Sons

Cherry, J. F. 1977. Investigating the political geography of an early state by multidimensional scaling of Linear B tablet data. In J. Bintliff (ed.), *Mycenaean Geography*, pp. 76–83. Cambridge: British Association for Mycenaean Studies

Cormack, R. M. 1971. A review of classification. *Journal of the Royal Statistical Society A* 134, pp. 321–67

Cowgill, G. L. 1977. The trouble with significance tests and what we can do about it. *American Antiquity* 42, pp. 350–68

Davis, J. C. 1986. *Statistics and Data Analysis in Geology*. 2nd edn. New York: John Wiley and Sons

Djindjian, F. 1980. *Construction de Systèmes d'Aide à la Connaissance en Archéologie Préhistorique. Structuration et Affectation*. Thèse de Doctorat de 3e Cycle, Université Paris 1, UER d'Art et d'Archéologie

Doran, J. and F. Hodson. 1975. *Mathematics and Computers in Archaeology*. Edinburgh: Edinburgh University Press

Durham, P., P. Lewis and S.J. Shennan. 1995. Artefact matching and retrieval using the Generalised Hough Transform. In J. Wilcock and K. Lockyear (eds), *Computer applications and Quantitative Methods in Archaeology 1993*, pp. 25–30. Oxford: Tempus Reparatum (BAR International Series 598)

Elmasri, R. and S. B. Navathe. 1989. *Fundamentals of Database Systems*. Redwood City, California: Benjamin/Cummings

Everitt, B. 1980. *Cluster Analysis*. 2nd edn. London: Heinemann

Everitt, B. and G. Dunn. 1983. *Advanced Methods of Data Exploration and Modelling*. London: Heinemann

Fieller, N. R. J. 1993. Archaeostatistics: old statistics in ancient contexts. *The Statistician* 42, pp. 279–95

Fieller, N. R. J. and A. Turner. 1982. Number estimation in vertebrate samples. *Journal of Archaeological Science* 9, pp. 49–62

Fienberg, S. E. 1980. *The Analysis of Cross-Classified Categorical Data*. 2nd edn. Cambridge, Mass.: MIT Press

Fletcher, M. and G. Lock. 1991. *Digging Numbers*. Oxford: Oxford University Committee for Archaeology

Gordon, A. D. 1981. *Classification: Methods for the Exploratory Analysis of Multivariate Data*. London: Chapman and Hall

Gower, J. C. 1971. A general coefficient of similarity and some of its properties. *Biometrics* 27, pp. 857–72

Greenacre, M. J. 1993. *Correspondence Analysis in Practice*. London: Academic Press

Gregg, S. A., K. W. Kintigh and R. Whallon. 1991. Linking ethnoarchaeological interpretation and archaeological data: the sensitivity of spatial analytical methods to post-depositional disturbance. In E. M. Kroll and T. D. Price (eds), *The Interpretation of Archaeological Spatial Patterning*, pp. 149–96. New York: Plenum Press

Hartwig, F. and B. E. Dearing. 1979. *Exploratory Data Analysis*. Beverly Hills and London: Sage

Healan, D. M. 1995. Identifying lithic reduction loci with size-graded macrodebitage: a multivariate approach. *American Antiquity* 60, pp. 689–99

Healy, M. J. R. 1988. *GLIM – An Introduction*. Oxford: Clarendon Press

Hodder, I. and C. Orton. 1976. *Spatial Analysis in Archaeology*. Cambridge: Cambridge University Press.

Hodson, F. R. 1977. Quantifying Hallstatt: some initial results. *American Antiquity* 42, pp. 394–412

Hodson, F. R. 1990. *Hallstatt: The Ramsauer Graves*. Bonn: Habelt

Isaaks, E. H. and R. M. Srivastava. 1989. *An Introduction to Applied Geostatistics*. New York: Oxford University Press

Jardine, N. and R. Sibson. 1971. *Mathematical Taxonomy*. London: John Wiley and Sons

Johnson, G. A. 1973. *Local Exchange to Early State Development in Southwestern Iran* (University of Michigan Museum of Anthropology, Anthropological Papers No. 51). Ann Arbor: University of Michigan

Johnston, R. J. 1978. *Multivariate Statistical Analysis in Geography*. London: Longman

Kampffmeyer, U. and W. R. Teegen. 1986. Untersuchungen zur rechnergestützten Klassifikation von Gefässformen am Beispiel der eisenzeitlichen Keramik des Gräberfeldes von Veis, Quattro Fontanili. *Die Kunde* 37, pp. 1–84

Kemp, B. 1982. Automatic analysis of Predynastic cemeteries: a new method for an old problem. *Journal of Egyptian Archaeology* 68, pp. 5–15

Kendall, D. 1977. Computer techniques and the archival map reconstruction of Mycenaean Messenia. In J. L. Bintliff (ed.), *Mycenaean Geography*, pp. 83–7. Cambridge: British Association for Mycenaean Studies

Kintigh, K. W. 1988. The effectiveness of sub-surface testing: a simulation approach. *American Antiquity* 53, pp. 686–707

Kruskal, J. B. and M. Wish. 1978. *Multidimensional scaling*. Beverly Hills and London: Sage Publications

Krzanowski, W.J. 1988. *Principles of Multivariate Analysis*. Oxford: Clarendon Press

Lewis, R. B. 1986. The analysis of contingency tables in archaeology. In M. B. Schiffer (ed.), *Advances in Archaeological Method and Theory* 9, pp. 277–310. New York: Academic Press

Lindsey, J. K. 1995. *Introductory Statistics: A Modelling Approach*. Oxford: Clarendon Press

McCullagh, P. and J. A. Nelder. 1989. *Generalized Linear Models*. London: Chapman and Hall

McDonald, J. and G. D. Snooks. 1985. The determinants of manorial income in Domesday England: evidence from Essex. *Journal of Economic History* 45, pp. 541–6

Madsen, T. 1988. Multivariate statistics and archaeology. In T. Madsen (ed.), *Multivariate Archaeology: Numerical Approaches in Scandinavian Archaeology*, pp. 7–28. Aarhus: Aarhus University Press (Jutland Archaeological Society Publications XXI)

Manly, B. F. 1991. *Randomization and Monte Carlo Methods in Biology*. London: Chapman and Hall

Martinsson-Wallin, H. 1994. *Ahu – The Ceremonial Stone Structures of Easter Island*. Uppsala: Societas Archaeologica Upsaliensis

Maschner, H. D. G. and J. W. Stein. 1995. Multivariate approaches to site location on the Northwest Coast of North America. *Antiquity* 69, pp. 61–73

Mather, P. M. 1976. *Computational Methods of Multivariate Analysis in Physical Geography*. London: John Wiley and Sons

Mathiesen, P., I. M. Holm-Olsen, T. Sobstad and H. D. Bratrein. 1981. The Helgøy project: an inter-disciplinary study of past eco-ethno processes in the Helgøy region, northern Troms, Norway. *Norwegian Archaeological Review* 14, pp. 77–117

Moore, C. and A. K. Romney 1994. Material culture, geographic propinquity and linguistic affiliation on the north coast of New Guinea: a re-analysis of Welsch *et al*. *American Anthropologist* 96, pp. 370–96

Moreno-Garcia, M., C. Orton and J. Rackham. 1996. A new statistical tool for comparing animal bone assemblages. *Journal of Archaeological Science* 23, pp. 437–53

Morrison, D. F. 1967. *Multivariate Statistical Methods*. New York: McGraw-Hill

Nance, J. 1983. Regional sampling in archaeological survey: the statistical perspective. In M. Schiffer (ed.), *Advances in Archaeological Method and Theory* 6, pp. 289–356. New York: Academic Press

Noreen, E. W. 1989. *Computer-intensive Methods for Testing Hypotheses: an Introduction*. New York: John Wiley and Sons

Orton, C. 1980. *Mathematics in Archaeology*. London: Collins

Orton, C. 1982. Computer simulation experiments to assess the performance of measures of quantity of pottery. *World Archaeology* 14, pp. 1–20

O'Shea, J. 1984. *Mortuary Variability: An Archaeological Investigation*.

Orlando: Academic Press

Parker, S. 1985. Predictive modelling of site settlement systems using multivariate logistics. In C. Carr (ed.), *For Concordance in Archaeological Data Analysis*, pp. 173–207. Prospect Heights, Illinois: Waveland Press

Peebles, C. S. 1972. Monothetic-divisive analysis of the Moundville burials – an initial report. *Newsletter of Computer Archaeology* 8, pp. 1-13

Petrie, W. M. F. 1899. Sequences in prehistoric remains. *Journal of the Anthropological Institute* 29, pp. 295–301

Plog, S. 1974. Settlement patterns and social history. In M. Leaf (ed.), *Frontiers of Anthropology*, pp. 68–92. New York: Van Nostrand

Plog, S. 1980. *Stylistic Variation in Prehistoric Ceramics*. Cambridge: Cambridge University Press.

Read, D. W. 1982. Towards a theory of archaeological classification. In R. Whallon and J. A. Brown (eds), *Essays in Archaeological Typology*, pp. 56–92. Evanston, Illinois: Center for American Archaeology Press

Read, D. W. 1989. Statistical methods and reasoning in archaeological research: a review of praxis and promise. *Journal of Quantitative Anthropology* 1, pp. 5–78

Read, D. W. 1994. What do we need to know to do quantitative archaeology? In I. Johnson (ed.), *Methods in the Mountains*, pp.1–6. Sydney: Department of Archaeology, University of Sydney

Read, D. W. and G. Russell. 1996. A method for taxonomic typology construction. *American Antiquity* 61, pp. 663–84

Renfrew, C. 1977. Alternative models for exchange and spatial distribution. In T. Earle and J. E. Ericson (eds), *Exchange Systems in Prehistory*, pp.71–90. New York: Academic Press

Robinson, W. S. 1951. A method for chronologically ordering archaeological deposits. *American Antiquity* 16, pp. 293–301

Schoknecht, U. (ed.). 1980. *Typentafeln zur Ur- und Frühgeschichte der DDR*. Weimar: Kulturbund der DDR

Scollar, I. 1994. WINBASP. Bonn: Unkelbach Valley Software Works

Shennan, S. J. 1985. *Experiments in the Collection and Analysis of Archaeological Survey Data: the East Hampshire Survey*. Sheffield: Department of Prehistory and Archaeology, University of Sheffield

Shennan, S. J. and J. D. Wilcock. 1975. Shape and style variation in Central German Bell Beakers: a computer-assisted study. *Science and Archaeology* 15, pp. 17–31

Sneath, P. and R. Sokal. 1973. *Numerical Taxonomy*. San Francisco: Freeman

Sorensen, M. L. S. 1992. Gender archaeology and Scandinavian Bronze Age studies. *Norwegian Archaeological Review* 25, pp. 31–49

Späth, H. 1980. *Cluster Analysis Algorithms*. Chichester: Ellis Horwood

Tainter, J. A. 1975. Social inferences and mortuary practices: an experiment in numerical classification. *World Archaeology* 7, pp. 1–15

Thompson, S. K. 1992. *Sampling*. New York: John Wiley and Sons

Tufte, E. R. 1983. *The Visual Display of Quantitative Information.* Cheshire, Connecticut: Graphics Press

Tufte, E. R. 1990. *Envisioning Information.* Cheshire, Connecticut: Graphics Press

van der Veen, M. and N. Fieller. 1982. Sampling seeds. *Journal of Archaeological Science* 9, pp. 287–98

Vierra, R. K. and D. L. Carlson. 1981. Factor analysis, random data and patterned results. *American Antiquity* 46, pp. 272–83

Wainwright, G. J. 1979. *Mount Pleasant, Dorset: Excavations 1970–71.* London: Society of Antiquaries

Walker, N. J. 1995. *Late Pleistocene and Holocene Hunter-gatherers of the Matopos.* Uppsala: Societas Archaeologica Upsaliensis (Studies in African Archaeology 10)

Wallin, P. 1993. *Ceremonial Stone Structures: the Archaeology and Ethnohistory of the Marae Complex in the Society Islands, French Polynesia.* Uppsala: Societas Archaeologica Upsaliensis

Wand, M. P. and M. C. Jones. 1995. *Kernel Smoothing.* London: Chapman and Hall

Warren, R. E. 1990. Predictive modelling in archaeology: a primer. In K. M. S. Allen, S. W. Green and E. B. W. Zubrow (eds), *Interpreting Space: GIS and Archaeology*, pp. 90–111. London: Taylor and Francis

Welsch, R. L., J. Terrell and J. A. Nadolski. 1992. Language and culture on the north coast of New Guinea. *American Anthropologist* 94, pp.568–600

Whallon, R. 1982. Variables and dimensions: the critical step in quantitative typology. In R. Whallon and J. A Brown (eds), *Essays in Archaeological Typology*, pp. 127–61. Evanston, Illinois: Center for American Archaeology Press

Whallon, R. 1984. Unconstrained clustering for the analysis of spatial distributions in archaeology. In H. Hietala (ed.), *Intra-site Spatial Analysis in Archaeology*, pp. 242–77. Cambridge: Cambridge University Press

Whallon, R. and J. A. Brown (eds). 1982. *Essays in Archaeological Typology.* Evanston, Illinois: Center for American Archaeology Press

White, J., A. Yeats and G. Skipworth. 1979. *Tables for Statistics.* London: Stanley Thornes

Winter, M. 1976. Excavating a shallow community by random sampling quadrats. In K. V. Flannery (ed.), *The Early Mesoamerican Village*, pp. 62–7. New York: Academic Press

Wishart, D. 1987. *CLUSTAN User Manual.* St Andrews: University of St Andrews

Wright, R. P. 1989. *Doing Multivariate Analysis and Prehistory: Handling Large Datasets with MV-ARCH.* Sydney: Department of Anthropology, University of Sydney

Zubrow, E. and J. Harbaugh. 1978. Archaeological prospecting: kriging and simulation. In I. Hodder (ed.), *Simulation Studies in Archaeology*, pp. 109–22. Cambridge: Cambridge University Press

APPENDIX

Tables A, B and E reproduced from D. V. Lindley and W. F. Scott, *New Cambridge Statistical Tables* (2nd edn), by permission of Cambridge University Press; Table C from J. White, A. Yeats and G. Skipworth, *Tables for Statisticians*, by permission of Stanley Thornes (Publishers) Ltd; Tables D and F by permission of the Biometrika Trustees.

TABLE A
Percentage points of the distribution of the number of runs.

Suppose that n_1 A's and n_2 B's $(n_1 \leq n_2)$ are arranged at random in a row, and let R be the number of runs (that is, sets of one or more consecutive letters all of the same kind immediately preceded and succeeded by the other letter or the beginning or end of the row). The upper P per cent point $x(P)$ of R is the smallest x such that $\Pr\{R \geq x\} \leq P/100$, and the lower P per cent point $x'(P)$ of R is the largest x such that $\Pr\{R \leq x\} \leq P/100$. A dash indicates that there is no value with the required property. When n_1 and n_2 are large, R is approximately normally distributed with mean $\dfrac{2n_1 n_2}{n_1+n_2} + 1$ and variance $\dfrac{2n_1 n_2(2n_1 n_2 - n_1 - n_2)}{(n_1+n_2)^2(n_1+n_2-1)}$. Formulae for the calculation of this distribution are given by M. G. Kendall and A. Stuart, *The Advanced Theory of Statistics*, Vol. 2 (3rd edition, 1973), Griffin, London, Exercise 30.8.

n_1	n_2	P			n_1	n_2	P		
		5	1	0.1			5	1	0.1
3	4	7	—	—	8	14	16	17	—
4	4	8	—	—		15	16	17	—
	5	9	9	—		16	16	17	—
	6	9	—	—		17	16	—	—
	7	9	—	—		18	16	—	—
5	5	9	10	—	8	19	16	—	—
	6	10	11	—		20	17	—	—
	7	10	11	—	9	9	14	16	17
	8	11	—	—		10	15	16	18
	9	11	—	—		11	15	17	18
5	10	11	—	—	9	12	16	17	19
6	6	11	12	—		13	16	18	19
	7	11	12	13		14	17	18	19
	8	12	13	—		15	17	18	—
	9	12	13	—		16	17	18	—
6	10	12	—	—	9	17	17	19	—
	11	13	—	—		18	18	19	—
	12	13	—	—		19	18	19	—
	13	13	—	—		20	18	19	—
	14	13	—	—	10	10	16	17	18
7	7	12	13	14	10	11	16	18	19
	8	13	14	15		12	17	18	20
	9	13	14	15		13	17	19	20
	10	13	15	—		14	17	19	20
	11	14	15	—		15	18	19	21
7	12	14	15	—	10	16	18	20	21
	13	14	—	—		17	18	20	21
	14	14	—	—		18	19	20	—
	15	15	—	—		19	19	20	—
	16	15	—	—		20	19	20	—
7	17	15	—	—	11	11	17	18	20
	18	15	—	—		12	17	19	20
	19	15	—	—		13	18	19	21
8	8	13	14	16		14	18	20	21
	9	14	15	16		15	19	20	22
8	10	14	15	17	11	16	19	21	22
	11	15	16	17		17	19	21	22
	12	15	16	—		18	20	21	23
	13	15	17	—					

		P	5	1	0.1
$n_1=11$	$n_2=19$	20	22	23
	20	20	22	23
12	12	18	19	21
	13	18	20	22
	14	19	21	22
12	15	19	21	23
	16	20	22	23
	17	20	22	24
	18	21	22	24
	19	21	23	24
12	20	21	23	24
13	13	19	21	23
	14	20	21	23
	15	20	22	24
	16	21	22	24
13	17	21	23	25
	18	21	23	25
	19	22	24	25
	20	22	24	26
14	14	20	22	24
14	15	21	23	24
	16	21	23	25
	17	22	24	25
	18	22	24	26

		P	5	1	0.1
$n_1=14$	$n_2=19$	23	24	26
	20	23	25	27
15	15	21	23	25
	16	22	24	26
	17	22	24	26
15	18	23	25	27
	19	23	25	27
	20	24	26	28
16	16	23	24	26
	17	23	25	27
16	18	24	26	28
	19	24	26	28
	20	25	26	29
17	17	24	26	28
	18	24	26	28
17	19	25	27	29
	20	25	27	29
18	18	25	27	29
	19	25	27	30
	20	26	28	30
19	19	26	28	30
	20	27	29	31
20	20	27	29	31

LOWER PERCENTAGE POINTS

		P	5	1	0.1
$n_1=2$	$n_2=8$	2	—	—
	9	2	—	—
	10	2	—	—
	11	2	—	—
	12	2	—	—
2	13	2	—	—
	14	2	—	—
	15	2	—	—
	16	2	—	—
	17	2	—	—

		P	5	1	0.1
$n_1=2$	$n_2=18$	2	—	—
	19	2	2	—
	20	2	2	—
3	5	2	—	—
	6	2	—	—
3	7	2	—	—
	8	2	—	—
	9	2	2	—
	10	3	2	—
	11	3	2	—

n_1	n_2	5	1	0.1
$n_1=3$	$n_2=12$	3	2	—
	13	3	2	—
	14	3	2	—
	15	3	2	—
	16	3	2	—
3	17	3	2	—
	18	3	2	—
	19	3	2	—
	20	3	2	—
4	4	2	—	—
4	5	2	—	—
	6	3	2	—
	7	3	2	—
	8	3	2	—
	9	3	2	—
4	10	3	2	—
	11	3	2	—
	12	4	3	—
	13	4	3	2
	14	4	3	2
4	15	4	3	2
	16	4	3	2
	17	4	3	2
	18	4	3	2
	19	4	3	2
4	20	4	3	2
5	5	3	2	—
	6	3	2	—
	7	3	2	—
	8	3	2	—
5	9	4	3	2
	10	4	3	2
	11	4	3	2
	12	4	3	2
	13	4	3	2
5	14	5	3	2
	15	5	4	2
	16	5	4	2
	17	5	4	3
	18	5	4	3
5	19	5	4	3

n_1	n_2	5	1	0.1
$n_1=5$	$n_2=20$	5	4	3
6	6	3	2	—
	7	4	3	—
	8	4	3	2
	9	4	3	2
6	10	5	3	2
	11	5	4	2
	12	5	4	3
	13	5	4	3
	14	5	4	3
6	15	6	4	3
	16	6	4	3
	17	6	5	3
	18	6	5	3
	19	6	5	3
6	20	6	5	4
	7	4	3	2
	8	4	3	2
	9	5	4	2
	10	5	4	3
7	11	5	4	3
	12	6	4	3
	13	6	5	3
	14	6	5	3
	15	6	5	3
7	16	6	5	4
	17	7	5	4
	18	7	5	4
	19	7	6	4
	20	7	6	4
8	8	5	4	2
	9	5	4	3
	10	6	4	3
	11	6	5	3
	12	6	5	3
8	13	6	5	4
	14	7	5	4
	15	7	5	4
	16	7	6	4
	17	7	6	4
8	18	8	6	4

	P	5	1	0.1			P	5	1	0.1
$n_1=8$	$n_2=19$	8	6	5	$n_1=12$	$n_2=18$	10	8	7
	20	8	6	5		19	10	9	7
9	9	6	4	3		20	11	9	7
	10	6	5	3	13	13	9	7	5
	11	6	5	3		14	9	8	6
9	12	7	5	4	13	15	10	8	6
	13	7	6	4		16	10	8	6
	14	7	6	4		17	10	9	7
	15	8	6	4		18	11	9	7
	16	8	6	5		19	11	9	7
9	17	8	7	5	13	20	11	10	8
	18	8	7	5	14	14	10	8	6
	19	8	7	5		15	10	8	7
	20	9	7	5		16	11	9	7
10	10	6	5	4		17	11	9	7
10	11	7	5	4	14	18	11	9	7
	12	7	6	4		19	12	10	8
	13	8	6	4		20	12	10	8
	14	8	6	5	15	15	11	9	7
	15	8	7	5		16	11	9	7
10	16	8	7	5	15	17	11	10	8
	17	9	7	5		18	12	10	8
	18	9	7	6		19	12	10	8
	19	9	8	6		20	12	11	8
	20	9	8	6	16	16	11	10	8
11	11	7	6	4	16	17	12	10	8
	12	8	6	5		18	12	10	8
	13	8	6	5		19	13	11	9
	14	8	7	5		20	13	11	9
	15	9	7	5	17	17	12	10	8
11	16	9	7	6	17	18	13	11	9
	17	9	8	6		19	13	11	9
	18	10	8	6		20	13	11	9
	19	10	8	6	18	18	13	11	9
	20	10	8	7		19	14	12	9
12	12	8	7	5	18	20	14	12	10
	13	9	7	5	19	19	14	12	10
	14	9	7	5		20	14	12	10
	15	9	8	6	20	20	15	13	11
	16	10	8	6					
12	17	10	8	6					

Percentage points of the Mann–Whitney distribution.

Consider two independent random samples of sizes n_1 and n_2 respectively ($n_1 \leqslant n_2$) from two continuous populations, A and B. Let all $n_1 + n_2$ observations be ranked in increasing order and let R_A and R_B denote the sums of the ranks of the observations in samples A and B respectively. This table gives lower percentage points of $U_A = R_A - \frac{1}{2}n_1(n_1 + 1)$; the function tabulated $x(P)$ is the largest x such that, on the assumption that populations A and B are identical, $\Pr\{U_A \leqslant x\} \leqslant P/100$. A dash indicates that there is no value with the required property. On the same assumption, $U_B = R_B - \frac{1}{2}n_2(n_2 + 1)$ has the same distribution as U_A, with mean $\frac{1}{2}n_1n_2$ and variance $\frac{1}{12}n_1n_2(n_1 + n_2 + 1)$. A test of the hypothesis that the two populations are identical, and in particular that their respective means μ_A, μ_B are equal, against the alternative $\mu_A > \mu_B$ is provided by rejecting at level P per cent if $U_B \leqslant x(P)$, and a similar test against $\mu_A < \mu_B$ is provided by rejecting at the P per cent level if $U_A \leqslant x(P)$. For a test against both alternatives one rejects at the $2P$ per cent level if U, the smaller of U_A and U_B, is less than or equal to $x(P)$. If n_1 and n_2 are large U_A is approximately normally distributed. Note also that $U_A + U_B = n_1n_2$.

Formulae for the calculation of this distribution (which is also referred to as the Wilcoxon rank–sum or Wilcoxon/Mann–Whitney distribution) are given by F. Wilcoxon, S. K. Katti and R. A. Wilcox, 'Critical values and probability levels for the Wilcoxon rank sum test and the Wilcoxon signed rank test', *Selected Tables in Mathematical Statistics*, Vol. 1 (1973), American Mathematical Society, Providence, R.I.

		P	5	2.5	1	0.5	0.1			P	5	2.5	1	0.5	0.1
$n_1= 2$	$n_2= 5$		0	—	—	—	—	$n_1= 2$	$n_2= 20$		4	2	1	0	—
	6		0	—	—	—	—	3	3		0	—	—	—	—
	7		0	—	—	—	—		4		0	—	—	—	—
	8		1	0	—	—	—		5		1	0	—	—	—
	9		1	0	—	—	—		6		2	1	—	—	—
2	10		1	0	—	—	—	3	7		2	1	0	—	—
	11		1	0	—	—	—		8		3	2	0	—	—
	12		2	1	—	—	—		9		4	2	1	0	—
	13		2	1	0	—	—		10		4	3	1	0	—
	14		3	1	0	—	—		11		5	3	1	0	—
2	15		3	1	0	—	—	3	12		5	4	2	1	—
	16		3	1	0	—	—		13		6	4	2	1	—
	17		3	2	0	—	—		14		7	5	2	1	—
	18		4	2	0	—	—		15		7	5	3	2	—
	19		4	2	1	0	—		16		8	6	3	2	—

$n_1=3$	$n_2=$	P 5	2.5	1	0.5	0.1
	17	9	6	4	2	0
	18	9	7	4	2	0
	19	10	7	4	3	0
	20	11	8	5	3	0
4	4	1	0	—	—	—
4	5	2	1	0	—	—
	6	3	2	1	0	—
	7	4	3	1	0	—
	8	6	4	2	1	—
	9	6	4	3	1	—
4	10	7	5	3	2	0
	11	8	6	4	2	0
	12	9	7	5	3	0
	13	10	8	5	3	1
	14	11	9	6	4	1
4	15	12	10	7	5	1
	16	14	11	7	5	2
	17	15	11	8	6	2
	18	16	12	9	6	3
	19	17	13	9	7	3
4	20	18	14	10	8	3
5	5	4	2	1	0	—
	6	5	3	2	1	—
	7	6	5	3	1	—
	8	8	6	4	2	0
5	9	9	7	5	3	1
	10	11	8	6	4	1
	11	12	9	7	5	2
	12	13	11	8	6	2
	13	15	12	9	7	3
5	14	16	13	10	7	3
	15	18	14	11	8	4
	16	19	15	12	9	5
	17	20	17	13	10	5
	18	22	18	14	11	6
5	19	23	19	15	12	7
	20	25	20	16	13	7
6	6	7	5	3	2	—
	7	8	6	4	3	0
	8	10	8	6	4	1

$n_1=6$	$n_2=$	P 5	2.5	1	0.5	0.1
	9	12	10	7	5	2
	10	14	11	8	6	3
	11	16	13	9	7	4
	12	17	14	11	9	4
	13	19	16	12	10	5
6	14	21	17	13	11	6
	15	23	19	15	12	7
	16	25	21	16	13	8
	17	26	22	18	15	9
	18	28	24	19	16	10
6	19	30	25	20	17	11
	20	32	27	22	18	12
7	7	11	8	6	4	1
	8	13	10	7	6	2
	9	15	12	9	7	3
7	10	17	14	11	9	5
	11	19	16	12	10	6
	12	21	18	14	12	7
	13	24	20	16	13	8
	14	26	22	17	15	9
7	15	28	24	19	16	10
	16	30	26	21	18	11
	17	33	28	23	19	13
	18	35	30	24	21	14
	19	37	32	26	22	15
7	20	39	34	28	24	16
8	8	15	13	9	7	4
	9	18	15	11	9	5
	10	20	17	13	11	6
	11	23	19	15	13	8
8	12	26	22	17	15	9
	13	28	24	20	17	11
	14	31	26	22	18	12
	15	33	29	24	20	14
	16	36	31	26	22	15
8	17	39	34	28	24	17
	18	41	36	30	26	18
	19	44	38	32	28	20
	20	47	41	34	30	21
9	9	21	17	14	11	7

P		5	2.5	1	0.5	0.1
$n_1=9$	$n_2=10$	24	20	16	13	8
	11	27	23	18	16	10
	12	30	26	21	18	12
	13	33	28	23	20	14
	14	36	31	26	22	15
9	15	39	34	28	24	17
	16	42	37	31	27	19
	17	45	39	33	29	21
	18	48	42	36	31	23
	19	51	45	38	33	25
9	20	54	48	40	36	26
10	10	27	23	19	16	10
	11	31	26	22	18	12
	12	34	29	24	21	14
	13	37	33	27	24	17
10	14	41	36	30	26	19
	15	44	39	33	29	21
	16	48	42	36	31	23
	17	51	45	38	34	25
	18	55	48	41	37	27
10	19	58	52	44	39	29
	20	62	55	47	42	32
11	11	34	30	25	21	15
	12	38	33	28	24	17
	13	42	37	31	27	20
11	14	46	40	34	30	22
	15	50	44	37	33	24
	16	54	47	41	36	27
	17	57	51	44	39	29
	18	61	55	47	42	32
11	19	65	58	50	45	34
	20	69	62	53	48	37
12	12	42	37	31	27	20
	13	47	41	35	31	23
	14	51	45	38	34	25
12	15	55	49	42	37	28
	16	60	53	46	41	31
	17	64	57	49	44	34

P		5	2.5	1	0.5	0.1
$n_1=12$	$n_2=18$	68	61	53	47	37
	19	72	65	56	51	40
	20	77	69	60	54	42
13	13	51	45	39	34	26
	14	56	50	43	38	29
13	15	61	54	47	42	32
	16	65	59	51	45	35
	17	70	63	55	49	38
	18	75	67	59	53	42
	19	80	72	63	57	45
13	20	84	76	67	60	48
14	14	61	55	47	42	32
	15	66	59	51	46	36
	16	71	64	56	50	39
	17	77	69	60	54	43
14	18	82	74	65	58	46
	19	87	78	69	63	50
	20	92	83	73	67	54
15	15	72	64	56	51	40
	16	77	70	61	55	43
15	17	83	75	66	60	47
	18	88	80	70	64	51
	19	94	85	75	69	55
	20	100	90	80	73	59
16	16	83	75	66	60	48
16	17	89	81	71	65	52
	18	95	86	76	70	56
	19	101	92	82	74	60
	20	107	98	87	79	65
17	17	96	87	77	70	57
17	18	102	93	82	75	61
	19	109	99	88	81	66
	20	115	105	93	86	70
18	18	109	99	88	81	66
	19	116	106	94	87	71
18	20	123	112	100	92	76
19	19	123	113	101	93	77
	20	130	119	107	99	82
20	20	138	127	114	105	88

TABLE C Areas of the standardised normal distribution.

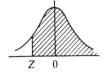

Z 0

Z	-0.09	-0.08	-0.07	-0.06	-0.05	-0.04	-0.03	-0.02	-0.01	-0.00
-3.9	0.99997	0.99997	0.99996	0.99996	0.99996	0.99996	0.99996	0.99996	0.99995	0.99995
-3.8	0.99995	0.99995	0.99995	0.99994	0.99994	0.99994	0.99994	0.99993	0.99993	0.99993
-3.7	0.99992	0.99992	0.99992	0.99992	0.99991	0.99991	0.99990	0.99990	0.99990	0.99989
-3.6	0.99989	0.99988	0.99988	0.99987	0.99987	0.99986	0.99986	0.99985	0.99985	0.99984
-3.5	0.99983	0.99983	0.99982	0.99981	0.99981	0.99980	0.99979	0.99978	0.99978	0.99977
-3.4	0.99976	0.99975	0.99974	0.99973	0.99972	0.99971	0.99970	0.99969	0.99968	0.99966
-3.3	0.99965	0.99964	0.99962	0.99961	0.99960	0.99958	0.99957	0.99955	0.99953	0.99952
-3.2	0.99950	0.99948	0.99946	0.99944	0.99942	0.99940	0.99938	0.99936	0.99934	0.99931
-3.1	0.99929	0.99926	0.99924	0.99921	0.99918	0.99916	0.99913	0.99910	0.99906	0.99903
-3.0	0.99900	0.99896	0.99893	0.99889	0.99886	0.99882	0.99878	0.99874	0.99869	0.99865
-2.9	0.99861	0.99856	0.99851	0.99846	0.99841	0.99836	0.99831	0.99825	0.99819	0.99813
-2.8	0.99807	0.99801	0.99795	0.99788	0.99781	0.99774	0.99767	0.99760	0.99752	0.99744
-2.7	0.99736	0.99728	0.99720	0.99711	0.99702	0.99693	0.99683	0.99674	0.99664	0.99653
-2.6	0.99643	0.99632	0.99621	0.99609	0.99598	0.99585	0.99573	0.99560	0.99547	0.99534
-2.5	0.99520	0.99506	0.99492	0.99477	0.99461	0.99446	0.99430	0.99413	0.99396	0.99379
-2.4	0.99361	0.99343	0.99324	0.99305	0.99286	0.99266	0.99245	0.99224	0.99202	0.99180
-2.3	0.99158	0.99134	0.99111	0.99086	0.99061	0.99036	0.99010	0.98983	0.98956	0.98928
-2.2	0.98899	0.98870	0.98840	0.98809	0.98809	0.98778	0.98745	0.98713	0.98679	0.98645	0.98610
-2.1	0.98574	0.98537	0.98500	0.98461	0.98422	0.98382	0.98341	0.98300	0.98257	0.98214
-2.0	0.98169	0.98124	0.98077	0.98030	0.97982	0.97982	0.97882	0.97831	0.97778	0.97725
-1.9	0.97670	0.97615	0.97558	0.97500	0.97441	0.97381	0.97320	0.97257	0.97193	0.97128
-1.8	0.97062	0.96995	0.96926	0.96856	0.96846	0.96712	0.96638	0.96562	0.96485	0.96407
-1.7	0.96327	0.96246	0.96164	0.96080	0.95994	0.95907	0.95818	0.95728	0.95637	0.95543
-1.6	0.95449	0.95352	0.95254	0.95154	0.95053	0.94950	0.94845	0.94738	0.94630	0.94520
-1.5	0.94408	0.94295	0.94179	0.94062	0.93943	0.93822	0.93699	0.93574	0.93448	0.93319
-1.4	0.93189	0.93056	0.92922	0.92785	0.92647	0.92507	0.92364	0.92220	0.92073	0.91924
-1.3	0.91774	0.91621	0.91466	0.91308	0.91149	0.90988	0.90824	0.90658	0.90490	0.90320
-1.2	0.90147	0.89973	0.89796	0.89617	0.89435	0.89251	0.89065	0.88877	0.88686	0.88493
-1.1	0.88298	0.88100	0.87900	0.87698	0.87493	0.87286	0.87076	0.86864	0.86650	0.86433
-1.0	0.86214	0.85993	0.85769	0.85543	0.85314	0.85083	0.84850	0.84614	0.84375	0.84134
-0.9	0.83891	0.83646	0.83398	0.83147	0.82894	0.82639	0.82381	0.82121	0.81859	0.81594
-0.8	0.81327	0.81057	0.80785	0.80511	0.80234	0.79955	0.79673	0.79389	0.79103	0.78814
-0.7	0.78524	0.78230	0.77935	0.77637	0.77337	0.77035	0.76731	0.76424	0.76115	0.75804
-0.6	0.75490	0.75175	0.74857	0.74537	0.74215	0.73891	0.73565	0.73237	0.72907	0.72575
-0.5	0.72240	0.71904	0.71566	0.71226	0.70884	0.70540	0.70194	0.69847	0.69497	0.69146
-0.4	0.68793	0.68439	0.68082	0.67724	0.67364	0.67003	0.66640	0.66276	0.65910	0.65542
-0.3	0.65173	0.64803	0.64431	0.64058	0.64058	0.63683	0.63307	0.62930	0.62172	0.61791
-0.2	0.61409	0.61026	0.60642	0.60257	0.59871	0.59483	0.59095	0.58706	0.58317	0.57926
-0.1	0.57535	0.57142	0.56750	0.56356	0.55962	0.55567	0.55172	0.54776	0.54380	0.53983
-0.0	0.53586	0.53188	0.52790	0.52392	0.51994	0.51595	0.51197	0.50798	0.50399	0.50000

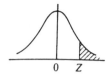

0   Z

Z	0.00	0.01	0.02	0.03	0.04	0.05	0.06	0.07	0.08	0.09
0.0	0.50000	0.49601	0.49202	0.48405	0.48006	0.47608	0.99996	0.47210	0.46812	0.46414
0.1	0.46017	0.45620	0.45224	0.44828	0.44433	0.44038	0.43250	0.43250	0.42858	0.42465
0.2	0.42074	0.41683	0.41294	0.40905	0.40517	0.40129	0.39743	0.39358	0.38974	0.38591
0.3	0.38209	0.37828	0.37448	0.37070	0.36693	0.36317	0.35942	0.35569	0.35197	0.34827
0.4	0.34458	0.34090	0.33724	0.33360	0.32997	0.32636	0.32276	0.31918	0.31561	0.31207
0.5	0.30854	0.30503	0.30153	0.29806	0.29460	0.29116	0.28774	0.28434	0.28096	0.27760
0.6	0.27425	0.27093	0.26763	0.26435	0.26109	0.25785	0.25463	0.25143	0.24825	0.24510
0.7	0.24196	0.23885	0.23576	0.23269	0.22965	0.22663	0.22363	0.22065	0.21770	0.21476
0.8	0.21186	0.20897	0.20611	0.20327	0.20045	0.19766	0.19489	0.19215	0.18943	0.18673
0.9	0.18406	0.18141	0.17879	0.17619	0.17361	0.17106	0.16853	0.16602	0.16354	0.16109
1.0	0.15866	0.15625	0.15386	0.15150	0.14917	0.14686	0.14457	0.14231	0.14007	0.13786
1.1	0.13567	0.13350	0.13136	0.12924	0.12714	0.12507	0.12302	0.12100	0.11900	0.11702
1.2	0.11507	0.11314	0.11123	0.10935	0.10749	0.10565	0.10383	0.10204	0.10027	0.09853
1.3	0.09680	0.09510	0.09342	0.09176	0.09012	0.08851	0.08692	0.08534	0.08379	0.08226
1.4	0.08076	0.07927	0.07780	0.07636	0.07493	0.07353	0.07215	0.07078	0.06944	0.06811
1.5	0.06681	0.06552	0.06426	0.06301	0.06178	0.06057	0.05938	0.05821	0.05705	0.05592
1.6	0.05480	0.05370	0.05262	0.05155	0.05050	0.04947	0.04846	0.04746	0.04648	0.04551
1.7	0.04457	0.04363	0.04272	0.04182	0.04093	0.04006	0.03920	0.03836	0.03754	0.03673
1.8	0.03593	0.03515	0.03438	0.03362	0.03288	0.03216	0.03144	0.03074	0.03005	0.02938
1.9	0.02872	0.02807	0.02743	0.02680	0.02619	0.02559	0.02500	0.02442	0.02385	0.02330
2.0	0.02275	0.02222	0.02169	0.02118	0.02068	0.02018	0.01970	0.01923	0.01876	0.01831
2.1	0.01786	0.01743	0.01700	0.01659	0.01618	0.01578	0.01539	0.01500	0.01463	0.01426
2.2	0.01390	0.01355	0.01321	0.01287	0.01255	0.01222	0.01191	0.01160	0.01130	0.01101
2.3	0.01072	0.01044	0.01017	0.00990	0.00964	0.00939	0.00914	0.00889	0.00866	0.00842
2.4	0.00820	0.00798	0.00776	0.00755	0.00734	0.00714	0.00695	0.00676	0.00657	0.00639
2.5	0.00621	0.00604	0.00587	0.00570	0.00554	0.00539	0.00523	0.00508	0.00494	0.00480
2.6	0.00466	0.00453	0.00440	0.00427	0.00415	0.00402	0.00391	0.00379	0.00368	0.00357
2.7	0.00347	0.00336	0.00326	0.00317	0.00307	0.00298	0.00289	0.00280	0.00272	0.00264
2.8	0.00256	0.00248	0.00240	0.00233	0.00226	0.00219	0.00212	0.00205	0.00199	0.00193
2.9	0.00187	0.00181	0.00175	0.00169	0.00164	0.00159	0.00154	0.00149	0.00144	0.00139
3.0	0.00136	0.00131	0.00126	0.00122	0.00118	0.00114	0.00111	0.00107	0.00104	0.00100
3.1	0.00097	0.00094	0.00090	0.00087	0.00084	0.00082	0.00079	0.00076	0.00074	0.00071
3.2	0.00069	0.00066	0.00064	0.00062	0.00060	0.00058	0.00056	0.00054	0.00052	0.00050
3.3	0.00048	0.00047	0.00045	0.00043	0.00042	0.00040	0.00039	0.00038	0.00036	0.00035
3.4	0.00034	0.00032	0.00031	0.00030	0.00029	0.00028	0.00027	0.00026	0.00025	0.00024
3.5	0.00023	0.00022	0.00022	0.00021	0.00020	0.00019	0.00019	0.00018	0.00017	0.00017
3.6	0.00016	0.00015	0.00015	0.00014	0.00014	0.00013	0.00013	0.00012	0.00012	0.00011
3.7	0.00011	0.00010	0.00010	0.00010	0.00009	0.00009	0.00008	0.00008	0.00008	0.00008
3.8	0.00007	0.00007	0.00007	0.00006	0.00006	0.00006	0.00006	0.00005	0.00005	0.00005
3.9	0.00005	0.00005	0.00004	0.00004	0.00004	0.00004	0.00004	0.00004	0.00003	0.00003

TABLE D Percentage points of the *t*-distribution.

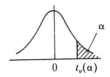

$$\Pr(T_\nu > t_\nu(\alpha)) = \alpha,$$
for ν degrees of freedom

Two-sided test

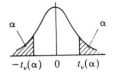

$$\Pr(T_\nu > t_\nu(\alpha) \text{ or } T_\nu < -t_\nu(\alpha)) = 2\alpha,$$
for ν degrees of freedom

$\alpha = 0.4$ ν $2\alpha = 0.8$	0.25 0.5	0.1 0.2	0.05 0.1	0.025 0.05	0.01 0.02	0.005 0.01	0.0025 0.005	0.001 0.002	0.0005 0.001
1 0.325	1.000	3.078	6.314	12.706	31.821	63.657	127.321	318.309	636.619
2 0.289	0.816	1.886	2.920	4.303	6.965	9.925	14.089	22.327	31.599
3 0.277	0.765	1.638	2.353	3.182	4.541	5.841	7.453	10.215	12.924
4 0.271	0.741	1.533	2.132	2.776	3.747	4.604	5.598	7.173	8.610
5 0.267	0.727	1.476	2.015	2.571	3.365	4.032	4.773	5.893	6.869
6 0.265	0.718	1.440	1.943	2.447	3.143	3.707	4.317	5.208	5.959
7 0.263	0.711	1.415	1.895	2.365	2.998	3.499	4.029	4.785	5.408
8 0.262	0.706	1.397	1.860	2.306	2.896	3.355	3.833	4.501	5.041
9 0.261	0.703	1.383	1.833	2.262	2.821	3.250	3.690	4.297	4.781
10 0.260	0.700	1.372	1.812	2.228	2.764	3.169	3.581	4.144	4.587
11 0.260	0.697	1.363	1.796	2.201	2.718	3.106	3.497	4.025	4.437
12 0.259	0.695	1.356	1.782	2.179	2.681	3.055	3.428	3.930	4.318
13 0.259	0.694	1.350	1.771	2.160	2.650	3.012	0.372	3.852	4.221
14 0.258	0.692	1.345	1.761	2.145	2.624	2.977	3.326	3.787	4.140
15 0.258	0.691	1.341	1.753	2.131	2.602	2.947	3.286	3.733	4.073
16 0.258	0.690	1.337	1.746	2.120	2.583	2.921	3.252	3.686	4.015
17 0.257	0.689	1.333	1.740	2.110	2.567	2.898	3.222	3.646	3.965
18 0.257	0.688	1.330	1.734	2.101	2.552	2.878	3.197	3.610	3.922
19 0.257	0.688	1.328	1.729	2.093	2.539	2.861	3.174	3.579	3.883
20 0.257	0.687	1.325	1.725	2.086	2.528	2.845	3.153	3.552	3.850
21 0.257	0.686	1.323	1.721	2.080	2.518	2.831	3.135	3.527	3.819
22 0.256	0.686	1.321	1.717	2.074	2.508	2.819	3.119	3.505	3.792
23 0.256	0.685	1.319	1.714	2.069	2.500	2.807	3.104	3.485	3.768
24 0.256	0.685	1.318	1.711	2.064	2.492	2.797	3.091	3.467	3.745
25 0.256	0.684	1.316	1.708	2.060	2.485	2.787	3.078	3.450	3.725
26 0.256	0.684	1.315	1.706	2.056	2.479	2.779	3.067	3.435	3.707
27 0.256	0.684	1.314	1.703	2.052	2.473	2.771	3.057	3.421	3.690
28 0.256	0.683	1.313	1.701	2.048	2.467	2.763	3.047	3.408	3.674
29 0.256	0.683	1.311	1.699	2.045	2.462	2.756	3.038	3.396	3.659
30 0.256	0.683	1.310	1.697	2.042	2.457	2.750	3.030	3.385	3.646
40 0.255	0.681	1.303	1.684	2.021	2.423	2.704	2.971	3.307	3.551
60 0.254	0.679	1.296	1.671	2.000	2.390	2.660	2.915	3.232	3.460
120 0.254	0.677	1.289	1.658	1.980	2.358	2.617	2.860	3.160	3.373
∞ 0.253	0.674	1.282	1.645	1.960	2.326	2.576	2.807	3.090	3.291

TABLE E(1) 5 per cent points of the *F*-distribution.

If $F = \dfrac{X_1/X_2}{\nu_1/\nu_2}$, where X_1 and X_2 are independent random variables distributed as χ^2 with ν_1 and ν_2 degrees of freedom respectively, then the probabilities that $F \geqslant F(P)$ and that $F \leqslant F'(P)$ are both equal to $P/100$. Linear interpolation in ν_1 and ν_2 will generally be sufficiently accurate except when either $\nu_1 > 12$ or $\nu_2 > 40$, when harmonic interpolation should be used.

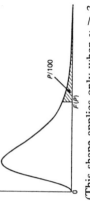

(This shape applies only when $\nu \geqslant 3$. When $\nu < 3$ the mode is at the origin.)

$\nu_1 =$	1	2	3	4	5	6	7	8	10	12	24	∞
$\nu_2 = 1$	161.4	199.5	215.7	224.6	230.2	234.0	236.8	238.9	241.9	243.9	249.1	254.3
2	18.51	19.00	19.16	19.25	19.30	19.33	19.35	19.37	19.40	19.41	19.45	19.50
3	10.13	9.552	9.277	9.117	9.013	8.941	8.887	8.845	8.786	8.745	8.639	8.526
4	7.709	6.944	6.591	6.388	6.256	6.163	6.094	6.041	5.964	5.912	5.774	5.628
5	6.608	5.786	5.409	5.192	5.050	4.950	4.876	4.818	4.735	4.678	4.527	4.365
6	5.987	5.143	4.757	4.534	4.387	4.284	4.207	4.147	4.060	4.000	3.841	3.669
7	5.591	4.737	4.347	4.120	3.972	3.866	3.787	3.726	3.637	3.575	3.410	3.230
8	5.318	4.459	4.066	3.838	3.687	3.581	3.500	3.438	3.347	3.284	3.115	2.928
9	5.117	4.256	3.863	3.633	3.482	3.374	3.293	3.230	3.137	3.073	2.900	2.707
10	4.965	4.103	3.708	3.478	3.326	3.217	3.135	3.072	2.978	2.913	2.737	2.538
11	4.844	3.982	3.587	3.357	3.204	3.095	3.012	2.948	2.854	2.788	2.609	2.404
12	4.747	3.885	3.490	3.259	3.106	2.996	2.913	2.849	2.753	2.687	2.505	2.296
13	4.667	3.806	3.411	3.179	3.025	2.915	2.832	2.767	2.671	2.604	2.420	2.206
14	4.600	3.739	3.344	3.112	2.958	2.848	2.764	2.699	2.602	2.534	2.349	2.131

15	4.543	3.682	3.287	3.056	2.901	2.790	2.707	2.641	2.544	2.475	2.288	2.066
16	4.494	3.634	3.239	3.007	2.852	2.741	2.657	2.591	2.494	2.425	2.235	2.010
17	4.451	3.592	3.197	2.965	2.810	2.699	2.614	2.548	2.450	2.381	2.190	1.960
18	4.414	3.555	3.160	2.928	2.773	2.661	2.577	2.510	2.412	2.342	2.150	1.917
19	4.381	3.522	3.127	2.895	2.740	2.628	2.544	2.477	2.378	2.308	2.114	1.878
20	4.351	3.493	3.098	2.866	2.711	2.599	2.514	2.447	2.348	2.278	2.082	1.843
21	4.325	3.467	3.072	2.840	2.685	2.573	2.488	2.420	2.321	2.250	2.054	1.812
22	4.301	3.443	3.049	2.817	2.661	2.549	2.464	2.397	2.297	2.226	2.028	1.783
23	4.279	3.422	3.028	2.796	2.640	2.528	2.442	2.375	2.275	2.204	2.005	1.757
24	4.260	3.403	3.009	2.776	2.621	2.508	2.423	2.355	2.255	2.183	1.984	1.733
25	4.242	3.385	2.991	2.759	2.603	2.490	2.405	2.337	2.236	2.165	1.964	1.711
26	4.225	3.369	2.975	2.743	2.587	2.474	2.388	2.321	2.220	2.148	1.946	1.691
27	4.210	3.354	2.960	2.728	2.572	2.459	2.373	2.305	2.204	2.132	1.930	1.672
28	4.196	3.340	2.947	2.714	2.558	2.445	2.359	2.291	2.190	2.118	1.915	1.654
29	4.183	3.328	2.934	2.701	2.545	2.432	2.346	2.278	2.177	2.104	1.901	1.638
30	4.171	3.316	2.922	2.690	2.534	2.421	2.334	2.266	2.165	2.092	1.887	1.622
32	4.149	3.295	2.901	2.668	2.512	2.399	2.313	2.244	2.142	2.070	1.864	1.594
34	4.130	3.276	2.883	2.650	2.494	2.380	2.294	2.225	2.123	2.050	1.843	1.569
36	4.113	3.259	2.866	2.634	2.477	2.364	2.277	2.209	2.106	2.033	1.824	1.547
38	4.098	3.245	2.852	2.619	2.463	2.349	2.262	2.194	2.091	2.017	1.808	1.527
40	4.085	3.232	2.839	2.606	2.449	2.336	2.249	2.180	2.077	2.003	1.793	1.509
60	4.001	3.150	2.758	2.525	2.368	2.254	2.167	2.097	1.993	1.917	1.700	1.389
120	3.920	3.072	2.680	2.447	2.290	2.175	2.087	2.016	1.910	1.834	1.608	1.254
∞	3.841	2.996	2.605	2.372	2.214	2.099	2.010	1.938	1.831	1.752	1.517	1.000

TABLE E(2) 1 per cent points of the F-distribution.

If $F = \dfrac{X_1/X_2}{\nu_1/\nu_2}$, where X_1 and X_2 are independent random variables distributed as χ^2 with ν_1 and ν_2 degrees of freedom respectively, then the probabilities that $F \geqslant F(P)$ and that $F \leqslant F'(P)$ are both equal to $P/100$. Linear interpolation in ν_1 and ν_2 will generally be sufficiently accurate except when either $\nu_1 > 12$ or $\nu_2 > 40$, when harmonic interpolation should be used.

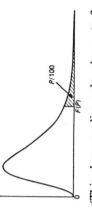

(This shape applies only when $\nu \geqslant 3$.
When $\nu < 3$ the mode is at the origin.)

$\nu_1 =$	1	2	3	4	5	6	7	8	10	12	24	∞
$\nu_2 = 1$	4052	4999	5403	5625	5764	5859	5928	5981	6056	6106	6235	6366
2	98.50	99.00	99.17	99.25	99.30	99.33	99.36	99.37	99.40	99.42	99.46	99.50
3	34.12	30.82	29.46	28.71	28.24	27.91	27.67	27.49	27.23	27.05	26.60	26.13
4	21.20	18.00	16.69	15.98	15.52	15.21	14.98	14.80	14.55	14.37	13.93	13.46
5	16.26	13.27	12.06	11.39	10.97	10.67	10.46	10.29	10.05	9.888	9.466	9.020
6	13.75	10.92	9.780	9.148	8.746	8.466	8.260	8.102	7.874	7.718	7.313	6.880
7	12.25	9.547	8.451	7.847	7.460	7.191	6.993	6.840	6.620	6.469	6.074	5.650
8	11.26	8.649	7.591	7.006	6.632	6.371	6.178	6.029	5.814	5.667	5.279	4.859
9	10.56	8.022	6.992	6.422	6.057	5.802	5.613	5.467	5.257	5.111	4.729	4.311
10	10.04	7.559	6.552	5.994	5.636	5.386	5.200	5.057	4.849	4.706	4.327	3.909
11	9.646	7.206	6.217	5.668	5.316	5.069	4.886	4.744	4.539	4.397	4.021	3.602
12	9.330	6.927	5.953	5.412	5.064	4.821	4.640	4.499	4.296	4.155	3.780	3.361
13	9.074	6.701	5.739	5.205	4.862	4.620	4.441	4.302	4.100	3.960	3.587	3.165
14	8.862	6.515	5.564	5.035	4.695	4.456	4.278	4.140	3.939	3.800	3.427	3.004

15	2.868	3.294	3.666	3.805	4.004	4.142	4.318	4.556	4.893	5.417	6.359	8.683
16	2.753	3.181	3.553	3.691	3.890	4.026	4.202	4.437	4.773	5.292	6.226	8.531
17	2.653	3.084	3.455	3.593	3.791	3.929	4.102	4.336	4.669	5.185	6.112	8.400
18	2.566	2.999	3.371	3.508	3.705	3.841	4.015	4.248	4.579	5.092	6.013	8.285
19	2.489	2.925	3.297	3.434	3.631	3.765	3.939	4.171	4.500	5.010	5.926	8.185
20	2.421	2.859	3.231	3.368	3.564	3.699	3.871	4.103	4.431	4.938	5.849	8.096
21	2.360	2.801	3.173	3.310	3.506	3.640	3.812	4.042	4.369	4.874	5.780	8.017
22	2.305	2.749	3.121	3.258	3.453	3.587	3.758	3.988	4.313	4.817	5.719	7.945
23	2.256	2.702	3.074	3.211	3.406	3.539	3.710	3.939	4.264	4.765	5.664	7.881
24	2.211	2.659	3.032	3.168	3.363	3.496	3.667	3.895	4.218	4.718	5.614	7.823
25	2.169	2.620	2.993	3.129	3.324	3.457	3.627	3.855	4.177	4.675	5.568	7.770
26	2.131	2.585	2.958	3.094	3.288	3.421	3.591	3.818	4.140	4.637	5.526	7.721
27	2.097	2.552	2.926	3.062	3.256	3.388	3.558	3.785	4.106	4.601	5.488	7.677
28	2.064	2.522	2.896	3.032	3.226	3.358	3.528	3.754	4.074	4.568	5.453	7.636
29	2.034	2.495	2.868	3.005	3.198	3.330	3.499	3.725	4.045	4.538	5.420	7.598
30	2.006	2.469	2.843	2.979	3.173	3.304	3.473	3.699	4.018	4.510	5.390	7.562
32	1.956	2.423	2.798	2.934	3.127	3.258	3.427	3.652	3.969	4.459	5.336	7.499
34	1.911	2.383	2.758	2.894	3.087	3.218	3.386	3.611	3.927	4.416	5.289	7.444
36	1.872	2.347	2.723	2.859	3.052	3.183	3.351	3.574	3.890	4.377	5.248	7.396
38	1.837	2.316	2.692	2.828	3.021	3.152	3.319	3.542	3.858	4.343	5.211	7.353
40	1.805	2.288	2.665	2.801	2.993	3.124	3.291	3.514	3.828	4.313	5.179	7.314
60	1.601	2.115	2.496	2.632	2.823	2.953	3.119	3.339	3.649	4.126	4.977	7.077
120	1.381	1.950	2.336	2.472	2.663	2.792	2.956	3.174	3.480	3.949	4.787	6.851
∞	1.000	1.791	2.185	2.321	2.511	2.639	2.802	3.017	3.319	3.782	4.605	6.635

TABLE F Percentage points of the chi-squared distribution.

The values tabulated are $\chi_\nu^2(\alpha)$, where
$\Pr(\chi_\nu^2 > \chi_\nu^2(\alpha)) = \alpha$, for ν degrees of freedom.

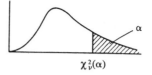

$\chi_\nu^2(\alpha)$

ν	$\alpha = 0.995$	0.990	0.975	0.950	0.900	0.750	0.500
1	392704.10⁻¹⁰	157088.10⁻⁹	982069.10⁻⁹	393214.10⁻⁸	0.0157908	0.1015308	0.454936
2	0.0100251	0.0201007	0.0506356	0.102587	0.210721	0.575364	1.38629
3	0.0717218	0.114832	0.215795	0.351846	0.584374	1.212534	2.36597
4	0.206989	0.297109	0.484419	0.710723	1.063623	1.92256	3.35669
5	0.411742	0.554298	0.831212	1.145476	1.61031	2.67460	4.35146
6	0.675727	0.872090	1.23734	1.63538	2.20413	3.45460	5.34812
7	0.989256	1.239043	1.68987	2.16735	2.83311	4.25485	6.34581
8	1.34441	1.64650	2.17973	2.73264	3.48954	5.07064	7.34412
9	1.73493	2.08790	2.70039	3.32511	4.16816	5.89883	8.34283
10	2.15586	2.55821	3.24697	3.94030	4.86518	6.73720	9.34182
11	2.60322	3.05348	3.81575	4.57481	5.57778	7.58414	10.3410
12	3.07382	3.57057	4.40379	5.22603	6.30380	8.43842	11.3403
13	3.56503	4.10692	5.00875	5.89186	7.04150	9.29907	12.3398
14	4.07467	4.66043	5.62873	6.57063	7.78953	10.1653	13.3393
15	4.60092	5.22935	6.26214	7.26094	8.54676	11.0365	14.3389
16	5.14221	5.81221	6.90766	7.96165	9.31224	11.9122	15.3385
17	5.69722	6.40776	7.56419	8.67176	10.0852	12.7919	16.3382
18	6.26480	7.01491	8.23075	9.39046	10.8649	13.6753	17.3379
19	6.84397	7.63273	8.90652	10.1170	11.6509	14.5620	18.3377
20	7.43384	8.26040	9.59078	10.8508	12.4426	15.4518	19.3374
21	8.03365	8.89720	10.28293	11.5913	13.2396	16.3444	20.3372
22	8.64272	9.54249	10.9823	12.3380	14.0415	17.2396	21.3370
23	9.26043	10.19567	11.6886	13.0905	14.8480	18.1373	22.3369
24	9.88623	10.8564	12.4012	13.8484	15.6587	19.0373	23.3367
25	10.5197	11.5240	13.1197	14.6114	16.4734	19.9393	24.3366
26	11.1602	12.981	13.8439	15.3792	17.2919	20.8434	25.3365
27	11.8076	12.8785	14.5734	16.1514	18.1139	21.7494	26.3363
28	12.4613	13.5647	15.3079	16.9279	18.9392	22.6572	27.3362
29	13.1211	14.2565	16.0471	17.7084	19.7677	23.5666	28.3361
30	13.7867	14.9535	16.7908	18.4927	20.6992	24.4776	29.3360
40	20.7065	22.1643	24.4330	26.5093	29.0505	33.6603	39.3353
50	27.9907	29.7067	32.3574	34.7643	37.6886	42.9421	49.3349
60	35.5345	37.4849	40.4817	43.1880	46.4589	52.2938	59.3347
70	43.2752	45.4417	48.7576	51.7393	55.3289	61.6983	69.3345
80	51.1719	53.5401	57.1532	60.3915	64.2778	71.1445	79.3343
90	59.1963	61.7541	65.6466	69.1260	73.2911	80.6247	89.3342
100	67.3276	70.0649	74.2219	77.9295	82.3581	90.1332	99.3341

v	$\alpha = 0.250$	0.100	0.050	0.025	0.010	0.005	0.001
1	1.32330	2.70554	3.84146	5.02389	6.63490	7.87944	10.828
2	2.77529	4.60517	5.99146	7.37776	9.21034	10.5966	13.816
3	4.10834	6.25139	7.81473	9.34840	11.3449	12.8382	16.266
4	5.38527	7.77944	9.48773	11.1433	13.2767	14.8603	18.467
5	6.62568	9.23636	11.0705	12.8325	15.0863	16.7496	20.515
6	7.84080	10.6446	12.5916	14.4494	16.8119	18.5476	22.458
7	9.03715	12.0170	14.0671	16.0128	18.4753	20.2777	24.322
8	10.2189	13.3616	15.5073	17.5345	20.0902	21.9550	26.125
9	11.3888	14.6837	16.9190	19.0228	21.6660	23.5894	27.877
10	12.5489	15.9872	18.3070	20.4832	23.2093	25.1882	29.588
11	13.7007	17.2750	19.6751	21.9200	24.7250	26.7568	31.264
12	14.8454	18.5493	21.0261	23.3367	26.2170	28.2995	32.909
13	15.9839	19.8119	22.3620	24.7356	27.6882	29.8195	34.528
14	17.1169	21.0641	23.6848	26.1189	29.1412	31.3194	36.123
15	18.2451	22.3071	24.9958	27.4884	30.5779	32.8013	37.697
16	19.3689	23.5418	26.2962	28.8454	31.9999	34.2672	39.252
17	20.4887	24.7690	27.5871	30.1910	33.4087	35.7185	40.790
18	21.6049	25.9894	28.8693	31.5264	34.8053	37.1565	42.312
19	22.7178	27.2036	30.1435	32.8523	36.1909	38.5823	43.820
20	23.8277	28.4120	31.4104	34.1696	37.5662	39.9968	45.315
21	24.9348	29.6151	32.6706	35.4789	38.9322	41.4011	46.797
22	26.0393	30.8133	33.9244	36.7807	40.2894	42.7957	48.268
23	27.1413	32.0069	35.1725	38.0756	41.6384	44.1813	49.728
24	28.2412	33.1962	36.4150	39.3641	42.9798	45.5585	51.179
25	29.3389	34.3816	37.6525	40.6465	44.3141	46.9279	52.618
26	30.4346	35.5632	38.8851	41.9232	45.6417	48.2899	54.052
27	31.5284	36.7412	40.1133	43.1945	46.9629	49.6449	55.476
28	32.6205	37.9159	41.3371	44.4608	48.2782	50.9934	56.892
29	33.7109	39.0875	42.5570	45.7223	49.5879	52.3356	58.301
30	34.7997	40.2560	43.7730	46.9792	50.8922	53.6720	59.703
40	45.6160	51.8051	55.7585	59.3417	63.6907	66.7660	73.402
50	56.3336	63.1671	67.5048	71.4202	76.1539	79.4900	86.661
60	66.9815	74.3970	79.0819	83.2977	88.3794	91.9517	99.607
70	77.5767	85.5270	90.5312	95.0232	100.425	104.215	112.317
80	88.1303	96.5782	101.879	106.629	112.329	116.321	124.839
90	98.6499	107.565	113.145	118.136	124.116	128.299	137.208
100	109.141	118.498	124.342	129.561	135.807	140.169	149.449

INDEX

$\alpha = 0.250$	0.100	0.050	0.025	0.010	0.005	0.001
ν						
1	1.32330	2.70554	3.84146	5.02389	6.63490	7.87944	10.828
2	2.77529	4.60517	5.99146	7.37776	9.21034	10.5966	13.816
3	4.10834	6.25139	7.81473	9.34840	11.3449	12.8382	16.266
4	5.38527	7.77944	9.48773	11.1433	13.2767	14.8603	18.467
5	6.62568	9.23636	11.0705	12.8325	15.0863	16.7496	20.515
6	7.84080	10.6446	12.5916	14.4494	16.8119	18.5476	22.458
7	9.03715	12.0170	14.0671	16.0128	18.4753	20.2777	24.322
8	10.2189	13.3616	15.5073	17.5345	20.0902	21.9550	26.125
9	11.3888	14.6837	16.9190	19.0228	21.6660	23.5894	27.877
10	12.5489	15.9872	18.3070	20.4832	23.2093	25.1882	29.588
11	13.7007	17.2750	19.6751	21.9200	24.7250	26.7568	31.264
12	14.8454	18.5493	21.0261	23.3367	26.2170	28.2995	32.909
13	15.9839	19.8119	22.3620	24.7356	27.6882	29.8195	34.528
14	17.1169	21.0641	23.6848	26.1189	29.1412	31.3194	36.123
15	18.2451	22.3071	24.9958	27.4884	30.5779	32.8013	37.697
16	19.3689	23.5418	26.2962	28.8454	31.9999	34.2672	39.252
17	20.4887	24.7690	27.5871	30.1910	33.4087	35.7185	40.790
18	21.6049	25.9894	28.8693	31.5264	34.8053	37.1565	42.312
19	22.7178	27.2036	30.1435	32.8523	36.1909	38.5823	43.820
20	23.8277	28.4120	31.4104	34.1696	37.5662	39.9968	45.315
21	24.9348	29.6151	32.6706	35.4789	38.9322	41.4011	46.797
22	26.0393	30.8133	33.9244	36.7807	40.2894	42.7957	48.268
23	27.1413	32.0069	35.1725	38.0756	41.6384	44.1813	49.728
24	28.2412	33.1962	36.4150	39.3641	42.9798	45.5585	51.179
25	29.3389	34.3816	37.6525	40.6465	44.3141	46.9279	52.618
26	30.4346	35.5632	38.8851	41.9232	45.6417	48.2899	54.052
27	31.5284	36.7412	40.1133	43.1945	46.9629	49.6449	55.476
28	32.6205	37.9159	41.3371	44.4608	48.2782	50.9934	56.892
29	33.7109	39.0875	42.5570	45.7223	49.5879	52.3356	58.301
30	34.7997	40.2560	43.7730	46.9792	50.8922	53.6720	59.703
40	45.6160	51.8051	55.7585	59.3417	63.6907	66.7660	73.402
50	56.3336	63.1671	67.5048	71.4202	76.1539	79.4900	86.661
60	66.9815	74.3970	79.0819	83.2977	88.3794	91.9517	99.607
70	77.5767	85.5270	90.5312	95.0232	100.425	104.215	112.317
80	88.1303	96.5782	101.879	106.629	112.329	116.321	124.839
90	98.6499	107.565	113.145	118.136	124.116	128.299	137.208
100	109.141	118.498	124.342	129.561	135.807	140.169	149.449

INDEX